BIOGRAPHICAL MEMOIRS OF FELLOWS, X

PROCEEDINGS OF THE BRITISH ACADEMY · 172

BIOGRAPHICAL
MEMOIRS
OF FELLOWS
X

Published for THE BRITISH ACADEMY
by OXFORD UNIVERSITY PRESS

Oxford University Press, Great Clarendon Street, Oxford OX2 6DP

Oxford New York
Auckland Bangkok Bogotá Buenos Aires Cape Town Chennai
Dar es Salaam Delhi Hong Kong Istanbul Karachi Kolkata
Kuala Lumpur Madrid Melbourne Mexico City Mumbai Nairobi
São Paulo Shanghai Singapore Taipei Tokyo Toronto

British Library Cataloguing in Publication Data
Data available
978–0–19–726490–4
ISSN 0068–1202

Typeset in Times
by New Leaf Design, Scarborough, North Yorkshire
Printed on acid-free paper by
CPI Group (UK) Ltd,
Croydon, CR0 4YY

The Academy is grateful to Professor Ron Johnston, FBA
for his editorial work on this volume

Contents

FRANK BARLOW

Frank Barlow
1911–2009

FRANK BARLOW was born on 19 April 1911, the eldest son of Percy Hawthorn Barlow and Margaret Julia Wilkinson, who had married in 1910. In his nineties he wrote a memoir, which is mostly devoted to describing his childhood and adolescence and his experiences during the Second World War, and which is now included among his personal and professional papers. He also kept many papers and memorabilia from his childhood and youth and he preserved meticulously his professional papers. His numerous publications include fifteen books and scholarly editions, of which many have turned out to be of quite exceptional long-term importance. He is notable above all for three outstandingly important historical biographies, for the excellence of his editions and interpretations of difficult Latin texts, and for a textbook that has remained in print for more than half a century. His interest in literature, present from an early age, and his belief that historical research and writing, while being conducted according to the most exacting scholarly standards, should be approached as a branch of literature, made him a historian whose appeal was literary as well as conventionally historical. He used biography as a means not just to understand an individual but also as the basis from which to interpret broad historical issues and to reflect on the mysteries of the human condition. In his hands, the edition of a Latin text was also a means to literary expression, with the text's meaning elucidated perceptively and imaginatively and the translation being every bit as much a work of literature as the original text. For much of his life he was a man of great energy and resilience, with a remarkably wide range of interests, both physical and intellectual.

Proceedings of the British Academy, **172**, 3–24. © The British Academy 2011.

Both of Frank's parents were elementary school teachers, with his mother, as was then customary, giving up work on marriage. In his earliest years, the family lived in rented accommodation at Porthill in the Potteries, between Stoke-on-Trent and Burslem, in a house that was in the middle of a terrace; the memoir records that they were prevented from buying a house by the outbreak of the First World War. On the ground floor the house had a scullery, a kitchen where meals were normally taken, a dining room and a sitting room at the front. Upstairs were two bedrooms and a bathroom. His parents would appear to have risen socially, at least to the extent of joining the professional classes, since his paternal grandfather had been a partner in a crate-making business (Barlow and Hall in Furlong Lane). Frank's father went on to be the headmaster of two elementary schools in the Stoke-on-Trent area, retiring in 1939 and moving to Rhyl, a favourite place for family holidays during Frank's childhood. In the copy of his first book, *The Letters of Arnulf of Lisieux* (London, 1939), that he presented to his parents, he thanked them in the following words: 'To mother and father, to whose belief in education I owe so much.'

What we know of Frank's father suggests a strong dedication to public service and a drive to self-improvement. He is described in a local newspaper article written at the time of his retirement as a genial and expansive man. An interest in science led him to take the London External B.Sc. without any access to laboratory facilities; as Frank says in the memoir, failure was as predictable as it was sad. Frank had two brothers. Alec, born soon after Frank, did not go to university; he excelled as a sportsman and remained resident in the Potteries until retirement, working in insurance. He died in the 1980s. (John) Philip, born some seven years after Frank, was called into the Navy in the Second World War and died in service in June 1943; he had followed Frank to St John's College, Oxford, where he took an outstanding First in History and then passed out top in the Civil Service entrance examinations. Both of Frank's parents lived into their eighties; Frank's mother dying in 1968 and his father in 1964.

Frank's parents were staunch Methodists. He appears to have attended services regularly with them at Hilltop Primitive Methodist Chapel throughout his childhood but, in his teenage years, to have eased himself out of what he came to see as social convention. The anticlericalism and lack of sympathy for institutionalised religion which were prominent among his attitudes in adult life, and which were rather surprisingly combined with a very sympathetic view of many churchmen, and especially of the two famous Archbishops of Canterbury, Anselm and Thomas Becket, cannot be truly explained from his surviving papers. All that can be said is that they do not appear to have been the result of any profound spiritual crisis in adult life, but rather to have stemmed from an adolescent rejection of childhood routine and a natural irreverence that was to become familiar to many who knew him. Nonetheless, that he could write with such understanding of sincere religious belief may be a reflection of his upbringing. Frank's parents are known to have set aside a special plot of land for him to cultivate, something that he regarded as the foundation for his later passion for gardening.

Frank was educated at home by his mother until the age of seven. After attending two elementary schools, he was admitted to Newcastle-under-Lyme High School (now Newcastle-under-Lyme School) on a scholarship. His school career was formidably industrious. He liked games and was good at a number of sports, playing rugby for the school's First XV for several years, starting as a full back and then becoming a forward. The memoir records physical courage; he dived off the high board for his house because no one else would do so. He continued to play rugby to a high level after leaving the Potteries for Oxford until an ankle injury while playing for Stoke-on-Trent sent him back to Oxford on crutches and led him to reduce his participation in sport. He retained his interest in sport throughout his life, scarcely ever missing a Test match on television. He was a sergeant major in the school's Officer Training Corps, receiving a military training that he believed made unnecessary the Pioneer Corps' training he received after call-up after the outbreak of the Second World War, and which was the basis of frequently expressed pride in later life; the ramrod upright posture that he retained into advanced old age was unquestionably in part associated with respect for the disciplines of military life. He edited the school magazine and contributed extensively to it. He was writing poetry at school and continued to do so at Oxford. He was also an accomplished photographer who developed and printed his own photographs, which had often been taken during long cycling tours around the country. Throughout his life Frank kept in touch with several of his school contemporaries. It is tempting, and perhaps excessively facile, to link the interest in his subjects' early lives that is a feature of his great biographies with his own attachment to the place and people of his early years; it is at least certain that he maintained to the end enduring and active links with individuals, families and institutions he had known in his childhood and adolescent years.

In the Preface he wrote in his last book, Frank refers to 'the admirable Mr. Lush' and 'the excellent History sixth form'. Although he apparently contemplated specialising in the sciences at one stage, history won out. In his memoir he drew attention to a special aptitude for French, and throughout his life he continued to read French literature in the original language. A visitor to the Barlow home at Kenton could view the well-thumbed volumes of Proust; a taste for that author's exploration of the nuances of social behaviour within a framework of class and institutions surely influenced the way Frank wrote history. Since his exceptional understanding of Latin is something that has impressed many who have used and benefitted from his work, it is arguably surprising that the memoir contains no mention of a Latin teacher. It is therefore likely that the qualities displayed above all in the editions and translations of the *Vita Ædwardi Regis* and *Carmen de Hastingae Proelio* derived from what was, in the 1920s, a good standard education in Latin language and literature, combined with an outstanding facility for language and a personal determination to do all things well. There is a section in the correspondence in 1956 between Frank and V. H. Galbraith about the edition of the *Vita Ædwardi* of the possibility of using a translator because, as Frank acknowledged, the text was extremely difficult. Having replied politely by agreeing to think about the suggestion, Frank manifestly ignored it completely; in 1958 he received a letter from Galbraith describing the translation as 'very fine indeed'.

An undoubtedly important formative episode in his life was the cycling tour of Normandy that Frank, his brother Alec and some friends made in 1929. The diary he kept survives. Of the visit to the Tapestry at Bayeux he notes: 'I had expected to be bored by it. I was conjuring up some gloomy drab tapestry, but instead of that there was a gaily coloured embroidery on white linen. It was in fine condition and hung at a convenient height. I was very interested in it.'

Frank went up to St John's College, Oxford, on an Open Scholarship in 1930, a considerable achievement, since St John's offered few Open Scholarships at that date. He had an outstanding Oxford career. A First was followed by a B.Litt. and a D.Phil. completed at remarkable speed in times when completion rates were not a political issue. Yet, in his last book *The Godwins* (Harlow, 2002) he recalled that his undergraduate tutor, A. L. Poole, had once accused him of laziness. He commented that he considered the charge 'a little unfair', but then also said that it rankled and that he had spent many years proving Poole wrong. As Frank implies, it is impossible to believe that he was actually lazy, even more so because letters to him from Gavin Bone, Fellow of St John's and Lecturer in English Language and Literature, whose verse translation of *Beowulf* was published posthumously in 1945, indicate that Frank learnt Old English as an undergraduate, reaching a level at which he could discuss *Beowulf* as a literary text. The incident surely has the character of a wake-up call against complacency after an outstandingly good sixth-form education. Frank continued his literary interests at Oxford, producing poetry and taking a prominent part in the St John's Essay Society, an organisation that was both literary and social. There is record of only one talk by Frank, given on 8 May 1932 with the Wildean title of 'The Prince of Darkness as a Gentleman'; the minutes of the Society inform us that it dealt with Manicheism, witchcraft and medieval belief. While at Oxford, he contemplated a career as a novelist and poet before turning to historical research. The legacy, a frequently expressed belief that history was a literary discipline, remained with him throughout his life. In later years he would offer the advice that a historian could often benefit more from reading Stendhal than from reading a history textbook.

In the Preface to his collected essays, *The Norman Conquest and Beyond* (1983), Frank described the influences on him of the three men who most shaped him as a historian: Poole, V. H. Galbraith and Sir Maurice Powicke. Poole is described as a supportive tutor who introduced Frank to Continental scholarship; Galbraith, his doctoral supervisor, as the man with whom he was regularly to discuss his work throughout his life and a patron who taught him that irreverent wit could be used to advantage. Some of his comments on Powicke are worth quoting in full, since they convey a meeting of minds and an intellectual sympathy that flourished even in the apparently formal setting of the lecture hall:

> ... for me he exemplified medieval scholarship at its best. From the moment I heard him lecturing on Bibliography in the Examination Schools, casually mentioning unknown masters, recommending incomprehensible foreign titles—my notes, when I looked at them many years later, were mostly gibberish—I was entranced. His combination of technical skills, a fine prose style, and acutely subtle understanding of the most hidden springs of behaviour—he was marvellously funny on Henry III and Simon de Montfort—set a standard to which I knew I ought constantly to aspire.[1]

Frank's first experience of research was in 1933–4 for a B.Litt. that involved editions of various Durham manuscripts, subsequently published in 1945 and 1950 as *Durham Annals and Documents of the Thirteenth Century* (Durham, 1945) and *Durham Jurisdictional Peculiars* (London,

---

[1] F. Barlow, *The Norman Conquest and Beyond* (London, 1983), Preface. For Powicke and biography, see further David Bates, Julia Crick and Sarah Hamilton (eds.), *Writing Medieval Biography: Essays in Honour of Frank Barlow* (Woodbridge, 2006), p. 7.

1950). There is clear evidence in their published versions of the mature independent-minded historian; his readiness to treat charters as literary texts that were a product of their times, rather than simply categorising them as 'authentic' or 'forged', was distinctly against the contemporary grain.[2] It was, however, in the published D.Phil. thesis, *The Letters of Arnulf of Lisieux*, that Frank's qualities as a historian and the interest in 'the most hidden springs of human behaviour' were first truly displayed. Also demonstrated there is the capacity to ground an edition within the frameworks of classical influences, theology and canon law that reappears in other contexts: the scholarly annotations are outstandingly good. The edited text is well-nigh perfect and only in the ordering of the manuscripts has any need for changes been suggested.[3] In the assessment of the turbulent and, ultimately, somewhat tragic Bishop Arnulf, examples appear for the first time in a published work of the type of comment that recurs again and again throughout Frank's later writings. Thus—to choose from several passages—of Arnulf's invective against the one notable French supporter of Anacletus II during the papal schism of the 1130s, Bishop Gerard of Angoulême, Frank comments that 'it secured notice beyond its merits', while of Arnulf Frank observed 'his mind, as often with good lawyers and administrators, seems not to have been complex, and he gives little signs of originality or of greatness'.[4] These passages are followed by other interesting inferences about Arnulf's character. The insertion of the editor's personal opinions in this way—opinions that are provocative and sometimes downright contentious—immediately seizes the reader's imagination; the same technique was to be employed in *The Feudal Kingdom of England* and in Frank's lectures to undergraduates and to a wider public. The correspondence associated with the publication of *The Letters of Arnulf* reveals how Frank's literary talents were encouraged at this stage of his career by others, with Powicke, Sir Frank Stenton and Christopher Cheney, the latter two respectively President and Literary Director of the Royal Historical Society, offering especially valuable advice. A readiness to take advice on difficult matters was to remain a feature of Frank's working method throughout his life.

[2] See above all, *Durham Jurisdictional Peculiars* (Oxford, 1950), pp. 2–3.
[3] Carolyn Poling Schriber, *The Letter Collections of Arnulf of Lisieux*, Texts and Studies in Religion, vol. 72 (Lewiston, Queenston and Lampeter, 1997), pp. xi–xii.
[4] *The Letters of Arnulf of Lisieux*, Camden, 3rd ser., lxi (London, 1939), xvi, xxi. The Camden series were (and are) Royal Historical Society editions of hitherto unpublished important historical texts.

Frank's doctoral research was funded by a Fereday Fellowship, a St John's fund available to descendants of its founder and to natives of Staffordshire. It was a relatively junior fellowship, offering neither accommodation in college nor participation in college government. It certainly did not guarantee a future in Oxford. Frank's application for, and appointment to, an assistant lectureship at University College London (UCL) in 1936 was a logical consequence of his astute assessment of his prospects. At about the same time as the move to London, Frank married Brigid Garvey, who was, like Frank, from the Potteries. Their marriage was to endure for seventy-three years, with Brigid, who was five years younger than Frank, outliving him by several months. Brigid's father was a doctor and the family were Roman Catholics of Irish origin. The flat in which they set up house in Guilford Street was within walking distance of UCL. Frank never spoke or wrote with much warmth or enthusiasm of his time at UCL, which lasted until 1940. There was a clash of personalities with the professor and head of department, the Tudor historian J. E. Neale, and Frank's time at UCL was apparently cut short on the latter's say-so. Yet links of enduring importance were formed there. One colleague at UCL was another medievalist with a distinguished future ahead of him, John Le Patourel (1909–81).[5] The eighteenth- and nineteenth-century historian Norman Gash (1912–2009), another St John's student and a life-long friend of Frank's, was an exact contemporary at UCL. An informant who attended Frank's lectures at UCL has described him as cutting a flamboyant and striking figure.

Frank was eventually drafted into the Army in 1941 and was subsequently commissioned into the Intelligence Corps, spending over three years in the Far East until 1946. He and Brigid initially stayed in London while he awaited call-up and he undertook the preparation of the first of the Durham books as a way of keeping his hand in during the first months of the war; the Preface of *Durham Annals* is dated 13 June 1940 at the flat in Guilford Street. The memoir also mentions duties as a shelter warden in nearby Mecklenburg Square. Frank and Brigid subsequently moved to the Potteries in November 1940 for greater security away from the bombing of London, with the memoir noting that they witnessed Coventry burning as they travelled north. There followed a summer term as a history master at Radley School, with Frank treasuring a testimonial from the headmaster that praised his discipline. Initial army training then

---

[5] See J. C. Holt, 'John Le Patourel (1909–1981)', *Proceedings of the British Academy*, 71 (1986), 581–96.

followed, with Frank passing out top of his group, before gaining a commission into the Intelligence Corps as a second lieutenant in the later
months of 1941. His memoir describes in some detail the journey by sea
to India, where he was stationed north of Calcutta (Kolkata) for over a
year before a transfer to Ceylon (Sri Lanka), which is where he was when
Japan surrendered. His main duties were to observe and assess the activity of the Japanese air force. After the end of the war, Frank was transferred to Singapore and employed monitoring independence movements
in the Dutch East Indies. He was promoted to the rank of major shortly
before demobilisation. In the memoir Frank notes that he 'decided to give
his life a purpose' and taught himself German with help from a fellow
officer; given how rare knowledge of German was at Oxford at the time
he studied there, this was a remarkable decision to have taken.[6] He later
spoke of army life as an invaluable formative phase, a time when he learnt
to delegate and acquired much worldly knowledge of human beings and
institutions.

On return from the Far East, Frank visited Galbraith, then Director
of the Institute of Historical Research, to consult him about his professional future. At least two interviews for posts followed, leading to
appointment in 1946 to a lectureship at the then University College of the
South West of England in Exeter. Frank's memoir records his being interviewed in military uniform, by John Murray, the ambitious and energetic,
if occasionally misguided, principal of the college from 1926 to 1951.[7] The
surroundings of the Gandy Street buildings that then accommodated the
six members of the History Department must have seemed a far cry from
Oxford and UCL. Frank and Brigid first lived in rented accommodation
in Topsham before buying a house in Devonshire Place, close to the
Streatham site on which the University College was beginning to expand.
Frank's and Brigid's two sons John and Michael were born during this
period. There is mention in the memoir of attempts to move elsewhere,
with possible openings at Durham and Oxford not coming to fruition. At
Exeter, as previously at UCL, he carried a heavy teaching load compris-
ing courses on English History 400–1500, History of Political Ideas,
Ancient and Medieval, English Economic History to 1600, and a Special
Subject on R. H. Tawney's and Eileen Power's *Tudor Economic Documents*
(London, 1924), three volumes with which he was entirely unfamiliar

[6] On this point, Janet L. Nelson, 'European History', in Alan Deyermond (ed.), *A Century of
British Medieval Studies* (Oxford, 2007), pp. 71–129, at 77–80.
[7] On Murray as Principal, see B. W. Clapp, *The University of Exeter: a History* (Exeter, 1982),
pp. 74–117.

before being asked to teach them. Among his colleagues were the historian of Victorian England W. D. (Bill) Handcock and the medievalist G. W. (George) Greenaway. From 1946 the professor and head of department was W. N. (Norton) Medlicott (1900–87), a man for whom Frank had great admiration and who seems to have been something of a model for him as a professorial head of department. When Medlicott left Exeter for the London School of Economics in 1953, Frank was appointed his successor after a somewhat tortuous appointments process.

It was Medlicott as General Editor of the Longmans History of England series who commissioned Frank to write *The Feudal Kingdom of England*. First published in 1955, *The Feudal Kingdom* is still in print fifty-six years later, having passed through five editions and, despite careful revision, not being greatly changed from its first edition; the book's importance, on both personal and professional grounds, was referred to many times by the participants during the 2003 conference held at Exeter in Frank's honour.[8] Frank made it clear in the Preface that his purpose in *The Feudal Kingdom* was to tell a story and this he did with great panache. Throughout, personalities and situations were evoked with compelling colour and economy. To read the two sentences—'The skeleton of an organised kingdom endured. And society took its own measures for protection.'—in the section devoted to King Stephen's reign in England, is to feel as if one is reading the prevailing orthodoxy of the early twenty-first century and then needing to remind oneself that the passage was written fifty years earlier.[9] Yet, for all the emphasis on the need to tell a good story, the reader is left in no doubt that momentous changes took place during the period between 1042 and 1216, and their general significance is explained with extraordinary clarity.

The genesis of this remarkable book is unclear from Frank's papers; the surviving notes are effectively the footnotes that the book does not have. Behind all must lie the remarkable literary talent evident from Frank's youth: the capacity when writing freely to produce clear, accessible and entertaining prose and a quite remarkable command of his subject. Teaching—above all the experience of lecturing and the ability to hold an audience, about which more will be said below—must have been an enormous stimulus. It is striking too how often the book anticipates in

---

[8] See further, Bates, Crick and Hamilton (eds.), *Writing Medieval Biography*.
[9] *The Feudal Kingdom of England*, 1st edn. (London, 1955), p. 225. It is noteworthy that the first of the two sentences survived every rewriting, but that the second disappeared in the 4th and 5th editions.

some way the opinions he expressed with greater finesse in later publications: Edward the Confessor, for example, is 'a weak man, riding—uneas-
ily and petulantly—political storms which he could not control', who
'nevertheless left the royal powers unimpaired; and from a mistaken view
of his character and piety was built a picture of a Christian king that
served as an ideal until the ideal itself lost favour'.[10] Yet at times we might
think the imaginative flamboyance overdone. What are we to make of the
assertion that 'Most medieval reigns end in ruin. The boyhood hero
becomes in time a broken old man. The unrestrained power which he has
acquired in his manhood cracks through the caprice and stubbornness of
his ageing brain:'[11] intended to be placed on an exam paper with the word
'Discuss' after it, perhaps? And the passage that follows it in all five editions and which in many ways epitomises Frank's approach to his sources
is where, writing of King John, Frank states: 'He was a cultivated man.
He died a papal vassal, a frustrated Crusader. Yet he was remembered as
an oppressor of the Church, as a tyrant. The standards of the monastic
chroniclers were simple and severe.'

In Frank's intellectual life, the period after the publication of *The
Feudal Kingdom* was dominated by engagement with the history of
England before the Conquest. *The English Church, 1000–1066* (London,
1963) was intended by Frank as the first volume of a series; Christopher
Brooke recalls a conversation with Frank in which he indicated that it
was his intention to produce an English equivalent to Albert Hauck's five-
volume history of the German Church.[12] Subtitled *A Constitutional
History* in its first edition, *The English Church* can nowadays seem old-
fashioned in the light of the subsequent development of religious history;
for example, it has little to say on matters such as spirituality and it only
acquired a chapter on monasticism in its second edition, published in
1979. But with notable strengths on matters of organisation, education
and jurisdiction, and containing potted biographies of all the major players, it made an important contribution to the historiographical rehabilita-
tion of the late Anglo-Saxon state, a hotly debated topic in those days,
but nowadays an orthodoxy contentious only in detail. Most interestingly, it set out forcefully how the twelfth century rewrote the immediately pre-1066 Anglo-Saxon past to the detriment of its reputation;

[10] *The Feudal Kingdom of England*, 1st edn. (London, 1955), p. 75.
[11] Ibid., p. 435. The passage survived through to the 5th edition, *The Feudal Kingdom of England*,
5th edn. (Harlow, 1999), p. 357.
[12] Albert Hauck, *Kirchengeschichte Deutschlands*, 5 vols. (Leipzig, 1887–1911); 2nd edn. (Leipzig,
1904–20).

William of Malmesbury, of whom Frank's opinion was much less favourable than that of many others has been since, was a particular target for him, while the writings of Goscelin of Saint-Bertin were exploited as rarely before. The second volume, *The English Church, 1066–1154* (London, 1979) was a book about which Frank at times expressed disappointment. It is nonetheless a remarkable quarry for detail, incisive in its interpretations, and as elegantly written as ever. While working on the first volume, Frank's interests were, however, diverted elsewhere to great profit towards producing an edition of the *Vita Ædwardi Regis*.

The idea of an edition of the *Vita* was under discussion with the editors of Nelson's Medieval Texts, V. H. Galbraith and Roger Mynors, in 1955. An introduction, text and translation were in existence by 1958. The fascination that this complex text exerted on Frank is evident from his papers: for example, in a typescript letter to Galbraith, dated 8 November 1958, he observed: 'This book is so madly interesting that one could reflect on it for ages.'[13] It is evident that he continued these reflections for the rest of his life, with the second Oxford Medieval Texts edition of 1992 containing changes that were unique in scale relative to everything else that Frank published; for all his other books, his standard method was to insert a preliminary essay assessing change or, at most, to rewrite selected passages without altering the basic framework. His papers contain one side of a remarkable correspondence with Galbraith about the *Vita*— Frank only occasionally kept a copy of his handwritten letters—which dealt with many of the central issues of the edition. Galbraith certainly reinforced Frank's assessment that the edition should divide the *Vita* into two books, something for which there is no warrant in the single surviving manuscript, and that he should be forthright on the matter of authorship by expressing scepticism about Goscelin's claims and arguing as forcefully as could reasonably be done for Folcard. Galbraith was, however, convinced that 'Book 2' was so different from 'Book 1' that it must in its final form date from the late eleventh century, a view that Frank rejected. It is also noticeable that the 1992 edition is less forthright in arguing the case for Folcard than the 1962 one had been; here as elsewhere, Frank became more cautious in the later decades of his life.[14]

---

[13] *The Life of King Edward, who rests at Westminster, attributed to a monk of St. Bertin*, Nelsons Medieval Texts (London, 1962); *Vita Ædwardi regis qui apud Westmonasterium requiescit: the Life of King Edward, who rests at Westminster, attributed to a monk of Saint.-Bertin*, Oxford Medieval Texts (Oxford and New York, 1992).

[14] The *Vita Ædwardi* and Frank's edition thereof have been much discussed since 1962. Frank dealt with criticisms in the 1992 edition, but discussion has continued. For the most recent

The 1960s was a remarkably productive period in Frank's career. Contemporaneous with the publication of the *Vita Ædwardi* in 1962 and *The English Church* in 1963, he was also Deputy Vice-Chancellor as well as Head of the Department of History, a range of activity and responsibility that would nowadays be thought impossible. He, Brigid, and the family moved to Middle Court Hall at Kenton in November 1965, a house where he could indulge to the full his passion for gardening; he came to possess a knowledge of plants that was akin to a botanist's. He had passed his driving test in 1963. There are thereafter numerous stories about his love of cars and his fast—many would say excessively fast—driving. By this time, he and Brigid were enjoying holidays in very good hotels in cities such as Paris, Rome and Madrid, something they continued to do for the rest of their active lives.

The publications of the decade, which culminated in the biography of Edward the Confessor in 1970, demonstrate a remarkable command of the sources for the tenth, eleventh and twelfth centuries. An article on Lanfranc published in 1965 has some of the qualities of the biographies to follow, although it is clear that Frank subsequently became more circumspect in his judgements of personality and character in the years leading up to the publication of *Edward the Confessor* in 1970.[15] At the same time Frank was also working on the sources for the Norman Conquest and, in 1966, published an essay on the poem the *Carmen de Hastingae Proelio*, attributed to Guy, Bishop of Amiens, in the Festschrift presented to Medlicott.[16] The profundity of this work deserves emphasis. Frank had clearly checked the two surviving manuscripts and collated his text against them, and he tackled all the issues about the poem that were subsequently to become controversial. Along with the Dutch scholar L. J. Engels's almost contemporary inaugural lecture, the article was the first serious modern study of the poem and, together with the 1999 edition, must be one of Frank's most important contributions to the study of the Norman Conquest.

---

arguments, see Simon Keynes and Rosalind Love, 'Earl Godwine's ship', *Anglo-Saxon England*, 38 (2009), 185–223, including discussion of Henry Summerson's earlier publication on the discovery of a lost section of the *Vita* in the same journal.

[15] 'A view of Archbishop Lanfranc', *Journal of Ecclesiastical History*, 16 (1965), 163–77 (repr. in *The Norman Conquest and Beyond*, pp. 223–38).

[16] 'The *Carmen de Hastingae Proelio*', in K. Bourne and D. C. Watt (eds.), *Studies in International History: Essays Presented to W. Norton Medlicott* (London, 1967), pp. 35–67 (repr. in *The Norman Conquest and Beyond*, pp. 189–222).

When this 1966 article is compared with Frank's definitive 1999 Oxford Medieval Texts edition, published when he was approaching his ninetieth year, it is remarkable how little his opinions needed to be revised. He took account of and carefully surveyed all the controversies of the intervening three decades. In the end, while accepting more recent palaeographical assessments of the manuscripts, completely changing his interpretation of 'the noble heir of Ponthieu' by accepting Engels's identification, and shifting his ground somewhat to make concessions to those who would date the poem earlier than 1068×1070, he changed little.[17] A remarkable file that starts in 1966, containing correspondence with R. H. C. Davis, who took a very different view of the date and character of the *Carmen*, but the stimulus of whose opinions Frank acknowledged in the 1966 article, along with all other significant participants in the debates that followed, is eloquent testimony to the thoroughness of Frank's working methods and to the courtesy with which he entered serious academic controversy. As in the case of the *Vita Ædwardi*, the elucidation of a difficult text became the work of a lifetime. From 1967 he gave a lot of encouragement and advice to Catherine Morton and Hope Muntz, who published an Oxford Medieval Texts edition of the poem in 1972, and in 1999 he defended their efforts and, in particular, their skill in establishing what he regarded as a reliable text; it is notable that he had sharp words for those who belittled their edition on the grounds that neither had held tenured academic posts. A final point about the 1966 article is that it attacked what Frank called the 'stock' synthetic narrative of the Battle of Hastings and the practice of giving priority to William of Poitiers' account; it has taken thirty years for others seriously to follow in his footsteps.

Frank played a very prominent part in the commemoration of the novocentenary of the Battle of Hastings. He also made a number of what would now be termed media appearances and gave many Historical Association lectures. His contributions generally stress that the Conquest brought about change, but change that largely occurred within the existing institutional framework, and of which the wider European dimensions needed to be taken into account. It is unlikely that Frank thought that the Conquest brought about a change for the better. The short book *William I and the Norman Conquest* was written quickly, and appeared in

---

[17] For 'the noble heir of Ponthieu', L. J. Engels, *Dichters over Willem de Veroveraar. Het Carmen de Hastingae Proelio. Openbare les gegeven bij het aanvaarden van het ambt van Lector in het Middeleeuws Latijn aan de Rijksuniversiteit te Groningen op dinsdag 21 Februari 1967* (Groningen, 1967), pp. 13–14.

1965 in advance of the anniversary year. Frank did not find the Conqueror especially interesting and almost certainly did not like him—he often portrayed him as a crude and illiterate soldier; the book's Prologue reminds us that 'It is a common fallacy ... that notable achievements must have involved notable men,' and its Epilogue describes William as 'a pot-bellied and blood-stained warrior, who was also a religious man and a lover of justice by the standards of the age'. Frank's attempt at a character sketch, as usual relating childhood experience to adult behaviour, is none-theless among the more interesting attempts to describe the Conqueror's personality.[18] His analysis of William's responsibility for the terrible events that followed the Battle of Hastings is, however, always judicious.

Edward the Confessor, first published in 1970, has since its publication dominated discussion of the reign. The first of his three major biographies that were together the inspiration for the 2003 conference and the 2006 volume based on it, this book exemplifies Frank's debt to literature and can reasonably be regarded as an innovative landmark in the writing of the biographies of medieval people. Since the contract for the book was not signed until 1965, *Edward* was written remarkably quickly, so much so indeed that he met the formal delivery date required by his contract, but on the basis of a lengthy reflection that had lasted two decades. Like *The Feudal Kingdom*, *Edward* is still in print. While publications subsequent to Frank's book can offer differing perspectives on several major issues, most notably on Edward's time in Normandy, on whether Edward was ever an effective ruler, and on the implications of the unity or otherwise of the *Vita Ædwardi*, Frank's achievement in placing the *Vita* at the heart of the complex reactions of a defeated elite to the catastrophe of 1066, and, on this basis, in insisting that Edward should be viewed above all as a secular ruler with no foreknowledge of the future development of a cult of sanctity, and in whose life austere religious values and behaviour in all probability did not take a central role, remains at the heart of all serious discussion of the reign.[19]

The book's preparation involved deep thought about the writing of biography and a remarkable level of self-reflection on the interpretation of sources; it arguably embodies a less forthright, but more profound and reflective, approach to human behaviour than had been evident in Frank's

---

[18] *William I and the Norman Conquest* (London, 1965), pp. xvi, 11–12, 191; cf., David Bates, 'The Conqueror's adolescence', *Anglo-Norman Studies*, 25 (2003), 1–18.
[19] For opinions, see Richard Mortimer (ed.), *Edward the Confessor: the Man and the Legend* (Woodbridge, 2009) and, in particular, Richard Mortimer's essay 'Edward the Confessor: the man and the legend', at pp. 1–41.

earlier work. This is above all exemplified firstly by the prefatory quotation from Anthony Powell and also by the cautious setting-out of differing interpretations and the search for revealing material outside the obvious main sources. Frank's personal papers and unpublished lectures contain remarks such as his justification of the book's length to Galbraith on the basis that the absence of sources required their thorough interpretation, and might therefore be deemed to justify an even longer book than he had written. Frank also noted the potential importance of an anecdote set in an unexpected context, a comment that has been seen as anticipating the much later sociological approach built around norms, scripts and rules. Published at a time when biography was relatively unfashionable and, arguably, in retreat under the assault from the *Annales* school of historical writing, it can now be cited as significant to the revival of biography as a form of historical writing.[20] Its negative treatment of Edward's claims to sanctity, which some found difficult at the time, also brought into the foreground Frank's drift in adolescence away from a conventional religious upbringing. While Frank was actually elected to the Fellowship of the Academy in 1970 shortly before *Edward's* publication, the near-coincidence of the two events seems appropriate; the book exemplifies the mixture of intimidating rigour, vivid imagination and strikingly original prose that characterises his best work. That he was also elected a Fellow of the Royal Society of Literature at around the same time illuminates yet again his literary qualities. He is known to have taken particular pleasure in a favourable review of *Edward* by the playwright Dennis Potter that contained comments such as 'This is a work of courage and imagination' and 'an intellectual exercise of the highest order.'[21]

Appointed in 1953 as the sole Professor of History and Head of Department until retirement, Frank's career until retirement in 1976 covered the granting of the University of Exeter's charter in 1955, the university's expansion on the Streatham site, the post-Robbins Report university expansion of the 1960s, and other changes of those times such as the advent of elected heads of department and consultative staff–student committees. He was a powerful force in the university throughout this period, important at the time of the granting of the charter and a member of the new university's first Council, and he subsequently held a series of major offices such as Dean of Arts, Deputy Vice-Chancellor and Public

[20] Bates, Crick and Hamilton (eds.), *Writing Medieval Biography*, pp. vii–x, 12–13; and also in this volume, Pauline Stafford, 'Writing the biography of Eleventh-Century Queens', pp. 99–109, and especially at 99, 108–9.
[21] *The Times*, 5 Nov. 1970.

Orator. He rode the crest of the wave of post-Robbins growth, almost trebling in size the Exeter History Department from the nine members of 1953 by the time of his retirement.[22] Around the time of retirement, he composed several essays reflecting on the changes that had taken place during his working life. In general, he believed that the expansion of the 1960s had not harmed the basic fabric of universities; the conditions for teaching and research had, if anything, improved. While believing that authority should always be challenged and that universities were by nature turbulent places, he was less sympathetic to the social and political changes of the time: he wrote scathingly about a middle-class elite that chose to ape the working classes who, he believed, had gained little from the post-Robbins expansion. He ended the text of one of these essays with the statement that the central mission of universities was 'Fundamental Research' and 'Fearless Teaching'; both these phrases were capitalised in the manuscript.

That Frank was the dominant power within the Department of History was clear even to the author of this memoir, who was at Exeter as an undergraduate and postgraduate in the 1960s. That what he accomplished was massively to its long-term benefit is undeniable. He lived long enough to see many of those he had appointed go on to outstanding careers; one of them, the late Professor Timothy Reuter, was, along with the author of this memoir, the driving force behind the early stages in the organisation of the conference that led to the publication of the Festschrift entitled *Writing Medieval Biography* in 2006. The creation in 1959–60 of one-year tutorial fellowships was in its day an innovation that supplied an invaluable stepping-stone from the doctorate to a permanent post. He encouraged the study of archaeology within the department, expanding the number of staff from the one inherited post of 1953 to three by 1976. He ensured that members of the department had time for research and, in relation to the balance of teaching and research, he provided an example that he expected to be followed, while also being explicitly aware of what was possible. His own regular regime involved teaching and departmental business in the mornings, gardening at home or, if required, service on university committees in the early afternoon, and writing in the late afternoon and evenings. After retirement he would tease a younger generation that he had never had, nor needed, study leave.

---

[22] This calculation takes into account the departure of some members to form the Department of Economic History in 1963–4.

Mischievous humour of this kind was deployed in all sorts of situations in a way that was unique to him; it would usually be preceded by a mounting crescendo of laughter. He could at times be so funny that some of his sayings have remained for good in the memories of many who knew him. While even his best friends and greatest admirers would acknowledge that there were times when his irreverence and love of repartee and, at times, lack of forethought could be felt as harsh by those on the receiving end, his essential good nature was usually recognised. In general, he was a source of excellent advice on all sorts of professional matters ranging, for example, from exam marking to survival in the labyrinth of university politics. Within the Department of History he permitted and encouraged discussion, and several of its members comment on how decisions were usually reached on a consensual basis. He had a powerful sense of occasion, usually, so it is recalled, wearing a bow-tie to examiners' meetings. He lectured in a gown. He and Brigid—and in this Brigid was of crucial importance—put a strong emphasis on departmental social life. There were annual departmental dinners and staff socialised in the evenings. Frank himself enjoyed dancing. The parties for the graduating finalists at Middle Court Hall were splendid affairs in marvellous surroundings. Frank's sociability also in the 1950s included turning out for the staff cricket team, 'the Erratics', captained by his close friend John Lloyd, the University Librarian.

He was a superb undergraduate lecturer, holding his audience with ease, conveying the essence of an argument with exemplary clarity, and illuminating what for the students might have seemed obscure subjects with a cascade of (sometimes dubious) modern analogies; the anecdote about the tenth-century nunnery of Wilton as a finishing school for royal daughters regularly visited by young bloods produced by Barbara Yorke at the 2003 conference is an illustration of this.[23] Former students with no specialist interest in medieval history have remarked on Frank's manifest and exemplary dedication to first-year lecturing, an expression of what was once deemed to be a central professorial role. At Special Subject level, classes were built around reading the texts in the original Latin. Here he made few concessions, while recognising in, for example, the Preface to *William Rufus* (London, 1983 and 2000) that the students must have found the Latin of someone like William of Malmesbury difficult. His

---

[23] Barbara Yorke, '"Carriers of the truth": writing the biographies of Anglo-Saxon female saints', in Bates, Crick and Hamilton (eds.), *Writing Medieval Biography*, pp. 49–60, at 49.

approach to postgraduate supervision was similar. He taught by example and he expected work of the very highest standard, making it abundantly clear, without explicitly saying so, that nothing less would be tolerated. With hindsight, it is clear that his insistence on the regular production of research essays, on technical accuracy in several languages, and the assumption that the research student was every bit as much a member of the professional community as the most distinguished of scholars, conveyed a mixture of discipline and seriousness that was extremely helpful. Supervisions were regular and frequent and, if discussion seemed often to drift towards gardening, cars or Frank's latest book, no one was at all unclear as to what was expected. To my knowledge, all his research students completed their theses, usually within the time-limits that the modern research councils regard as mandatory—as indeed Frank himself had done.

Frank played a massive and committed part in the life of the university and the city, a role that he continued beyond retirement. He was clearly someone who was called upon when important and difficult business had to be done. He oversaw the publication of *Exeter and Its Region*, a volume to which almost every senior member of the university contributed, for presentation to the British Association for the Advancement of Science when its annual conference was held in Exeter in September 1969. He also played a prominent part in institutions such as the Devonshire Association, the Devon and Exeter Institution and the Devon and Cornwall Record Society, and, for some most memorably, successfully chaired the cathedral's Technical Advisory Committee between 1978 and 1987 when the renovation of some of the building's west front and south tower was under contentious discussion. A selective list of some of the contributions Frank made throughout his life to major academic projects that were for the benefit of others makes remarkable reading. His edition of the Statutes of Bishop Peter Quinil (Quivil) (1280–91) for *Councils and Synods*, edited by Powicke and Christopher Cheney (Oxford, 1964), on which he was working in the early 1950s, might reasonably be identified as an additional and sixteenth book. He contributed an edition of the Winchester surveys to the important Winchester project overseen by his former Exeter colleague Martin Biddle. He rescued the Exeter Episcopal Acta volumes when the two editors were unable to fulfil their obligations, and was an active and enthusiastic member of the British Academy's Episcopal Acta Committee, a project initiated by his friend Christopher Cheney; he expresses most warmly his enjoyment of the Committee's meetings in the Preface to his second volume of Exeter

acta.[24] He contributed to the 1972 and 1986 celebrations of Exeter cathedral's two most famous manuscripts, the Exeter Book and Exon
Domesday, and he was later to write the Introduction to the Devon volume
of the Alecto facsimile edition of Domesday Book. He took very seriously
the responsibilities of the reviewer; his reviews of books are a model of
rigour. Frank also benefited in significant ways from Exeter. In many of
his books, he acknowledges George Greenaway for reading the manuscript in draft. The exact nature of George's contribution is unclear; a
speculative suggestion made during the preparation of this memoir was
that George, a profoundly committed Christian, might at times have counter-
balanced Frank's religious scepticism. Other notable advice came from
the Professor of Classics, F. W. (Fred) Clayton on the technicalities of
Latin verse in advance of Frank's 1966 article on the *Carmen*. Frank was
generous in his thanks to those who he thought had helped him.

   William Rufus, first published in 1983, and for many his finest book,
has in common with *Edward* the search for the man beneath the veneer
imposed by monastic historians and their nineteenth-century successors.
As in *Edward*, Frank sought to engage with the thought-world of lay society. It has the same magisterial command of detail combined with a clear
general perspective. Although others have followed Frank in writing about
Rufus, his biography dominates, and has indeed completely reshaped,
modern discussion. It is a celebration of kingship in which Frank—typically—could not resist citing Christopher Marlowe's *Tamburlaine*, both
as a preface to the book and in the text; *William Rufus* is a portrait of
triumphant kingship cut short when the king was on the verge of still
greater triumphs. The book is a portrait of a military world, of the successful continuation of the Conqueror's achievements in trying circumstances, of a rather dissolute court full of witty and intelligent men, and of
a boisterous, confident and clumsy king whose values were those of the
soldiers whose company he often shared. In the book's 2000 edition,
Frank claimed that he had been trying to write 'total history', by which he
meant that he had read widely in the new kinds of social history that were
becoming current in the 1970s. His claim was, if anything, an excessively
modest one: his originality as a biographer was already based securely
on the establishment of context, and what he was doing in *Rufus* was

---

[24] Frank Barlow (ed.), *English Episcopal Acta, xii: Exeter, 1186–1257* (Oxford, 1996), p. x ('Finally,
I have greatly enjoyed and profited from the company of my fellow members of the British
Academy Committee at our meetings in Cambridge and of my fellow editors at our periodic
reunions in York').

merely extending his method to encompass up-to-date types of historical writing.

The book also enabled him to put St Anselm's life and Eadmer's *Historia* in what Frank thought was their rightful place without distorting the record; Anselm's high principles and moral sensitivity are often portrayed as irritating to Rufus and to all the churchmen who supported the king, but at the same time Frank notes Anselm's magnanimity and nobility; it was he after all who wept at the news of the king's death. If some, at the time and subsequently, have thought that Frank had treated Rufus too kindly, especially with regard to his relations with the great magnates and the rapacity of his financial exactions, the portrait remains fundamentally persuasive. It is clear too that Frank thought Rufus the most attractive of the four kings about whom he wrote most. And in the book's last sentence we have again the sort of enigmatic—and actually in its context somewhat incomprehensible—comment that managed to bring together the kinds of verdict that might have emanated from the monastic world that Frank wanted to penetrate beyond and the military world he wanted to portray: 'To deprive a hero of a hero's death was the most terrible punishment that God could inflict.'

In *Thomas Becket*, first published in 1986, Frank returned to the interests of his postgraduate years, something that in the book's Preface he said he had always wanted to do. The contract had been signed in 1973; in all likelihood the work on it and on *William Rufus* overlapped. Although there is nothing in his papers to indicate as such, it is possible that the idea of producing a non-partisan account that concentrated on the human beings in the story must in the context of the historiography of the time have appealed to his irreverent anticlericalism. As so often, Frank went immediately to the heart of the matter by quoting first of all the famous passage from St Augustine of Hippo: 'it is not the penalty which makes true martyrs, but the cause'. *Thomas Becket* is a magisterial detailed narrative, a remarkable *tour de force* especially notable for its narrative of the archbishop's long period of exile. Yet, while in its declared intention to concentrate on telling the story, Frank apparently distinguishes *Becket* from *Edward the Confessor* and *William Rufus*, the biographer who wrote those books is nonetheless very much in evidence. Frank was clearly determined to link a young man who he believed to have been an extremely intelligent, but inadequately educated, Parisian student, to the adult chancellor and prelate. The 'conversion' that has baffled every one since 1162 was to be explained in terms of psychological insecurity. After 1145 Becket was always the outsider, with the archbishopric meaning that he had at last obtained an independent power-base; in that post 'he had all the failings of the typical parvenu'.[25]

The overall story that Frank tells is a human one: the sad and ulti-mately tragic quarrel between two men, both of whom Frank said he admired. With the emphasis on the people and the events, the battle of ideas that is clearly there in the *Letters* is arguably left rather to one side. While *Thomas Becket* has subsequently been judged by some to be more pro-Henry than pro-Becket, no one who reads Frank's book can be left in any doubt of his grasp of the complexity of the human, theological, moral and legal issues that the events involved.[26] The account of the events of the Council of Clarendon and their implications is a notably sensitive portrayal of a situation in which no one could control the conflicting loyalties, emotions and principles that were unleashed. And Henry is not spared criticism, above all because he pushed proposals that were mani-festly unacceptable to leading contemporaries, and because of his subse-quent determination to ruin Thomas. In places Frank was noticeably more sympathetic to Thomas than might be expected from the book's early sections, as in the passages that portray him as doomed by his past and a victim of circumstances; the earlier comments describing him as 'a liability, even a menace' were actually a perception of how contemporar-ies might have seen him, while the later comments expressed Frank's per-sonal view.[27] Set-pieces such as Herbert of Bosham's appearance before Henry II at Angers in 1166 and Thomas and Henry's meeting for the first time after a period of over six years at Fréteval in 1170 bring out fully the drama of the occasions. And Frank's final positive assessment of Thomas conveys exceedingly well the judgement that ideas can indeed be mightier than the sword. Yet here again there is also the sense of the enigmatic that is typical of Frank; for, in giving voice to Peter of Celle through his letter to John of Salisbury, he invites his readers to ponder the eternal mystery of how the archbishop's triumph through violent death had come about.[28]

Frank became increasingly frail physically in his last years, and Brigid's retirement to a nursing home in 2002 left him vulnerable and uncertain. He was fortunate in that an old friend Marjorie Bowen agreed to care for him at home. As a result, he was able to stay at Middle Court

[25] *Thomas Becket* (London, 1986), p. 89.

[26] A different approach to Thomas and Henry is set out in Anne Duggan, *Thomas Becket* (London, 2004).

[27] Barlow, *Becket*, pp. 97, 119.

[28] *The Letters of Peter of Celle*, ed. Julian Haseldine, Oxford Medieval Texts (Oxford, 2001), no. 174.

Hall almost to the end; he died on 27 June 2009. At his last public appearance, the presentation at the University of Exeter in 2006 of the volume of essays published in his honour, *Writing Medieval Biography*, Frank delivered a typically well-prepared speech, in which he surveyed his career and warmly thanked the friends and well-wishers who were present, as well as some who could not be. He told the audience how much he had enjoyed his life. He also joked that the gods might not have loved him; the good do after all die young. One might remark that the gods of this world had indeed loved him; to the Fellowships of the British Academy and of the Royal Society of Literature were added an Honorary Doctorate from the University of Exeter in 1981, a CBE in 1989, and an Honorary Fellowship of St John's in 2002. Arguably too, the gods must have loved someone who was still active and publishing at the highest level in the tenth decade of his life. Yet the joke also has that unknowable—except to Frank—mixture of simple wit, perversity and ambiguity with which he loved to tantalise his readers and his friends.

DAVID BATES
University of East Anglia

Note.   The author wishes to thank John Barlow and Marjorie Bowen for discussions of Frank's life and for access to Frank's papers at Middle Court Hall. They, Christopher Brooke, Bob Higham, Jinty Nelson, Elisabeth van Houts, and Barbara Yorke have all read earlier drafts of this memoir and have discussed it with the author. I must also thank Julie Barrau, Martin Brett, Julia Crick, Anne Duggan, Reg Erskine, John Greenaway, Robert Greenhill, Michael Morten, Nicholas Orme, Michael Riordan, Ivan Roots, Richard Sharpe, Ian Short and John Thurmer for discussions and assistance with the memoir, as well as everyone else to whom I have talked about Frank during its writing.

JOHN BARNES

John Arundel Barnes
1918–2010

JOHN BARNES was an intellectual and a scholar who truly spanned disciplines. He taught, did field research, and contributed significantly to the development of theoretical and methodological approaches in both sociology and social anthropology. He was elected a Fellow of the British Academy in 1981 and was a member of the Sociology, Demography and Social Statistics Section (S4), although he would have been equally at home in Anthropology and Geography (S3). Indeed, often sociology and social anthropology coalesce in his work. He was also a Fellow of the Australian Academy of the Social Sciences, and he contributed to the development of social sciences in both Australia and the United Kingdom. In the 1974 *Register of Members* of the Association of Social Anthropologists of the Commonwealth, Barnes listed his interests as Asia and Oceania (regional), and ecology, politics and economics, culture, and the ethics of social enquiry (theoretical).[1] This makes clear his ever-changing concerns. He had already made his name in European and African ethnographic studies, in network analysis and mathematical modelling, in kinship theory, in the politics of 'race relations' in Africa, and in many other fields. Later he would make contributions in several other areas, but he was perhaps most at home in the eclectic style of social science that spanned conventional sociology and social anthropology and gave prominence to a history which embraced both social change and continuity, to relations

---

[1] *Register of Members* (London, Association of Social Anthropologists of the Commonwealth, 1974), p. 21.

Proceedings of the British Academy, **172**, 27–45. © The British Academy 2011.

between structure and individual action, and to the nature of virtually all contemporary societies.

Barnes privately published his autobiography in 2008.[2] Other auto-biographical material includes an interview by Les Hiatt, a video interview by Jack Goody, a short note in the Australian Anthropological Society Newsletter, and a shorter memoir.[3] Material gathered from some of these is included in his autobiography, and his warm personality and great sense of humour come through wonderfully in the Goody interview. In 1990, Barnes published a valuable selection of his best essays, with a concentration on his ideas on the modelling process in social science research.[4] And in the same year, colleagues presented him with a Festschrift published as a special issue of *The Australian Journal of Anthropology*.[5] The latter dealt exclusively with the reinterpretation of Barnes's famous and seminal paper, 'Genetrix: genitor : : nature: culture?'.[6] At least for some social anthropologists, this remains his most inspiring and enduring work.

I

John was born in Reading, Berkshire, on 9 September 1918. The family soon moved to a different part of town, but he recalled that when he was about five or six his mother pointed out his birthplace to him and his brother Irwin: 27 Coley Hill, 'a rather forbidding terrace house near the central shopping area'.[7] His parents had moved from London, in the case

[2] J. A. Barnes, *Humping My Drum: a Memoir* (Raleigh, NC). Available at www.lulu.com
[3] Les Hiatt, 'An interview with John Barnes', *Australian Anthropological Society Newsletter*, 63 (1986), 4–15. Interview of John Barnes by Jack Goody, 19 Dec., 1983 <www.alanmacfarlane. com/ancestors/barnes.html>. J. A. Barnes, 'Where lies the truth?', *Australian Anthropological Society Newsletter*, 64 (1986), 4–9. John Barnes, 'Looking back and hardly believing', in Geoffrey Gray (ed.), *Before It's Too Late: Anthropological Reflections, 1950–1970*, Oceania Monographs, 51 (Sydney, 2001), pp. 147–51.
[4] J. A. Barnes, *Models and Interpretations: Selected Essays* (Cambridge, 1990).
[5] Warren Shapiro (guest editor), 'On the generation and maintenance of the person: essays in honour of John Barnes', *The Australian Journal of Anthropology*, 1 (2/3): Special Issue 1 (Sydney, 1990).
[6] J. A. Barnes, 'Genetrix: genitor : : nature: culture?', in Jack Goody (ed.), *The Character of Kinship* (Cambridge, 1973), pp. 61–73.
[7] Barnes, *Humping My Drum*, p. 1. Without further notes, I shall draw on Barnes's memoir for much of the biographical material presented here, and also for his own recollections of career decisions. The memoir is extensive and incredibly detailed; it numbers 464 printed pages. As he suggests in the 'Preamble' there, it may be incorrect at times, but at least is based (mainly) on his own recollections.

of his father, and from Bath, in the case of his mother, around 1912. John's father, Thomas Daniel Barnes, known as Tom, had a music shop in Reading and before that worked as a piano tuner in Bath and then in London. Tom's father, James, lived with John's natal family in Reading. Grandfather James was one of twelve siblings, at least two of whom were said to have been last seen working in a quarry in New South Wales. Tom's own brother was called Irwin, and John's brother was named after him. Irwin the elder, after having worked as a surveyor in Africa, emigrated to Australia (also NSW) to practise that profession not long after 1900. John himself would follow his Uncle Irwin, but as an anthropologist, to Africa in 1946 and to Australia in 1956. The Barnes family belonged to the Baptist Church and Tom sang in the choir, although John learned later in life that Tom had rejected his Christian beliefs, and John eventually did the same.

John's mother, Mabel Grace Nash, known as Grace, was the daughter of a Bath publican. One of her sisters, embarrassed by their father's occupation, used to tell people that their father was 'a traveller in hops'. Grace once told John and Irwin that he been a great traveller and had even been to the South Pole. Later they learned that 'The South Pole' was a pub near Bath Spa railway station, and that as a child Grace had lived above it. Grace's mother had been an alcoholic, and the family were active in the Congregational Church and the temperance organisation, the Band of Hope. Before she married John's father, Grace was manager of a milk shop in Bath. She lived to the age of 97, and in later life became 'pleasantly confused'.

At the age of six, in 1924, John started school. Clooneavon House School had been a small school for girls. To expand its intake it had opened its doors for boys that year, and for the whole of that year John was the only boy. After two and a half years there, he moved to the junior section of Reading School. He came top of his class in many subjects, but did 'dismally' in religious knowledge. He won a scholarship to Christ's Hospital, a well-known boarding school near Horsham in Sussex. Because of his Baptist upbringing he had not yet been christened, but at school he was duly baptised and confirmed in the Anglican Church. John joined the Christian Union, whose evangelical leanings later turned out to be of some practical benefit when he came to work closely with evangelical missionaries during his anthropological fieldwork in Central Africa, Norway, Australia and Papua New Guinea. He was not much good at games, but excelled academically, especially at mathematics. His skills in mathematics also turned out to be useful later in his anthropological career,

when he came to deciphering the intricacies of 'Murngin' (Yolngu) kinship structures that had eluded analysts and ethnographers, if not
Yolgnu Aborigines themselves.[8] They also earned him (after an entrance
examination) a scholarship to Cambridge.

John entered St John's College, Cambridge, in 1936. He started in
mathematics but expressed a desire to switch to economics, which was
refused on the grounds that his scholarship was in mathematics. His college allowed him to skip to Part Two of the Mathematics Tripos for his
first two years and read for Part Two of the Economics Tripos in the
third. This would require him to work on Part One of the Economics
Tripos in his spare time during his first two years. However, he found
economics dull. He dabbled in astronomy too, although the course proved
to consist mainly of the kind of mathematics he least liked. He therefore
settled on the Archaeology and Anthropology Tripos for his third year.

His formal Director of Studies was the archaeologist Glyn Daniel, but
he decided to study social anthropology as his main interest, with East
Africa as his 'special area'. He worked closely with Jack Driberg, a colourful former colonial officer who reportedly had supported his own
anthropological training, at the London School of Economics, by playing
poker.[9] Driberg had spent considerable time in the Anglo-Egyptian Sudan
and in Uganda, and John would later follow him to Central Africa, where
he made his name as an ethnographer of the Ngoni of Fort Jameson of
what was then Northern Rhodesia. Through Driberg, John met a number
of anthropologists based at Oxford, including A. R. Radcliffe-Brown,
E. E. Evans-Pritchard, Meyer Fortes and Max Gluckman.

At Cambridge, John became secretary of the Student Christian
Movement, and despite, by his own admission, lacking musical talent,
joined the choir of the Cambridge University Socialist Club. He had been
a pacifist, but the rise of Hitler dissuaded him from keeping his pacifist
principles, although he maintained his broadly left-wing beliefs. He also,
gradually it seems, became an atheist. It was at Cambridge that he met
Frances Bastable, whom he married, at Kingsclere, in Hampshire, on
16 December 1942 when John was on leave from the Royal Navy. They
spent more than sixty years together and had four children—though a

---

[8] I refer here to his short but important monograph, J. A. Barnes, *Inquest on the Murngin*, RAI
Occasional Paper No. 26 (London, Royal Anthropological Institute of Great Britain and
Ireland, 1967). The 'Murngin' (Yolngu) are an Aboriginal people whose impenetrably
complicated kinship system could perhaps only really be understood by Barnes, who believed
that, at least in a certain sense, it did not exist.

[9] See also Ray Abrahams, 'Jack Herbert Driberg (1888–1946)', *Journal of the Anthropological
Society of Oxford*, NS 2(1–2) (2010), 74–82.

honeymoon eluded them, as John had to head quickly to his ship at Greenock, on the Clyde.

Just before the war, John had been awarded a small grant, of £30, to go with a friend to Scandinavia to explore possibilities for ethnographic fieldwork. They had planned to travel across Germany to France, and to meet up with Frances in Paris. However, while they were in Norway, the United Kingdom declared war on Germany, and that put an end to the plan. When he returned to the UK he caught up with his recruiting board. He joined the Royal Navy and, after training as an air navigator, served with the aircraft carrier HMS *Victorious* (which, for a time as part of the United States Navy, also doubled as USS *Robin*). The ship sailed through the Atlantic, the Pacific and the Indian Oceans, and gave John not only the chance to see the Pacific and the African coast, but even, in New York in 1942, a chance to meet briefly with Ruth Benedict and Ralph Linton, two of the most prominent members of Franz Boas's team at Columbia University. Boas himself had died earlier that year. John served in the navy from 1940 to 1946.

II

Barnes earned his BA in 1939. In the same year he was offered a Fellowship at the Peabody Museum of Harvard University, but because of the war was not able to take it up. After the war, he studied briefly (in 1946) with Isaac Schapera, as a postgraduate student at the University of Cape Town. Max Gluckman, then Director of the Rhodes-Livingstone Institute (RLI), had sent him to work with Schapera as part of his RLI apprenticeship. Barnes completed his D.Phil. in social anthropology at Oxford in 1951. His earlier appointments were numerous, and he often held more than one at the same time. They included Research Officer at the Rhodes-Livingstone Institute (1946–8), Lecturer in Anthropology at University College London (1949–51), Fellow of St John's College, Cambridge (1950–3), Simon Research Fellow at the University of Manchester (1951–3), Honorary Research Assistant at University College London (1951–4), Reader in Anthropology at the London School of Economics (1954–6), Professor of Anthropology at the University of Sydney (1956–8), Professor of Anthropology at the Australian National University (ANU) (1958–69), Fellow of Churchill College, Cambridge (1965–66, 1969–2010), and Professor of Sociology at the University of Cambridge (1969–82).[10]

[10] *Register of Members*, p. 20.

Among Barnes's many early achievements were the Wellcome Medal, awarded by the Wellcome Trust in 1950, and the Rivers Memorial Medal of the Royal Anthropological Institute in 1959. He was elected to the Association of Social Anthropologists of the Commonwealth in 1950. He was an active member of several anthropological and sociological associations and a stalwart of anthropology and sociology in both Australia and the United Kingdom. By the time he returned to the UK in 1969, he had served as Chairman of the Australian Branch of the Association of Social Anthropologists of the Commonwealth, President of Section F of the Australian and New Zealand Association for the Advancement of Science, and President of the Sociological Association of Australia and New Zealand, as well as an Executive Member of the Interim Council of the Australian Institute of Aboriginal Studies.[11]

Through his career, Barnes was offered many jobs, and of course he accepted several. One he turned down was a post at Rhodes University, Grahamstown, in 1950—because he did not want to raise his family in South Africa. He spent some time in South Africa after the war, and the National Party government was elected in 1948. He later lectured on South African 'race relations', in Australia and in Hawaii, although he never claimed expertise in that field. His arrival in Cape Town in 1946 was alone, because his wife Frances was pregnant with their first child and keen to complete her medical studies. John met his son Rory for the first time when Frances and Rory arrived in Livingstone, in then Northern Rhodesia, some months later. His base in the Federation was at Fort Jameson (now Chipata) in the Eastern Province, where he worked with the Ngoni, a displaced offshoot of the Zulu kingdom who had reached that part of what is now Zambia and Malawi (with some also in Tanzania and Mozambique) in the mid-nineteenth century. From Fort Jameson, he visited Max Gluckman in Barotseland, Elizabeth Colson among the Plateau Tonga, Max Marwick among the Cewa, and J. Clyde Mitchell among the Yao. Barnes enjoyed visiting colleagues and students in the field, and later he regretted that his department at Sydney in the 1950s had no money for such trips.

After his stint at the RLI Barnes returned to England to write up his field notes and complete his D.Phil. Officially, his supervisors were Max Gluckman, Meyer Fortes and E. E. Evans-Pritchard (in succession, apparently each doing a term at a time). Eventually, Max Gluckman, with whom he had started, was his only supervisor, although his comments on

---

[11] *Register of Members*, p. 20.

the thesis itself were limited. Isaac Schapera, though, worked systematically through the thesis and became one of his two examiners (the other
being J. G. Peristiany). Schapera had recently left Cape Town and taken
up the second chair in anthropology at the London School of Economics,
and Barnes drove him to Oxford for his own viva—the formal exam lasting less than a minute. In those days, the group associated with the RLI
met in their own seminar once a week at the Royal Anthropological
Institute in London. The seminar was also attended by Evans-Pritchard,
although reportedly he often dozed off on the sofa at the far end of the
room. Barnes also attended two other seminars in his Oxford days, both
at the London School of Economics: the lively intercollegiate anthropology
seminar chaired by Raymond Firth, and the rather more sedate sociology
seminar chaired by Morris Ginsberg.

When in 1952 Barnes began his fieldwork in Norway, he was holding
down three posts: a Simon Fellowship at Manchester, a college fellowship
at St John's College, Cambridge, and an honorary research assistantship
at University College London (UCL). It seems that he had also recently
been offered, but turned down, a lectureship at Cambridge (and in any
case, it transpired that no lectureship was actually available at Cambridge
at that time). His decision to leave them all for fieldwork at the small
settlement of Bremnes (later part of Bømlo, in southwestern Norway) was
accepted by Daryll Forde, head of anthropology at UCL, who assisted
Barnes in getting free Norwegian tuition at UCL. It also pleased Max
Gluckman, who had been appointed Professor of Social Anthropology
at Manchester in 1949. Gluckman had been director of the Rhodes-
Livingstone Institute from 1941 to 1947, and the dynamic theoretical
approach that Gluckman, Barnes and their colleagues fostered became
known as the Manchester School (though it could as easily have become
known as the RLI School).[12] The Manchester School was more than a
theoretical school though, as it entailed a number of specific methodological tools useful in both fieldwork and analysis. Among these the extended
case study method and network analysis were the most prominent, and the
latter was associated with Barnes, who gave it its name.[13]

---

[12] Raymond Firth, 'Max Gluckman, 1911–1975', *Proceedings of the British Academy*, 61 (1975),
479–96. Richard P. Werbner, 'The Manchester School in South-Central Africa', *Annual Review
of Anthropology*, 13 (1984), 157–85. T. M. S. Evans and Don Handelman (eds.), *The Manchester
School: Practice and Ethnographic Praxis in Anthropology* (New York, 2006).
[13] The extended case study emphasised a small number of cases to illustrate ethnographic
generalities, whereas network analysis emphasised individual associations rather than the place
of an individual within a social structure.

The Norwegian fieldwork gave Barnes the chance to take part in local activities, perhaps in a way that had not been as easy in Central Africa. Ultimately, it gave him comparative insights on Africa and points on which he would ultimately draw comparisons based on later visits, for example, to New Guinea, where he noted the relative isolation of communities, similar to that experienced in Bremnes. Fieldwork in Bremnes, as well as his development of network analysis, also gave Barnes an entry into the discipline of sociology which was to become as significant to him as social anthropology.

In 1954 he was given a Readership at the London School of Economics, but the post was short-lived. In 1956, he took the opportunity to take his first chair, at the University of Sydney. The Department of Anthropology there was Australia's most famous one, established by its first professor, A. R. Radcliffe-Brown, in 1925. Barnes was unhappy at Sydney though and apparently suffered disagreements with some of his colleagues. Meanwhile, the Australian National University (ANU), at Canberra, was keen to replace Siegfried Nadel, who had died early in 1956 and whose post remained vacant. An attempt to entice Edmund Leach to ANU fell through. The Vice-Chancellor offered Barnes the job, but prematurely, and Barnes had to keep the offer secret from colleagues, including close friends, at both Sydney and ANU—including Jim Davidson, who happened to be convener of the search committee. Barnes, still an Africanist and a northern Europe specialist, was happy at ANU despite ethnographic specialisations in other parts of the world (notably Australia and New Guinea). And he was delighted with life in Australia.

Barnes's unexpected decision to return to Cambridge in 1969, his choice of a newer college over an older one, and above all his decision to abandon an anthropology chair for a sociology one, all caused bemusement in some circles. He later revealed that the decision to change jobs and countries had had to do with the fact that he feared doing so later in life would have been impossible, although his documented disagreements with his colleague Derek Freeman at ANU perhaps also played a part. Barnes was a peace-loving man, and he shied away from academic politics when he could. For Barnes, the unexpected thing was that he should have been chosen for the Cambridge post at all. He was concerned that some might say that Meyer Fortes, who was William Wyse Professor of Social Anthropology there at the time and a member of the appointment committee, had acquired a second chair of anthropology through the back door. This led him to resist, at first, the invitation to teach an anthropology course at Cambridge, although later he did so. His decision for

Churchill over St John's reflected, at least in part, his wish to be part of what he perceived as a younger and more vibrant institution. He never regretted that momentous decision—although he had calculated that Fellows of Churchill would, before long, be the same age as Fellows at St John's, and mused over the fact that he may indeed enjoy growing older there, along with his fellow Fellows.

After thirteen years as Professor of Sociology at Cambridge, in 1982, the year after his election to the British Academy, Barnes took early retirement and returned to Australia. By his own admission, his heart lay there, although he carried both British and Australian passports—having acquired Australian nationality in 1987. He was Visiting Fellow at ANU (1978–9, 1984–92) and subsequently Programme Visitor (1993–8). His career was long, and he loved travelling and indeed travelled widely, throughout much of Australia, many parts of Asia and the Pacific, North America, Africa and Europe. He also enjoyed hill walking, even after, in 1997, he was diagnosed with Parkinson's disease.

His clever and subtle humour (and his raucous, infectious laugh) won him many friends and delighted his postgraduate students, whom he visited in their fieldwork sites when he could. He was a private and shy person, it seems, but had great influence on his students, to whom he was always steadfastly helpful. They were indeed his students, not his disciples, and their work continues some of his interests in both Australia and the UK. He was utterly devoted to his wife and children. He returned to England in 1998, and he died 'in exile' (as he signed his own memoir[14]) in the village of Histon, near Cambridge, on 13 September 2010. His wife Frances died a few weeks later in Leeds, where she had gone to be with their daughter. They were survived by their four children (one in Australia, three in England), and eight grandchildren.[15]

III

To many of us today, social anthropology and sociology are very different disciplines. To John Barnes, they never were, and perhaps for this reason some social anthropologists came to regard him as more of a sociologist, while sociologists often saw more the anthropologist in him.

[14] Barnes, *Humping My Drum*, p. 454.
[15] Michael W. Young, 'John Arundel Barnes (1918–2010)', *The Australian Anthropological Society Newsletter*, no. 120 (Dec. 2010), 2–6. Ray Abrahams, 'John Arundel Barnes (1918–2010)', *Anthropology Today*, 26(6) (Dec. 2010), 27.

Although he made great contributions to both subjects, he found such disciplinary boundaries distasteful, and the rigid separation of sociology and anthropology in the minds of others perhaps marginalised his work more than it might have. He may have resented this, although, it seems, he never explicitly said so.

In Barnes's early training in social anthropology, the mainstream view was Radcliffe-Brown's, and Radcliffe-Brown saw anthropology as a kind of sociology, which he perceived as static in nature.[16] Barnes and his fellow fieldworkers based at the Rhodes-Livingstone Institute gradually came to reject the static view of society that that sociological view implied. They focused instead on a dynamic approach, looked for conflict and contradiction in social structure and to social organisation over social structure. Barnes was part of this movement, and partly through his own work sociology came to follow similar lines, with the eventual rejection of structural-functionalism in favour of other perspectives and methods— not least, network analysis. Network analysis was to find its way into the heartland of the Manchester School through the work of fieldworkers in Central Africa, including particularly J. Clyde Mitchell and A. L. (Bill) Epstein.[17] Ironically perhaps, it had its most direct origins in Barnes's Norwegian fieldwork, and it served too to assist Gluckman in his desire to bring sociology together with social anthropology at Manchester. Rapidly too, it was to take prominence in sociology, particularly in the United States.

So what of J. A. Barnes the sociologist? The choice of the best of his articles among practitioners of that discipline would certainly include 'Class and committees in a Norwegian island parish'.[18] It is still the most cited of his articles, and was influential in sociology, as indeed it was also in anthropology within the Manchester School. The reason for its significance, however, is not apparent in its title, nor even in its subject matter. Its classic status derives from the fact that this short article virtually established a subdiscipline: that of network analysis. Barnes was in fact the first to use phrases such as 'network analysis' and 'social networks'. 'Class and committees' was published in 1954, and many years later, in 1987, he remarked that in spite of the abundance of formal organisations, 'most

---

[16] See, for example, A. R. Radcliffe-Brown, *Structure and Function in Primitive Society* (London, 1952).
[17] See Lynn Schumaker, *Africanizing Anthropology: Fieldwork, Networks, and the Making of Cultural Knowledge in Central Africa* (Durham, NC, 2001), pp. 152–89.
[18] J. A. Barnes, 'Class and committees in a Norwegian island parish', *Human Relations*, 7 (1954), 39–58.

individuals appeared to make decisions with reference to personal contacts that often cut across organizational boundaries'. Barnes 'tried to capture this configuration with the label "network"', which he applied particularly to the 'class system'.[19]

The paper was published after initial presentation at the 1953 meeting of the Association of Social Anthropologists of the Commonwealth, to which Barnes had been admitted three years before. Barnes's main appointment at the time was with the University of Manchester, but he soon moved to the London School of Economics. There he found that Elizabeth Bott was encountering a similar phenomenon in her work on relationship patterns among couples and families in London. Soon she was to publish, using the same term: 'network'.[20] Clyde Mitchell and others from the Manchester School also followed suit and developed the methodologies with which to explore network analysis, both in Central Africa and elsewhere.[21] Ultimately, the journal *Social Networks* was to follow, and a professional body, the International Network for Network Analysis, and much later, social networking websites. Barnes, who now has a posthumous *Facebook* page, remarked in 1987 that though his interests in sociology moved away from network analysis towards the sociology of knowledge, nevertheless he tried to keep in touch with those still practising what he had started.[22] And by 2007, a journalist would have to enlighten American readers with the fact that '"Social network" is not a *Facebook* term. Sociologist J. A. Barnes coined the phrase in 1954 to explain ....'[23]

The content of the 1954 article is not in fact confined to networks. It really has two main themes: networks and leadership. Barnes once remarked that even in Africa he did not find what he was supposed to find: corporate groups, such as agnatic lineages, dominating the social life of the Ngoni.[24] Agnatic ideology was not replicated in group structure. When he started fieldwork in Norway, then, he had expected groups to be more formally organised than in Central Africa. Here he would find his corporate groups, but in fact it was the networks that proved more important than

---

[19] J. A. Barnes, 'This Week's Citation Classic: "Class and committees in a Norwegian island parish"', *Current Contents / Social & Behavioral Sciences*, 23 (8 June 1987), 18.

[20] Elizabeth Bott, *Family and Social Network* (London, 1957).

[21] J. C. Mitchell (ed.), *Social Networks in Urban Situations: Analyses of Social Relationships in Central African Towns* (Manchester, 1969).

[22] Barnes, 'This Week's Citation Classic', p. 18.

[23] Monica Hesse, 'An unmanageable circle of friends', *The Washington Post* (Sunday, 26 Aug. 2007), M10.

[24] Barnes, *Models and Interpretations*, p. 67.

local government organisations, producers' cooperatives or other groups. The second theme, though rather rarely cited, concerns patterns of leadership. Barnes uncovered in Bremnes patterns of decision-making that emphasised discussion and consensus. Rivalries, pressures and divided loyalties were in evidence, but committees avoided public displays which might be awkward, such as voting.

Barnes's work in sociology of course includes a great deal of other material, though it is fair to say that although a professor of sociology for thirteen years, his output in social anthropology was greater, at least in number of books and papers. Among his most interesting contributions to sociology, though, was his Inaugural Lecture as Professor of Sociology at Cambridge, delivered in the wake of the era of student protest.[25] One reviewer did comment that 'it will hardly set the Cam on fire', but Barnes answered with characteristic reason coupled with humour that this had not been his intention. Rather, he 'had merely hoped to explain to the university why its sociology students might try to burn its buildings'.[26]

Barnes began his Inaugural Lecture by noting that he was the first Professor of Sociology at Cambridge. This of course exempted him from having to pay tribute to pioneers, as is customary on such an occasion. But the novelty of the subject in that university did require him, as he saw his duty, to justify its existence there. He pointed out that the subject had been taught in some American universities since the 1880s and at the London School of Economics since 1907. But of course sociological thought had existed in other guises at Cambridge, as elsewhere, long before 1969, and he pointed this out. Disciplines such as social anthropology, politics, economics and history, all then well-represented at Cambridge, employ ideas and even methods commonly regarded as belonging to sociology. Furthermore, he noted, a sustained analysis of the relations between the status of women, marital discord, and problems in bringing up children made it inevitable either that sociology should be present at Cambridge, or that these need not be concerns for Cambridge and its students. Likewise, poverty, war, overpopulation and the social consequences of environmental degradation, he argued, merit study. This may seem quite obvious today, but the paper is eminently readable and a good argument to be put before a new generation of undergraduates. Indeed, it is hard to think of it as a product of its time, since it remains current even now.

---

[25] J. A. Barnes, *Sociology in Cambridge: an Inaugural Lecture* (Cambridge, 1970).
[26] Barnes, *Models and Interpretations*, p. 182.

During his tenureship of the Cambridge chair, Barnes published two books that fall within the disciplinary milieu of sociology, with a third some years later.[27] All three hint, in their different ways, at the lack of clear disciplinary boundaries in what Barnes saw as social science, rather than as sociology or anthropology. They are also, in curious ways, related works, and they show Barnes's concern with both the practicality and the philosophy of ethical issues, and the relations between the practical and the philosophical.

Of these the first, *The Ethics of Social Inquiry*, is the most clearly socio-logical. Yet, its subtitle, *Three Lectures*, gives a hint of the origin if not the content of this short monograph. The three lectures were presented at the Institute for Social and Economic Change (ISEC), at Bangalore in South India. The invitation to South India had come from M. N. Srinivas, India's premier sociologist, who was in fact an Oxford-trained anthro-pologist: in India, the two disciplines are in any case often merged. The invitation specifically to the ISEC had come from its director, V. K. R. V. Rao, an economist and later a politician. Barnes urged his listeners to study the process of social inquiry itself, as well as to heed the words of E. E. Evans-Pritchard (with whom both Srinivas and Barnes had been former associates at Oxford), 'He who sups with the administration needs a long spoon.' He also commented on the difference between social and natural science, in that the former is specifically concerned with human society and thus has a more direct relevance for ethical concerns. Barnes drew examples from classical anthropological and sociological sources, as well as employing what were then topical examples from Chile and Vietnam.

The second book to fall within the disciplinary domain of sociology, *Who Should Know What?*, covers dilemmas and problems of covert and overt data-collection, of privacy and anonymity, and of dealing with writ-ten documents. It also touches on cultural formulations of the latter: in Scandinavia, documents are generally open; in other countries, they are surrounded by a legally enforced secrecy that ends arbitrarily at some exact date. The most interesting point in all this is shown through a his-torical example related to the dissemination of results. This is the example of the notion of the natural science paradigm within the social sciences, and Barnes uses the case of A. C. Haddon's decision on publication of the

[27] J. A. Barnes, *The Ethics of Inquiry in Social Science: Three Lectures* (Oxford, 1971). J. A. Barnes, *Who Should Know What? Social Science, Privacy and Ethics* (Harmondsworth, 1979). J. A. Barnes, *A Pack of Lies: Towards a Sociology of Lying* (Cambridge, 1994).

results of the Cambridge Torres Straits Expedition of 1898–9.[28] These were published not in the Torres Straits, nor even in Australia, but in Cambridge. And some were not published until 1935—of little use either to the Torres Straits inhabitants or their administrators.

The last of the three sociological works, humorously entitled *A Pack of Lies*, was written after Barnes taught a course on lying at Flinders University in Adelaide in 1990. It is the only one of his books with 'sociology' in the title or subtitle. Yet his examples and discussion ranges from sociology to social anthropology, to philosophy, psychology, linguistics and literary studies, and even to primatology (can non-human primates lie?).

IV

If the Manchester School had its roots in the RLI and its ethnographic tradition, then so too did network analysis. In another sense, as with the Norwegian case, the theory lies within the social organisation itself. A good deal of his work touches on the inapplicability of 'African models', and this applies even within Africa itself. While others (including E. E. Evans-Pritchard, Meyer Fortes, Daryll Forde and Jack Goody) tended to emphasise rigid structures, particularly lineages and clans, Barnes and his RLI colleagues saw African society in rather different terms. These different, more fluid forms of social organisation were prevalent especially, but by no means exclusively, in Central Africa. This may stem partly (but only partly) from the fact that Central Africa was perceived as being in the throes of 'social change'.

Barnes published a number of papers in this genre, and two book-length works. The latter two were, respectively, a monograph on marriage and one on politics.[29] *Marriage in a Changing Society* begins with a discussion of marriage before 1898, when Britain took control of the region. Historical evidence from documentary sources, as well as comparative examples from other Nguni-speaking groups such as Zulu and Swazi, provided a baseline. The Fort Jameson Ngoni (like other Nguni-speakers) married through the exchange of various payments: ideally a 'snuff-box' (a handful of tobacco), followed by 'bridewealth' (eight head

---

[28] Barnes, *Who Should Know What?*, pp. 32–3.
[29] J. A. Barnes, *Marriage in a Changing Society: a Study in Structural Change among the Fort Jameson Ngoni* (Cape Town, 1951). J. A. Barnes, *Politics in a Changing Society: a Political History of the Fort Jameson Ngoni* (Cape Town, 1954).

of cattle) and a 'legalisation payment' (e.g. an ox, a chicken or a cloth). A hierarchical system of polygyny, leviratic marriage, and segmentation by 'houses' (residential units, each headed by a different co-wife) all occurred. (Schapera suggested that a group of co-wives be called a 'bevy', but his suggestion came too late for Barnes to change the text, and Barnes called them 'bands'.[30]) At Fort Jameson, colonial rule changed all this. The Ngoni kingdom and its army were defeated, and a British settlement was established in its centre. Large villages were burnt, people were dispersed and cattle were looted. Clans were never that important for Ngoni, but the agnatic lineages that did exist lost some of their significance. Migrations in the twentieth century, both to the towns and to the mines, brought changes too, and Barnes vividly documents many aspects of social life with textual description, accompanied by statistical evidence, and through fourteen short 'case histories'. Barnes's contribution to the use of statistics, for example in divorce rates, was seminal, and led to subsequent suspicion whenever any anthropologist dared utter such then-common vagaries as 'divorce is rare' or 'divorce is frequent'. Though little read today, *Marriage in a Changing Society* remains a tour de force of ethnographic writing.

Politics in a Changing Society follows a similar form. It is less a history in the conventional sense, and more an anthropological (or sociological) analysis of processes in which changing social relations are more important than historical events. It also begins with a baseline, from both documentary and comparative material, and follows this with analytical use of field data. There was a trend at the time in examining change in more sophisticated and systematic ways, for example by Edmund Leach and Aiden Southall,[31] and Barnes's contribution was appreciated by many both in the Manchester tradition and outside it. Indeed Manchester University Press later reprinted both *Marriage in a Changing Society* and *Politics in a Changing Society*.[32]

Among J. A. Barnes's most important articles in social anthropology are such gems as 'African models in the New Guinea Highlands',[33] 'Time flies like an arrow',[34] and 'Genetrix: genitor : : nature: culture?' Probably

[30] Barnes, *Marriage in a Changing Society*, p. iii.

[31] E. R. Leach, *Political Systems of Highland Burma: a Study of Kachin Social Structure* (London, 1954). Aidan W. Southall, *Alur Society: a Study in Processes and Types of Domination* (London, 1956).

[32] In 1954 and 1957 respectively.

[33] J. A. Barnes, 'African models in the New Guinea Highlands', *Man*, 62 (1971), 5–9.

[34] J. A. Barnes, 'Time flies like an arrow', *Man*, NS 6 (1971), 537–52.

most social anthropologists would agree that all of these remain important for the discipline. They are still cited and assigned as undergraduate readings. Indeed, many of Barnes's works—thirteen of which were included in his collection *Models and Interpretations*—have stood up well to time. What is perhaps more striking, though, is that so many of them are linked to his earlier interests in Northern Rhodesia and to the time he spent there.

'African models in the New Guinea Highlands' was first published in *Man* in 1962. It was presented the year before at the Tenth Pacific Science Conference in Honolulu. Ironically, considering its subsequent celebrity, the paper was initially rejected by three other journals, and later attacked by various critics, not least for being a 'red herring'.[35] Yet it had a sobering impact on the Melanesia specialists, caught out by this Africanist's amazement at the use of simplified African-derived models to account for social phenomena in colonial New Guinea. Such models do not even characterise many African societies very well, especially if viewed through time. Melanesianists were looking for patrilineal descent systems, with all that documented examples like the Nuer of the Anglo-Egyptian Sudan or the Tallensi of the Gold Coast (Ghana) might imply. The article's beauty lies in its generality—written as it was on board ship, and citing no references. It was certainly not detailed, but it did give eight reasons why Highland New Guinea society was *not* characterised by stereotypical 'African' descent systems. It would take twenty years before the misleading application of African models in Africa would be similarly debunked, at least at a theoretical level.[36]

'Time flies like an arrow' was first published in the newly revamped *Man* (then merged with the former *Journal of the Royal Anthropological Institute*), in 1971. It was written to celebrate and to comment on the work of Claude Lévi-Strauss. It is an intellectually challenging piece, and for that very reason it requires contemplation as much as it demands close reading. Barnes contrasts Radcliffe-Brown's notion of synchronic analysis (concerned with enduring characteristics) with Lévi-Strauss's (concerned with Saussurian principles of regularity), and likewise Radcliffe-Brown's notion of diachronic analysis (characterised by a search for systematic change) with Lévi-Strauss's (characterised by a recognition of the partic-

---

[35] See Barnes, *Models and Interpretations*, p. 44.
[36] The debunking of African models within Africa can be attributed to several scholars writing about the same time, but the most indicative is Adam Kuper, 'Lineage theory: a critical retrospect', *Annual Review of Anthropology*, 11 (1982), 71–95.

ular and the accidental). Consequently, notions of structure and process may be quite different in the two implied traditions of anthropology. Moreover, although both British and French structuralists were more interested in the synchronic than the diachronic, they perceived it differently. Barnes was apparently thinking of Radcliffe-Brown as his exemplar of 'British structuralists', but a concern with Edmund Leach's brand of British 'French-style structuralism' (Lévi-Straussian but focused on single societies rather than human universals) would add another dimension.

'Genetrix: genitor : : nature: culture?' appeared in 1973 in *The Character of Kinship*, a Festschrift for Meyer Fortes. It uses Western, Australian Aboriginal, Melanesian and African examples. It shows the intricacies of kinship, as a product of both nature and culture, and culture itself as consisting of layers of culturally constructed social realities. The simple Latin distinctions between *genetrix* and *mater* and between *genitor* and *pater* imply precision, but they hide the fact that far from 'knowing' the 'biological facts' of reproduction, neither the Romans nor probably many in the West knew much at all about how conception occurs. Spermatazoons were discovered in 1677, although what they had to do with fertilisation was not at first clear. Mammalian ova were discovered in 1828, although how they combined with spermatazoons only became known (to a small group of scientists) in 1875. So much for Western 'knowledge'. Barnes criticised the ideas of David Schneider, then leading a new approach in kinship studies that maintains a clear distinction between science (which Schneider saw as based on facts) and culture (which he saw as consisting of symbols).[37] Barnes's own specific contribution lay in distinguishing three levels: the true genetic mother and true genetic father, the culturally recognised genetic mother (genetrix) and culturally recognised genetic father (genitor), and the culturally recognised social mother (mater) and culturally recognised social father (pater).[38] When new reproductive technologies were invented along with techniques for putting them into practice, the field opened further, although theoretical discussions of the nature of kinship were already being informed by the diverse notions of Melanesians, Australian Aborigines and early Christian theologians concerning how reproduction occurs. Some of these issues were dealt with in the special issue of *The Australian Journal of Anthropology* which was dedicated to Barnes.

[37] David M. Schneider, *American Kinship: a Cultural Account* (Englewood Cliffs, NJ, 1972).
[38] J. A. Barnes, 'Physical and social kinship', *Philosophy of Science*, 28 (1961), 296–9. J. A. Barnes, 'Physical and social facts in anthropology', *Philosophy of Science*, 31 (1964), 294–7.

Barnes produced a number of other works in the field of kinship. *Three Styles in the Study of Kinship* was intended as his final gesture in this area.[39] Essentially a pedagogical work, although highly analytical too, it outlines in great detail the approaches to kinship study of George Peter Murdock, Claude Lévi-Strauss and Meyer Fortes. Their main works were all published in 1949. Schneider's now-classic study of 'American kinship' had only just been published as Barnes was completing *Three Styles*, and moving back to Cambridge to take up the chair in sociology. However, an invitation to return to the fray (for a conference in India), along with the growing interest in Schneider's approach, required Barnes to comment. In a paper delivered there and published in 1980, Barnes chose to set 'the current state of play' in historical terms (and kinship studies had begun in earnest in 1871).[40] He concluded, perhaps enigmatically, that a coming synthesis might involve a combination of Lévi-Straussian structuralism and Raymond Firth's brand of micro-sociology (by which Barnes meant his studies of kinship in London rather than his much better-known work on the Pacific island of Tikopia). It was not, in other words, to come from Schneider's work, which he regarded with great suspicion.

V

John Barnes's groundbreaking work spans sociology, anthropology and the formal study of kinship structures—arguably a discipline separate from both. His best-known work in sociology was in methodology and in network analysis, and much of his work in anthropology was also related to that interest. He lives on in anthropology through the one-letter symbols now used by virtually all anthropologists (except for some in the North American kinship tradition), F, M, B, Z, S, D, H, W, P, G, C, E (respectively, father, mother, brother, sister, son, daughter, husband, wife, parent, sibling, child, spouse): a system thought up by Barnes, with others, on the train from Cape Town to Livingstone in 1946.[41] He put it

---

[39] J. A. Barnes, *Three Styles in the Study of Kinship* (London, 1971).

[40] J. A. Barnes, 'Kinship studies: some impressions of the current state of play', *Man*, NS 15 (1980), 219–303.

[41] Used in strings of possessives, for example MMBDD (mother's mother's brother's daughter's daughter)—one of four permitted-spouse genealogical positions for female alters and male egos, out of sixteen possible female second-cousin genealogical positions for female alters and male egos, in some Australian Aboriginal kinship systems.

to exemplary use in his most 'serious' venture into kinship studies, his Royal Anthropological Institute occasional paper *Inquest on the Murngin*.

John lives in our folk memory also through phrases we now take for granted: network analysis (which he invented in 1953) and structural amnesia (which he invented in 1947). Perhaps only anthropologists will know the latter, which refers to *forgetting* ancestors who are unimportant, for example, in defining one's lineage, and *remembering* those who are important in that way. J. A. Barnes defines an intellectual lineage for many social scientists, and his descendants in both sociology and anthropology are abundant.

ALAN BARNARD
Fellow of the Academy

Note. I am grateful to Ray Abrahams and Tim Ingold for their comments on an earlier draft and for their assistance with the preparation of this memoir.

GERALD COHEN

Gerald Allan Cohen
1941–2009

G. A. COHEN, universally known as Jerry, died unexpectedly on 5 August 2009. Born on 14 April 1941, he had recently retired as Chichele Professor of Social and Political Thought at Oxford University, and had taken up a part time post as Quain Professor of Jurisprudence at University College London. UCL was where he had begun his lecturing career in 1963, before being elected in 1984 at a youthful 43 to his Oxford Chair, which had previously been held by G. D. H. Cole, Isaiah Berlin, John Plamenatz and Charles Taylor. He took up the Chair in 1985, the same year in which he was also elected to the British Academy.

The question of who would be appointed to the Chichele Chair was, somewhat surprisingly, a matter of discussion in the national press. Cohen was relatively unknown and an unlikely candidate, at that time the author of just one book, *Karl Marx's Theory of History: a Defence* (Oxford, 1978) and a handful of papers. On his appointment the satirical magazine *Private Eye* speculated that the committee may have been influenced by Cohen's reputation as a wit and raconteur, and the need to enliven the quality of dinner table conversation at All Souls. Certainly Cohen had a unique and memorable gift for entertaining those around him—his conversation crackled with jokes, snatches of show tunes, and impressions of great philosophers, real and imagined—but in truth, the committee understood that he also had a rare, perhaps unique, philosophical talent, and their confidence in him was amply rewarded.

Cohen was born into a Jewish Marxist family, and his life and character were woven into his philosophical work in an unusual way, to the point

where some of these writings contain extended descriptions of his upbringing and family. For example, chapter 2 of his 1996 Gifford Lectures *If
You're an Egalitarian How Come You're so Rich?* (Cambridge, MA, 2000)
is entitled 'Politics and religion in a Montreal communist Jewish childhood' and paints a moving picture of his childhood, his parents, their
convictions and their social milieu as factory workers and, in the case of
his mother, communist party member and activist.[1] To read it is to be
transported into another world: the world of a cold-war Canadian child,
from an immigrant family, first convinced of the truth of Marxism and the
moral superiority of Soviet Communism, but later trying to come to terms
with the behaviour of the Soviet Union in the 1950s. Cohen's upbringing,
his family, his Jewishness (as distinct from Judaism) and his need to position his own beliefs in relation to Marx and to Soviet Communism were
central to his life and work, both in terms of its content and, often, its
presentation.

Equally important to his work was his training in philosophy, especially at Oxford, where he moved from undergraduate study in McGill, in
1961. There he came under the influence—the 'benign guidance'[2]—of
Gilbert Ryle and received a thorough grounding in the techniques of analytical philosophy, with its emphasis on rigour and fine distinctions. It was
armed with such techniques that Cohen began his earliest project, resulting in his Isaac Deutcher Memorial Prize-winning book *Karl Marx's Theory
of History: a Defence* (*KMTH*).[3] Later he said it was a type of 'repayment
for what I had received. It reflected gratitude to my parents, to the school
which had taught me, to the political community in which I was raised.'[4]
It was an attempt to state and defend Marx's theory of history in a fashion that met the standards of rigour and clarity of contemporary analytic
philosophy, in the face of criticisms from Plamenatz and others that this
could not be done. The project proceeded relatively slowly. Cohen first
published a number of papers on Marx-related themes. These include two
papers on what might be thought of as social epistemology. One, his first
published paper, considers the question of whether one's social role should
determine what one can think and believe; Cohen argues that human freedom requires one to believe as a human being, rather than attributing

---

[1] G. A. Cohen, *If You're an Egalitarian, How Come You're So Rich?* (Cambridge, MA, 2000),
pp. 20–41.
[2] G. A. Cohen, *History, Labour and Freedom* (Oxford, 1988), p. xi.
[3] G. A. Cohen, *Karl Marx's Theory of History: a Defence* (Oxford, 1978, expanded edn., 2000).
[4] *History, Labour and Freedom*, p. xi.

one's beliefs to a social role that one plays.[5] A second paper asks how a Marxist understanding of the materialist production of ideas affects the question of whether any such ideas can be regarded as true.[6] This is clearly a matter of huge importance for a Marxist philosopher, and, no doubt, a question Cohen felt he had to settle before taking any further steps. His response is that while other classes need, falsely, to represent their ideas as universal, in the sense of being in the interest of the great majority, the proletariat have no such need of pretence or deception. For their ideas really are in the interest of the majority.

Both these papers are, in a way, prefatory to his project of defending Marx's theory of history, in that they are questions that need to be answered in order to carry out the project with confidence. A third paper from the period, however, is much more closely aligned to the book-length project. Published in 1970, it is called 'On some criticisms of historical materialism' and was presented to the Joint Session of the Aristotelian Society and Mind Association at its annual meeting.[7] Here Cohen responds to some earlier criticisms of historical materialism by H. B. Acton and John Plamenatz, and Acton then replies to Cohen's paper.

Although published some years before *KMTH*, several of the innovative themes of that work are foreshadowed here. First, Cohen praises Acton for applying the standards of rigour of analytical philosophy to Marxism, and suggests that in his own work he will apply even higher standards. For this reason, arguably, this 1970 paper may well be the first appearance of what was later to be called 'Analytic Marxism', using the techniques of analytical philosophy and formal economics and social science to defend Marxism, rather than to criticise it. Second, Cohen takes Marx's 1859 *Preface to the Contribution to a Critique of Political Economy* as the central source for his reading of Marx's theory of history. Finally, he presents a sketch of how the device of functional explanation can be used to overcome some difficulties in the formulation of the theory, which was to become one of the central aspects of his later reconstruction. The main topic of the symposium is the question of the relation between the economic base and the legal and political superstructure in historical materialism. The economic base is understood to be the set of relations of

[5] G. A. Cohen, 'Beliefs and roles', *Proceedings of the Aristotelian Society*, lxvii (1966–7), 17–34.
[6] G. A. Cohen, 'The workers and the word: why Marx had the right to think he was right', *Praxis* (Zagreb), 3/4 (1968), 376–90.
[7] G. A. Cohen, 'On some criticisms of historical materialism', *Supplementary Volume, Proceedings of the Aristotelian Society*, xliv (1970), 121–41.

production, such as the relations between capitalists and workers, or masters and slaves, within the economy. Thus the base is, broadly speaking, the economic system. Plamenatz had argued that it was impossible to characterise economic relations of production except in terms of legal powers. For example, a proletarian is someone who has the right to sell his or her labour, unlike the serf or slave who has no such right. Yet to use the language of rights is to use a set of concepts belonging to the superstructure, and hence, so it is argued, it is impossible to define the economic structure except in superstructural terms. If this is so, then, it is argued, it cannot be the case that the economic structure has explanatory priority over the superstructure, as orthodox Marxism dictates.

Cohen does not question Plamenatz's claim that it is necessary to provide an independent account of the economic structure for it to play the role Marx requires of it. Rather he takes on the challenge of providing such an account—what he calls a 'rechtsfrei' interpretation. He argues that the economic base should be understood, strictly speaking, as constituted by powers, rather than rights. The superstructure, as a set of legal rights, exists in order to consolidate the powers belonging to the economic base. This is a direct and explicit appeal to functional explanation. The superstructure exists because it has a function: the function of protecting economic power. The solution is elegant. The base and superstructure can be characterised independently of each other, and while the superstructure has a causal effect on the base, it exists in order to have that effect. Therefore the economic base has explanatory priority even though causal influence goes in the opposite direction.

Although many of the elements were in place by 1970, and other important papers on Marx were published in 1972 and 1974,[8] it was not until 1978 that Cohen published *KMTH*. Part of the reason for delay was his perfectionism in trying to get the details as precisely right as he could. But another explanation was that he was faced with a much more urgent project. In 1973 Robert Nozick published a long article in *Philosophy and Public Affairs*, which was to become the heart of the libertarian political philosophy elaborated in *Anarchy, State, and Utopia*.[9]

Cohen reports that Nozick's ideas were first drawn to his attention by Gerald Dworkin in 1972, and, in an important episode in his life, in 1975

[8] G. A. Cohen, 'Karl Marx and the withering away of social science', *Philosophy and Public Affairs*, 1 (1972), 182–203, G. A. Cohen, 'Marx's dialectic of labour', *Philosophy and Public Affairs*, 3 (1974), 235–61, and G. A. Cohen, 'Being, consciousness and roles', in C. Abramsky (ed.), *Essays in Honour of E. H. Carr* (London, 1974).
[9] Robert Nozick, *Anarchy, State, and Utopia* (New York, 1974).

he visited Princeton for a semester, lecturing on Nozick and making important connections with Tom Nagel and Tim Scanlon.[10] On encountering Nozick's arguments Cohen felt a need to divert his focus from his work on Marx, for the time being, to answer Nozick. Nozick, of course, sets out a natural rights based form of libertarianism, defending a minimal state, and condemning any form of redistributive transfer as coercive and unjust. For many left-liberals, Nozick's was a dazzling defence of an obviously false and heartless view: a view that required attention because of the intellectual strength, wit and elegance of many of the arguments of the book but not because the overall doctrine presented gave them any cause to doubt their own heartfelt convictions. For Cohen, however, the situation was quite different. As he later put it, in a paper revealingly entitled 'Marxism and contemporary political philosophy, or: why Nozick exercises some Marxists more than he does any egalitarian liberals',[11] Cohen's Marxist-inspired critique of capitalism was based on the idea that the relation between capitalist and worker is exploitative, because it involves 'the theft of another person's labour time'. Yet in *Anarchy, State, and Utopia* Nozick argues that redistributive taxation has exactly that character. According to Cohen, Marxists such as himself at that time believed in the principle of self-ownership, that people are the rightful owners of their own powers, but exactly this principle is argued, by Nozick, to yield not communism but a stark form of capitalist individualism. Refuting this view, then, became another essential 'ground-clearing' task in the defence of Marxism, but also very important for its own sake.

Cohen's classic paper on Nozick, 'Robert Nozick and Wilt Chamberlain: how patterns preserve liberty' was published in 1977.[12] (A slightly revised version was published in 1995 in *Self-Ownership, Freedom and Equality*. Like many of his reprinted papers the later version contains a number of small corrections and amendments.) Nozick vividly argued that any attempt to introduce a 'pattern' of distributive justice, such as equality, will require the state to prevent individuals from making voluntary transactions that might disrupt the pattern. Yet if the state were to do this, it would restrict individual liberty, needing to coerce individuals into conformity to the designated distribution, and so those who value liberty should resist any attempt to try to implement a pattern. Cohen makes many points in criticism of Nozick's argument, but his main response is

[10] G. A. Cohen, *Self-Ownership, Freedom and Equality* (Cambridge, 1995), p. 4.
[11] Ibid., pp. 144–64.
[12] G. A. Cohen, 'Robert Nozick and Wilt Chamberlain: how patterns preserve liberty', *Erkenntnis*, 11 (1977), 5–23.

that Nozick has overlooked the fact that a distribution of property is already a distribution of liberty. One person's ownership of an item of property entails that other people are not at liberty to use it without the owner's permission. Therefore it can be the case that a pattern is needed to preserve the liberty of those who would otherwise suffer in an unpatterned distribution. Hence, Cohen argues, patterns preserve liberty. He notes that Nozick attempts to avoid this, by redefining liberty as, essentially, the freedom to do what one has a right to do, and so a non-owner's inability to use the property of its owner is no longer a detriment to liberty. But if this move is made it then becomes question-begging to try to defend a view of private property in terms of liberty, for any account of liberty already assumes a view of justified property. This critique is arguably the most powerful and influential of those that attempted to engage with Nozick's argument.

Cohen finally published *KMTH* in 1979, as well, that year, as publishing a brilliant, critical examination of Marx's labour theory of value and its relation to the theory of exploitation.[13] On the publication of *KMTH* Cohen established his position as among the world leading interpreters of Marx's thought. The book is a considerable extension of the earlier paper 'On some criticisms of historical materialism', and sets out a clear account of the core of Marx's theory of history. According to Cohen the two central theses of historical materialism are the 'development thesis' and the 'primacy thesis'. The development thesis states that society's productive forces tend to develop throughout history, in the sense that human productivity tends to become more powerful over time. The primacy thesis is a combination of two claims: that the nature of the productive forces explains the economic structure, and that the nature of the economic structure explains the superstructure (the claim we saw explicated and defended in the earlier paper). Put together, this is a form of technological determinism: the ultimate explanatory factor for all other significant facts about society is the nature of technology available. As Marx himself puts it, in *The Poverty of Philosophy*, 'the hand-mill gives you society with the feudal lord, the steam mill society with the industrial capitalist'.

This theory is distinctively Marxist in that it divides history into epochs—pre-class society, slavery, feudalism, capitalism, and communism—and understands the transition from epoch to epoch as the result of class struggle and revolutionary change. The claim is that an economic

---

[13] G. A. Cohen, 'The labour theory of value and the concept of exploitation', *Philosophy and Public Affairs*, 8 (1979), 338–60.

structure, such as capitalism, will persist for as long as it is optimal for the development of the productive forces (an application of functional explanation) but eventually it cannot contain all the growth it has stimulated. At that point the economic structure 'fetters' the development of the productive forces and must give way, to be replaced by a new economic structure that will continue the development of the productive forces.

Although the basic theory can be stated simply, *KMTH* is a complex book. First, it enters into many disputes regarding the detailed understanding of Marx, attempting to settle contested points of textual interpretation. Second, Cohen builds detailed and ingenious arguments for many of the positions taken. The book, after all, is an interpretation of Marx and a defence of the view. Accordingly the discussion encompasses questions not raised by Marx, such as how to formulate and deploy the central device of functional explanation, or how to argue for the claim that the forces of production tend to develop throughout history.

On publication the book received wide acclaim. At the same time, naturally enough, it received various forms of criticism. Some of this criticism was aimed at the interpretation of Marx. One oft-made charge was that Marx's theory of history was not, at bottom, one of technological determinism. Some of these critics pointed out that Cohen had downplayed Hegel's influence on Marx and, accordingly, had not taken seriously dialectical forms of reasoning. However, Cohen's project of incorporating analytic philosophy into Marxism was designed precisely to overcome what he saw as the damaging obscurantism of Hegelian Marxism, especially that transmitted via the work of Althusser.[14] A related, and less doctrinaire, criticism was that Cohen allowed only a relatively minor role for class struggle. In Cohen's reading, class struggle is the agent of change from epoch to epoch, rather than the engine of history at all times, as appears to be indicated by Marx's remark that 'history is the history of class struggle'. Yet Cohen was convinced that his interpretation of Marx was correct on this point, accepting that class struggle is the 'immediate driving power of history' but not its 'underlying' driving force.[15]

Other lines of criticism concerned the theory itself, rather than whether it was a true depiction of Marx's thought. Jon Elster, for example, strongly criticised the use of functional explanation, arguing that it retained an unacceptable teleology. As Elster observes, suggesting that economic structures rise and fall as they further or impede human productive power

---

[14] *Karl Marx's Theory of History*, extended edn., p. xxi.
[15] *History, Labour and Freedom*, p. 16.

seems to assume that history is goal directed, or even that there is some sort of external agency ensuring that progress continues to be made.[16] Andrew Levine and Erik Wright took issue with Cohen's argument that the development of the productive forces can be explained in terms of what they call 'rational adaptive preferences'. They suggest that Cohen does not take sufficiently into account problems of collective action.[17] Joshua Cohen made similar criticisms and adduced evidence that there have been long stretches of history in which the productive forces declined in strength (most notably on the fall of the Roman Empire).[18] Richard Miller pointed out that the account of fettering was unclear.[19] Did the productive forces have to stop developing, or was it enough that they developed more slowly than they would under some other economic structure? Furthermore, the use of the productive forces and their development are quite different. One could argue that capitalism greatly develops the productive forces but uses them poorly. Is this fettering or not?

Each of these criticisms brought forward important responses and further clarifications of the theory. In response to Elster, Cohen pursued the analogy with the Darwinian use of functional explanation in evolutionary biology, which does not presuppose teleology or 'nature's purposes'.[20] In response to Joshua Cohen, and Levine and Wright, Cohen, together with Will Kymlicka, wrote a detailed rebuttal of their argument,[21] and, in response to Richard Miller, Cohen broadly accepted the criticism that the theory of fettering was unclear, and wrote a detailed clarification, which was first published in *History, Labour and Freedom* and was ultimately incorporated as an additional chapter in the extended edition of *KMTH*.

Yet in the face of these criticisms and reformulations Cohen began to see that the theory was not as clear-cut as he had thought. He also had begun to develop reservations of his own, especially about historical materialism's neglect of people's apparent need for self-definition: that is, the need to identify with groups in society that are less than the whole. This in turn leads Marxism to a dismissive and reductionist approach to religion

---

[16] Jon Elster, 'Cohen on Marx's theory of history', *Political Studies*, 28 (1980), 121–8, Jon Elster, *Making Sense of Marx* (Cambridge, 1985).

[17] A. Levine and E. Wright, 'Rationality and class struggle', *New Left Review*, 123 (1980).

[18] Joshua Cohen, 'Book Review: *Karl Marx's Theory of History*', *Journal of Philosophy*, 79 (1982), 253–73.

[19] Richard Miller, 'Productive forces and the forces of change: review of *Karl Marx's Theory of History*', *The Philosophical Review*, 90 (1981), 91–117.

[20] G. A. Cohen, 'Functional explanation: reply to Elster', *Political Studies*, 28 (1980), 129–35.

[21] G. A. Cohen and W. Kymlicka, 'Human nature and social change in the Marxist conception of history', *Journal of Philosophy*, 85 (1988), 171–91, repr. in *History, Labour and Freedom*.

and nationalism. These anxieties are recorded in two other papers that also appeared first in *History, Labour and Freedom* and then in the expanded edition of *KMTH*: 'Reconsidering historical materialism' and 'Restricted and inclusive historical materialism'. Others might, at this point, have seen the enterprise as a 'degenerating research programme'. Instead of using the theory to illuminate and explain ever more aspects of empirical reality, it appeared to require increasingly intricate internal development, specification and qualification to defend it against criticism, thereby reducing its explanatory power. Indeed, Cohen explains that his attitude to historical materialism had changed on completing the book. While writing it he was sure that Marx's theory of history was correct. After, he said, it was not so much that he believed it to be false, but that he did not know how to tell whether or not it was true.[22]

During this time Cohen was a founder and very active member of the Non-Bullshit Marxism Group (later called the September Group), which was a remarkable, interdisciplinary group of scholars who first met in 1979 and again 1980, to discuss exploitation. They then met annually, and then biennially, to discuss wider themes. The core membership of the original group, aside from Cohen, were Jon Elster, John Roemer, Hillel Steiner, Philippe van Parijs, Robert van der Veen, Adam Przeworski, Erik Olin Wright, Pranab Bardhan and Robert Brenner, although the membership changed considerably over the years.

The September Group was founded to discuss themes within Marxism, but their allegiance to the themes lasted longer, typically, than their allegiance to Marx. This development was foreshadowed, to some degree, by Cohen's earlier paper 'The labour theory of value and the concept of exploitation' in which he had argued that the concept of exploitation does not rest on the labour theory of value. As Cohen continued to work in the 1980s and beyond, one might characterise his writings as working out how to formulate his opposition to capitalism and allegiance to socialism without the underpinnings of Marx's theory of history. As he put it, 'In the past, there seemed to be no need to *argue* for the desirability of an egalitarian socialist society. Now I do little else.'[23]

This next phase in his career takes up themes that emerged in his criticism of Nozick: the relation between capitalism, socialism and freedom, and the nature and consequences of the thesis of self-ownership. These are the topics of the last few papers reprinted in *History, Labour and*

---

[22] *History, Labour and Freedom*, p. 132, *Karl Marx's Theory of History*, expanded edn., p. 341.
[23] *Self-Ownership, Freedom and Equality*, p. 7.

Freedom, and all of his next collection, *Self-Ownership, Freedom, and Equality.*

Cohen in the 1980s was especially exercised by the Marx-inspired question of how to understand the unfreedom of workers under capitalism, given that they exist in a structure which places freedom of choice at its centre, and no worker is forced, so it appears, to work for any particular capitalist. Yet at the same time there seems to be a vital sense in which workers in the capitalist system remain unfree. One important part of the analysis is to provide a definition of being forced to do something in which saying that a person is forced to do something does not mean that it is the only option available to him or her, but that any other options he or she has are not acceptable or reasonable.[24]

One obvious response to the claim that workers are forced to sell their labour-power to the capitalists, on this definition, is that workers do have an acceptable alternative; they can become petty bourgeois shop owners or self-employed in some way. Here Cohen accepts that this escape route is available to some workers, yet, he argues, although any individual worker is free to leave the proletariat, the proletariat is collectively unfree, for there are nothing like as many escape routes as there are members of the proletariat.[25]

The notion of the worker's right to freedom and the thesis of self-ownership are linked through the idea of a person's right to control their actions and labour. Cohen characterises self-ownership as the thesis that 'each person enjoys over herself and her powers, full and exclusive rights of control and use, and therefore owes no service or product to anyone else that she has not contracted to supply'.[26] This is, of course, qualified by the condition that rights of self-ownership do not permit one to interfere coercively into the lives of others. In a series of papers Cohen considered the relation between self-ownership and what he refers to as 'world-ownership': rights over those parts of the world that are not persons. Essentially Cohen set out to rebut the Nozickian argument that rights to self-ownership entail rights to world-ownership (i.e. individual property rights) that are in principle unrestricted. Nozick had argued that any attempt to redistribute worldly resources in effect conscripts one person, willingly or not, to work for another.

Cohen notes that those who are in favour of redistribution have the option merely to deny self-ownership, and assume that we have non-

[24] *History, Labour and Freedom,* p. 247.
[25] Ibid., pp. 239–304.
[26] *Self-Ownership, Freedom and Equality,* p. 12.

contractual duties of non-interference. Yet he argues that a stronger defence is to accept, for the purposes of argument, the thesis of self-ownership, and show that the Nozickian conclusion does not follow. In a now-classic discussion of Nozick's account of justice in initial acquisition, Cohen points out that it is essential to Nozick's argument that the external world is, initially, unowned, and therefore available for initial acquisition. However, Nozick does not show that the world is not jointly owned by all human beings. If that were the case the conditions for appropriation would be much more strict, and would not yield the type of property rights favoured by libertarians. Hence, at the least, Nozick has not shown that radically unequal distribution can follow from self-ownership. Furthermore, even if the world is not jointly owned, Cohen argues that Nozick's defence of initial appropriation—roughly, an appropriation is acceptable as long as it makes no one worse off—contains a strong element of paternalism that Nozick would reject in other circumstances.[27]

As his work on this topic developed Cohen seemed close to endorsing the thesis of self-ownership, especially, as we noted above, because he saw it as very similar to the views that underlie the Marxist opposition to exploitation. Yet he came to believe that self-ownership and an attractive form of egalitarianism were in conflict. In 'Are freedom and equality compatible?'[28] he argues that assuming that egalitarianism should be characterised by the thesis that the world is jointly owned by everyone is far too restrictive. It would require everyone else's consent before anyone could use anything at all. This, Cohen argues, thereby renders self-ownership 'merely formal' (a criticism that also applies to libertarianism, for the self-ownership of those without property is also merely formal and they would have to rely entirely on the cooperation of others for survival). He continues with the argument that the egalitarian alternative of parcelling the world into equal individual shares fares no better, at least from an egalitarian point of view, as it will allow outcomes to be strongly determined by the exercise of differential talent, and fails to guarantee support for those who cannot produce for themselves.

Eventually, therefore, he found the principle of self-ownership unhelpful, and in a pair of papers published for the first time in *Self-Ownership, Freedom and Equality* he came to accept the position that many of his liberal egalitarian friends and colleagues had urged upon him for years: the rejection of the principle. While he defends the coherence of the idea

---

[27] Ibid., pp. 67–91.
[28] Ibid., pp. 92–115.

of self-ownership, he argues against its adoption. His position is not so much to find a direct argument against the thesis, but rather to demonstrate that the motivations that lead in the direction of self-ownership do not take one all the way. That is to say, one can oppose slavery, advance autonomy and object to treating a person as a means without adopting self-ownership.[29]

Self-Ownership, Freedom and Equality largely pursues a single theme: the thesis of self-ownership—and it is something of an anticlimax that the work ends on a largely negative note. Yet this should not detract from the point that the essays together add up to the most powerful and influential detailed rebuttal of Nozick's libertarianism that has been produced, one that is unlikely to be surpassed. The essays, executed with supreme rigour, are full of insight and interest even when their point is to warn against a wrong turning, rather than build a new construction.

Modestly Cohen characterised himself as essentially a reactive philosopher. This, as a more general conception of philosophy, comes out clearly in a remarkable paper, 'How to do political philosophy', written for use in teaching a graduate class in Oxford, where it is clear that Cohen conceives of philosophy as an activity that takes place against an opponent.[30] In the first phase of his career Marx was the clear inspiration, and the opponents were analytic critics of Marx, such as Plamenatz, and obscurantist defenders, such as Althusser. The second phase was dominated by the need to answer Nozick's libertarianism. In the third phase Ronald Dworkin was the focus of his reflections, and in particular Dworkin's two seminal articles on equality of welfare and equality of resources.[31] Cohen found himself very sympathetic to what later came to be called 'luck egalitarianism'. Dworkin's achievement, said Cohen, in a much quoted passage, was to perform 'for egalitarianism the considerable service of incorporating within it the most powerful idea in the arsenal of the anti-egalitarian right: the idea of choice and responsibility'.[32] Indeed, there is a strong residue of Cohen's earlier reflections on Nozick in this comment.

The leading idea of luck egalitarianism is to make a distinction between those aspects of one's fate for which one is responsible, and those aspects

[29] *Self-Ownership, Freedom and Equality*, pp. 209–44.
[30] G. A. Cohen, 'How to do political philosophy', in Michael Otsuka (ed.), *On The Currency of Egalitarian Justice, and Other Essays* (Princeton, NJ, 2011), pp. 225–35.
[31] Ronald Dworkin, 'What is equality? Part 1, equality of welfare', *Philosophy and Public Affairs*, 10 (1981), 185–246, and 'What is equality? Part 2, equality of resources', *Philosophy and Public Affairs*, 10 (1981), 283–345.
[32] G. A. Cohen, 'On the currency of egalitarian justice', *Ethics*, 99 (1989), 906–44, repr. in *On the Currency of Egalitarian Justice and Other Essays*, pp. 3–43.

for which one is not. Dworkin makes a distinction between 'brute luck' and 'option luck' and on this view the project is to set out principles that allow people to reap the benefits, but also suffer the burdens, of good and bad option luck, but at the same time to insulate people from the effects of good and bad brute luck. There are, at least, two central questions that must be answered in order to settle how this doctrine is to be formulated. One is the question of how exactly to define the 'cut' between those factors for which a person is to be held responsible, and those they are not. A second is the 'currency' of justice: should equality be defined in terms of welfare, resources, capabilities, or something else again? Dworkin is very clear on the second question: equality of resources is the right currency. His response to the first question—how exactly to draw the cut—was less easy to discern from his writings.

Cohen's contribution to this debate was initially set out in two papers, 'On the currency of egalitarian justice', mentioned above, and 'Equality of what? On welfare, goods and capabilities'. [33] Cohen broadly accepts Arneson's characterisation of Dworkin's theory as one of equality of opportunity for resources.[34] However, in opposition to Dworkin and Arneson, Cohen's preferred position is one of 'equality of access to advantage', of which the more important modification is 'advantage' instead of 'resources' or 'welfare'. Cohen's point is that an egalitarian must be sensitive to certain types of resource deficiency, however they impact on welfare, as well as certain types of welfare deficiency, however they impact on resources. Accordingly he defines a new notion—advantage—which straddles resources and welfare (although he does not attempt to specify how the two elements are to be combined).

One primary issue between Cohen and Dworkin comes down to the question of whether low welfare should engage egalitarian concerns. Dworkin admits the immediate appeal of such a view, but marshals a range of considerations to put it into doubt. Perhaps surprisingly, the focal example for deciding between different cases is that of 'expensive tastes'. If a person cannot enjoy those things others typically take pleasure in—beer and hen's eggs, say—but, to achieve comparable levels of enjoyment, they must consume expensive champagne and plover's eggs,

---

[33] G. A. Cohen, 'Equality of what? On welfare, goods and capabilities', *Recherches Economiques de Louvain*, 56 (1990), 357–82, and in M. Nussbaum and A. Sen (eds.), *The Quality of Life* (Oxford, 1983), pp. 11–29, repr. in *On the Currency of Egalitarian Justice*, pp. 44–60.
[34] Richard Arneson, 'Equality and equal opportunity for welfare', *Philosophical Studies*, 55 (1989), 77–93.

should they receive a social subsidy so that they can achieve the same level of enjoyment as the rest of the population?

Dworkin's position is that one should not receive a subsidy for expensive tastes, unless they are a form of compulsion or craving, akin to mental illness. Cohen, by contrast, argues that there is a difference between those people who find themselves with expensive tastes, by bad brute luck, who should be subsidised, and those who deliberately cultivated them, and who, in the spirit of luck egalitarianism, should be required to bear the consequences of their freely made choice. Dworkin argues that the key factor for deciding whether or not subsidy is due is whether the person identifies with their tastes. It would be 'alienating' to offer people subsidy for aspects of what they regard as their personality. In reply Cohen makes the important distinction between identifying with the taste and identifying with its cost. One can fully identify with the taste yet regret that it is expensive. If one has not deliberately cultivated it then, in Cohen's view, subsidy is due. The debate between Dworkin and Cohen went through several exchanges, both making strong and plausible arguments and neither side prepared to concede ground.[35]

When luck egalitarianism—in all its versions—came under attack from Elizabeth Anderson[36] and others for its apparent inhumanity, such as its 'abandonment of the irresponsible' (those who have freely chosen paths with disastrous consequences and would therefore have no claim for help) Cohen took pains to point out that his project was only to define and argue for a theory of equality as an account of distributive justice, and not to argue that any society should adopt an unmodified principle of equality. Rather, he reminded his readers of a point that he had made explicit in his earlier paper. He accepts that concerns other than those of egalitarian justice could turn out to be more important in practice.[37] In making this point he develops an early version of a distinction that, as we will see, became important in the last period of his work: the distinction between theories of justice and what he was to call 'rules of regulation'.

The next phase in Cohen's work began with three papers that stand with *Karl Marx's Theory of History*, and the critique of Nozick, as the

[35] G. A. Cohen, 'Expensive tastes and multiculturalism', in R. Bhargava, A. K. Bagchi and R. Sudarshan (eds.), *Multiculturalism, Liberalism and Democracy* (New Delhi, 1999); R. Dworkin, *Sovereign Virtue* (Cambridge, MA, 2000); G. A. Cohen, 'Expensive taste rides again', in J. Burley (ed.), *Dworkin and his Critics* (Oxford, 2004), pp. 3–29, repr. in *On the Currency of Egalitarian Justice*, pp. 81–115. R. Dworkin, 'Replies', in *Dworkin and his Critics*.
[36] Elizabeth Anderson, 'What is the point of equality?' *Ethics*, 109 (1999), 287–337.
[37] G. A. Cohen, *Rescuing Justice and Equality* (Cambridge, MA, 2008), p. 271.

high points of his career. These are the Tanner Lectures of 1992, 'Incentives, inequality and community',[38] 'The Pareto argument for inequality' (1995),[39] and 'Where the action is: on the site of distributive justice' (1997).[40] The last of these papers was also included in Cohen's superbly readable and engrossing book *If You're an Egalitarian How Come You're So Rich?* and together they also comprise the first three chapters of his final major book, *Rescuing Justice and Equality*. The essential question is how, as a believer in equality, should one behave in one's personal economic life? In particular Cohen is concerned to question how it could be consistent both to pursue a high income and to espouse egalitarianism. Much of this work is aimed at the criticism of one particular attempt to defend such a combination to be found in the work of John Rawls, who, in effect, became Cohen's last philosophical opponent. Rawls's famous 'Difference Principle' states that inequalities in income and wealth are justified when they are to the greatest possible benefit of the worst off.[41] An apparently naïve reply to Rawls is to question how inequalities could ever be to the benefit of the worst off. Inequalities can be removed by transferring money from the richer to the poorer, thereby achieving equality by making the worst off better off. The Rawlsian reply is that such a transfer would, of course, be better if it were possible. But the Difference Principle also anticipates situations where such a beneficial transfer is not possible; that is where equalising would make everyone worse off, at least in the longer term. Broadly this doctrine is thought to be sensitive to the economic argument that everyone can be better off if the highly productive are provided with material incentives to work harder. This, in turn, leads to inequalities that are to the advantage of all.

Cohen, however, pushes the argument to another stage. How can there be circumstances where equality is impossible at a higher level for all? Presumably, only because those who are well off will not contribute as much effort at a lower level of income. This may be an understandable response, if not admirable, for those who do not believe in equality. Yet one of the conditions of Rawls's account of a 'well-ordered society' is that everyone should believe in the Rawlsian principles of justice, and in

[38] G. A. Cohen, 'Incentives, inequality, and community', in Grethe B. Peterson (ed.), *The Tanner Lectures on Human Values*, 13 (Salt Lake City, UT, 1992), pp. 261–329.

[39] G. A. Cohen, 'The Pareto argument for inequality', *Social Philosophy and Policy*, 12 (1995), 160–85.

[40] G. A. Cohen, 'Where the action is: on the site of distributive justice', *Philosophy and Public Affairs*, 26 (1997), 3–30.

[41] John Rawls, *A Theory of Justice* (Oxford, 1971, rev. edn., 1999).

particular endorse the principle that the worst off should be made as well off as possible. Therefore people in a Rawlsian society should not seek higher wages than others, unless there is some special reason why they cannot (as distinct from will not) be more productive on the same income as others. Therefore, Cohen argues, the Difference Principle justifies much less inequality than it is often thought to do, and that Rawlsian principles of justice must be supplemented by an 'egalitarian ethos' to guide choices in everyday life.

There are several resources in Rawls to try to combat this line of argument, although Rawls himself never confronted it in detail. One important response is that the Difference Principle is intended to regulate the 'basic structure' of society, rather than personal behaviour. This, and several other strategies, are discussed, and rebutted in detail, in the first half of *Rescuing Justice and Equality*. The second part of the book, while still engaged with Rawlsian theory, changes tack, extending an argument first presented in a paper entitled 'Facts and Principles'.[42] Here the project is to attempt to show that basic principles of justice must be 'fact free' in the sense of not depending on any empirical facts. This contrasts with a Rawlsian 'constructivist' approach in which facts about human nature and society are taken into account at the most basic level in formulating principles of justice. Here Cohen accuses Rawls and his followers of failing to respect the distinction mentioned above between rules of regulation and (pure) principles of justice.

Although this work has attracted respectful and detailed attention, many readers have been surprised by this turn in Cohen's work. Although it is the fruit of several years of sustained endeavour, in contrast to most of his other work it is much less clear what the payoff is, as his opponents are not convicted of any substantive error regarding what is to be done, as distinct from conceptual confusion regarding the nature of justice. However, for Cohen conceptual clarity for its own sake was of supreme importance.

Nevertheless, certainly for the chapters in Part One, the book is already a classic in political philosophy, and it may well be that in time the significance of Part Two will come to be better understood. Furthermore, in presenting his ideas in book length form Cohen came to reflect on a number of items that are foreshadowed in earlier work but explicitly clarified here. For example, there is a short discussion of Cohen's attitude to

---

[42] G. A. Cohen, 'Facts and principles', *Philosophy and Public Affairs*, 31 (2003), 211–45

moral realism,[43] and a more explicit endorsement of pluralism than is found elsewhere.[44]

Cohen's final book, *Why Not Socialism?*, was completed before he died but published posthumously.[45] The book is very short, and published in small format. It begins with an account of a camping trip and persuasively argues that under such circumstances the trip would be much more enjoyable for all participants, and more efficient, if the campers adopted certain anti-individualist principles of community and equality that could fairly be described as socialist, rather than capitalist market principles, to govern their interactions. The book continues with the question of why it should be that such socialist principles are not adopted in broader social and economic life. Here Cohen refuses to accept the pessimism about human nature that suggests that natural human selfishness makes socialism impossible. Rather, he points out, we have not (yet?) been able to devise social mechanisms that allow ourselves to organise large-scale economic interaction on the basis of human generosity, in contrast to the capitalist free market, which can turn individual greed and fear to general advantage, although, of course, it has many disadvantages too.

At his death Cohen left a number of works in progress as well as a series of lectures on moral and political philosophy that he had intended to prepare for publication. Much of this work will be published in the next few years. One of the most intriguing as yet unpublished papers is called 'One kind of spirituality'. The importance of Cohen's Jewish background has already been remarked upon, but many assumed that he had no interest in any issues of religion or spirituality, especially given what he has described as his 'anti-religious upbringing'. However two of three children, Gideon and Sarah, took a different direction, Gideon adopting Rastafarianism and moving to Ethiopia, and Sarah spending much of her time in an Ashram in the southern Indian state of Kerala. Cohen's love and respect for his children no doubt encouraged him to take their views seriously. In his Gifford Lectures for 1996—normally given on a theme in Philosophy of Religion—Cohen stated that he was agnostic, not an atheist. But more surprisingly for many readers, he revealed himself as a long-standing and regular Bible reader of both testaments. In the lectures he showed a respectful and tolerant attitude to religion, and especially Christianity.

---

[43] *Rescuing Justice and Equality*, pp. 230, 257
[44] Ibid., pp. 3–6.
[45] G. A. Cohen, *Why Not Socialism?* (Princeton, NJ, 2009).

It should be clear from the foregoing how important family was to Cohen. His first major philosophical project was seen as a type of repayment to his parents, to whom his first book was dedicated. He married Margaret Pearce in 1965 and they had three children, Gideon, Miriam (who now teaches philosophy in London) and Sarah. The marriage was dissolved but Cohen remained on very good terms with Maggie, and both remarried, Cohen to Michèle Jacottet in 1999. His second marriage was a very happy one, spent in the company of what was now a complex and growing extended family.

Cohen's contribution to political philosophy has been extensive, defending what many would regard as the most thorough-going and radical egalitarianism to be found among analytical philosophers. However, his own positive view was not developed in the detail of other leading figures such as John Rawls, Ronald Dworkin or John Roemer. Rather, as noted, Cohen considered himself more of a reactive than an individually creative philosopher. In this his skill was unrivalled. His style is often that of an expert demolition worker: finding what might look like a rather banal difficulty, but probing and probing until the edifice collapses. Cohen knew exactly where to locate his criticism, and how to develop it to greatest effect. At first sight the criticisms can look pedantic or fussy, but as the arguments develop something of great power emerges. Those who have the instinct to defend the views he attacks find themselves with a much more difficult task than they first assumed.

Cohen will be remembered for his work, but just as much for his wit and his support for other people. Even in prestigious public lectures he would crack jokes, burst into song, or imitate other philosophers. He would do the same thing in restaurants, drawing waiting staff or diners at other tables into the fun and good-natured mischief. His valedictory lecture at Oxford in 2008 included a series of imitations or parodies of many well-known philosophers, and was said by many members of the audience to be the funniest and most entertaining lecture they had witnessed. Fortunately some video and audio recordings of Cohen survive, most notably a TV programme, *No Habitat for a Shmoo*, made in 1986, some videos of lectures and impersonations delivered in Madison Wisconsin in 1998, and an imperfect audio recording of the valedictory lecture.[46]

---

[46] The text of this lecture will appear in one of the forthcoming volumes of Cohen's work, edited by Michael Otsuka. An enhanced version of the recording will possibly be made available on the internet.

In 2009, about half a year before his death, a conference at Oxford was held in celebration of his work and career. In remarks at the end of the conference Cohen observed how odd it is that in this country we honour people by attempting to rip their work to pieces. But in these remarks he also made clear how extremely proud he was of his former students—of how confident they had become, and of how much they had become their own people. Cohen was extraordinarily generous with his time, and not only for his own students, and not only on his own topics. His native intelligence—honed by tutorials with Gilbert Ryle—enabled him to grapple with any topic put to him, and fifteen minutes with Cohen would leave anyone understanding both more and less about their own view or argument. All of those who met him, or read his work, will realise what a gap his unexpected death has left. He gave so much, yet he still had so much more. Any attempt to express how much he will be missed by his family, friends, colleagues and even those who never met him, will seem trite or formulaic.

JONATHAN WOLFF
University College London

Note. My thanks to Miriam Cohen Christofidis, Veronique Munoz Dardé, Michael Otsuka, Michael Rosen, Hillel Steiner, and Arnold Zuboff for very valuable comments on an earlier version. A few paragraphs of this piece appeared previously in an obituary I published in *The Philosophers' Magazine*. I thank the editors for permission to reuse the material.

JOHN COWDREY

Herbert Edward John Cowdrey
1926–2009

HERBERT EDWARD JOHN COWDREY (always known as John) was born in Basingstoke on 29 November 1926. His father, Herbert Cowdrey, was head gardener at Moundsmere, a stately home in Hampshire, and from him John learned a love of gardening that stayed with him for the rest of his life. In his own statement written for the British Academy, John drew attention to the fact that both his parents came from North Hampshire workers' families. Towards the end of his life, he was clearly proud of his roots in the English countryside. But it cannot have been particularly easy for him, in the class-bound society of England in the 1940s, to move from home into the environment into which his talents took him.

John's primary education was at Church Oakley Church of England School near Basingstoke, where he must have impressed his teachers. In 1937 he won a scholarship to Queen Mary's School, Basingstoke. It is unfortunate that few records of his education at this ancient grammar school in the town remain. But it was surely at Queen Mary's that John's remarkable abilities not only as an historian but also as a linguist were given their opportunity to develop. He excelled in all subjects except, ironically, divinity (at this stage in his life he professed himself an atheist). At the end of Michaelmas Term 1943, when he was only just seventeen, he won an open scholarship in Modern History at Trinity College, Oxford. Of this he later remarked that it marked him out 'as one of the last generation of old-style scholarship boys'. In 1944, having chosen the navy as his national service destination, he experienced Oxford in wartime at a Services Short Course, that strange blend of academic endeavour and preparation for war that was offered to young men who could not be spared from call-up for more than a few months. Here he began his historical studies.

John then spent most of his national service, 1945–7, on *HMS Mauritius*, a cruiser tasked with preserving British interests in the eastern Mediterranean. In the last months of the Second World War, the German threat in this area had almost died out. But there was a need to contain any possible Russian thrust into the region and to assist anti-Communist forces in Greece and the Southern Balkans. There were moments of real danger, most notably on 22 October 1946 in the Straits of Corfu. John was on *HMS Mauritius* when, accompanied by the cruiser *HMS Leander* and the destroyers *HMS Saumarez* and *HMS Volage*, they found themselves completely unexpectedly in a minefield off the Albanian coast. Both destroyers were seriously damaged, and forty-four men were killed. Much later, in conversation with Graham Loud, John recalled that he had at the time of the explosions been in one of *HMS Mauritius'* magazines, so might well not have survived had the cruiser hit a mine. Less dramatically, he also was conscious of living dangerously when he made his first visit to Palestine in 1947, because all Britons there were under threat of assassination in that last year of the Mandate. Despite these short periods of tension, John enjoyed the navy and credited his time in the Eastern Mediterranean with kindling in him a lasting interest in the history, peoples and places he had first encountered then.

In 1947 John returned to Trinity College, Oxford, to finish off his historical studies, concentrating at this time on the modern period, post-1760. He later recalled with gratitude the contrasting styles and interests of his three tutors, Michael MacLagan, Bruce Wernham, and Philip Williams. Together they gave him the confidence to take a First Class degree in 1949. At this point, John made one of the most important decisions of his life, to read for a second degree in Theology instead of continuing with historical research. His tutor in this subject was the distinguished philosophical theologian, Austin Farrer, then chaplain of Trinity. Farrer was famous for his preaching, and may well have had a significant influence on John's decision to devote himself to theological studies. It was important for the development of John's later interests that the Theology curriculum allowed him to do a Special Subject on the medieval papacy, for which he was able to choose his own set texts. This constituted his real entrée into medieval studies and especially into the world of Gregory VII and eleventh-century reforms. John valued his second degree not just for this but also for the breadth of insight into history across the centuries and the windows into other civilisations and states than Western European ones that it gave him.

He also benefited from adding to his already extensive list of languages Biblical Hebrew and Greek. Long afterwards, at John's funeral, Gerald Hegarty, chaplain of St Edmund Hall, attested to his lifelong habit of reading a part of the Old Testament in Hebrew every other day until failing eyesight prevented it.

While he was still studying for his second degree, John began to work towards taking Anglican orders at St Stephen's House, Oxford. St Stephen's House was founded to provide training for clergy of the High Anglican persuasion, in which community John found himself at ease for the rest of his life. He felt gratitude to the then Principal, A. H. Couratin, for the thorough training provided, and for the good grounding in biblical, doctrinal and liturgical studies he acquired there. He was ordained in 1953, when he took up the position of chaplain and teacher of Old Testament and Christian doctrine at St Stephen's House. Although he moved from there in 1956, he remained a firm supporter of that institution, later serving on its governing body and towards the end of his life receiving its Fellowship

In November 1956 John was elected chaplain of St Edmund Hall, a job to be combined with teaching in the Modern History school for the medieval part of the syllabus. He remained at St Edmund Hall for the rest of his life, resigning the chaplaincy in 1976 but continuing to teach medieval history until his retirement and election as an emeritus fellow in 1994. The point at which John joined the Hall was an exciting one because in February 1957 it acquired its new Statutes, under which it became a proper college, its government vested in the hands of its Principal and Fellows. John was distinctly proud to have been one of the foundation fellows and keen to nurture a sense of collegiality in the changed institution. In the brief history of the college he wrote (which still appears on the college website), he said of it: 'Unique among the Colleges by reason of its history, it combines the maturity and confidence of long, rich and resilient experience as a Hall with the modernity and adaptability of its new way of life as a college.' When college archivist, he said of the archives: 'The whole story of the Hall's gradual deliverance from tutelage and its growth into the great and glorious college that it now is, is richly documented.'[1] The acute awareness of how institutions evolve over time, with particular moments of rapid development, was to be a notable feature of John's historical scholarship. Perhaps his later portraits of Cluny and Montecassino were shaped in part by his own experience at the Hall in 1957.

[1] *St Edmund Hall Magazine*, 1981–2, p. 11.

John preserved a marked reverence for and knowledge of the 1957 Statutes, and later also for the by-laws, in the framing of which he had played a considerable role. Occasionally in later times when modifications of the original Statutes were mooted, he struck his colleagues as rather over-zealous in protecting what he saw as their essence. Indeed, he described the by-laws as intended to lock the collegial management of the Hall's business into an unchanging template. This attitude could irritate those who favoured even small changes. But by then few of the fellows could themselves remember the major revolution that had been achieved in 1957.

The Hall that John joined was small, both in terms of physical space (the Emden and Kelly buildings that transformed it were the work of the 1960s) and as a community—he was the eleventh fellow to be elected. In that number were two other clerical fellows. One of these was John Kelly, Principal of the college, who encouraged and supported John in his early years. It was in token of this that John wore Kelly's robes when he took his Doctor of Divinity degree in 2000. He also formed a long-lasting alliance with the other history fellow, George Ramsay, whose geniality combined with high academic standards made him an excellent colleague. It was from this time forward that John began to see himself as a college, rather than a faculty or university, man. Nevertheless, he scrupulously fulfilled all his obligations to the History faculty, as a lecturer, as a dedicated exam-iner of both undergraduate and graduate students, as a supervisor (on which more will be said below), and as a member of the History board. The faculty board responded to this and to his growing reputation as a researcher by appointing him to a Special Lectureship for five years in 1979, an appointment that led him to give up the office of chaplain in the Hall (though not of course his tutorship in medieval history).

When John was originally appointed chaplain, a programme of restor-ation was already on-going in the late seventeenth-century chapel. He was in office when it reached its climax in 1957–8, with the installation of a new altar-piece, the Supper at Emmaus, painted by Ceri Richards and commissioned by the undergraduates at the time. Although there were those who preferred the old altar-piece (now kept in the Old Library), John was probably in the majority in thinking the Richards painting entirely appropriate to the building, both in colour and in form. He was impressed that the artist had spent several hours sitting in the chapel before sketching out the picture, time which he thought well spent.[2] Since

---

[2] I am indebted to the late Revd Gerald Hegarty for this information.

its installation the altar-piece has attracted much admiration. Richard Harries, then Bishop of Oxford, in 2005 regarded it as the equal of Graham Sutherland's famous *Noli me tangere* for Chichester Cathedral, and praised it for the way in which Richards had avoided excessive literalism in the depiction of the risen Christ. In the restored chapel, John fulfilled his duties towards the collegiate community, including regular invitations to other clergy to come and preach at the Sunday evening services. The 1950s and 1960s were relatively calm decades for chaplains of Oxford colleges. More challenging times began with the increasingly secular mood of the 1970s.

The other part of John's original job was the teaching. The move from St Stephen's House to St Edmund Hall meant the abandonment of any teaching of Theology. From now on, he confined himself to History. But in what he most enjoyed he drew rather more on what he had learned under Austin Farrer and A. H. Couratin than on his History degree. In those days—and indeed for long afterwards—fellows of poor colleges were obliged to give tutorials for at least twelve hours a week. Although John as chaplain did not initially have to fulfill this obligation, after the end of his Special Lectureship he had to take on what external teaching he could find in order to make up his hours. Like all Oxford tutors, he sometimes felt burdened. But he enjoyed a reputation among his pupils both for punctiliousness in the performance of his duty and for real kindness. At the retirement dinner the college gave for him in 1994 when he became an emeritus fellow, his old pupils 'united in their appreciation of Mr. Cowdrey as not only an excellent history tutor but also an exceptionally kind man'.[3] One of them recorded that, overcome with nerves before taking his final examinations, he turned to John, who took him away from Oxford for a day or two on a walking holiday, which made all the difference both to his feelings and, he was sure, to his performance. John's kindness was also remarked by his surprisingly small number of research students, in particular by Graham Loud, who praised John as an exemplary supervisor. Not only did he read carefully and quickly all that was submitted to him, providing excellent analysis, but he was generosity itself in writing references and offering support in any way he could. Among his colleagues in college he was remembered as the person who was always willing to lend his room in vacations to those ejected from their own by building work.

---

[3] *St Edmund Hall Magazine*, 1993–4.

In 1959 there came another major change in John's life: he married a musician, Judith Watson Davis, with whom he subsequently had two daughters and a son. Not long after the marriage the pair moved to Old Marston, to a house with a fairly large garden where John put his skills to good use. From then on, he could be seen regularly cycling in across the Marston Ferry Road, through North Oxford and down to St Edmund Hall. This move also marked the beginning of his close involvement in the church of St Nicholas, Old Marston, where he was to act as deputy to the vicar for many years. For as long as he was able, he presided over the 8 a.m. communion on Sunday mornings in the church, and was well known to all the congregation. It seems appropriate that a man of strong traditionalist views should have served in a church where worship is known to have taken place at least from the early years of the twelfth century, and probably occurred further back than that. It is extraordinary that, with so much already on his plate, John still had the energy to spend part of every summer vacation, at least into the mid 1980s, as an A-level examiner and delegate for the Oxford Local Examinations Board, and also to participate actively in the Henry Bradshaw Society, devoted to the study of medieval liturgy, of which he became Chairman of Council in 1985–6. Perhaps the huge demands he placed on himself went some way to explain the reticence he always preserved. John was an intensely private person. Everyone held him in great respect; very few of the university community, if any, felt they knew him well.

Once installed in St Edmund Hall, John began to turn his mind to the kinds of research for which his combination of historical and theological training best fitted him. The first problem to which he was attracted was essentially theological, although it had clear historical implications: that of the doctrine and discipline behind reordinations in the western church, 400–1300. In 1963, supported by John Kelly, he received a British Academy grant to enable him to follow through the major sources for this huge project. His work gave him the opportunity to study intensively the authors of the early middle ages, particularly those of the Carolingian age. If the original intention had been to produce a book on the subject, this was abandoned. What John achieved saw the light of day in two articles, one on the dissemination of St Augustine's teaching on reordinations,[4] and the other on Pope Anastasius II's use of St Augustine's doctrine of holy orders.[5]

---

[4] *Journal of Theological Studies*, 20 (1969), 448–81; repr. in *Popes, Monks, and Crusaders* (London, 1984).
[5] *Studia Patristica*, 11 (1972), 311–15; repr. in *Popes, Monks, and Crusaders*.

These articles demonstrated the breadth of John's knowledge, his familiarity with all the sources, and his ability to pick out changes in emphasis in later readers' use of St Augustine's teaching.

In the meantime, and probably under the influence of his undergraduate teaching, John's interests had turned back to the eleventh century and the work he had done for his Special Subject in the Theology school. This century was to remain his overwhelming preoccupation for the rest of his scholarly career. It fascinated him because he could detect in it major developments in thought among the clergy, both regular and secular. It was also a period which he knew had left some evidence not fully exploited by previous generations of historians. Besides, he had an instinctive sympathy for the form of Benedictine monasticism that reached its apogee in that century. He was drawn to the ritual, the penitential discipline, the sense of solidarity that characterised the inward lives of these stable, aspirational communities, and yet permitted them to spread their influence well beyond their walls. He wanted to understand them better and to pass on his new knowledge to others. He saw much to do, and much reason to feel excitement about what might be discovered there. In 1966 and 1968 he published three articles, all apparently concerned with a narrow geographical focus, the city of Milan, but all vital to the broader problem that was to occupy him for many years, that of what was known then as the Gregorian reform movement in the church. Without a knowledge of the local politics in Milan, it was impossible to comprehend the appearance of the Patarenes or the part they played in the rift between Pope Gregory VII and King Henry IV. These articles were the first building bricks of John's later book on Gregory VII, interesting in themselves and more significant for later developments

It was in 1970 that John's publications first brought him to the attention of all medieval historians. It was a great year for him. The first of the three notable pieces to appear was entitled 'The Peace and the Truce of God in the Eleventh Century'. This article treated—admittedly more obliquely than in later work—a theme that is instantly recognisable as a major Cowdrey preocccupation—the impact of Benedictine monasticism on the wider world. The article remains forty years later the most reliable and most persuasive discussion of the Peace and Truce in English. The argument developed is well nuanced, dependent on the drawing of careful distinctions; despite its complexity it is expressed with crystal clarity; it covers the whole of western Europe in its scope; it is scrupulous in its use of sources. The footnotes attest to John's wide reading in French, German and Italian secondary literature. In the first footnote summarising the existing work on the subject, John included Bernard Töpfer's remarkable *Volk und Kirche zur Zeit der beginnenden Gottesfriedensbewegung im Frankreich*,[6] recording of it that it is 'a particularly stimulating and valuable Marxist interpretation'. In the course of the article, he paid homage to Töpfer's conclusions on the coherence of the peace movement and its appeal to all classes. John was certainly not narrow-minded in his approach to what he read. But much of the article went well beyond the secondary literature. John's understanding of the church's ritual brought to the subject the kind of insight often aspired to by those trained in anthropology, as witnessed in his words: 'The concluding of peace under episcopal sanctions was … part of a pattern of events which began with the sign of God's wrath, continued with healing by the intervention of the saints, and ended with men's answering contract of peace and justice.'[7] Altogether, the article was and remains a *tour de force*. Later, he added a brief article entitled 'From the Peace of God to the First Crusade', as a response to Marcus Bull's contention, in *Knightly Piety and the Lay Response to the First Crusade* (Oxford, 1993), that there was no connection between the Peace and the Crusade. John's conclusion was typical: he agreed with Bull's arguments, but thought there was more to be said: 'If the Aquitanian assemblies lapsed, the underlying aspirations of which they were temporary expressions continued.'[8] There was, therefore, a connection, though not at the obvious level. The 'underlying aspirations' of which John speaks here constituted a longing for *iustitia*, righteousness, which he came to regard as the hallmark of eleventh-century intellectuals.

The second major work to be published in that year was John's first book: *The Cluniacs and the Gregorian Reform* (Oxford, 1970). The theme was the effects of eleventh-century monasticism on the outside world. The book was a contribution to an on-going debate, largely conducted by German scholars, on the question of whether the great Benedictine monastery of Cluny played a central or at best a peripheral role in the ecclesiastical reform that characterised the second half of the eleventh century, normally associated particularly with Pope Gregory VII. In the introduction to the book, John summarised the debate for his readers. The first thing that strikes the eye was his easy familiarity with German scholar-

---

[6] Berlin, 1957.

[7] *Past and Present*, 46 (1970), 42–67, at 50; repr. in *Popes, Monks, and Crusaders.*

[8] 'From the Peace of God to the First Crusade', in L. García-Guijarro Ramos (ed.), *La Primera Cruzada, novecientos anos después: el concilio de Clermont y les origines del movimiento cruzado* (Castello d'Impresseo, 1997), pp. 51–61, at 53; repr. in *The Crusades and Latin Monasticism in the Eleventh and Twelfth Centuries* (Aldershot, 1999).

ship. It is perhaps not surprising that a young man with linguistic gifts being educated during the Second World War should have regarded it as essential to read German fluently. But John had not had the opportunity of long—or even short—residence in that country; it was all done by innate flair and determination. The introduction to *The Cluniacs* provided for many English-speaking readers their first appreciation of the importance of the school of Tellenbach in European historiography.

The Cluniacs and the Gregorian Reform is remarkable for drawing on an unusually wide range of sources and for its broad geographical scope. On sources, the book provides the first glimpse of what was to be one of John's most noted characteristics, his willingness to edit for the use of others documents he had found, which were now difficult of access but valuable for the insights they provided. So in an appendix to *The Cluniacs* he provided editions of three papal letters found in Pierre Simon's *Bullarium sacri ordinis Cluniacensis* of 1680, an exceedingly rare work. Two of these letters had played a considerable role in John's reassessment of the relationship between Cluny and the papacy; they were there as *pièces justicatives*. But they also marked the start of what was to be an important part of John's *oeuvre*, editing medieval Latin letters. On geographical scope, the book is unusual in searching for Cluny's influence far beyond the bounds of southern and eastern France. This breadth did arouse criticism; could Hirsau and its dependencies really be called Cluniac? If so, what exactly made a house Cluniac? Was a debt to Cluny's foundation charter, its customs, its guidance and its prestige enough? Or did the adjective demand subjection to Cluny? These remain points of dispute, as John himself acknowledged. But John's incisive arguments on the influence of Cluny in Spain have had a lasting influence on later writers. So, too, has his acute awareness of change and development within the mother house itself. Few would now argue with his careful statement:

> By its origin the Cluniac Reform was much older than the Gregorian; but, so far as its coming to maturity is concerned, it was much more nearly contemporary with it.[9]

This insight was crucial to his argument for the growing interdependence of Cluny and the papacy, which has generally found favour among historians. The occasional critic thought that the Gregorian Reform was perhaps more precisely defined in the author's mind than it had been in that of any contemporary. But any uneasiness felt on this score was soothed by

---

[9] *The Cluniacs*, p. xxiv.

the promise made in a footnote that John intended in the future to produce a full-scale study of Gregory VII (which he did in 1998). All reviewers
agreed in praising the clarity with which John stated his subtle arguments
in modification of the Tellenbach school's views on Cluny. His first was a
well-received book.

The third and final piece of John's work to see light of day in 1970 was
probably the most widely read of anything he wrote. It was 'Pope Urban's
preaching of the First Crusade'.[10] In it, he carefully subjected to scrutiny
Carl Erdmann's well-known view that Urban's main aim in launching the
crusade was to free the eastern churches from the Turkish yoke. After
examining a vast array of sources—chronicles, charters, contemporary
letters, Urban's own letters, and evidence for preaching of the crusade—
John concluded that Erdmann was wrong. The liberation of Jerusalem by
military force was the goal of the crusade, and from the outset Urban
offered to those who were willing to attempt this liberation the spiritual
benefits of pilgrimage. John's conclusions have hardly been questioned
since then; his article has found its way on to reading lists in universities
across the world. On a personal level, the article paved the way for John's
participation in a large number of conferences dedicated to the crusades,
at which he met and became friendly with all the great names in the field.
In the summer of 1977 he went to Israel to lecture at various universities
there and to see crusader sites. It was a small-scale beginning of the travels
so conspicuous in his later years. His involvement in crusader scholarship
and with those who studied the crusades resulted in a series of articles
originating in conference papers devoted to the themes of holy war and
crusade, which appeared at regular intervals for the next thirty years.
Perhaps the most influential of the early articles were 'The genesis of the
Crusades: the springs of western ideas of the Holy War';[11] 'Pope Gregory
VII's "Crusading" plans of 1074';[12] and 'Martyrdom and the first Crusade'.[13]
Several other articles were reprinted in *The Crusades and Latin Monasticism
in the Eleventh and Twelfth Centuries*. In the Preface to this collection,
John said: 'The Crusade articles are particularly concerned with the trans-

---

[10] *History*, 55 (1970), 177–88; repr. in *Popes, Monks, and Crusaders*.
[11] In T. P. Murphy (ed.), *The Holy War* (Columbus, OH, 1974), pp. 9–32; repr. in *Popes, Monks and Crusaders*.
[12] In B. Z. Kedar, H. E. Mayer and R. C. Smail (eds.), *Outremer: Studies in the History of the Crusading Kingdom of Jerusalem presented to Joshua Prawer* (Jerusalem, 1982), pp. 27–42; repr. in *Popes, Monks and Crusaders*.
[13] In P. Edbury (ed.), *Crusade and Settlement* (Cardiff, 1988), pp. 45–56; repr. in *The Crusades and Latin Monasticism*.

formation in western attitudes to the bearing of arms and in the quest for internal and external peace and security.' In other words, much of John's work in the crusading field was inspired by, and developed or modified, ideas culled from Carl Erdmann's great *Die Entstehung des Kreuzzugsgedankens*,[14] a book he much admired if he did not always concur with everything in it—he was later to speak of Erdmann's 'fine intelligece and immaculate scholarship'.[15] The excitement of the later eleventh century lay, for both of these historians, in its transformation of underlying thought patterns, its new way of configuring religious ideals. For both of them, the run up to and the aftermath of the First Crusade were fascinating illustrations of just this transformative power.

John's next published book, *The Epistolae vagantes of Pope Gregory VII*,[16] was another homage to Erdmann, who had intended to edit these letters but had died before achieving this. For John, it was also a preparatory task for his own eventual study of Gregory VII. In a footnote on page 168 of the *Cluniacs*, he had called attention to the fact that many of Gregory VII's letters had escaped registration, and that some of these were not included in Jaffé's *Epistolae collectae*. Here he added to Jaffé's work a number of letters found by other historians in the intervening hundred years, but excluded from it letters that had recently appeared in Santifaller's edition of Gregory's privileges.[17] The intention was that *The Epistolae vagantes*, along with the edition by Caspar of Gregory's *Register*,[18] and Santifaller's volume, should provide historians with all the Latin letters of Gregory that survive. The amount of scholarship that lay behind this edition was enormous. In 1970, supported to some extent by the British Academy, John made his first scholarly visit to Rome, carrying an introduction to the Prefect of the Vatican Library written for him by John Kelly. This visit allowed him, among many other things, to study the manuscript Caspar used for his edition of Gregory's *Register*, Reg. Vat. Lat. 2. The scholarly apparatus to *The Epistolae vagantes* demonstrates the skill with which John was able to order the 'stray' letters by reference to those in the Register, which he seems almost to have known off by heart. Other footnotes show his easy familiarity with the chronicles and

---

[14] Stuttgart, 1935.

[15] *Epistolae vagantes*, Preface, p. vi.

[16] Oxford, 1972.

[17] Leo Santifaller, *Quellen und Forschungen zum Urkunden- und Kanzleiwesen Papst Gregors VII, Teil 1, Quellen: Urkunden, Regesta. Facsimilia* (Vatican City: Biblioteca apostolica vaticana, 1957).

[18] *Monumenta Germaniae Historica. Epistolae selectae*, 2 vols. (Berlin, 1920–3).

letters written by other contemporaries which modern scholars must have in mind in order to understand the content of Gregory's letters. Others again highlight his exemplary listings of the manuscripts and printed sources in which each of these letters had made earlier appearances.

The footnotes are intended for scrutiny by well-informed readers. But because *The Epistolae vagantes* was published in the Oxford Medieval Texts series, John was required to provide an English translation for each letter. These translations were clear, precise and unambiguous. Yet from what he said in the Introduction, John at this time had in mind assisting only those who found the Latin difficult; he did not intend to translate for those who were incapable of reading the original. But the decline of Latinity among undergraduates in the following decades slowly convinced him that there was a need for a translation of Gregory's work for those whose interest in the subject was quite unmatched by their linguistic skills. Therefore in 2002 John produced an English translation of Gregory's *Register*,[19] relying on Caspar's edition. His long familiarity with the contents of the *Register* will have made this a relatively easy task for him. Again, the clarity and precision of the English rendering attracted praise from reviewers. This time the introduction and footnotes were clearly intended both for students and for scholars. In the Introduction, readers were brought to face the difficulties posed by the text, warned that there was apparently no logic about which letters were registered and which not, brought to realise that sometimes the most important part of a message might be conveyed verbally by the messenger, not by the script, and told to trust their own judgement on which letters brought them closest to Gregory's own mind, personality and purposes. At no point was John intent on ramming his own interpretation down his readers' throats. But whereas the English translation of *The Epistolae vagantes* was alone in the field, John's translation of the *Register* had been preceded by Ephraim Emerton's *The Correspondence of Pope Gregory VII: Selected Letters from the registrum.*[20] With forty years of thinking about Gregory VII behind him, the advantage of having much recent scholarship to draw on, and most obviously the value of covering the whole register, there was little doubt that John's was, from the scholarly point of view, a substantial improvement on Emerton's work. On the other hand, it did not put a huge amount of new material into the orbit of students who could not read Latin.

[19] Oxford, 2002.
[20] New York, 1932.

Having tried his hand at it with *The Epistolae vagantes*, John found he wanted to edit yet more little-used texts, and to go further now by pointing out their historical value. He fixed on material illustrative of the activities of two consecutive abbots of Cluny, Hugh and Pontius. In 1978 he produced the texts of two lives of Abbot Hugh, along with various of his letters; and also an analysis of the sources relating to Pontius.[21] Two of Abbot Hugh's letters were of particular interest to John, in that they set out guidance for the activities of monks-bishop, a group which always intrigued John.[22] The sources he made accessible for Hugh provided amplifications rather than serious modifications of that great man's career. The material relating to Pontius was of greater value. It permitted John to reassess the early years of his abbacy, showing him as a mediating figure between the pope and the emperor Henry V. There was, however, no getting away from the disasters at the end of his career, which John attributed to his autocratic temperament, given too free rein by the customs of Cluny. Pontius's failures reinforced John's belief that Cluny and its dependencies had grown too fast in the reign of Hugh for it to be ruled effectively by one man, however able. The deposition of Pontius was simply one sign among many that by the second decade of the twelfth century the great age of Cluny was over.

If editing texts was an occasional pleasure, writing articles was a daily activity. There can be few scholars who have produced as many as John. The majority of these were reprinted in three collections, *Popes, Monks and Crusaders*; *The Crusades and Latin Monasticism in the Eleventh and Twelfth Centuries*; and *Popes and Church Reform in the Eleventh Century. Essays around Gregory VII*. Admittedly some articles, particularly perhaps in the last volume, were either earlier or more extended treatments of questions discussed elsewhere in his books. But some were major contributions to knowledge in their own right. For example, 'The Anglo-Norman *Laudes Regiae*' drew on liturgical texts (which he also edited) to give form to political concepts current in the Anglo-Norman realm.[23] Of the 1068 *Laudes Regiae*, John pointed out that they 'expressed to perfection the "political theory" of the Norman Conquest'. They showed William, confident of his place on earth and in heaven, ruling over one people, both Norman and English, in harmony with his bishops. But their triumphant and propagandist aspect was appropriate only to the immediate aftermath

---

[21] *Studi Gregoriani*, 11 (1978), 13–298.

[22] Epp. 4, 6, pp. 145–9, 151–2.

[23] *Viator*, 12 (1981), 37–78; repr. in *Popes, Monks, and Crusaders*.

of his military victory. The *Laudes Regiae* used for feasts and coronations in the twelfth and thirteenth centuries appear to have been more low-key, more adaptable to rather less dramatic times. Here John's characteristically careful reading of unusual sources was combined with an imaginative approach derived from his own participation in the rituals of the Church, to offer an insight more secular historians could only envy. [24] Imagination of a different kind was evident in his 'Towards an Interpretation of the Bayeux Tapestry'[25] of which one of the more remarkable features is John's reading of the marginal figures in the Tapestry, along with his ability to detect elements in the scenes designed to appeal to Englishmen as much as Normans. Both of these articles—and indeed several more—seem originally to have been inspired by the teaching of English history John was obliged to do in conformity with the then Oxford undergraduate syllabus. The question of what constituted Englishness in the eleventh century, an important theme in his last book on Lanfranc, was one that he had clearly pondered on for years before.

Nevertheless, his main preoccupation in these years was with his projected study on Gregory VII. In 1983 there was published his *The Age of Abbot Desiderius. Montecassino, the Papacy, and the Normans in the Eleventh and Early Twelfth Centuries.*[26] As John explained in the Preface, this was deliberately designed as a preliminary to the major work on Gregory VII he was projecting. Its aim was to reflect on the papacy of the reform era, especially in the 1080s, from the perspective of the south: 'Did Montecassino and the reform papacy have compatible—though not perhaps identical—aims, interests and policies?'[27] The book's secondary aim was to produce a portrait of the interactions between the great southern monastery of Montecassino and the outside world as a parallel to the study on Cluny he had already achieved. In this secondary aim, John was somewhat inhibited by the fact that the American historian Howard Bloch had already written some seminal articles on the subject and had for a long time been projecting a book. John therefore concentrated much more on the first and more political aim, focusing particularly on Abbot Desiderius who became Pope Victor III on the death of Gregory VII. But the preservation of at least a modicum of material about Montecassino as a cultural power-

---

[24] As he said in 'Urban II and the idea of Crusade' (*Studi medievali*, 36 (1995), 721–42; repr. in *The Crusades and Latin Monasticism*), 'Nothing embeds religious imagery more deeply in the mind than regular liturgical recitation', p. 730.

[25] *Anglo-Norman Studies*, 10 (1988), 49–65.

[26] Oxford, 1983.

[27] p. xxvii.

house and centre for South Italian religious sentiment, while the main focus was clearly on the South Italian politics of its abbots, proved a difficult balance to hold. The book perhaps lacks the inner logic and superb organisation of material that characterised *The Cluniacs*, and which was to be so conspicuous a feature of *Gregory VII*.

Its virtues are, however, evident. It is based on careful analysis of the available literary and legal sources; it weighs their importance in the light of the fact that artists, canon lawyers, and chroniclers all had their own axes to grind; it goes out of its way to identify what contemporaries would have judged to be 'sound conservative principles' at any point; it takes for granted that the objectives of the reform popes varied over time; it examines the pressures, in particular those exercised by Norman princes, that caused both popes and abbots to react defensively; it therefore finds no problem with the occasional sharp fluctuations in relationship between the abbots of Montecassino and the popes (especially when there was also an antipope); and it gives due weight to the importance of Montecassino to Gregory VII at the end of his life. The last chapter of the book is concerned with the election of Victor III and his very brief pontificate. On this, contemporary opinions were so divided that the task of steering a path through the thicket was almost impossible. But John's conclusion that Victor was by then an active and convinced Gregorian seems persuasive. And there can be no doubt that *The Age of Abbot Desiderius* allowed John to incorporate a more southern perspective into *Gregory VII*.

The books, the articles, and the editions thus far described brought about John's election to the British Academy in 1991, an event which gave him great pleasure. The speech he gave at the dinner in his honour in St Edmund Hall following his election was remembered for its wit and good humour. To a man so withdrawn, so inclined normally to preserve silence, the public recognition of his abilities was doubly sweet. It is said that he was particularly delighted to have attained the same distinction as the two earlier St Edmund Hall medievalists, John Kelly and A. B. Emden.

It was not until 1998 that *Pope Gregory VII, 1073–1085* first saw the light of day.[28] The first full-length study of that pope for more than fifty years, it was at once recognised as a masterpiece. Because it had been known to be in preparation for nearly thirty years, it was eagerly anticipated; and it certainly did not disappoint. Henry Mayr-Harting said of it: 'As a meticulous exposition of a complex story, done with vast learning, control and lucidity, it is a tour de force.' He went on to comment that

[28] Oxford, 1998.

John's picture of Gregory's personal devotion 'comes from the heart as well as from the head'.[29] Nevertheless, the Gregory that emerged from these pages was rather far from the conventional autocrat with revolutionary tendencies that many medievalists automatically summoned up when hearing his name. As John saw him, Gregory VII, occasionally rash in his support for his allies, only completely lost his sense of proportion when sorely provoked. He was a man of whom it could be said that he normally harboured 'concern to temper justice with mercy and to seek peace and agreement wherever they could be found' (p. 330). In Central Italy, 'his exercise of authority ... was firm, moderate and statesmanlike' (p. 279). In France, Gregory's 'studied moderation ... won him willing hearers' (p. 422); 'Gregory had an exceptional capacity to inspire personal loyalty and devotion even in those who, in important respects, differed from him' (p. 690).

Those acquainted with John's preliminary articles cannot have been surprised at the emergence of this relatively conciliatory figure. Two essays in particular pointed to such a portrait. The first was 'The spirituality of Gregory VII', which stressed the emphasis the pope continued to lay on monastic obedience, his concern with pastoral matters in his high position, his devotion to the Virgin, and his personal asceticism.[30] The second was 'The Papacy and the Berengarian controversy' (a subject that Erdmann had also tackled). After looking at all the evidence, John was struck by Gregory's 'enquiring and conciliatory approach to liturgical and sacramental matters'.[31] As he said, 'this is not the usual modern perception of Gregory'. Jonathan Riley-Smith, in his review of the book, described John's Gregory as having 'the air of an old-fashioned Anglican clergyman, conservative in many ways, moderate and sensible for most of the time ... on the high side but with initial doubts about the real presence in the eucharist'.[32] John himself summed him up thus: 'The deepest springs of Gregory's thought and action are not to be found in any politician's urge to wield power and to humble his adversaries ... Before all else, his motives were religious.'[33]

Hardly surprisingly, so radical a representation evoked a measure of dissent. This was understandable, since John himself produced much evi-

[29] *English Historical Review*, 116 (2001) at 139.
[30] *Analecta Carthusiana*, 130 (1995), 1–22; repr. in *The Popes and Church Reform*.
[31] In P. Ganz, R. B. C. Huygens, and F. Niewöhner (eds.), *Auctoritas et Ratio. Studien zu Berengar von Tours* (Wiesbaden, 1990), pp. 109–38, at 132; repr. in *The Popes and Church Reform*, p. 132.
[32] *Times Literary Supplement*, 14 May 1999, 30.
[33] *Gregory VII*, p. 695.

dence on which his opponents could build their case. No one could maintain that Gregory was consistent throughout his career, either in rhetoric or in action. Circumstances sometimes ruled out calm reaction as, for example, after the council of Brixen in 1080. But John struck the balance on the side of moderation. Perhaps he was thinking of what some of his critics had said when he remarked, in his Introduction to the English translation of Gregory's *Register*, that in the last resort the judgement over which of the letters get closest to Gregory's own mind, and which were written by clerks without close personal supervision, has to be subjective.[34] Nevertheless, the question of why a man of moderate temperament should employ an intransigent legate like Hugh of Die does need answering and is not answered in the book. On the other hand, there is much more evidence for moderation, for monastic caution, than the conventional portrait would allow and, perhaps more unexpectedly, also for Gregory's capacity to excite loyalty. As a result of John's work it is very unlikely that historians of the future will content themselves with a purely political approach to Gregory's leadership of the church.

For very few figures in the eleventh century is it possible to create a full context. It was John's extraordinary achievement to reveal the whole background against which Gregory lived his turbulent life and to explain so complex a picture in crystal-clear terms. From the first chapter of *Gregory VII*, in which Rome is set before the reader in all its material desolation but nurturing its image of past grandeur and present holiness, to the twelfth chapter describing his exile and death among the Normans, the book has a coherent internal dynamic. Themes touched upon at various times in the narrative are brought together at the end. Personal relationships, for example that with Peter Damiani, are revealed in all their complexities. Even Henry IV and the German princes are seen as caught in uncomfortable dilemmas from which they sometimes sought to escape by negotiation rather than force. Guibert of Ravenna, later the antipope Clement III, had what appeared to be a legitimate grievance against Gregory in 1078.[35] John neither over-simplified nor drew his characters only in black and white. The great strength of the book lies, as with all John's work but especially with this, his masterpiece, in the amazing range of sources with which he was familiar, in the extended geographical scope of his discussion, and in his inherent sympathy with those caught up in events which they could not control.

[34] p. xvi.
[35] p. 310.

John's last book, *Lanfranc. Scholar, Monk, and Archbishop,*[36] was an interesting choice of subject. Although Lanfranc was a monk before his elevation to Canterbury, a circumstance which automatically aroused John's interest, he had been the determined opponent of Berengar of Tours, for whom John had exhibited a certain sympathy, and he was firmly neutral between Gregory VII and Clement III from the latter's papal coronation in 1084, a time when Gregory needed all the allies he could get. Whereas there had been no biography of Gregory VII for more than fifty years before he wrote, Margaret Gibson had produced her *Lanfranc of Bec* in 1978.[37] John thought that, although Lanfranc's scholarship had received justice, his deeds as archbishop had been rather underestimated. He wanted to rescue him from the shadow that had been cast by Sir Richard Southern's towering *Saint Anselm*,[38] to argue that Lanfranc, at least as much as Anselm, understood the English people over whom he was called to be primate. For John, Lanfranc's knowledge of canon law, Old English law, and ecclesiastical history made him an admirable leader to guide the English church firmly into the wider church of western Christendom. He laid foundations on which others could build. He was to be praised above all for 'the enduring character and benefit of his government of the English church, both in itself and as an aspect of national life'.[39]

During all the time John was writing solidly, he was also travelling. The *St Edmund Hall Gazette* listed the various places he had lectured each year in the 1990s. For example, in 1991–2, he gave papers in Moscow, Berlin, Serra San Bruno in Calabria, and Palermo. In 1992–3 he was lecturing in Austria, Italy and New South Wales. But perhaps the most interesting journey was in 1983, when, as a guest of the East German Academy of Sciences, he visited history departments in East Berlin, Halle, Jena and Leipzig. This was presumably in some way connected with the Martin Luther celebrations, a time when the Evangelical Church in the German Democratic Republic cooperated with the state in holding up for admiration a progressive revolutionary, and when the Church of England extended a hand of friendship to the Evangelical Church.

---

[36] Oxford, 2003.
[37] Oxford, 1978.
[38] R. W. Southern, *Saint Anselm: a Portrait in a Landscape* (Cambridge, 1990).
[39] p. 231.

In his later years, John fell victim to Parkinson's Disease, which slowly robbed him of his powers to research and travel. The last five years of his life were a time of growing disability. He died on 4 December 2009.

JEAN DUNBABIN
Fellow of the Academy

Note. I am grateful for the help of Mr Justin Gosling, formerly Principal of St Edmund Hall; Dr Nicholas Davidson, archivist of St Edmund Hall; the late Revd Gerald Hegarty, Chaplain of St Edmund Hall; Professor Graham Loud; Professor Blair Worden; Professor Henry Mayr-Harting; Mr Alexander Murray; Ms Clare Hopkins, archivist of Trinity College; and Mr John Dunbabin, Emeritus Fellow of St Edmund Hall.

RALF DAHRENDORF

Ralf Gustav Dahrendorf
1929–2009

THE YEAR 1944 was an even bleaker one for the Dahrendorfs than it was for most German families. Father Gustav had been sentenced to seven years' imprisonment for his activities in the German resistance, culminating in the plot to assassinate Adolf Hitler in that year. He had already been in trouble for having been one of the Social Democratic members of the 1933 Reichstag who had voted against Hitler's seizure of power. One of the family's sons, 15-year-old Ralf, was starving in a concentration camp, to which he had been sent for circulating leaflets to his contemporaries urging them not to fight in Hitler's army. That these two brave people survived the period at all was a remarkable stroke of fortune. But Ralf was released suddenly, in one of those impenetrable arbitrary actions to which dictatorships are liable, though he remained in hiding. In April 1945 the Russians arrived in Berlin, where the family was living, and Gustav too was restored to the family.

Gustav Dahrendorf, who had been a trade-union and political activist since his own teenage, now became one of the Social Democrats charged with negotiating workable political arrangements with the Soviet Union and German Communists in the divided city and country. He refused to accept the absorption of Social Democracy within the Russian-backed Socialist Unity Party, and in 1946 the British smuggled him and the family back to their native Hamburg, in the new western Federal Republic of Germany. He died in 1954. Ralf lived on to have an extraordinarily rich and diverse career as an intellectual, politician and administrator spread across Germany, the European Union, the UK and the USA, until his death in 2009.

Proceedings of the British Academy, **172**, 93–111. © The British Academy 2011.

Stressful experiences in youth often leave a mark of restless energy and enduring discomfort, and it is possible to trace such a story in Ralf Dahrendorf's life. Two of his three marriages ended in divorce (his second and third wives both outlived him). He completed university studies in philosophy at Hamburg in 1952 with a doctoral thesis on the concept of justice in Karl Marx, and then went to the London School of Economics and Political Science, where he completed a second Ph.D. thesis in 1956, in sociology, on unskilled labour in Britain. By the following year he had also completed his Habilitation in sociology at the University of Saarbrücken, his *Habilitationsschrift* being the major treatise *Soziale Klassen und Klassenkonflikt in der industriellen Gesellschaft*,[1] translated into English within two years. By the age of 28 therefore he had become a full German professor, and had written a book that was to become a modern sociological classic. In the 1950s and 1960s he seemed almost to commute between posts in German and North American universities (Hamburg 1957–60, Columbia 1960, Tübingen 1960–4, Vancouver and Konstanz 1966–9, Harvard 1968).

Originally, like his father, an active member of the Social Democratic Party of Germany (SPD)—he was even born on May Day—he moved to the Free Democratic Party (FDP) in 1966. (In the 1990s he transferred his political support to the British Liberal Democrats—at the time that he made it, a different kind of party from the FDP, despite their both belonging to the European Liberal family; for a time he sat as a Liberal Democrat member of the House of Lords, but later moved to become a crossbencher.) He had left academia in 1968 to become a member of the Landtag of Baden-Württemberg, then of the Bundestag in 1969, serving as a junior foreign minister in the SPD–FDP coalition of Willi Brandt for a year before leaving to accept a post in Brussels as one of Germany's European Commissioners. An ardent Europeanist, he nevertheless found himself at loggerheads with many of his colleagues in the bureaucracy, and wrote some anonymous articles attacking the Commission, the authorship of which was discovered. He was publicly attacked in the European Parliament, where he viewed with amusement—given his father's experiences with Communists—the fact that his only supporters were the Italian Communist Party.

He was 'rescued' from Brussels by the offer of the directorship of the LSE. There followed ten years of directing the institution where he had been a graduate student in the 1950s, several of whose great figures, and particularly Karl Popper, had been deep inspirations in his life. He became

---

[1] Ralf Dahrendorf, *Soziale Klassen und Klassenkonflikt in der industriellen Gesellschaft* (Stuttgart, 1957); *Class and Class Conflict in Industrial Society* (Stanford, CA, 1959).

embedded in British public life, giving the Reith Lectures in 1974, serving on official commissions (the Hansard Society's Committee on Electoral Reform 1975–6; the Royal Commission on Legal Services 1976–9; the Wilson Committee on the Functioning of Financial Institutions 1977–80), being elected a Fellow of the British Academy in 1977 (of which he was Vice-President, 1982–3), and becoming a knight in 1982. As Sir Huw Wheldon, at that time chairman of the Court of Governors of the LSE, remarked, he had become Britain's most popular German since Prince Albert. When his term of office at the LSE ended, in 1984, he returned to Konstanz as professor of sociology, but came back to Britain two years later to become Warden of St Antony's College, Oxford for a 10-year term of office. He accepted British citizenship in 1988, and was appointed a Member of the House of Lords in 1993—where the peer who introduced him, Lord Annan, had been the 30-year-old major who had engineered the Dahrendorfs' escape from Berlin to Hamburg in 1946. He seemed now to have become thoroughly British, though he had never relinquished German citizenship. But at the last the earlier identity claimed him and, aged 76, he returned to Germany as a research professor at the Wissenschaftszentrum Berlin in 2005. Whereas the works of his lengthy 'middle period' were primarily written first in English, though often then translated into German, he never abandoned writing in his native language, and returned to it fully in his last years, producing at least five books and collections of essays that remain at the time of writing not translated into English.[2] His final months were spent living in Cologne, where he was welcomed as a visitor at the Max Planck Institute for the Study of Societies.

As his final return to Germany probably showed, Ralf Dahrendorf's restlessness was not just a frequent revision of decisions about where and what to be. He occasionally revised that fundamental choice between the exercise of choice itself and surrender to the claims of loyalties and identities. This latter he called, in his contributions to social theory, 'ligatures'. But restlessness and even discomfort were not qualities that disturbed him; he believed in them. His vision of the good society and the good life were in no way whatsoever states of rest; creative conflict and disagreement were fundamental to it. He hated the idea of utopia—'Out of Utopia' was the title of one of his essays.

This was the fundamental issue that led him to abandon his own and his father's social democracy for liberalism, and later to speak with some

---

[2] Among them is a non-chronological, self-ironic autobiographical work, *Über Grenzen: Lebenserinnerungen* (Munich, 2002).

contempt of the social democracy of both Britain and Germany in the 1970s. By that time it had become, in Dahrendorf's eyes, more a matter of weary bureaucratic regulation, drab egalitarianism and neocorporatist evasion of conflict than wide-eyed utopianism—though it was also central to his analysis that drabness and utopia were closely related. To some extent this made him more in sympathy with the neoliberalism of the 1980s, and the waves of deregulation and increased inequality that have characterised both his countries and many others since. But he was deeply critical of the consequences for both the rich and the poor that neoliberalism created. At a profound level he never suppressed his social democratic instincts, and he remained, again consistently with his social theory, willing to accept and work with the conflicts and tensions that resulted from the relationship between them and his dominant liberalism; a tension with which he grappled, in another of his slightly quaint terms, in his discussions of the relationship between 'entitlements' and 'provisions'.

Throughout his life he maintained a poise between the academic and political worlds; it is probably not a coincidence that the two positions that claimed him with most consistency for a decade each—as director of the LSE and as warden of St Antony's—were posts that combined the two, the leadership of academic institutions. His formal political career was not successful, but he was active in many public institutions. He spent several years as a board member of the Ford Foundation, and after the fall of the Soviet bloc took a highly active role in many initiatives to assist intellectual and civil society institutions in central and eastern Europe. He was, for example, closely associated with George Soros's Open Society Foundation and Central European University in Budapest. Much of his writing too retained that increasingly difficult balance between academic seriousness and popular readability; he wrote frequently for newspapers, with regular columns in *Die Zeit* and *La Repubblica*. He was a genuine 'public intellectual'.

I have here set up an approach to understanding Ralf Dahrendorf's intellectual contributions that is rooted in his life and normative positions. One does this, not just because it was a life that obviously demands to be addressed as one of moral action in public life far more than is the case with those who remain in academia all their lives, but also because it was something else that he believed one should do. In his early, characteristically bold, work, *Homo Sociologicus*,[3] he condemns a social science that

---

[3] Ralf Dahrendorf, *Homo Sociologicus* (Cologne, 1959; second edn., 1965; English trans., London, 1973).

seeks to abstract human life so that it loses sight of the actual person. One can best approach his contribution in terms of four always related, always both scholarly and normative, themes, at each of which the above has already hinted: the rejection of both utopia and *homo sociologicus*; the wholehearted embrace of conflict; the exploration of entitlements and provisions; and of options and ligatures.

Openness versus system: against utopia and an abstracted view of mankind

A rejection of the search for utopia was common among perceptive individuals who had witnessed both fascist and communist forms of that search at close quarters. To Ralf Dahrendorf we can add, among others, George Orwell and Karl Popper. When the young Dahrendorf arrived as a doctoral student at the LSE in the exciting post-war atmosphere of the 1950s, Popper was already one its dominant presences.[4] Unlike Friedrich von Hayek, another formidable LSE presence with whom he is often linked, Popper did not respond to totalitarianism by fully embracing the free market. For him, all total systems were suspect; the important thing was to retain an open mind, to keep being willing to learn from many sources, and to move forward cautiously and variously.[5] He called his approach 'social engineering', thinking of the pragmatic adjustments that engineers make—a term which has come to be misunderstood as meaning just about the opposite. The young Dahrendorf absorbed this approach to the full, and its profound lessons informed all his contributions to social theory and stayed with him the rest of his life. In 1990, in his reflections on the final collapse of the Soviet regime in Eastern Europe,[6] he again rejected Hayek's insistence on the absolute priority of the free market as a search for a perfect closed world that was inconsistent with Popperian openness. In particular, he saw Hayek's desire to give constitutional status to a free-market economy as virtually and ironically a kind of totalitarianism—and also deeply anti-entrepreneurial. Much earlier, in 'Out of utopia', he had

[4] Dahrendorf describes that atmosphere in his own official history of the LSE (Ralf Dahrendorf, *LSE: a History of the London School of Economics and Political Science, 1895–1995* (Oxford, 1995).
[5] Karl Popper, *The Open Society and Its Enemies* (London, 1945).
[6] Ralf Dahrendorf, *Reflections on the Revolution in Europe: in a letter intended to have been sent to a gentleman in Warsaw* (London, 1990).

already grasped the paradox that economic theory's search for equilibrium was hostile to many of the things for which it seemed to stand: 'the
assumption of certainty implicit in all equilibrium theories ... turns out to
be a deadly weapon against individual freedom in a living, changing
society'.[7]

The search for utopia rested on a belief that somewhere was to be
found a resolution to constant uncertainty. That, for Dahrendorf (and for
Popper), was a profound mistake, as it envisaged a time of *stasis*, when
debate, change and revision would no longer be necessary. That would be
at best dreary and boring, and at worst a new totalitarianism, as those
who questioned the reality of utopia would have to be dealt with.

As with Popper, this essentially normative position was linked to one of
social scientific methodology. The German book-length expansion of 'Out
of utopia' has a subtitle claiming it to be a work of methodology.[8] While
Popper concentrated on outlining the rules of scientific method consistent
with his approach of permanent scepticism and doubt, Dahrendorf turned
much of his attention to criticising the search for system in sociological
theory. Systems are, virtually by definition, closed, self-perpetuating: 'We
have to choose between systems and the open society', he would write
much later.[9] And in a particularly striking passage, commenting on Francis
Fukuyama's *The End of History*:[10]

> The battle of systems is an illiberal aberration . . . if capitalism is a system, then
> it needs to be fought as hard as communism had to be fought. All system means
> serfdom, including the 'natural' system of a total 'market order' ...[11]

He was here addressing a certain 'Polish gentleman' with whom he had
been discussing, in 1990, the collapse of communism and the rebuilding
of economy, polity and society; the target in this passage is clearly Hayek,
who was being much admired in central and eastern Europe. The much
vaunted German social market, he reminded his reader, was not at all a
designed system—though many writers have mistaken it for such—but an
unplanned hybrid. (Fukuyama's idea of an end of history was of course
highly uncongenial to Dahrendorf, who mischievously entitled a set of

[7] Ralf Dahrendorf, 'Out of utopia', *American Journal of Sociology*, 54 (1958), p. 148.
[8] Ralf Dahrendorf, *Pfade aus Utopia: Arbeiten zur Theorie und Methode der Soziologie* (Munich, 1967).
[9] Dahrendorf, *Reflections*, p. 61.
[10] Francis Fukuyama, *The End of History and the Last Man* (New York, 1992).
[11] Dahrendorf, *Reflections*, p. 37.

late essays on politics from the fall of the Berlin wall to the Iraq war as 'The restarting of history'.[12])

An approach to social theory and research that was dedicated to expounding and discovering the properties of systems came therefore from the same thought world as the search for utopia. He expounded his critique of—at times attack on—this approach in a series of lectures and papers written in the 1950s and early 1960s, addressed variously to German and US audiences, the primary example of which was *Homo Sociologicus*.[13] This bold work, written when he was 30, was an attack on most of the luminaries of early post-war German social science, his supporting champions coming from Anglophone traditions.

In the name of a scientific sociology, the human person was being analysed as a series of roles, stripped of several layers until nothing is left—like an onion, though Dahrendorf did not make use of Kierkegaard's powerful image. Whole persons never appeared, just bearers of positions and players of roles; but the whole, free-will person was more than the sum of the roles. He saw a way out of the problem without sacrificing the meth- odological usefulness of the role concept. Roles became social when these were seen, not just as parts to be acted out, but as responses to expectations from others. Crucially, these expectations came in different orders of obli- gation indicated by different modal verbs: *Muß-, Soll und Kann-Erwartungen* (must, ought and can expectations). Freedom consisted in the whole per- son having a multiplicity of these and him/herself being able to exploit the differences between the different degrees of obligation. This was scientific- ally important, because it was only by grasping the whole person behind the cluster of roles that we could observe how people did this. We therefore needed a highly complex model of all activities and expectations of a per- son's roles, using opinion research and many other data sources. The person and the scientific abstraction must be kept alongside each other: science with art, history with sociology, psychology with sociology. Conflicts and contradictions among a person's roles and associated expectations would be particularly important. This would not make for a comfortable sociology; society should not appear to the sociologist as fact (*Tatsache*), he states, but even as a nuisance or irritant (*Ärgernis*).[14]

This was guidance for how to conduct social research, though after his London Ph.D. thesis Dahrendorf did not undertake any empirical research

---

[12] Ralf Dahrendorf, *Der Wiederbeginn der Geshichte* (Munich, 2004).
[13] Ibid., it and others were later all translated into English and published as *Essays on the Theory of Society* (London, 1968).
[14] Dahrendorf, *Homo Sociologicus*, p. 95.

himself. But there is also an undisguised, proclaimed moral purpose here. It is only through such an approach that sociology can be true to Kant's insistence on the moral quality of the human person. Dahrendorf was always a Kantian though, again like Popper, definitely not someone who received that philosopher by way of Hegel.

His singling out of German social science as particularly guilty of this losing sight of the human in scientific abstraction seems odd, given the directions being taken by Anglo-American linguistic philosophy and economics at that time and ever since, and the fact that the absolutely dominant form of sociological systems thinking in the 1950s was a US product, albeit one forged under strong German influence: the structural functionalism of Talcott Parsons. Dahrendorf was in fact well aware of this, and the young German visiting scholar to the US attacked this school too during the period when it was fully hegemonic, in a number of articles in US journals.[15]

In praise of conflict

Something else was really in his mind when he singled out his fellow Germans for criticism here, and it was a critique to be directed at the whole nation, not just its sociologists. The idea of utopia as at best dreary was associated for Dahrendorf with the idea of an 'extremism of the centre'. This paradoxical phrase had been devised by Seymour Martin Lipset,[16] one of that great post-war generation of US sociologists whom Dahrendorf met during his American visits. Extremists of the centre, often reacting against totalitarianism, sought to avoid conflicts and extremist threats by depoliticising social questions, by fudging rather than tackling challenges. This kind of behaviour was anathema to the young Dahrendorf and, as he journeyed to and fro across the Atlantic and the Channel, it seemed to him to represent a contrast between the political and intellectual approaches of his native Germany and the Anglo-American tradition to which he was increasingly drawn. It led him to develop his critique of the 'unpolitical German', first in a 1960 article in the first issue of *The European Journal of Sociology*, then in a very substantial book, *Gesellschaft und Demokratie in Deutschland*, translated into English soon afterwards.[17]

[15] See several essays in *Essays*.
[16] Seymour Martin Lipset, 'Social stratification and "right-wing extremism"', *British Journal of Sociology*, 10 (1959), 346–82.
[17] Ralf Dahrendorf, 'Demokratie und Sozialstruktur in Deutschland', *European Journal of Sociology*, 1 (1960), 86–120; *Gesellschaft und Demokratie in Deutschland* (Munich, 1965); *Society and Democracy in Germany* (London, 1968).

This work suggested that the search for quiet and the avoidance of all tension that characterised German politics, society and academy in the decades after the Second World War was not just a temporary reaction to the traumas of Nazism and the other nightmares of the first half of the German twentieth century, but a deep historical response to far earlier periods of turbulence (like the Thirty Years War) and a mass of different forms of autocratic rule. Germans had responded to this history through such movements as Pietism, that Lutheran search for inward piety that tended to ignore the social conditions surrounding it. The German Enlightenment, so daringly critical in its early manifestations, had become similarly inward-looking, a penetrating, inquiring life of the mind and spirit cut off from having any critical implications in the outside world, epitomised in the figure of Johann Wolfgang von Goethe becoming an obedient civil servant basking in court life at Weimar. The journey from *Sturm und Drang* to the comfort of Biedermeyer was one of escape, and a rather unhealthy form of escape. Ostensibly so different from the phenomenon of Nazism, Dahrendorf saw this as in fact its mirror image, as both shared a view that open conflict was dangerous. By the time one reached Hegel and the admonition that human striving can be sublimated into the work of the state, which then relieved individual persons of the need to reach beyond themselves unaided, the link started to become clear. Soon after Dahrendorf had published his book, the relatively young Federal Republic was briefly being governed by the Große Koalition of the two main parties, the Christian Democrats and Social Democrats. This seemed to be the epitome of non-political, conflict-avoiding, German society; but he had also traced what he saw as excessive consensus-building in the preceding period of CDU–FDP government.

One might consider Dahrendorf's concept of social conflict as part of the discussion of utopia and system, as it is so much a logical part of the same coherent approach, but it represents such a significant component of his contribution to social theory that it merits a section of its own. As already noted above, he had burst upon the world with his *Soziale Klassen und Klassenkonflikt in der industriellen Gesellschaft* in 1957. Its translation into English by a US university press in 1959 was an extraordinary feat for a German still in his twenties. It was common for non-Marxist sociologists of that time, especially in the US, to deny the continued relevance of class; such denial was methodologically part of Parsonian system theory and politically part of the dominant atmosphere of a cosy, achieved utopia— both of course the reverse of what Ralf Dahrendorf believed in. But in its turn the Marxist image of class conflict comprising massive confrontations of hegemonic blocs was also profoundly unsatisfactory to him. At one level he contested the *reductio ad minimum* of the Marxist idea of the proletarian, equipped with absolutely no resources other than those with which the Communist Party could furnish him. (His LSE Ph.D. thesis had been a study of so-called 'unskilled' labour in London, revealing that few if any workers were really so devoid of their own resources.) At another, and more obviously prominent, level, he considered that the Marxist concept of class and the consequent totality of its associated conflict could be valid only if people's relation to the means of production defined all their access to power resources. Once it was possible to have distinctions between economic and other forms of power that could produce such a phenomenon as a trade unionist mayor, this had broken down. Here Dahrendorf extended Max Weber's division of class into political, economic and social to include a myriad other dimensions.

Yes, therefore, for Dahrendorf Marxists were right to see conflict rather than perfectly functioning systems as endemic to industrial societies. But they were wrong to see such conflicts in massive, homogeneous, history-defining terms, as might perhaps have been appropriate in many forms of pre-industrial society. Conflict was endemic but fragmented. Further, both Marxists and functionalists were wrong in seeing the possibility of a society in which conflict would be transcended. Its endemic nature was permanent, and, moreover, this was not a matter for regret, as eternal conflict was the crucible of human creativity.

This was a quintessentially liberal position, not an anarchist one. The very fragmentation of conflict would produce, not chaos, but stability, as institutional boundaries prevented conflict in any one arena slipping over into and aggregating with others. This image of institutionalised conflict was common among post-Marxist scholars of the time, and it has had an enduring influence. Among political scientists it produced a sociologically enriched model of the older constitutional idea of pluralism. For sociologists it made possible a kind of reconciliation between Parsonianism (the idea of institutional constraints) and Marxism (continuing conflict). Dahrendorf's version of it was particularly vigorous and thoroughgoing, and also set up a model of institutionalised conflict in which conflict was not so much to be tamed as to be enabled to act as a major fount of human creativity. But these institutional boundaries did not exist in a kind of 'natural' way, like a Hayekian catallaxy; they were the work of human activity, building forms of separation and boundary that wrapped themselves around specific conflictual fields in the way that insulating material is wrapped around electric wires. Not every society had experienced this work of institution-building, but democratic industrial societies had a strong chance of doing so. This is what Marx had not foreseen, which is why he had predicted the culmination of conflicts in one catastrophic class alignment; and it was in the interests of human freedom and creativity that Marx's expectation was false. *Class and Class Conflict* was certainly an anthem in praise of conflict, but conflict of a subtly constrained kind. It became one of the founding texts of today's post-Marxist study of institutions.

Although this work was to prove highly influential, it never succeeded in replacing a concept of class as fundamentally economic. The centrality of the economic in relation to other aspects of life, and the capacity of economic elites to maintain a strong influence over others, rendered the model of total fragmentation unrealistic. Dahrendorf acknowledged much of this twenty years later,[18] pointing out that his approach had been guilty of the empty formalism of which he was so critical. After 1957 his own use of class gradually reverted to its commonly accepted socio-economic meaning. We can understand why he wanted to fragment it and send it across a mass of different institutions when we see his idea in the general context of his belief in the benign role of fragmentation (up to a point to which we shall later return), and the avoidance of so defining people that they could be mobilised by a totalising political party.

While his concept of the benign nature of conflict was partly developed as a reaction to Germans' tendency to avoid it, and although he liked British and American societies for what he saw as their greater willingness to embrace it, he also made some shrewdly critical comments on the British approach. For the British, he wrote, conflict is a cup tie, a zero-sum game.[19] One certainly has a conflict, but then it is over; there is a clear winner, and the loser goes away—for a while. It applies very directly of course to British political ideas like 'first past the post' and opposing benches in the House of Commons. It is different from German proportional representation and fan-shaped parliamentary assemblies. But it is also different from Dahrendorfian conflict, where no loser ever goes away, the whistle never blows to signal the end of the match; because if they do, society starts to stagnate.

But the fragmented image of conflict almost does away with the idea of power; everyone seems to be so equally endowed with a resource of some kind. Dahrendorf was relatively soon to come partly to terms with

[18] Ralf Dahrendorf, *Life Chances: Approaches to Social and Political Theory* (London, 1979), ch. 3.
[19] Ralf Dahrendorf, *On Britain* (London, 1982).

this, in particular in his defence of Thrasymachus, the crude visitor who, in one of Plato's dialogues, gatecrashes one of Socrates' sessions and shouts that in the end everything is resolved by unequally distributed power.[20] Socrates gets rid of him quickly and treats him as a figure of ridicule. Characteristically, Dahrendorf takes his side, not only in terms of asserting the role of power as such, but also its corollary: that through their use of power, in conflict with each other, human beings can make their history; they are not in the grips of ineluctable forces. But the inequality of power remained a problem for him until he divided inequality into two forms, relating to 'entitlements' and 'provisions'.

Entitlements and provisions

He does this in the same place where he returned fully to the theme of conflict of his first book, thirty years later, in *The Modern Social Conflict*.[21] Dahrendorf's command of the English language was total; one could tell it was not his native language only because his grammar and syntax were more perfect than most of those for whom it is a mother tongue. One must therefore assume that the definite article in that title, which would be normal in German but sounds slightly odd in English, was deliberate, and that it implies identification of a specific conflict, characteristic of modernity. (The book was first written in English and only later did he translate into German.) This is therefore designed to be a major statement about conflict, and so it is. He addresses two kinds of conflict, for which he uses the slightly unusual terms: 'entitlements' and 'provisions'. The first refers to the struggle for rights to access things from which people have been barred by not being, or by being, members of certain categories. This is the familiar territory of the concept of citizenship as it was developed by another of the giant figures of early post-war London sociology whose influence he always recognised, T. H. Marshall. Conflict over provisions is the struggle for material goods; it becomes possible on a mass scale only in modern societies, where mass aspirations for large quantities of goods have become feasible for the first time in history.

There is nothing much original in the identification of these two objects of conflict. What is original is the insight into the conflict between these two conflicts and the changing dynamics in their relationship, and that is

---

[20] Ralf Dahrendorf, 'In praise of Thrasymachus', in *Essays*, ch. 5.
[21] Ralf Dahrendorf, *The Modern Social Conflict* (London, 1988).

what makes it 'the' modern social conflict. The time of writing, the mid-1980s, is significant. In the late 1970s Dahrendorf had shared the widespread tendency to denounce the bureaucracy, neocorporatism, dreariness and lack of opportunities for unequal entrepreneurial rewards that had become associated with social democracy. It was the furthest he had moved from the political position of his father and his own youth, and it was a position from which he would never subsequently resile. (As late as 1990 he was willing to tell a worried Polish social democrat—contemplating the wave of Americanisation that he expected now to engulf his country—that he wanted Poland and the rest of Central Europe to have 'trashy culture', because that is what people wanted. And he wanted them to have a tough wave of neoliberal economic policy before they started to rebuild some social values from scratch.[22])

However, by the mid-1980s he had seen several years of the reaction against social democracy in the West, the phenomenon that he and many others called 'Thatcherism', in action. Although the emergence of new material inequalities in general and the privileged position of persons working in secondary and derivative financial markets were then in their infancy and had reached nothing like the levels they attained by the early twenty-first century, Dahrendorf had perceived their direction of travel, one which he had in principle welcomed, and had not liked what he saw. His social democratic 'ligature' remained within his overriding liberalism. Also, although he had become highly critical of social democracy's achievements, he never relinquished his support for the value of citizenship, including Marshall's idea of the social citizenship of the welfare state, and regretted the contemporary trend to relate citizenship rights to willingness to work. Social citizenship rights, he reflected ruefully, were becoming seen as 'non-wage labour costs (and taxes)', and 'as reducing national competitiveness'.[23]

True as ever to his own theories, this discomfort was not a problem but spurred him on to new creativity, as he tried to distinguish between benign and malign inequalities.

The great struggles for democracy of the nineteenth and twentieth centuries had been struggles for inclusion and entitlement among excluded groups; and there was no end-point for such struggles other than equality. These were also necessarily collective struggles, in which one worked as a

[22] Ralf Dahrendorf, 'The strange death of socialism and the mirage of a "Third Way"', in *Reflections*.
[23] Dahrendorf, *The Modern Social Conflict*, p. 128.

member of a category with a shared identity. Social democracy's struggle for equal entitlements he regarded as having been achieved in 1968, with the collapse of nearly all remaining symbols of superior social status. Material struggles, conflicts over provisions, did not have a logical end, certainly not in a state of equality. Material struggles were also individualistic. Inequality in the pursuit of provisions was the spur to constant dynamism—an argument he had first made as long ago as 1961[24]—so insistence on equality of provisions had negative effects. But the search for an equality of entitlements, the constant extension of citizenship rights and domestication of power, expanded human scope and was therefore benign.[25] However, given an end to most (if not all) conflicts over entitlement, there would be, at least for a time, a concentration on conflicts over provisions, for which Thatcherism was far better suited than social democracy.

This all sounds superficially similar to sentiments expressed in a number of contemporary clichés. Is it not similar to saying 'equality of opportunity is fine, but not equality of outcomes'? Or 'people no longer need collective and political struggle, because they have achieved democratic rights, while there is no end to the shopping they can do'? But this was not the end of Dahrendorf's story; he never saw an end to history. He saw how the inequalities of provisions being intensified in British and American society (Germany had not yet started its own journey towards greatly increased inequalities) were creating new problems of entitlement among newly defined excluded groups. But—and here was a distinctive twist—their problem was made that much worse by the fact that the dominant class that was excluding them was what he termed and believed to be the 'majority class',[26] the victors of social democracy's earlier struggles. (It is notable that since the 1950s he had switched from seeing a multitude of classes to now being unable to see any class or entitlement differences between the financial and corporate elite and the mass of the population.)

Overall his perception of the complex links between entitlements and provisions comes fairly close to the concept of 'capabilities' that Amartya Sen was developing at the same time.[27] Dahrendorf acknowledges Sen's concept of 'entitlements', but had not embraced 'capabilities'. In Dahrendorfian terms, one could consider capabilities to constitute interdependent combinations of entitlements and provisions, without both parts of which a person

---

[24] Ralf Dahrendorf, 'On the origin of inequality among men', in *Essays*, ch. 6. The essay had earlier existed in a number of forms, in both English and German.
[25] Dahrendorf, *The Modern Social Conflict*, p. 124.
[26] Ibid., p. 154.
[27] Amartya Sen, *Commodities and Capabilities* (Amsterdam, 1985).

cannot act effectively. This stance incorporates but transcends the better known idea that there can be no equality of opportunity if there is extreme inequality of outcome. Neither Dahrendorf nor Sen is concerned with career opportunities alone, but with a far broader range of capacities to act and to be included in society. Of course, Dahrendorf does not offer us a model of a desirable balance between the egalitarian struggle for entitlements and the inegalitarian struggle for provisions; that would be utopian. He identifies the conflict for us, makes a few suggestions of his own, which now inevitably sound dated, but leaves us with a necessarily and desirably unresolved issue.

Options and ligatures

One form of what Dahrendorf saw as sources of desirable inequalities were the identities and loyalties that bind us, give us meaning and an escape from anomy. These identities and loyalties are not necessarily unequal in the sense of being hierarchical, though many are. But there is nearly always an inequality involved in saying that because A is a member of category X and B is not, A will have certain entitlements from which B will be excluded. B might of course be a member of category Y, which will have some different entitlements from which A is excluded; but X and Y do not necessarily offer equally valuable membership packages. The characteristic modern approach to this question is to combat the contention that category membership should have any implications at all. This abolition of identity-conferring membership can constitute one of the sources of drabness of which social democracy stands accused; under a communist system it reaches the point where no identities at all are permitted except those with party and state. Fascism tended to move in the opposite direction, and insist on identities, to the extent of denying the right to life of the possessors of some of them. It therefore ended in the same place, with no identities among the survivors. To add to the complexity of the issue, collective identities are often seen as egalitarian forces when set against the strivings of individuals who acknowledge no loyalties in their bid for personal advance.

The classic liberal solution to the dilemma is indeed to stress the rights of the individual stripped of all identity-conferring characteristics like gender, race or religion—the *citoyen individu* of French republicanism. In particular, the advantages of the individual in the gender-blind, race-blind, free market will be emphasised. One might have expected to find

Ralf Dahrendorf, the ultimate liberal, absolutely dedicated to personal freedom and liberation from constraints, to have fully endorsed that position. But he was a sociologist, not an economist, and where he saw a dilemma he would never let either himself or his readers escape either of its horns. The labels he placed on this particular pair of horns was 'options' (freedom, the ability to choose free from constraint) and the curiously named 'ligatures', the bonds that tie us, constrain us, but in so doing give our lives a meaning that the repeated exercise of choice prevents us from having. The idea of ligatures is most fully developed in his book *Life Chances.*[28]

The phrase 'life chances' has passed into everyday speech, but its origins lie in Max Weber's idea of *Lebenschancen*, where, as Dahrendorf points out, 'chance' has almost the opposite meaning from its current English usage by itself as closely related to luck as in 'games of chance'. Weberian (and Dahrendorfian) life chances are the socially structured probabilities that an individual will have certain experiences and opportunities rather than others. The individual is active and choosing among options, though by no means with infinite possibilities, but constrained by various social bonds or ligatures. Life chances are therefore a combination of options and ligatures.[29] But—up to a point—these ligatures are necessary to choice itself, as options without them are meaningless and make no sense. A strategy of expanding options without expanding, and perhaps even by destroying, ligatures will therefore have negative consequences for the quality of life. In *On Britain*, Dahrendorf reflected that the British might have come close to such a position.[30] Both the social democratic search for equality and Thatcherite neoliberalism pursued a 'universal insistence on discontinuity'; he even wondered whether the decline of the old class system would threaten values of cohesion and solidarity that it had once guaranteed.

Of course, if identity made it impossible for blacks in the USA to have equal civil rights with whites, one would fight against that implication, and accept that certain ligatures would be destroyed in the process. But what does one do when large parts of a young generation, white and black, in large cities, find their only identity in the anomy of a drugs culture? And what part did various destructive searches for options, not to mention pursuits of unequal provisions, play in the creation of that predica-

---

[28] Dahrendorf, *Life Chances*. This book was based on his Reith Lectures, 'The New Liberty', 1975.
[29] Ibid., pp. 29–30.
[30] Dahrendorf, *On Britain*, p. 36.

ment? One needs somehow to try to maximise options and ligatures together, and not present them as part of a zero-sum encounter. He therefore rejected the economist's welfare function, that sought to maximise what could be achieved by individuals within a taken-for-granted social structure, and sought what he called an 'active liberalism', 'one which anchors opportunities for human growth in patterns of social structure without overlooking the desirability of personal satisfaction'.[31] Again, this is an idea that comes close to Sen's idea of capabilities. Dahrendorf saw it as the nearest one might come to the idea of meaning in historical development, though it was no Hegelian idea, but a history made by a mass of actions by ordinary people, and by no means a unidirectional and irreversible one.

The idea of ligatures can be seen as related to that idea in *Class and Class Conflict*, that conflict arenas need forms of institutional protection to separate them from each other and ensure fragmentation and diversity. These varied components of social structure cannot be set in place by plan or *Diktat*, but it is possible for conscious political and social action to support or retard them. Dahrendorf developed his idea of a creative tension between options and ligatures as a form of 'active liberalism', distinguished from the 'passive liberalism' of defenders of the market order. But it is also a social democratic and conservative idea: social democratic in its concern for the impact of social structure on individuals; conservative in its fears for the consequences of destroying the albeit incoherent accumulation of past bonds and loyalties. What is typically Dahrendorf is the way in which he accepts the need to confront the inconvenient virtue of ligatures.

It is here that the biography of the man, never far away from the academic *oeuvre*, is most difficult to separate from it. He acted to exercise 'option' to change his life on a grand scale more often than most people can even contemplate: in personal relationships, in political identity, in career, in nationality. But he clearly also experienced the cost of that and knew what identity meant, if sometimes in its loss. How else do we explain the member of the British House of Lords, at the end of his life, leaving the country where he had won more appreciation than anywhere else, and returning to Germany, knowingly to die there? He never relinquished his pride in his father's bravery, even though he himself abandoned Gustav's political path. Towards the end of his period as director of the LSE, that institution where he had found so much intellectual identity in the 1950s,

---

[31] Dahrendorf, *Life Chances*, pp. 22–3.

he declared at a formal meeting 'I love the LSE.' A few weeks later at a similar meeting he recalled that a president of the German Federal Republic, Gustav Heinemann, had been challenged by a television interviewer to say whether he loved his country. The president had replied that he loved his wife; one could not use the same verb for a country. Could one really 'love' an institution?, Dahrendorf mused. Yes, he loved the LSE. He also loved the whole of London, not just its school of economics, and identified with it. He identified strongly as a European, while acknowledging that the European Union had not yet formed the identities to which most people could feel loyalty. This freedom-loving man understood the pull of ligatures.

Ralf Dahrendorf used to observe that very few decisions presented a case of 100 per cent on one side of the case and zero on the other. Indeed, 60/40 decisions were very common. Although one always had to go with the 60 per cent, the 40 per cent did not then go away. The options one had not taken remained to confront one from time to time. In his conceptual pairs—entitlements versus provisions and options versus ligatures—one sees that succinct observation set out at length and explored in difficult detail. He helps us give labels to and recognise the full implications of troublesome choices that we have dimly perceived. He never lost his optimism or belief in the potential of human striving, and continued careers as a man of action rather than of contemplation alone until very late in his life. But it was an intellectually informed optimism. Because he combined his worldly careers with unceasing reflection on the problems that Marshall, Popper, Weber, Marx, and in the background always Kant, had left him, he produced contributions to both sociology and practical politics that take us more deeply into the world's problems than most of the utterances of those who remain with just one of these career options; and he continuously felt the pull of both sets of those ligatures too.

Ralf Dahrendorf, born 1 May 1929 in Hamburg, died 17 June 2009 in Cologne

Personal postscript

I first encountered Ralf Dahrendorf when he came to the LSE as director and I was a very junior lecturer there. Shortly after his arrival he planned some changes to the administration that I and a few others thought would be damaging. We campaigned against him; we lost; and I was the most junior of the conspirators. He might have totally ignored me, so insignificant had it all turned out to be; or he could have been quite vindictive, as some would have been. Instead, however, he bothered to talk about the issue with me, and took a friendly interest in me from that time on. He was true to his beliefs and theories; conflict was healthy, even if it meant opposing him. During the various small student rebellions that took place at the School in those years he always acted in the same way. Whereas other directors might have taken disciplinary action, or smoothed everything over with bland avuncular words, Dahrendorf would engage in argument with the students, saying where he disagreed; combating them certainly, but in a manner that showed respect for their right to argue, to wage conflict, and to be treated as worthy sparring partners.

Several years later, by which time he had become a knighted figure of the British Establishment, I happened to ask him about some mutual acquaintance: 'Oh', he said, 'he has sadly become a *großer Ordinarius*'—a term used to describe a German professor who has become pompous and full of his own dignity. 'No one', I thought to myself, 'will ever be able to say that about Ralf.' The last time I saw him, a few months before his death, was at the Max Planck Institute in Cologne, where he had called in to chat to some of the doctoral and postdoctoral students there. He was telling them about the House of Lords and its quaint customs, in the way that members of that House do. But the mood of self-irony was clear; the slightly mischievous twinkle that was so often in his eye was prominent, though he was by then, in his own words, 'much reduced'. Never *ein großer Ordinarius*, but always *ein großer Mensch*.

COLIN CROUCH
Fellow of the Academy

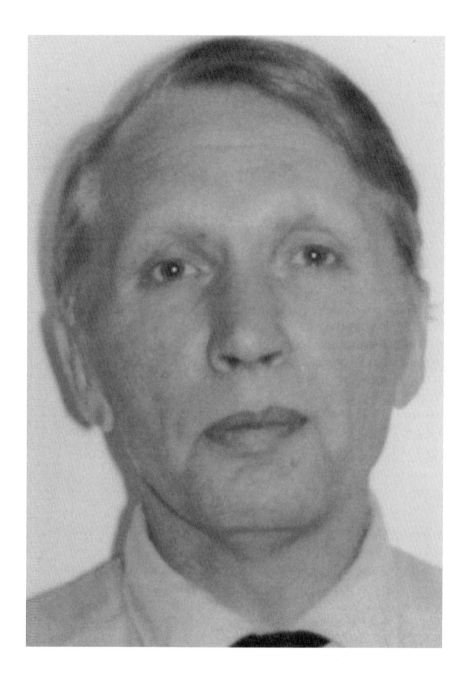

ROBIN DONKIN

Robert Arthur Donkin
1928–2006

ROBERT ARTHUR ('ROBIN') DONKIN was an exceptional scholar in both style and substance. Setting for himself very high standards of research and teaching, he expected others to do likewise for themselves. Meticulous in his search for answers to geographical questions about the past, he was so committed to a specific kind of historical geography and so convinced of its authenticity that he pursued it with total dedication and with disdain for the modish currents in Geography that ebbed and flowed around him. His firmly held ideas about historical geography and how to pursue it resulted in a significant body of original scholarship that will only slightly and slowly, if at all, be reshaped by subsequent researchers.

Formative years

Robin Donkin was born in his grandparents' house in Morpeth, Northumberland, on 28 October 1928. His father, Arthur, at the time of Robin's birth was a draper and shopkeeper but he had—and was to have—strong military associations. On leaving school in Morpeth, Arthur Donkin had enlisted in the army and was in the trenches in France during the Great War and then served with the British Army of Occupation in the Rhineland until 1919. Enlisted again in 1939, Arthur was posted to India and Burma where his unit was reported for nine months as 'missing'. Against that military background, Robin had a stable, modest, home life at Monkton in Jarrow that was both musical and bookish. Both of his parents played musical instruments—they first met as members of Morpeth Town

Proceedings of the British Academy, **172**, 115–139. © The British Academy 2011.

Orchestra. His mother, Elizabeth Jane (*née* Kirkup), had left school when she was 15, trained as a secretary and then worked for a solicitor in Newcastle. His father, a largely self-educated man, read widely and accumulated a large collection of books that included works by Darwin, Kipling, T. E. Lawrence and Galsworthy. Family holidays—Robin had two younger sisters—were spent either on the Northumbrian coast or inland helping out on the farms of relatives. It seems that young Robin also went youth hostelling in the Lake District. With his families on both maternal and paternal sides being staunch Anglicans, Robin was for many years a choirboy.

From the local elementary school at Monkton, Robin went to Jarrow Grammar School and in 1947 took his Higher School Certificate in English, Geography and History. He then read Geography at King's College, Newcastle upon Tyne, when it was still under the aegis of Durham University. The first of his many publications was an essay on pioneer settlement that appeared during his first year as an undergraduate in the *King's College [Newcastle] Geographical Society Magazine*. He graduated in 1950 with a First Class degree and enrolled at Durham as a research student. The first of Robin's many adventurous travels abroad was as a postgraduate student: he acquired a motorcycle and in 1951 went with a companion to North Africa, sleeping rough alongside the bike *en route* in France and then in Tunisia and Libya. As an undergraduate, he had been most impressed by the teaching and writings of M. R. G. Conzen, who had fled Germany in the mid-1930s to escape the National Socialist regime. Conzen applied exacting standards to his painstaking research on what he called 'the cultural landscape' (a German geographical concept that embraced the natural landscape and its modification by human activities). He argued that such landscapes were best interpreted in terms of their forms or morphologies, their functions, and their changes through time. Robin was especially stimulated by Conzen's work on medieval towns and it was to him that he turned for a supervisor for his own doctoral research on the contribution of the Cistercians to the geography of England in the twelfth and thirteenth centuries. In practice, he consulted Conzen rarely about his doctoral research, preferring to beaver away independently in libraries, mainly that of the British Museum.

With the prospect of National Service looming, Robin resolved to complete his thesis in three years and was awarded a Ph.D. in 1953. While a research student, he had participated in the 1952 Durham University Exploration Society's expedition to Morocco: his later travels were to be solo affairs, except, of course, those undertaken while doing his National Service between 1953 and 1955. After training at Rhyll, Oswestry and

Woolwich, Robin was—to the immense delight of his father—commissioned as a lieutenant in the Royal Artillery and posted to the Canal Zone in Egypt. He always claimed that he learned to drive in the desert and when taking a few days leave purchased a camera and drove to Cairo and to the Pyramids. Proud of his military connection, in later life he often wore his regimental tie and had the bearing of an army officer.

Looking beyond his time as a conscript, Robin had applied for and was awarded a King George VI Memorial Fellowship to enable him to spend 1955–6 at the University of California, Berkeley. This was to be an especially formative experience but his precise reasons for going to Berkeley cannot be established with certainty. Some forty years later, he claimed that it was as an undergraduate that he had

> stumbled on Sauer's writings—two classic papers, both published in 1941, 'Foreward [*sic*] to historical geography' and 'The personality of Mexico', and, a little later, his long chapter on 'Cultivated plants' in the *Handbook of South American Indians*. Here were new pastures and a new approach, culled from the living world, for which I wasn't then prepared; but I determined to return in mind and, if possible in body, when the opportunity arose, as in fact it did in 1955.[1]

Robin took a boat across the Atlantic and then trains across the United States to California. His time there during 1955–6 was to have a profound impression upon him and his research projects. He fell completely under the spell of Carl Sauer and the Berkeley school of historical and cultural geography. Sauer's graduate seminars on topics as varied as the domestication of plants and animals, the impact of early human settlement in the Americas, and the Spanish conquest of Latin America enthralled him. Intriguingly, his time at Berkeley went unrecorded in Sauer's voluminous correspondence, except for one occasion when Sauer, who was on a preretirement sabbatical in Europe, enquired of his secretary, Westher Hess, about his graduate students. After itemising the progress of some of them, she added: 'We do not see much of Donkin, he spends most of his time in the [Bancroft] Library.' It was there, as a follow-up to his study of the Cistercians, that he researched the contribution of the Franciscan missions to the settlement of southern California between 1769 and 1823.[2] It was clearly Robin's sojourn in Berkeley that laid the solid foundations for the interests he was later to pursue in the historical geography of Latin

---

[1] R. A. Donkin, 'A "servant of two masters"?', *Journal of Historical Geography*, 23 (1997), 247–66.
[2] R. A. Donkin, 'The contribution of the Franciscan missions to the settlement of Alta California colonisation 1769–1823', *Revista de Historia de América*, 52 (1961), 373–93.

America and in the domestication of plants and animals globally. In a rare published statement about influences on his career, Robin admitted much later that it was geographers at Berkeley who first turned his interests toward the aboriginal New World.[3] But those interests had to lie relatively dormant until he had established himself in the British university system and until he had satisfied himself that he had published all that he had to say about the Cistercians in England.

Edinburgh 1956–1958 and Birmingham 1958–1970

On returning to the United Kingdom in 1956, Robin took up a post as Assistant Lecturer in the Department of Geography at the University of Edinburgh. He was the only historical geographer in that department, which was then led by J. Wreford Watson, a regional geographer sensitive to the role of historical explanation in geography. While busily preparing new lecture courses, Robin initiated what was to become a massive record of publications.[4] During his two years at Edinburgh, he published six papers on the Cistercians and one on an early nineteenth-century source for studying the geography of California.

In 1958 Robin moved to an Assistant Lectureship in Geography at the University of Birmingham, being upgraded the following year to a full Lectureship, a post that he held until he took up a Lectureship in Cambridge from January 1971. With teaching historical geography at Birmingham largely the domain of Harry Thorpe, he found himself mainly delivering general courses on human geography. He put a Sauerian stamp on them. His first year course ranged very widely in time and space, covering the origins of life on earth, the early dispersal routes of mankind, the domestication of plants and animals, the development of the world's agricultural systems, of urbanism and of early civilisations. For most freshmen undergraduates, such an introduction to human geography was a cultural shock. It was an introduction to the rigorous scholarship and intellectual curiosity of Robin rather than to the current fashions and fads of the 'new geography' being taught in most British universities in the 1960s. His third year course on 'advanced human geography' reflected strongly his experience of Sauer's teaching at Berkeley. It consisted of two

---

[3] R. A. Donkin, *Agricultural Terracing in the Aboriginal New World* (Tucson, AZ, 1979), p. xi.
[4] There is no published comprehensive listing of his publications so one is provided at the end of this memoir.

parts, a set of lectures by Robin and of seminars presented by individual students. His lectures having provided an in-depth study of agricultural origins and dispersals and their impacts on cultural landscapes, the seminars focused on changes to landscapes associated with the introduction of particular plants and animals. Philip Jones recalls that his seminar topic was 'French colonisation in Algeria with special reference to the introduction of viticulture'. For such seminars, Robin allowed students access to his vast card indexes and encouraged them to prepare comprehensive handouts for their own seminars, including maps, statistical tables and extensive bibliographies. Other members of staff often attended these seminars, which many undergraduates came to regard as highlights of their Birmingham days. Robin also taught some shorter courses on the conservation geography of Mediterranean lands and, within the School of History, on the historical geography of the Americas. He issued students with unforgettably long reading lists and expected them to read widely and thoughtfully before proffering their own views and conclusions. In the intimate setting of his tutorial groups, his style was forensic, a constant flow of penetrating questions educating students into a deep suspicion of shallow explanations.

Students were not only inspired by Robin's high standards of teaching but also by his lifestyle and approachability. A dashing, dapper and somewhat eccentric bachelor figure in his thirties, he stood out from his colleagues by his smart country wear, his smoking of small cigars and his driving a large, Burgundy coloured, and convertible, Alvis car. He was a tutor at one of the university's halls of residence, Manor House, a huge mock Tudor house given to the university by the local chocolate making company, Cadburys, and set in bosky suburbs. He enjoyed the company of students. In his book-filled flat, he hosted sherry evenings for groups of students, not least for the graduate students of the Department of Geography, whether they were physical, contemporary human or historical geographers. As one former student put it, Robin's 'conversations were always unthreatening, with a line in mock sarcasm to deal with things he was not so sure about, and we came away flattered by his interest in us and thinking more carefully than before'. Another said that 'to those who did not know Robin well, he was a shy and rather distant member of staff with a formidable reputation' but 'on a one-to-one basis he was a "different" person—warm, encouraging, constructively critical and supportive'.

While at Birmingham, Robin travelled a great deal. His interest in travel and exploration led him to join the Hakluyt Society in 1962. He took undergraduate field classes to Wales, the Lake District, Brittany and

Provence; he travelled independently during the vacations to Italy, Sardinia, Provence, Spain and Portugal. He went to Seville for Spanish language courses. But he also began to build on his Latin American interests developed at Berkeley. A Leverhulme Research Fellowship held in 1966–7 enabled him to travel to Middle America, where he worked in libraries in Mexico City, La Paz, Lima, Bogotá and Caracas and in the field in Mexico, Guatemala and the northern and central Andes. In the field he travelled using local transport and also walked long distances, staying in basic accommodation with local people. Transport was clearly an enjoyable challenge for Robin: he travelled from England to Middle America from Port Sunlight, courtesy of a Shell oil tanker, and at the end of his trip he returned with Shell from Curaçao to Rotterdam. Another Latin Americanist, Jock H. Galloway, arranged for Robin to be an invited Visiting Associate Professor of Geography at the University of Toronto for 1968–9. His teaching there completed, he took the opportunity from June to September to work in the library of the Institute of Latin American Studies at the University of Texas at Austin and then to undertake field work in Haiti, the Dominican Republic and Mexico. In the field, he again made the point of using local transport—including mules—and basic accommodation.

Throughout his years at Edinburgh and Birmingham, Robin pursued two research strands: one was a continuation of his doctoral work on the Cistercians, the other was the initiation of his work on Latin America. By the time he left Birmingham, in December 1970, he had almost closed down his research on the Cistercians, so it will be appropriate to consider that work before following him to Cambridge.

But before doing so, there is one very personal consequence of Robin's sojourn at Birmingham that demands attention. Among the undergraduates who attended his lectures when she arrived at Birmingham in 1960 was Jennifer Kennedy, whom Robin married ten years later. After graduating in 1963, Jennifer undertook Voluntary Service Overseas for two years in the Anglo-French Condominium of the New Hebrides (Vanuatu), Western Pacific, and for a short period worked in the British Council Library at Suva, Fiji; during 1965–6 she was a library trainee at the University of St Andrews and at the University of British Columbia; during 1966–7 she obtained a postgraduate Diploma in Librarianship and Archives from University College London and for the next three years was an Assistant Librarian at York University. In 1970 Jennifer was offered a post in the library of the newly founded University of the South Pacific in Fiji but by then she had for some years been in touch with Robin and they were married on 12 September 1970, a few months before he took up his new post in Cambridge in January 1971. Jennifer was Assistant Librarian at Fitzwilliam College from 1971 until 1976. Their daughter, Lucy, was born on 6 April 1977.

The Cistercians

Publications did not flow from Robin's 1953 doctoral dissertation on the Cistercians until after he had completed his National Service and his visit to Berkeley. Then, between 1957 and 1969, intensifying and extending his doctoral research, he published twenty papers on the geographical impact of the Cistercian Order in Europe (but especially in England and Wales) during the medieval period. Robin was, of course, building on a corpus of earlier work on Cistercian settlement by medieval monastic historians like David Knowles. The Order's objectives of livelihood self-sufficiency and physical isolation had attracted the attention of many historians but their work lacked the geographical perspective that he brought to the topic. A succession of articles addressed the many ways in which the Cistercians impacted upon landscape, economy and society: they included the Cistercians' highly profitable trade in wool and cattle; marshland rec-lamation and woodland clearance; forest management; settlement and depopulation; investment in urban properties; markets and fairs; and the foundation of granges, the granaries in which were stored the large quan-tities of cereals harvested from reclaimed lands. His work on the Cistercians was usefully summarised in three publications: a valedictory article, a bibliography and a book.

In 1963 Robin published 'some conclusions' about the Cistercians in medieval England as landowners, pioneers, stockmen and traders, stress-ing those conclusions which modified the then prevailing view of the Order.[5] He argued that the monks were not only pioneers and innovators but also catalysts of wide change throughout the twelfth and much of the thirteenth centuries. His approach was that of an historical geographer: his detailed attention to development through time was illustrated by his histogram of Cistercian foundations in Europe and the Near East between 1100 and 1500, while his detailed attention to spread through space was demonstrated in, for example, distribution maps of medieval Benedictine

[5] R. A. Donkin, 'The Cistercian Order in Medieval England: some conclusions', *Transactions and Papers of the Institute of British Geographers*, 33 (1963), 181–98.

and Cistercian monasteries in England and Wales, of Cistercian houses with tanneries and/or vaccaries, of Cistercian houses with fulling mills, and of Cistercian houses with property in London. That Robin had perhaps intended this to be his valedictory paper on the Cistercians is indicated not only by its titular stress upon his 'conclusions' about their activities but also by the fact that the only references cited were to fourteen of his own papers. This highly unusual but perfectly logical device is itself indicative of his somewhat eccentric but carefully considered approach. In fact, however, he had not finished with the Cistercians. He went on to publish two further papers on them and two other major works.

In 1969 Robin published a *Cistercian Bibliography*, at the time a pioneering bibliography of printed works relating to the Cistercian Order as a whole and to the Houses of the British Isles in particular. This bibliography, of more than 100 pages and 1,500 items, revealed the extensive range of printed works from the fifteenth century onwards, not only in English but also in many other languages that he used as the source materials for his work. Then, in 1978, he brought together his final thoughts on the Order in his 242-page book dedicated to his parents: *The Cistercians: Studies in the Geography of Medieval England and Wales.* This was, in effect, a massive updating of his doctoral thesis written twenty-five years previously. Its first chapter traced the spread of the Order throughout Europe and described the changes that occurred as a result of resiting by houses in England and Wales. The following chapter considered the question of depopulation and the grange as the key to the Cistercian economy. The next two chapters focused on pastoral farming and the winning of new land at the expense of woodland, waste and fen. Questions relating to trade, the ownership of markets and urban property were addressed in the penultimate chapter. A final postscript examined the role of the white monks as agents for the diffusion of new ideas and technologies and showed how the Order became involved in affairs of state when, towards the end of the thirteenth century, abbots in considerable numbers were called to parliament. Eleven appendices tabulated—to the benefit of future Cistercian scholars—the detailed factual scaffolding Robin had painstakingly erected to enable him to reveal the geography of the Cistercians in twenty-five maps and a meticulously crafted text. This culmination of his work on the Cistercians represents the peak of a mountain of the highest-quality historical and geographical scholarship. A widely admired enterprise, it influenced strongly D. M. Robinson's 1980 study *The Geography of Augustinian Settlement in Medieval England and Wales.*[6]

---

[6] Published in two volumes in Oxford as *British Archaeological Reports*, 80 (1980).

While gradually closing down his Cistercian enterprise, Robin was opening a new Latin American project and his move from Birmingham to Cambridge was pivotal in that transformation. With hindsight, he concluded that his charting of the contribution of the Cistercian Order to the geography of medieval England was perhaps closer to the tradition of Berkeley than to that established by H. C. Darby in England.[7]

Cambridge 1971–1996

During 1970, funding became available at Cambridge for a Lectureship in the Geography of Latin America, one of the by-products of the Parry Committee's urging of central government to promote study of the region. Professor H. C. Darby, a leading historical geographer who was then head of the Department of Geography at Cambridge, admired Robin's work on the Cistercians and had engaged him while at Birmingham to write the chapter on changes in the early Middle Ages for his new, edited, historical geography of England, published in 1973. Darby knew that Robin's interests were turning towards Latin America and so invited him to apply for the new Lectureship. Robin did so and in August 1970 he was appointed to the Lectureship from 1 October 1970. But he was obliged to give one Term's notice to Birmingham and so Cambridge agreed to his request to defer taking up his appointment until 1 January 1971. He was subsequently promoted to be Reader in Historical Geography from 1 October 1990 and two years after that he was approved by Cambridge for the Litt.D. degree. In 1972 he had been elected as a Fellow of Jesus College, Cambridge and in 1985 as a Fellow of the British Academy.

At Cambridge, Robin was able to give lecture courses closely related to his own research interests. He taught a first year course on 'human geography' (later more trendily marketed by the Department as 'environment and resources') which focused on the domestication of plants and animals and on the development of basic systems of agriculture and animal husbandry. He contributed a few lectures on Latin America to a course on contemporary economic development but took sole responsibility for a full course on the cultural geography of Latin America. In addition, he delivered a few lectures on the monastic orders in Robin Glasscock's course on the geography of medieval Britain and two lectures on Carl Sauer and the Berkeley school of cultural geography embedded within a shared course on geographical ideas and methods.

[7] Donkin, 'A "servant of two masters"?', p. 247.

To undergraduates, Robin's empirical lectures on agricultural origins and indigenous peoples were a contrast in their subject matter to the kind of geography they had learned at school and in their style to the quantitative and theoretical geography being promoted by many lecturers at Cambridge in the 1970s and 1980s. Former students remember him as a fluent and polished lecturer, articulating precisely many memorable phrases in a seemingly spontaneous manner even though they had been meticulously prepared. To his rapt student audience, he conveyed a depth of enthusiasm and a breadth of scholarship that marked him apart from many of his colleagues. His lectures were authoritative, inspirational, thought-provoking and clearly grounded in his own deep and genuine intellectual curiosity. For many undergraduates at Cambridge—as also for many at Birmingham—his lectures opened windows onto new worlds and did so in ways that they remember with warmth and gratitude today.

It was also a very memorable experience to be taught by Robin in small groups of two to four students in a 'supervision'. His office, where he conducted supervisions from behind a desk covered in papers and his Olivetti typewriter, was full of books, of curious artefacts collected on his travels, of files for thousands of record cards, and of smoke from his cherished pipe. He continued to use his beloved Olivetti, on which he had typed his doctoral dissertation in 1953, until his death fifty-three years later.

More important than the stage setting for Robin's supervisions was the drama enacted by him and his students, for some of whom supervisions were a daunting experience. Robin set high standards of scholarship for himself and expected undergraduates to do so for themselves. He engaged very positively with students who had read and thought about the topic in hand but he made it clear that he thought that students who had not prepared thoroughly for the occasion had let both themselves and him down. He cared about students both in the Department and at Jesus College, even if some of them did not share his high standards of scholarship and morality or find it easy to deal with what, on a first encounter, seemed to be an austere and shy persona. Although he could be hard-edged with students academically, he was also—as one his former undergraduates put it— 'someone with a very gentle, open and caring attitude'.

Robin impressed not only many undergraduates but also, for a variety of reasons, many of his Cambridge colleagues. For them, he was first and last a serious scholar with very high standards. None could question that in relation to his research but it could and did lead him into differences of opinion with his colleagues over some other issues. Three examples come to mind. First, when examining for the Geographical Tripos, Robin was very reluctant to award many Firsts on the grounds that a First Class at Cambridge was the 'gold standard' and should not be devalued. At meetings of the Board of Examiners he would mount spirited opposition to awarding a First to a candidate whose work included a spread of Second Class marks. 'You have known these students for three years', he would challenge his co-examiners, 'how many really first class minds are there amongst them?' Second, in June 1995 Robin wrote to complain to Dr Keith Richards, Head of the Department of Geography, that he had just spent a week marking scripts for the paper on 'Environment and Resources' for Part IA of the Tripos and that it was an experience he did not wish to repeat: 'I am unsuited to marking essays on "environmental policy" (read *politics*) which seem to permeate every answer. Many bear the marks of prepared statements to rehearsed questions, PR style, starved of natural science and of originality … I am unwilling to act as an examiner for Part IA of the Geographical Tripos, 1996.' Despite Dr Richards' pleading, Robin held to his principles and he was not a tripos examiner in 1996, his final year as a university officer. Third, in early 1993 the Degree Committee of the Faculty of Earth Sciences and Geography was recommended by two examiners to approve the award of a Ph.D. degree to a candidate for his submitted dissertation. Robin, a member of the Committee, had read the dissertation and voted against the recommendation. He found himself in a minority of one, because the Committee accepted the recommendation by 11 votes to 1, with two abstentions. Three days after the Committee's meeting, he wrote to the Secretary of the Committee, resigning his membership from both the Degree Committee and the Faculty Board on the grounds that, in his opinion, the reports of the two examiners did not justify their joint recommendation. As Head of Department at the time, I asked Robin to reconsider his position. I made two points: first, that the Committee's decision had been reached democratically and that to find oneself in a minority on a university committee was not a sufficient ground for resigning (if all university officers were to act in such a way, the business of a university would soon grind to a halt); and second, that his stand on a matter of principle would in practice mean additional work for the colleague who would have to be found to replace him on the committee. On my advice and at my request, he generously withdrew his resignation. He was high-minded but not intransigent.

Robin's teaching and research gave him reason to be proud but he was a modest man easily embarrassed by what he considered to be too much attention. When Geoffrey Harcourt, a Fellow of Jesus College,

congratulated him on his being promoted as a Reader, Robin dismissed
the comment saying that there was no cause for any such remark. It might
have been that he attached little value to what Harcourt, a left-wing economist, thought about him. But such self-effacement was characteristic of
Robin. Another such incident throws further light on his personality. As
Robin approached retirement, the Head of Department (Keith Richards)
wanted to mark it in some appropriate way. The idea of a special lecture
by a distinguished scholar was floated. But Robin wrote to Richards on
29 March 1996: 'On reflection, I have gone off the idea of a lecture. It would
take time and trouble to prepare, and, in any case, I cannot at the moment
think of anyone who could reasonably be approached, who is "geographical" (for the sake of the occasion and the audience), and who [*sic*] I particularly wish to hear ... Least trouble would be (as you kindly suggested)
a glass of wine after the final staff meeting of the year, provided there are
no speeches.' Richards understandably followed convention and organised a collection among Robin's colleagues and on 30 October, shortly
after Robin's tenure had expired, wrote to him to ask for a time when he
and his wife could attend a very informal gathering in the Head of
Department's office, just to toast him on his retirement. Richards told
Robin that there had been a collection for him and that he enclosed, paid
for from that source, two tickets for a London performance of Georges
Bizet's opera *The Pearl Fishers*—an ingenious but ill-judged gesture that
Richards thought would be appreciated because Robin was at that time
writing a book on pearl fishing from its origins to the Age of Discoveries.
Robin's reply, on 4 November 1996, returning the tickets, is illuminating:
'Your letter left me feeling very uncomfortable. I hoped that my wishes
would be accepted—that there would be no presentation and no gather-
ing. We cannot use these embarrassingly expensive tickets. Now I fear that
I have offended you all, which I much regret.' Richards could not let the
matter rest there—the money collected on Robin's behalf had to be used
for its intended purpose. So, on 8 December, Richards delivered to him at
Jesus College an eminently suitable two-volumes' 1868 edition of Charles
Darwin's *The Variation of Animals and Plants under Domestication* together
with a 'best wishes' card signed by his colleagues in the department. Robin
wrote to Richards on 18 December: 'The Darwin volumes! How very, very
kind—a quite perfect parting gift and, along with the signed card, so much
appreciated. I am most grateful and honoured. The immediate pleasure
was all the keener since it came after a long and not particularly rewarding
day in the B.L.[British Library]! You will, I know, convey my warmest
thanks to the Department as a whole.'

In dress, demeanour and discussion Robin was a distinctive and apparently incongruous visitor to the common room of the department. His deceptively quiet, other-worldly, appearance had an 'old England' touch about it: he was smartly dressed, often in what some considered to be old-fashioned brown tweed suits, proudly wearing his 'Gunner' tie and sporting a silk handkerchief in his breast pocket: this at a time when many 'dons'—aping undergraduates—were much less formerly attired. In contrast to the often raucous badinage of some of his colleagues in the department's common room, Robin's quiet (unless broken by his extraordinarily loud and body-shaking laugh) conversations with his colleagues were intellectual, showing interest in their endeavours and relating them often to his own. Bill Adams, an Africanist, recalls Robin asking him what he knew about early Portuguese descriptions of Africa or archaeological debates about the plough in the Sahel or about the spread of the banana in East Africa. All of which was a contrast with discussions elsewhere in the common room about the weekend's football results or the latest frontier or model in geography. Mark Billinge, another of Robin's colleagues, recalls that he 'was distinctly old-fashioned: polite, moral, judgemental, erudite and proper. He was also enormous fun: irreverent, cheeky, full of fun.' Adams remembers that Robin's most censorious put-down of other geographers whose work he considered to be insufficiently scholarly was to say: 'I haven't seen him/her in the UL [University Library] recently.' Robin conveyed what another of his colleagues, Derek Gregory, described as 'an artfully cultivated image of a civilised man marooned amidst the barbarisms of the modern world'. But to some extent Robin himself undermined that image, for sometimes outside the common room was parked his sand-coloured (officially, a geographically appropriate 'Limestone') and somewhat battered-looking, short wheelbase, Land Rover. Robin sold his Alvis for about £50 in 1970, on leaving Birmingham, and at Cambridge in early 1971 purchased his Land Rover for £1,600, presumably subscribing to the description in the company's brochure that 'the man who buys a Land Rover wants something more than an ordinary car'. He held on to the vehicle during his lifetime. Although an expeditionary vehicle, he never took it abroad. Perhaps on the three miles' journey between his home in the village of Barton and the university he dreamed of far away places! He did take the Land Rover on frequent 'expeditions' to the Lake District, where the Donkin family owned a house and where Robin had great enjoyment tending the fell-side garden.

Whenever Robin was in the common room of the Department of Geography, he was usually on his way by bicycle to or from Jesus College or the University Library, his 'second home'. Although he played his full part as a lecturer and as an examiner for the Geographical Tripos, and as a member of the Faculty Committee and of the Degree Committee, he never taught any practical classes nor did he lead any field classes while at Cambridge. His expertise and knowledge, he was able to claim, lay else-where—thereby reserving to himself more time for research in the University Library and in 'his' special field in Latin America and other foreign places.

During his almost twenty-six years in the Department of Geography at Cambridge, Robin used a number of sabbaticals to travel abroad to work in libraries and in the field. In 1972 he went to Bolivia, Argentina, Ecuador and Brazil and in 1979–80 to Mexico and Guatemala. With his research interests broadening beyond Latin America, he travelled in 1987 to India, Goa, China, Hainan Island, Macau and Hong Kong and in 1994 to Pakistan, going through the Karakorum Pass to Gilgit, the Hunza val-ley and to the oasis city of Kashgar in remote northwest China. As was his custom, he travelled alone, using local transport and basic accommo-dation. Jennifer, his wife, never travelled with him, in part because she remained at home to look after their daughter, Lucy, and in part because Robin preferred to travel on his own to his research outposts with their often-limited facilities. Jennifer thinks that Robin's self-reliance when travelling perhaps reflected his awareness of the physical hardships that his father had had to endure in the trenches of the First World War and in Burma when he went missing during the Second World War. Whatever the reason, there can be no doubt that such travels abroad combined with tramping the long corridors of the University Library in Cambridge enabled Robin to produce an extraordinary corpus of scholarship.

Latin America and beyond

While at Berkeley during 1955–6, Robin launched his research interest in Latin America by travelling to Mexico, Guatemala and Cuba. But it did not really gain momentum until 1966–7, much of which he spent in Middle and South America, to be followed by a further six months' sojourn there in 1969. But although initially based in Latin American countries, Robin's research interests were essentially thematic and he soon moved beyond those countries to embrace many areas of the globe in his quest to dis-cover more about the early domestication of plants and animals and related interactions between the Old and New Worlds. These issues fired Robin into producing a remarkable set of meticulously researched monographs.

The first to be published, *Spanish Red*, in 1977, had as its subject cochineal, a red dye-stuff that Mexican and Peruvian Indians had for centuries obtained from an insect (a species of the genus /*Dactylopius*/). Robin argued that cochineal was 'the most widely traded and, next to gold and silver, the most valuable product of the Spanish Indies. Moreover, in no other colonial enterprise were the aboriginal associations so pronounced; production was left almost entirely in the hands of the Indian population.' With astonishing diligence, he traced information from the beginning of the sixteenth century onwards on the rearing of the insect in the highlands of Middle and South America and on the preparation of the dyestuff, mining *codices* of native origin, natural histories, official reports and historico-geographical surveys. For the Old World, his sources included herbals, floras, and diverse scientific reports; state papers; trading records and commercial directories; travellers' accounts; and, from about 1820, pamphlets written to advise prospective farmers. With the information laboriously harvested from such sources, Robin mapped the extent of cochineal culture in the New World and the introduction of insects and their host cacti in the Old World. Detailed lists of published references to the raising of cochineal from pre-Hispanic times to the mid-twentieth century were accompanied by distribution maps of such references. He produced an astonishing story of an historically rare phenomenon, the domestication of dye insects. Within about a hundred years of the conquest of Mexico, cochineal was being employed in the textile- and leather-working cities of Eurasia and North Africa. The cochineal 'industry' prospered, with cochineal becoming one of most valued commodities carried to the Old World from its colonies until its use was eclipsed during the nineteenth century by the use of aniline (synthetic) dyes.

A very different focus is found in Robin's second monograph, *Agricultural Terracing in the Aboriginal New World* (1979). This was much more concerned with the cultural landscape and was based on considerable work in the field as well as in libraries. It was a close examination of the evidence for extensive agricultural terracing in Middle and South America: it embraced, breathtakingly, terracing in the arid and semi-arid highlands of Mexico, Guatemala, Honduras, Venezuela, Colombia, Ecuador, Peru, Bolivia, Chile and Argentina. Robin combined his own observations in the field with references to agricultural terracing diligently excavated from the topographical, ethnographical and archaeological literature of the New Word. Detailed descriptions of specific sets of terraces, many of them abandoned, were set within a general discussion of the fundamental characteristics of pre-Hispanic agriculture and of its range of field implements. Evidence for the construction, use and abandonment of these agricultural terraces was carefully weighed. Although having similar forms, they might have had different origins and functions. Abandonment might have been a product of climatic or demographic change. Although his study could not answer conclusively all of the questions that such terraces pose, his work remains the definitive statement about them. The broad scope of this study of terracing in the aboriginal New World as a whole connected with regional and local studies of terracing conducted by William Denevan and his students in Peru, Bolivia, and Venezuela both before and after Robin's work.

Those who consider Robin's concerns to have been esoteric find strong support in his next monograph, *Manna: an Historical Geography* (1980). The description 'manna' has no uniform or precise meaning, nor is it applied exclusively to any one substance. It is used to refer to any sweet substance or honey-like gum either exuded from the branches or leaves of plants or trees (occasioned by unusually high atmospheric temperatures or by the punctures of insects or artificial incisions) or excreted by insects in the form of honey-dew or, exceptionally, of protective cocoons. The cultural use of manna has not involved domestication: in the hot dry lands of the Old World, with which it has been chiefly referenced, it has simply been collected. Following his now familiar 'method' (although he would never have referred to it as such), Robin searched with extreme diligence for reports on manna in printed works from the sixteenth century onwards. He discovered some 250 species of Old World plants associated with the product, principally in the hot and dry lands of western and west-central Asia. He found very few references to manna in the Americas. He showed that manna was used both as a sweetener and as a medication. Furthermore, he demonstrated that the nature of the substance was apparently nowhere properly understood until the early medieval period, and even until much later it was widely held to be some kind of dew, condensed from the atmosphere. Its mysterious origins invited speculation and it acquired a reputation as a supernatural 'gift' or 'bonus'—as nectar or ambrosia of the gods—throughout and well beyond the main areas of supply. The relatively recent spread and ultimately dominance of cane sugar have not entirely displaced the use of manna, Robin argued, because their properties differ and local recipes and traditional remedies have preserved the preferences and knowledge of past centuries.

During the next twenty-five years, Robin published six more mono-graphs and there was another completed typescript with a publisher at the time of his death in 2006. In *The Peccary* (1985) he traced the history and geography of the New World peccary. Primarily a forest or woodland ani-mal, the peccary was never domesticated (that is, bred regularly in captiv-ity) by traditional societies but it was hunted as perhaps their single most important source of meat. Europeans valued their meat but even more their hides. He suggested that the conditions and processes that might have led to their domestication were disrupted by the European conquest of the Americas and by the associated introduction of the domesticated Old World pig. His historical geography of the peccary covered a wide range of topics: for example, he mapped the local and regional names given to the animal; he detailed both the techniques used to hunt them and the products of the kill; and he explored the peccary in ceremony and myth. In this monograph, he made a rare (for him) excursion into com-parative analysis. He pointed out how distinctive was the process of animal domestication in the humid tropics, where grazing animals were not present until introduced from elsewhere. Management of animals involved, in all three tropical regions of the world, the rearing or full domestication of one pig-like scavenger and one or two large bird scavengers, with all the animals being attracted to sedentary horticultural settlements in which some surplus food was available. He simply noted this as a pattern, with-out attempting any kind of explanation. A former colleague, Tim Bayliss-Smith, thinks that this was and remains 'an original observation of almost Sauerian scope, but characteristically Robin tossed it out and never (I think) attempted again this kind of global synthesis'.

In the Preface to his next monograph, *The Muscovy Duck, Cairina mos-chata domestica: Origins, Dispersal, and Associated Aspects of the Geography of Domestication* (1989), Robin provided a justification for writing it: 'Years ago, in the first issue of *Acta Americana* (1943), Carl Sauer called for infor-mation about the Muscovy, where and why it was kept. This monograph is a belated and inadequate response to that request.' Here is evidence both of his indebtedness to Sauer and of his own modesty. The New World had few domesticated animals but among them was the Muscovy duck which, together with the guinea pig and the turkey, had been introduced into Europe by the middle of the sixteenth century. He mapped the recorded distribution of the Muscovy duck, wild and domesticated, in the Americas before detailing its introduction and diffusion in Europe and west-central Asia, in Africa and in southern Asia and Oceania.

There followed four studies in similar vein: (1) of the anthropogenic dispersal of the guinea fowl (*Meleagrides: an Historical and Ethnographical Study of the Guinea Fowl*, 1991)—which Robin dedicated to Carl Sauer; (2) of pearls and pearl-fishing from its origins to the Age of Discoveries (*Beyond Price: Pearls and Pearl Fishing*, 1998)—this time dedicated to his wife and daughter; (3) of the Indonesian origins and diffusion of camphor, the source of a powerful perfume (*Dragon's Brain Perfume: an Historical Geography of Camphor*, 1999)—dedicated to 'the editors of countless primary sources and to the librarians around the world who have made these and much else available to me, 1948–1998'; and (4) the Indonesian archipelago of the Moluccas and the traffic in spices until the arrival of Europeans in the fifteenth century (*Between East and West: the Moluccas and the Traffic in Spices up to the Arrival of the Europeans*, 2003)—dedicated to James Parsons, a distinguished Berkeley geographer in the Sauerian tradition who died in 1997 and with whom Robin had been in contact since his Californian visit in 1955–6. The last two of these books signalled his developing interest in geographical discovery and trade. It comes as no surprise that at the time of his death in 2006 he had completed a book on maritime exploration in the Atlantic and Indian Oceans before 1500: it is to be published posthumously by the American Philosophical Society. Robin had also begun work on his intended next book, on maize. He had by then moved a long way from the Cistercians where his own scholarly explorations had begun in Durham in 1950 and even moved a long way beyond his Latin American expeditions launched seriously in Cambridge in 1971.

An independent scholar

That Robin was in the Rare Books Room of Cambridge University Library on the day before he died on 1 February 2006 is symptomatic of his almost obsessive dedication to research. His retirement years saw the publication of three monographs, the writing of a fourth and research begun for a fifth one. Even so, his productivity in retirement was stalled by a serious accident in July 1997, when he was knocked off his bicycle by a car near to Barton, his village home just outside Cambridge, sustaining arm, leg and rib fractures as well as concussion. His injuries required medical attention for almost three years but, typically, he bore his misfortune with great fortitude.

Robin was unequivocally an eminent historical geographer whose work embraced an astonishing range of historical, archaeological, anthropological, zoological, botanical and iconographical evidence. Moreover, his work was remarkably international in terms of both its evidential base and the countries in which his monographs were published (Canada, the Netherlands, the United Kingdom, and the USA). His prodigious work both on the impact of the Cistercians on the medieval English landscape, economy and society and on the cultural significance, in carefully tracked periods and places, of particular exotic plants and animals stands as an impressive memorial to a life dedicated to historical and geographical scholarship of the highest order. His was a life of historical and geographical discovery, in many ways like those of the explorers and travellers upon whose observations he based his own work. 'Facts about origin, expansion and distribution, how man's artefacts and possessions come to be where they are', Robin wrote, 'lie at the heart of Human Geography as taught by [Friedrich] Ratzel, [Paul] Vidal [de la Blache] and Sauer. Such facts are not usually to be found in convenient blocks of readily mappable surveys, but rather eclectically in the literature and in the field, not strictly random but difficult to recover and to assimilate.'[8] He saw his task as that of recovery and assimilation. He collected, sorted, and dated and then tabulated and mapped masses of data drawn from an amazing array of printed sources. In the case of the Cistercians, he assimilated his painstakingly discovered 'facts' into a synthesis of his findings and his interpretation of them. No such overarching synthesis emerged from Robin's individually important work on agricultural terracing, on the historical geography of some exotic plants and animals, and on exploration and trade. Instead, his fascination with each topic seems to have totally absorbed him. While his monographs do set their specific matters of concern within broader contexts, he did not venture far into 'big picture', generalised, portrayals.

Professional caution and personal modesty probably restrained him from doing so: for Robin, a scholar's work could never claim with justification to be definitive, there would always be more work to be done. He offered his monograph on agricultural terracing as 'a preliminary study', saying in a postscript to it that 'the study of agricultural terracing in the New World has scarcely begun'; he cautioned that his study of cochineal, with its 800 or so references, 'must necessarily be regarded as provisional' and his study of manna, with a similar number of citations, concluded

---

[8] R. A. Donkin, *The Muscovy Duck* (Rotterdam, 1989), p. vii.

that 'further research is needed on the mannas of the New World'; while his work on the peccary, citing about 1,000 sources, had as a concluding sentence a suggestion of what 'future research may show'.[9] In one sense, it was a pity that Robin did not take his own advice: instead, having produced a monograph on one subject he moved onto another.

What enthralled Robin, he confessed in a letter of 13 October 2004 to a former Cambridge colleague, Tim Bayliss-Smith, was 'esoteric knowledge' of the kind he had encountered at Berkeley some fifty years earlier, knowledge acquired in 'the old German historico-geographical tradition' as taught by Conzen, his own research supervisor. He admitted that, 'for better or worse', he had missed the 'New Geography' of quantification and model building. He simply admired the way in which, as he saw it, at Berkeley people asked 'questions of the kind that interested (and still interest) me, but no-one worried about how you set about answering them'. He had little time for discussions of the nature and methodology of geography. He was only once seduced into discussing such matters, by a former Cambridge colleague, David Stoddart, who arranged for him to give the Carl O. Sauer Memorial Lecture at Berkeley in 1995. Robin explained how he had become 'a servant of two masters', history and geography.[10] He had been 'born and brought up in the Anglo-Scottish Border, where reminders of a turbulent past are rarely out of sight—formidable castles, fortified churches, ruined monasteries, not to mention the greatest of all Roman defence-works'. So he 'determined to be a medievalist'. But even as a youngster, he was 'chiefly interested in how things—primarily then medieval things—came to be where they are, or were, or took place where they did'. He was thus enthused by history and geography well before he first heard the term 'historical geography'. As a research student at Durham, Robin set out to chart the contribution of the Cistercian Order to the geography of medieval England, doing so in what he later judged to be perhaps closer to the Sauerian tradition of cultural geography at Berkeley than to the Darbian tradition of historical geography in England. He set his own work unquestioningly within the distributional or locational tradition of geography. His focused curiosity, interpreted from Sauer, was chiefly the territorial expansion and contraction of cultural artefacts and practices around perceived or postulated centres of origin, and any consequential changes in economy and society.

[9] R. A. Donkin, *Agricultural Terracing in the Aboriginal New World*, p. 134; *Spanish Red* (Philadelphia, PA, 1977), p. 3; *Manna: an Historical Geography* (The Hague, 1980), p. 116; *The Peccary* (Philadelphia, PA, 1985), p. 102.
[10] Donkin, 'A "servant of two masters"?'.

For Robin, research should be driven by questions—specifically for him questions about 'why there and why then?'. While he accepted that attempts to answer questions could lead to 'preferred procedures' for doing so, anything redolent of 'methodology' was anathema to him. Answering questions about historical and geographical distributions, he demonstrated, requires interdisciplinary enquiry. But he also concluded that what he termed 'geographical questions'—by which he meant questions about distribution or location—are being increasingly posed and pursued in other disciplines. This led him, somewhat pessimistically, to ask whether, if 'geography' as an academic discipline did not exist today, there would be a case for inventing it. Nine years after delivering the Sauer Memorial Lecture, Robin wrote to Tim Bayliss-Smith: 'No-one would now invent Geography, in practice held together by tradition, inertia and vested interests.' A week earlier he had written in exactly the same terms to Ron Johnston, a Fellow Academician, adding that 'the putative combination of interests in Geography is largely illusory'. There is also an apocryphal story that, when retiring from his university post in Cambridge, he wrote to the central administration suggesting that the Department of Geography could—perhaps should—be disbanded, with its staff distributed readily and comfortably among other departments, notably those of Earth Sciences, Economics and History.

That jaundiced view reflects the extent to which the practice of geography generally and by Robin himself had come to emphasise its systematic perspectives, so obviously shared with other disciplines, rather than its regional or area emphasis, the traditional core of geography as a distinctive discipline. By the time Robin retired in 1996, he was far from being primarily concerned with the geography of Latin America, the *raison d'être* of his being appointed to Cambridge in 1970. His increasingly sceptical view of geography also reflects and explains the extent to which he set himself aside from the academy of geographers and set himself up as an almost independent scholar working on the fringes of a number of disciplines. While he joined a number of professional societies of scholars (including the Institute of British Geographers, the Royal Geographical Society, the Society for Latin American Studies, and the Royal Anthropological Institute), he never became closely involved in their organisation or even their activities. During his half-century as a prolific scholar, Robin attended very few academic conferences, almost certainly no more than could be counted on the fingers of one hand. He declined more than one invitation to deliver a research paper to an after-dinner, college-based, seminar in historical geography that I co-organised throughout most of his time in

Cambridge. He refused, modestly but mistakenly asserting: 'No one will be interested in the esoteric work that I do.' He attended hardly any of those seminars to hear papers by others. During his almost twenty-six years as a member of staff of the Department of Geography at Cambridge, he supervised only two doctoral research students and both were, in a sense, forced upon him: one, Rodney C. Watson, having been awarded a Canada Council research studentship, came to Cambridge in 1979 to work on a Latin American topic (he never completed his doctoral dissertation, but he did publish some papers derived from his research on the historical geography of late-colonial Chiapas, Mexico); the other, Ursula H. Barrow, working on the development of small businesses in Belize, became Robin's student in January 1988 during her third year because Graham Chapman, her supervisor until then, had moved to take up a post elsewhere in Britain (she was awarded her Ph.D. in 1991 and continued her career in the diplomatic service of Belize).

Robin did not have his work followed up by a string of graduate students and nor did he undertake any collaborative work with any colleagues in Cambridge or indeed elsewhere. Nor, in his many monographs or articles, did he provide substantial critical reviews of, or commentaries upon, work by other modern scholars related to his own interests. Nor did he normally include in his monographs any acknowledgements to other scholars for information they had provided him or for the comments on his work that he had sought from them. Only in his monograph on agricultural terracing did he record his personal indebtedness to other scholars; in a few of the others he acknowledged simply technical assistance given to him by cartographers, secretaries, librarians and archivists. When Robin travelled abroad to pursue his researches, he did so alone. He liked to be independent and self-contained. He preferred to work on his own and on topics that he had decided merited his attention. He did so with a self-confidence that never mutated into arrogance. He valued highly his academic freedom and repaid the academic community with scholarship of the highest order. While preparing this memorial, one former colleague from the Department of Geography in Cambridge described him as 'a scholar's scholar, one of a kind who could not survive in the university world of today'; another, from Jesus College, described him as 'the last of the great scholars'. While those positive judgements on Robin personally are entirely appropriate, we must hope that the negative contexts in which they are set prove not to be true.

ALAN R. H. BAKER
Fellow of the Academy

Note. I am grateful to the following for their assistance in the preparation of this Memoir: W. M. Adams, T. P. Bayliss-Smith, M. D. Billinge, M. D. I. Chisholm, M. C. Cleary, I. Edwards, J. H. Galloway, N. Gates, R. E. Glasscock, B. Giles, D. J. Gregory, J. D. Hamshere, G. Harcourt, P. N. Jones, G. Kearns, J. Langton, R. Munton, L. Newson, K. S. Richards, D. J. Robinson, M. Sharp, R. M. Smith, T. Spencer, J. Stargardt, C. W. J. Withers, and P. A. Wood.

I am also grateful for permissions granted to consult unpublished documents in the Department of Geography and at the University Library, Cambridge, and at Jesus College, Cambridge. I benefited from reading the 2,000 words for a Memoir on Robin Donkin that Michael Williams had provisionally drafted before his own death. I have also benefited from the obituary by Robin Glasscock published in *The Independent* (10 May 2006).

I wish to express my thanks also to Tim Bayliss-Smith and David Harris for their individual and very helpful comments on a draft of this Memoir. I am especially grateful to Jennifer Donkin, who very willingly answered my many questions about Robin.

Bibliography of works by Robin Donkin

Donkin, R. A. (1948), 'Pioneer settlement: a problem in human geography', *King's College [Newcastle] Geographical Society Magazine* (April 1948), 13–16.

Donkin, R. A. (1956), 'Geographical report—three studies in the geography of Morocco: Some Moroccan villages and house types; The Ksar, a completely nucleated settlement; shops, stalls and trading pitches in Morocco; Appendix I A Moroccan oil press and mill', *Extract from the Report of the Durham University Exploration Society's Expedition to French Morocco 1952* (Newcastle upon Tyne), pp. 4–47.

Donkin, R. A. (1957), 'The disposal of Cistercian wool in England and Wales during the 12th and 13th centuries', *Cîteaux in de Nederlanden*, 8: 109–31 and 181–202.

Donkin, R. A. (1957), 'Localisation, situation économique et rôle parlementaire des abbés cisterciens anglais (1295–1341)', *Revue d'Histoire Ecclésiastique*, 52: 832–41.

Donkin, R. A. (1956–8), 'The *Diseño:* a source for the geography of California 1830–1846', *Mid-America*, 40: 92–105.

Donkin, R. A. (1958), '*Bercaria* and *Lanaria*', *Yorkshire Archaeological Journal*, 39: 447–50.

Donkin, R. A. (1958), 'Cistercian sheep-farming and wool-sales in the 13th century', *Agricultural History Review*, 6: 2–8.

Donkin, R. A. (1958), 'The marshland holdings of the English Cistercians before *c.*1350', *Cîteaux in de Nederlanden*, 9: 1–14.

Donkin, R. A. (1959), 'The site changes of mediaeval Cistercian monasteries', *Geography*, 44: 251–8.

Donkin, R. A. (1959), 'The urban property of the Cistercians in mediaeval England', *Analecta Sacri Ordinis Cisterciensis*, 15: 104–31.

Donkin, R. A. (1960), 'The Cistercian settlement and the English Royal Forests', *Cîteaux: Commentarii Cisterciensis*, 11: 39–55 and 117–32.

Donkin, R. A. (1960), 'Settlement and depopulation on Cistercian estates during the 12th and 13th centuries, especially in Yorkshire', *Bulletin of the Institute of Historical Research*, 33: 141–65.

Donkin, R. A. (1961), 'The contribution of the Franciscan missions to the settlement of Alta California colonization 1769–1823', *Revista de Historia de America*, 52: 373–93.

Donkin, R. A. (1962), 'Cattle on the estates of mediaeval Cistercian monasteries in England and Wales', *Economic History Review*, 15: 31–53.

Donkin, R. A. (1962), 'The markets and fairs of mediaeval Cistercian monasteries in England and Wales', *Cistercienser Chronik*, 59: 1–14.

Donkin, R. A. (1962), 'Some aspects of Cistercian sheep farming in England and Wales', *Cîteaux*, 13: 296–310.

Donkin, R. A. (1963), 'The Cistercian order in medieval England: some conclusions', *Transactions and Papers of the Institute of British Geographers*, 33: 181–98.

Donkin, R. A. (1964), 'The Cistercian grange in England in the 12th and 13th centuries, with special reference to Yorkshire', *Studia Monastica,* 6: 95–144.

Donkin, R. A. (1964), 'The English Cistercians and assarting *c.*1128–*c.*1350'. *Analecta Sacri Ordinis Cisterciensis*, 20: 49–75.

Donkin, R. A. (1967), 'The growth and distribution of the Cistercian order in medieval Europe', *Studia Monastica*, 9: 275–86.

Donkin, R. A. (1967), 'Ambiente y poblamiento precolombinos en el altiplano de Boyaca-Cundinamarca, Colombia', *Boletin de la Sociedad Geografia de Colombia*, 26: 199–207.

Donkin, R. A. (1969), 'The Cistercian order and the settlement of Northern England', *Geographical Review*, 59: 403–16.

Donkin, R. A. (1969), *Cistercian Bibliography: a Check-list of Printed Works relating to the Cistercian Order as a Whole and to the Houses of the British Isles in Particular*, (Rochefort, Belgium, *Documentation Cistercienne*).

Donkin, R. A. (1970), 'Pre-Columbian field implements and their distribution in the highlands of Middle and South America', *Anthropos*, 65: 505–29.

Donkin, R. A. (1973), 'Changes in the early Middle Ages', in H. C. Darby (ed.), *A New Historical Geography of England* (Cambridge), pp. 75–135.

Donkin, R. A. (1974), '*Bixa orellana*: "The eternal shrub"', *Anthropos*, 69: 33–56.

Donkin, R. A. (1977), 'The insect dyes of western and west-central Asia', *Anthropos*, 72: 847–80.

Donkin, R. A. (1977), 'Spanish Red: an ethnographical study of Cochineal and the *Opuntia* cactus', *Transactions of the American Philosophical Society*, 67: 1–84.

Donkin, R. A. (1978), *The Cistercians: Studies in the Geography of Medieval England and Wales* (Toronto).

Donkin, R. A. (1979), *Agricultural Terracing in the Aboriginal New World* (Tucson, AZ).

Donkin, R. A. (1980), *Manna: an Historical Geography* (The Hague).

Donkin, R. A. (1985), 'The peccary: with observations on the introduction of pigs to the New World', *Transactions of the American Philosophical Society*, 7(5): 1–152.

Donkin, R. A. (1989), *The Muscovy Duck,* Cairina moschata dometica: *Origins, Dispersal and Associated Aspects of the Geography of Domestication* (Rotterdam).

Donkin, R. A. (1991), Meleagrides: *An Historical and Ethnographical Study of the Guinea Fowl* (London).

Donkin, R. A. (1997), 'A "servant of two masters"?', *Journal of Historical Geography*, 23: 247–66.

Donkin, R. A. (1998), *Beyond Price: Pearls and Pearl Fishing: Origins to the Age of Discoveries* (Phildalphia, PA).

Donkin, R. A. (1999), *Dragon's Brain Perfume: an Historical Geography of Camphor* (Leiden).

Donkin, R. A. (2003), *Between East and West: the Moluccas and the Traffic in Spices up to the Arrival of the Europeans* (Philadelphia, PA).

Donkin, R. A. (forthcoming), *To the Cape: Exploration in the Atlantic and Indian Oceans to c. AD 1500* (This monograph, completed before Robin's death, has been accepted for publication by the American Philosophical Society, Philadelphia, PA: date for publication not yet known.)

FRED HALLIDAY   *Maxine Molyneux*

Simon Frederick Peter Halliday
1946–2010

Fred Halliday (as he was always known), who died from cancer in Barcelona on 26 April 2010, was a writer, teacher and public intellectual whose work spanned two closely related fields: the post-colonial societies of the Middle East, and international relations. Although he was not afraid to change his mind on key matters, there is one strand that runs through all of the forty-plus years of his writing career: his belief in linking theory and practice. For him they were never separate realms. Concepts must always be tested in the crucible of events; and events must always be understood not just as a jumble of facts, but with their interlinkages, purposes and conceptual frameworks all part of the picture. He battled increasingly against the threefold fault of much public discussion of international issues: lack of historical depth, lack of linguistic skills, and lack of feel for the complexities of dealing with other societies. He travelled to one troubled society after another, always with the aim of developing a more profound understanding. His command of languages was legendary. He may even have understated it when he wrote in his CV in 2006: 'Fluent: German, French, Italian, Spanish. Working knowledge: Russian, Portuguese, Persian, Arabic, Latin. Elementary: Modern Greek, Dutch.' In his last years he also learned Catalan.

In his writing and research he owed a debt, which he readily and frequently acknowledged, to Maxine Molyneux. She was inspirer, partner and critic. They met in 1971 and married in 1979. Throughout her academic career she has had a particular interest in gender, development and human rights issues. Since 1994 she has been at the Institute for the Study of the Americas at the School of Advanced Study (University of London) where

Proceedings of the British Academy, **172**, 143–169. © The British Academy 2011.

she is Professor of Sociology and Director of the Institute. Many of the enduring themes of Fred's work were strongly shared with Maxine. These can be roughly summarised in a series of interlinked propositions. (1) The global market is not, as dependency theorists present it, merely a force for underdevelopment and impoverishment: it is also a force for development, and one that stimulates new political and social forces. (2) The politics of specific states have to be understood within a broader regional and global whole. (3) The state has to be understood sociologically: both state and society respond in complex ways to the international environment in which they operate, and for example the ethnic homogeneity of states is a myth that impedes serious analysis. (4) The role of women is a critically important factor in understanding any society, including its role in international relations. (5) Revolutions have major repercussions internationally as well as domestically, and are as important as other more familiar factors in international relations. (6) Outside powers, even when they intervene militarily, have only very limited ability to change the political and social order within a society.

It was my pleasure and privilege to have known Fred for about forty years. I always found his take on international issues to be both challenging and refreshing: this was partly because he approached problems from a different political angle from that of many colleagues, myself included, but also because he had deep knowledge of different societies, especially in the Middle East. In this short survey I cannot do justice to all his work: he published some twenty books in English, over eighty-five chapters in books, and more than 100 journal articles, as well as countless contributions in the electronic and print media. Nor can I trace all the influences in his intellectual journey. His path has been seen, in one provisional assessment, as from 'revolutionary socialist' to 'critical liberal'.[1] Perhaps it could be better viewed as from an initially Olympian revolutionism to a richer and more diverse form of internationalism. Such characterisations inevitably fail to capture the full picture. The purpose of this memoir is simply to sketch and appraise some of the main landmarks of his life and published work.

Early life and education

Fred, was born in Dublin on 22 February 1946. His father, Arthur Halliday, a Yorkshireman from an austere Methodist and Quaker background, ran

[1] Alejandro Colás and George Lawson, 'Fred Halliday: achievements, ambivalences and openings', *Millennium: Journal of International Studies*, 39 (2010), 235–58.

a successful shoe-manufacturing business in Dundalk in the Republic of Ireland and was highly respected as a good employer. His mother, Rita (née Finigan) was a local Roman Catholic from a middle class background. Both families, despite their very different backgrounds and loyalties, came from what Fred would later call, with pride, the 'dissident middle classes'.[2] His parents' wedding—controversial because 'mixed'—had taken place in a church far from Dundalk, with some local gravediggers as the only witnesses.

Fred was the youngest of three brothers, whose naming involved complexities.[3] The eldest, Frederick David Patrick (born 1937), known as David, went into the shoe business. The second, John Arthur George (born 1939), known as Jon, became a well-known writer on international politics. Jon was critically important, especially in Fred's early years, in helping to shape Fred's future evolution: Fred and Jon came to share a passionate interest in international politics, one that did not diminish with time.

The Halliday family home was in Dundalk, the main border town with Northern Ireland, which has a tradition of sympathy with the Irish republican cause and indeed was the headquarters of the Irish Republican Army (IRA). Fred was to remember, with fear, the onset of the IRA campaign of 1956–62 and its effects on a divided community. Thus began a lifelong interest in conflict, and a sense of obligation to understand it. In 2005 he was to say: 'If I had to sum up what is for me the bedrock, personal, political experience, it is the Irish question. I grew up in Ireland. I think troops out of Ireland was a completely irresponsible slogan, just as I think troops out of Afghanistan was an irresponsible slogan.'[4]

It was a standard condition for a wedding between a Catholic and a non-Catholic that the children should be brought up Catholic. Fred's first school, from 1950 to 1953, was the Marist School in Dundalk—the primary school for St Mary's College.[5] In 1953–63 his Catholic education

[2] In a lecture at the LSE, 30 Jan. 2008.

[3] The naming of the children was one of several areas of contestation between Fred's parents. It had been a temporary success for Arthur that the eldest had as his first name Frederick—which came from his family in Yorkshire: however, it was a success for Rita when the boy came to be known by his second name, David. When the third child was born in 1946 he got 'Frederick' as his second name. This time, as 'Fred', it stuck.

[4] In a long and illuminating interview with Danny Postel, Chicago, 23 Nov. 2005, published in *Salmagundi*, Skidmore College, Saratoga Springs, New York, Summer 2006 issue, and available on <http://www.opendemocracy.net/columns/halliday_21.jsp>, accessed 9 Jan. 2011.

[5] The primary school for St Mary's College, Dundalk. St Mary's College secondary school, established by the Marist Fathers in 1860–61, was the first foundation of the Society of Mary in Ireland. More information at <http://www.maristdundalk.com/History.html>. See also the website

continued at Ampleforth College—the fee-paying monastic boarding school attached to the Benedictine monastery of Ampleforth, at a very isolated spot on the edge of the North Yorkshire Moors. This famous school, which aimed to provide well-to-do Catholic pupils with skills appropriate to an elite, was also attended by his brothers. Sending the boys there was a compromise between two potentially contradictory pressures: their father's attachment to Yorkshire and their mother's Catholic faith. Until 1957 Fred attended the preparatory school, at Gilling Castle, across the valley from the school and abbey. Then he went to the main site of Ampleforth, starting at age 11 in the separate Junior House. A fellow-pupil and lifelong friend, Edmund Fawcett, recalled their meeting there in 1957: the other boys were mainly taken up 'in field games and keeping rabbits. Fred was preoccupied with the Chinese occupation of Tibet. That's the boy I want to be *my* friend, I thought. To my lasting good fortune, Fred was.'[6] In a subsequent response to an enquiry from me he provided a fuller picture of the Ampleforth years 1957–63 and Fred's subsequent 'gap year':

> Fred's home life was not easy, which kept him I think on edge, and he threw himself into school. Not into sports, hobbies or the cadet corps, but into books and debating. He shone at both. He led the school team that won the Inter-Schools Debating Competition. He played the piano moderately well but did not, that I recall, paint or act. The school was a funny mix: English establishment (which Fred reacted against) and Benedictine learning (which he took to). He was a critic, not a rebel. He was deputy head of his house and became a school monitor.
>
> Clever boys did maths or classics. Fred's gifts were more linguistic than mathematical. So Latin and Greek were as good as given. His most eminent teacher was Walter Shewring, an Italianist and translator of Homer. The one he liked most, I suspect, was Philip Smiley, a stickler for accuracy and mocker of authorities. Both were lay teachers. The librarian, Fr Dominic Milroy, I recall, encouraged argument on all topics, including religion.
>
> When he left the school he was still thinking of becoming a priest. At 16 or 17 he joined a school party of boys and monks that visited Lourdes to help the sick. It was the time of Vatican II. Social-minded radicalism, marching for peace and liberal Catholicism seemed a natural mix.
>
> Fred was internationalist by experience. Irish boys, as they were known, arrived at school on a different train from the rest of us. Small countries under the thumb were a natural, if precocious, interest. When we met at 11 Fred was already a close follower of the news. As a big issue, anti-colonialism was cutting across the Cold War. He was up on Dien Bien Phu and Suez. Lumumba was a

---

of the Marist Fathers in Ireland, <http://www.maristfathers.org/ministries.html>. Both accessed 27 Dec. 2010.

[6] Edmund Fawcett, introductory remarks at the tribute to Fred Halliday held in Beveridge Hall, Senate House, London, 4 May 2010.

hero. He spent the summer of the 1961 Algerian crisis in Paris learning French. His reading then was more Fanon than Marx. In 1963 we visited Prague together and met dissident writers. I'd say Fred's outlook was anti-imperialist, but not nationalist. Of course, that landed him in interesting puzzles. He was, after all, being schooled in the least national, some would say most imperial, of faiths. Tibet was an interesting case. Hazily I recall that he wasn't for *retardataire* Tibetan monks. On the whole he was for Chinese imperialism because he was against the American kind. He entertained us with a ditty: 'Let's liberate Formosa, let's liberate it now. Let's take it away from Chiang Kai-shek and give it back to Mao.' China appealed to Fred at school also as an anti-Soviet power— thus opening up for him a winding path to Trotsky and the New Left.

He spent his gap year learning German in Munich, where he found a very beautiful Iranian girlfriend. His Catholic faith was already weakening. To the priest in a confessional at the Theatinerkirche on Odeonsplatz, Fred told me later, he owned up to the temptations of 'Materialismus'.[7]

This picture of Fred at Ampleforth was confirmed after Fred's death by the above-mentioned Father Dominic: 'Fred was a towering and passionate thinker from an early age, impatient of complacency and shallowness, and a rivetingly good speaker. In a very wide-ranging and compelling way, he anticipated the "Student Revolution" of 1968 by an entire decade.'[8] Even at the time, his teachers saw that Fred was exceptional. As the school's reference for him in his application to Oxford University stated, he was in

> ... a group of wide and varied interests, which led them to argue more about music, D. H. Lawrence, atom bombs, and the sins of their elders, than about the rival merits of Sophocles and Euripides.... He has perhaps not turned out quite as good a Classical scholar as we hoped: but he is a good linguist and has an interest and flair for modern tongues.
>
> He is an earnest Irishman, with a gift for debating and a fund of honest indignation about the wrongs of others; but he usually generates more light than heat, and he is saved by humour and geniality from celebrating wrongs of his own. He will be an able man when he has grown to full stature and will make his mark in some good cause: a most conscientious person of high ideals and admirable performance.[9]

He went on to study Philosophy, Politics and Economics (PPE) at Queen's College, Oxford, 1964–7. He had applied to the college for a modest scholarship intended to enable men from any of a dozen schools in the north to train for the priesthood—and had received in response a modest cash award of £12 but not the title of scholar, and apparently no priestly

---

[7] Edmund Fawcett, email, 30 Dec. 2010.
[8] Obituary in *The Ampleforth Journal*, vol. 114 (Sept. 2009–July 2010), p. 89.
[9] Signed by Rt Revd William Price, Headmaster of Ampleforth, 25 July 1963, on Fred's Oxford Colleges Admissions Office application form.

obligation.[10] He was a deeply interested and engaged student: for example, he kept full notes on lectures given by Thomas Hodgkin, the writer on pre-colonial and colonial history who in 1965–70 held a lectureship in the government of African states.[11] In his first year he became Political Editor of *Isis*, the weekly student magazine, contributing a regular column about conflicts and crises around the world. In his second year he became President of the Oxford University Labour Club, in which capacity he organised a meeting in March 1966 addressed by Colonel Caamaño, former President of the Dominican Republic—believed to have been the last time that Caamaño appeared in public.[12] It was at Oxford that he first met some of the leading figures of the New Left. He took part in weekly meetings at the Oxford Union with Tariq Ali, Mary Kaldor and others. To some contemporaries he appeared to be very earnest: others already saw the witty side which was later to be a striking feature of his public persona. He gained a very good First in his final examinations in 1967.

He then proceeded directly to do an M.Sc. in Middle East Politics at the School of Oriental and African Studies (SOAS) in London, 1967–9. He was awarded a distinction mark. At SOAS he studied under some very different teachers. Those with whom he engaged intellectually included P. J. Vatikiotis, the historian of Egypt, who was anything but a Marxist; and Bill Warren, who was one, but, in a variant of traditional Left condemnations of imperialism, argued that capitalism and imperialism could be engines for development in the Third World, and who also emphasised the central truth that there are no simple answers.[13]

New Left start

Even as a student, Fred embarked on a career of study, writing and advocacy that hardly followed a standard academic pattern. In 1968, while studying at SOAS, he became a member of the editorial committee of *New Left Review* (*NLR*). He worked actively in this capacity until 1983.[14]

[10] I am grateful to Michael Riordan, Archivist, the Queen's College, for this information and for showing me the Ampleforth reference.

[11] Later Fred made these notes available to Thomas Hodgkin's biographer, Michael Wolfers, who confirmed to me on 12 Jan. 2011 how much he appreciated this assistance.

[12] This meeting is described in the introduction to Fred's last book, *Caamaño in London: the Exile of a Latin American Revolutionary* (London, 2011).

[13] See Bill Warren's posthumous work *Imperialism, Pioneer of Capitalism* (London, 1980).

[14] His brother Jon had been a member of the *NLR* editorial committee since early 1967. Fred's name first appeared in issue no. 47 (Jan.–Feb. 1968).

At the same time he made major contributions of his own on a range of controversial and difficult international topics.[15] His long involvement in the New Left, crucially important though it was to the development of his thinking, proved ultimately to be disappointing.

He was also briefly on the editorial committee of the irregularly appearing and short-lived paper *Black Dwarf*, edited by Tariq Ali. An issue in June 1968 had the headline, across the whole front page: 'WE SHALL FIGHT, WE WILL WIN. PARIS, LONDON, ROME, BERLIN.'[16] In 1970 there was a parting of the ways, and Fred later recalled the *Black Dwarf* episode as unhappy. He then became the full-time Foreign News Editor of *Seven Days,* from October 1971 to May 1972, when it folded. There he shared an office with Maxine, also a full-time staff member as Arts and Culture Editor.

The commitment to the New Left involved extensive writing and editorial work. In the first of many contributions he would make to collective works, he wrote a chapter, 'Students of the World Unite', in a book edited by New Left comrades that was inspired by the events of 1968.[17] He would later think of this chapter as embarrassing and 'ultra-leftist', but it has also been deservedly praised as 'astonishing for its global breadth of knowledge'.[18] From about 1971 until 1975 he had a close association with New Left Books (NLB), the degrees of involvement varying greatly due to his other commitments. Already in 1970 he had translated for NLB *Marxism and Philosophy*, by Karl Korsch (1886–1961), an independent Marxist thinker from Germany who had emigrated to the USA in 1936.[19] Fred's Introduction to Korsch's book was scholarly and illuminating.

Another publication in 1970, when he was only 24, was an edited collection of writings by Isaac Deutscher, *Russia, China and the West*. This was very much part of his *NLR* activity: after Deutscher died in 1967, Perry Anderson of *NLR* had proposed that Tamara Deutscher ask Fred to edit this posthumous collection. Fred did this with great professionalism, his editorial contributions always clear and to the point. He refers

[15] See e.g. his first really substantial journal article, 'The Ceylonese insurrection', *NLR*, 69 (Sept.–Oct. 1971), pp. 55–89.
[16] Facsimile of *Black Dwarf*, 1 June 1968, available at <http://www.1968andallthat.net/node/43>, accessed 7 Jan. 2010.
[17] Alexander Cockburn and Robin Blackburn (eds.), *Student Power: Problems, Diagnosis, Action* (Harmondsworth, 1969), pp. 287–326.
[18] Stephen Howe in his excellent article 'Son of the Bani Tanwir: the work of Fred Halliday (1946–2010)', available at <http://www.opendemocracy.net/author/fred-halliday>, accessed 22 Jan. 2011.
[19] Karl Korsch, *Marxism and Philosophy* (London, 1970).

positively to Karl Marx's journalistic writings, and it is not difficult to detect the influence of their style and approach in much that Fred himself would write in the next four decades. Indeed, Fred's enduring commitment to serious scholarly journalism was based on admiration for many distinguished exponents of this art, including not only Karl Marx and Isaac Deutscher, but also Conor Cruise O'Brien and Eric Rouleau. Fred wrote about Isaac Deutscher, as he might have written, *mutatis mutandis,* about Marx—or indeed as others might later write about Fred himself:

> Deutscher was not always correct in his predictions; no writer on current affairs ever could be. But the value of his analysis and predictions, true or false, lay in his constant awareness of the broader significance of individual events and of their relationship to underlying political trends in Soviet history....
>
> The immediacy and freshness of current affairs is fused with the long-term perspective of history.[20]

In 1975 he was appointed to the largely advisory position of Fellow and Assistant European Director of the Transnational Institute (TNI) in Amsterdam; and from 1979 to 1983 he was Senior European Fellow.[21] Founded in 1973—and working closely with a partner organisation, the Institute for Policy Studies (IPS) in Washington DC—TNI was committed to a transformative agenda and to supporting various activist and liberation movements. In 1976 Fred had a horrific reminder of the perils of activism. Orlando Letelier, previously Chilean foreign and defence minister and ambassador to the US, had been appointed director of TNI. Deeply opposed to the rule of General Pinochet in Chile, he had persuaded the Dutch government to cancel a $60 million loan for Chilean industrial development. On 21 September 1976 Letelier—together with Ronni Moffitt, a young fund-raiser at IPS—was assassinated by a car bomb in Washington DC. Investigations revealed the involvement of the Chilean secret police. Despite this searing experience, Fred's association with TNI was relatively unproblematic. He remained based in London, and although his responsibilities at TNI were far from negligible they left time and opportunity to do the research and writing on the Middle East

---

[20] Isaac Deutscher, *Russia, China, and the West: a Contemporary Chronicle, 1953–1966*, ed. Fred Halliday (London, 1970), p. xiii.

[21] His CV of December 2006 lists the period with TNI as 1975–83. So does his entry in *Who's Who.* However, TNI itself says: 'Fred was a TNI fellow for 12 years, between 1973 and 1985.' <http://www.tni.org/article/former-tni-fellow-fred-halliday-dies-age-64>, accessed 28 Dec. 2010. Probably the term 'fellow' was being used flexibly to encompass different degrees of involvement. Fred certainly maintained a close association with TNI for many years after 1983.

and East–West relations that was his real calling, and on which he was beginning to publish extensively.[22]

Interpreter of revolution: Arabia, Ethiopia and Iran

Fred was sufficiently attracted by the concept of revolution to base most of his published work around that theme, but his scholarly devotion to facts, in all their awkwardness, gave his work a flavour very different from, indeed opposed to, the shrill advocacy of much writing on the Left.

His first major book, published in 1974, was *Arabia without Sultans*.[23] The very title, engaging and prescriptive, proclaimed his anti-mystificatory intent. He presented Arabian society, not in terms of tribal oligarchies or (in the case of Iran) militarised monarchy, but in the context of capitalist development and exploitation, and with a focus on local elites seeking to maximise their positions within a global market. This book established Fred as an important and attractive writer about the Middle East, particularly because he had an analysis of politics in which radical movements faced the enmity of regional conservative states; and a vision of change that was distinct from most of those currently on offer in the region, including from the USA and USSR. It was based on first-hand experience, including of Dhofar, where he had joined the guerrillas as a reporter in 1970, supporting their struggle against the Omani state. The book made his reputation, and appeared subsequently in Arabic, Italian, Japanese, Persian and Turkish translations.

However, as he handsomely conceded nearly thirty years later in the second edition of *Arabia without Sultans*, its analysis had limitations as well as virtues:

> *Arabia* partook not just of the perspective, but also of the tone and language of the revolutionary left of this epoch: in this sense it is a document of its time. It did, on a number of issues, notably nationalism and 'underdevelopment', seek to distance itself from the prevailing views on the left, but it partook, nonetheless, of the Marxist perspective of the late 1960s and early 1970s. It reflects some of the rhetorical delusion of that outlook. More than one critic commented, justly, on its haphazard use of the concept 'imperialism'.[24]

---

[22] One key outlet for his writings from 1976 to 2001 was Middle East Reports (Merip). For details see <http://www.merip.org/mer/mer255/halliday_ouevre.html>, accessed 22 Jan. 2011.

[23] Halliday, *Arabia without Sultans* (Harmondsworth, 1974).

[24] Halliday, *Arabia without Sultans*, 2nd edn. (London, 2002), 'Introduction to the Second Edition', p. 2.

He went on to enumerate some key respects in which the book, and the critical perspective of that period, retained their validity. However, this led him into further self-criticism. The book had deliberately focused on the revolutionary movements of South Arabia, especially in North and South Yemen and Dhofar:

> But here, above all, history was to overtake the book. The year after *Arabia* was published (1974), the guerrilla movement in Dhofar, which had been the revolutionary pivot of the book, was crushed by an Omani state reconsolidated after the coup of 1970, and by a combination of British, Iranian and Jordanian intervention.... in the face of external pressure and internal divisions alike, the South Arabian revolutions were, from the mid-1970s, forced into a retreat from which they never recovered.[25]

Such setbacks did not stop Fred's interest in revolutions, either in the short run or in the longer term. It had been his continuing interest in revolutions, including in Dhofar after the setback of 1975, that informed his 1977 pamphlet criticising the UK government's line on mercenaries:

> The British government is not opposed to mercenaries as such, only to people fighting in wars of which the government disapproves....
>
>   The British Empire may be all but gone, but the role of Britain ... in counter-revolution and counter-insurgency throughout the world is still a considerable one.... Socialists have therefore a continuing, if not increased, duty to reveal and oppose activities of this kind.[26]

If the revolutionary cause had failed in Dhofar, there were other places where it could be picked up. In the events in Ethiopia from 1974 onwards, and in Iran in 1977–9, his belief that revolutions remained an important part of international politics found vindication. What was much more in question is whether either of these revolutions could be seen as historically progressive. Fred knew both these countries, and wrote about both of them with characteristic incisiveness. He published a work on Iran first, then one on Ethiopia.

In Iran, the popular revolt against the Shah's rule, which began with university protests in October 1977, led to the Shah's departure in January 1979 and then to Ayatollah Khomeini's return to Iran on 1 February. Fred's book *Iran: Dictatorship and Development*, was completed in 1978 and appeared in 1979. In its final sentence he correctly foresaw the Shah's departure, but not what came after: 'It is quite possible that before too

---

[25] Halliday, *Arabia without Sultans*, 2nd edn. (London, 2002), 'Introduction to the Second Edition', pp. 4–5.
[26] Halliday, *Mercenaries: 'Counterinsurgency' in the Gulf* (Nottingham, 1977), pp. 10 and 22.

long the Iranian people will chase the Pahlavi dictator and his associates from power, will surmount the obstacles in its way, and build a prosperous and socialist Iran.'[27] In an afterword written in 1979 after the fall of the Shah he wrote: 'The Shah and his associates have been driven from power through a mass mobilization which must rank among the most epic chapters of the international revolutionary movement in this century.' He added: 'It cannot be emphasized often enough that the Islamic character of the movement, and in particular Khomeini's leadership, were relatively late in establishing themselves.'[28]

Fred's next book concerned a social revolution that had begun long before the fall of the Shah. In Ethiopia, social unrest in February–September 1974 led to the ousting of Emperor Haile Selassie, who had ruled the country since 1930. The left-wing military junta which took over—the Provisional Military Administrative Council (the Derg)—presided over a revolution of sorts. Fred and Maxine visited the country in 1977 and 1978, and in their book *The Ethiopian Revolution* they identified some similarities with France in 1789 and Russia in 1917:

> As in the earlier cases, those who began the process did not complete it. But among those actors one—the radical military—was able to displace its political competitors and consolidate a new post-revolutionary order. If such resulting conditions were not the product of some original intentionality, they cannot be seen either as purely contingent and haphazard, or as betrayals of some alternative post-revolutionary system that would otherwise have been easily attainable. It is precisely in the balance between structural causation and purposive action that the outcome of these revolutions can be discerned.[29]

How did Fred and Maxine react to the many problems associated with the period of Derg rule—including killings without trial (especially intense in 1974 and 1977–8), the Ogaden War against Somalia (1977–8) and the secessionist movements in Eritrea and Tigray? They addressed these issues directly, raising sharp questions both about the use of terror and violence and about the depth of the social transformation involved.[30] At the same time, the book recognised frankly the vagueness of such socialist ideas as informed the policies of the Derg. It explored the regime's consequent vulnerability to outside ideas and assistance: those imported from the Soviet Union were not always appropriate to Ethiopia's circumstances. Above all, the book is a notable exploration of the whole idea of revolution

[27] Halliday, *Iran, Dictatorship and Development*, 1st edn. (Harmondsworth, 1979), p. 309.
[28] Halliday, *Iran, Dictatorship and Development*, 2nd edn., 'Afterword', pp. 310 and 317.
[29] Fred Halliday and Maxine Molyneux, *The Ethiopian Revolution* (London, 1981), p. 15.
[30] Ibid., pp. 30, 37, 41 and 122–3.

in the Third World: the forms it can assume, the types of social arrangement sought, and the dangers inherent in the process. The book thus
addresses the very areas on which revolutionary theory has traditionally
been weakest, and is for that reason a notable contribution.

With the wisdom of hindsight it would be easy to say that *The Ethiopian
Revolution* did not see the extent of failure of the revolutionary regime in
Ethiopia: the huge famine of 1984–5, the withdrawal of Soviet assistance,
and the eventual collapse of the regime in 1991. However, the authors did
recognise at least some of the limits of what had been achieved in Ethiopia.
The concluding chapter is a remarkable mixture of doubt and certainty. It
contains a classic expression of honest doubt within a Marxist framework: 'The outcome of the Ethiopian revolution could be that the country
embarks on a transition to socialism. Alternatively, Ethiopian society
could, after a period of oscillation, become one in which capitalist social
relations predominate.' At the same time it is confidently assertive on some
general conceptual issues, for example: 'Socialism is a period of transition
between capitalism and communism.'[31] The tension that is so evident here
between core principles and observed practice continued, sometimes even
in accentuated form, in Fred's later writings. A puzzle remains, not just in
this book, about how he adjudicated between the costs of revolutions and
the progress they sought.

The 'Second Cold War'

In the early 1980s, at a time of considerable Western concern about perceived Soviet advances from Angola to Afghanistan, Fred produced a
short book which brought much of his thinking about crisis and revolution together, relating it to broader themes of international politics.
Originally published in the US under the title *Soviet Policy in the Arc of
Crisis*,[32] a revised and retitled edition, published by Penguin in the following year as *Threat from the East?*, gained a wider readership.[33] It was based,
as he said in the preface, on visits to the countries concerned, including
South Yemen (1977), Ethiopia (1977, 1978), Iran (1979), Iraq (1980) and
Afghanistan (1980). A sustained critique of Western, especially US, policy,
it reinforced Fred's reputation as a public intellectual of the Left. He

[31] Fred Halliday and Maxine Molyneux, *The Ethiopian Revolution* (London, 1981), p. 269.
[32] Halliday, *Soviet Policy in the Arc of Crisis* (Washington DC, 1981).
[33] Halliday, *Threat from the East? Soviet Policy from Afghanistan and Iran to the Horn of Africa* (Harmondsworth, 1982).

defined the 'arc of crisis' as 'running from Afghanistan through Iran and the Arab Middle East down to the Horn of Africa'. It denoted 'as much an anxiety in the human mind as a delimited territory'. His book was based on two assumptions: first, that 'the sources of political change within these countries lie as much in factors operating within them as they do in the operations of external states'; and second, that 'analysis of the ways in which events in the region affect East–West relations' should be combined with 'evaluation of the manner in which the policies of major outside powers affect developments within the countries of the region'.[34] He argued throughout that a 'New Cold War' was taking place, and that 'the positing of a "Soviet threat" as an explanatory tool for understanding the events in the Arc during the late 1970s, or as a means of legitimating US policy, cannot survive critical analysis'.[35] On the Russians in Afghanistan he said (wrongly, as we know with the benefit of hindsight): 'They will only leave when the Kabul government itself is strong enough to cope with the rural opposition that remains.' Yet he was very critical of much in the Soviet record: 'The Soviet Union has not just given general support to the regimes it favours, but has done so in such a way as to condone or support some of their more repressive characteristics.'[36] He concluded this notably prescriptive essay:

> The lessons of this study can therefore be summarized as follows: the events of the Arc of Crisis cannot be reduced to a simple picture of Soviet trouble-making, and Soviet policy is one that permits substantial negotiation between East and West on issues of concern in the region. A straightforward adversary policy is not justified by the facts, and fails to realize the potential for reducing tension that exists.[37]

1983 saw the publication of his last book to appear while he was a TNI Fellow, *The Making of the Second Cold War.*[38] Its core argument was that the East–West détente of the early 1970s had been dangerous for the two main power blocs in the world. The USA in particular felt threatened, not just by the development of Soviet military power, but by revolutionary movements in Asia, Africa and Latin America. While the New Right in the US along with other political forces in the West reinforced a sense of economic and military threat, a socialist Europe might yet emerge to undermine the political legitimacy of both the USA and the USSR. His

---

[34] Ibid., pp. 7 and 9.
[35] Ibid., p. 16.
[36] Ibid., pp. 116 and 117.
[37] Ibid., p. 129.
[38] Halliday, *The Making of the Second Cold War* (London, 1983).

book was open to some obvious criticisms: in particular, that the conflicts and tensions of the early 1980s, serious as they were, were hardly comparable to those of the late 1940s; that it presented an oversimple view of their causes; that its coverage of the East–West military balance avoided some hard issues that had contributed to concern in the West; that it was notably weak on eastern Europe, especially Czechoslovakia; and that, in characterising the British role in the 1982 Falklands War as 'patriotic carnage', it had failed to make any reference to the key international principles which Britain claimed to be defending.[39] It was not his best book, but it appealed to readers who wanted to be able to set their criticisms of Reagan's and Thatcher's policies—for example over the Euromissiles controversies of the time—in a broader international perspective.

Arrival at LSE, departure from *NLR*

In 1983, at age 37, Fred left the TNI. He took up what was initially a temporary teaching post at the London School of Economics (LSE). This was the start of a momentous change in his life that was to bring him to the heart of a major national and international institution. The new direction had many origins. It had been at the suggestion of Philip Windsor, Reader in International Relations at LSE, that in 1982–3 Fred became a visiting fellow at the LSE's Centre for International Studies. During that year it was Professor Susan Strange, at that time Convenor of the International Relations Department, who encouraged him to start teaching. Like Fred, she had a background in journalism, practice, and academe, and liked to stir things up. Other reasons for the change included the need for a more regular source of income than freelance writing could provide.

Later in the same year, 1983, he left the editorial committee of *New Left Review* on which he had served for fifteen years. This departure was bitter, relating as it did both to the way *NLR* had been run and to broader ideological issues. Perry Anderson, editor of *NLR* from 1962 until he stepped down formally at the end of 1982, and still the dominant influence, had been critical of him on a number of grounds, one being in connection with his writing in the 'bourgeois media' such as *The Guardian*. This implicitly challenged Fred's deep commitment to serious journalism, and accentuated his not-so-latent concerns about the way *NLR* had been

---

[39] I made these points in a review in *New Society*, London, no. 1075 (23 June 1983), p. 481. Such criticisms were not a problem between us: Fred regarded disagreement as entirely normal.

run. A reply from Fred with proposals for reform included the memorable phrase: 'Quite simply the NLR ... takes itself far too seriously ... There is an element in our discussions and in our Themes of a self-appointed general staff without any troops at our command.'[40] He regretted what he saw as the scheming which created a difficult emotional atmosphere that had affected his work for NLB as well as *NLR*. There was also an underlying issue between revolutionary and somewhat theoretical perspectives on the one hand and the radical incremental reformist type of politics to which Fred had been moving on the other. In late 1983, Fred, who believed in a more open engagement with the outside world than *NLR* was taking, felt he had to resign. Anthony Barnett, who was also writing regularly in the *New Statesman* and *The Guardian,* and who had earlier worked with Fred on *Black Dwarf* and *Seven Days*, resigned as well. Both were members of the small group of regulars who had run the *NLR* editorial committee, decided the journal's contents, and produced it. Eight other members of the nineteen-strong editorial committee resigned with them.[41] For Fred, however difficult things at *NLR* had been, it was still a wrench. It was not a total break: he did write some further articles for *NLR*. Yet the resignation was also an escape from an ideological ghetto.

The departures from TNI and *NLR* were the beginning of a new phase in his life: for the next twenty-five years he would be in the UK's (and arguably the world's) largest department of International Relations, with all the pressures and rewards of teaching large numbers of undergraduate and postgraduate students. He would be working with colleagues, and students, with very different backgrounds, intellectual frameworks, political positions and preoccupations. For Fred's intellectual development and public profile, the change was highly beneficial.

He was hardly a newcomer to LSE. In October 1978 he had registered to do a Ph.D. in LSE's Department of International History, with which he was to have a less than happy experience. So while he had been working on other topics—including Iran and Ethiopia—he had an uncompleted thesis weighing him down. He had eventually fixed on South Yemen's

---

[40] The reference to 'Themes' is to the editorial section of *NLR*, which had this title. The September 1983 letter is mentioned in Colás and Lawson, 'Fred Halliday: Achievements, Ambivalences and Openings', p. 237, n. 2.

[41] The other eight were Jon Halliday, John Merrington, Juliet Mitchell, Roger Murray, Tom Nairn, Lucien Rey (Peter Wollen), Bob Rowthorn and Gareth Stedman Jones. A brief note about the resignations of the ten appeared in *New Left Review*, no 142 (Nov.–Dec. 1983), p. 4. For one account, see Duncan Thompson, *Pessimism of the Intellect? A History of New Left Review* (Monmouth, 2007), pp. 123–32.

foreign policy as its subject, completing the thesis in 1985.[42] The revised version, published five years later, is mentioned below.

From the start of his teaching there in 1983, Fred warmed to LSE. In early 1985 events took a surprising turn. Having applied for a full lectureship and been beaten to the post for it by Christopher Coker, he was then encouraged by some friends among his colleagues to apply for a new professorship. His appointment was controversial, meeting some resistance at LSE. A colleague in another department phoned me to say how outraged he was that a Trotskyite had been appointed a professor at LSE. *And* he hadn't even got his doctorate yet! *And* he had been turned down for a lectureship only shortly before! This colleague asked what was to be done about it. I said he should wait and see: Fred had an interesting mind and a unique approach, and would prove over time the appointment was the right one.

In response to a congratulatory note from me, Fred suggested a meeting: 'I need to orientate myself in my new position, and would welcome your advice on a number of questions.' He added that he could be found at home 'quite a lot of time at the moment: baby + scripts = domesticity.'[43] His life had indeed changed, especially with the birth of his and Maxine's son Alex on 21 March 1985. As he told me when we met in Oxford that June, 'in a single year I became a professor, a doctor, a father and an orphan'. He wondered whether he was the same person at the end of that year as he had been at the beginning. He was, thank goodness. But at the same time he was never afraid to develop intellectually. One year later, when I was appointed to the Montague Burton Professorship at Oxford, he wrote to me: 'Clearly, in addition to the other more established conditions, an unorthodox past is now a sine qua non for holding a chair in international relations. An equally unorthodox future must surely follow.'[44]

Fred himself gave us many revealing indications of how his underlying views on international relations developed. LSE was central to this. It was very different from the places where he had previously worked. His inaugural lecture in 1987, appropriately on the subject of internationalism, conveyed a subtle understanding of the need for, and pitfalls of, internationalist approaches.[45]

[42] S. F. P. Halliday, 'Aspects of South Yemen's Foreign Policy, 1967–1982', Ph.D. thesis, LSE, 1985. A copy is held in the LSE Library's theses collection.
[43] Halliday, letter to the author, 2 June 1985.
[44] Halliday, letter to the author, 18 April 1986.
[45] Halliday, 'Three concepts of internationalism', *International Affairs,* London, 64 (1988), 187–98.

In his characteristically witty and rich remarks made at his LSE retirement dinner in 2008, he described the huge effect that immersion in International Relations at LSE had on him after arriving there in 1982–3: 'My induction into IR came as a severe intellectual shock.... Of the theoretical landscape of IR I was wholly innocent.'[46] As well as attending lectures by two role models, Michael Banks and Christopher Hill, 'I studied, and found myself in some considerable agreement with, the main tenets of the English School.'[47]

To some this must have sounded as shocking as if Richard Dawkins were to confess that he had become a Roman Catholic. But actually there is a logic in it: the 'English School's' emphasis on interest as a guide to state behaviour; its recognition of the diversity of experiences, forms and beliefs of different societies; its belief in studying history, including the history of ideas; and its scepticism about grand schemes for the total reform of international relations—all these can be seen as positions to which Fred had been moving anyway.

It would be wrong to attribute all of the intellectual changes that Fred underwent from 1983 onwards to the LSE alone. During Fred's twenty-five years at LSE, events—especially the end of the Cold War, discussed further below—continued to impinge on his thinking. In any case, to present Fred's development simply as an LSE-assisted induction into the 'English School' would do less than justice to the richness and complexity of Fred's world-view. As Christopher Hill put it at the memorial event at LSE:

> Fred himself accepted that the subject of IR was virtually new to him on appointment as Professor in the Department, and he worked enormously hard to master its literature. Being the person of talent and enormous productivity that he was, this did not take him long. It led him to be attached to the subject, as he was to the Department as an institution, and to many individual colleagues, to say nothing of the hundreds of students in whose development he played a major part. But Fred had too broad interests, and too strong a commitment to sociological understandings of the world, to be satisfied with a pure English School approach, even assuming that this has indeed been the orthodoxy in recent decades in the Department—which has to be doubted. He was, however, consistent throughout his time in the Department in placing great emphasis on both the *international*, which he thought all other subjects should learn from, and on the importance of *the state* as a counter-balancing factor to

[46] Halliday, 'Personalities, Events, Ideas: Twenty-five Years in the LSE Department of International Relations', revised text of remarks made at IR Department Dinner marking departure of FH from LSE, Cooper's Restaurant, Lincoln's Inn Fields, 22 May 2008, p. 3.
[47] Halliday, 'Personalities, Events, Ideas', p. 4.

more structural understandings of the world, whether materialist or ideational. And he saw the Department as the institutional guarantor of these two, inter-linked, perspectives.[48]

He loved International Relations as taught at LSE—the tension between realism and idealism, the interest in theory without forcing colleagues or students to fall into one or another paradigmatic camp; the commitment to studying most if not all the continents, and most if not all of the ideas. But he loved the department more for its potential than its achievements. It had lacked strong links with other disciplines at LSE. It was his strong presence that changed its standing in the School. As Hill has said, 'Fred was himself a lion, the defender of the pride whom we needed to lift our status and our activity onto a more confident plane. It was the combination of intellect, drive and charisma which set him apart.'[49] He did his stint as convenor of the department, and served on some of the major committees of the school. He continued to be notably productive. In the 2001 Research Assessment Exercise, covering the years 1996 to 2000, he submitted four single-author works: a performance that must have taken a personal toll. He went on to publish five more books in the next five-year period.

End of the Cold War

How did the end of communism in Europe, and the concomitant end of the Cold War, impinge on Fred's life and work? This was perhaps the greatest change on the global political landscape in his professional life-time, comparable in importance to the process of decolonisation from the 1940s onwards, and it presented challenges to those who, like Fred, had been at least as critical of Western policies as they had of Soviet ones.

Until the 1980s, Fred had written virtually nothing about European international politics. Shortly after the 1968 invasion of Czechoslovakia he told me that eastern European countries had not interested him much because they had never had real revolutions, communist rule having been imposed on them largely from outside. This was the very reason that they did interest me, but that's another story.

---

[48] Christopher Hill, 'Tribute to Fred Halliday', LSE, 3 Nov. 2010, p. 2. Available at <http://www2.lse.ac.uk/internationalRelations/pdf/CJHtributetofred.pdf>, accessed 29 Dec. 2010.
[49] Ibid., pp. 3–4.

Perhaps because his interest in eastern Europe was limited, he misread some of the signs of the end of the Cold War. As late as 1989 he said of the US–Soviet competition about how societies (especially in the Third World) should be organised: 'This competition, far from disappearing, was continuing through the late 1980s on the terrain most central to it, around the forms of government and socio-economic system to be found in third world societies, and, by extension, in the more developed world ... There was little in the negotiations of the late 1980s to suggest that this underlying conflict had ended.'[50] The subsequent collapse of Communist Party systems in Europe forced him into a rethink, not least about revolutionary socialism, which he pronounced dead.[51]

The events of 1989–91 also threw up specific issues that forced him to stake out new positions. The Iraqi invasion, occupation and annexation of Kuwait in August 1990 was the occasion of a dramatic shift. In *Arabia without Sultans* he had described Kuwait as 'a viciously reactionary state with an untarnished record as a supporter of imperialist interests'.[52] Sixteen years later, when it was attacked by Saddam Hussein's Iraq, he was absolutely clear in his support for the US-led coalition. To many it was a shock to find Fred, anti-imperialist to his finger-tips, actually favouring a Western incursion into Arab lands to restore oil-rich Kuwait's sovereignty. Yet his reasons were powerful. It was partly a matter of interstate morality—if one state could invade, occupy and annex another with impunity, the result would be tragedy. And it was partly also a matter of political systems—Fred could recognise a thug when he saw one, and Saddam Hussein was one such.

His political stances had consequences for him. During and after the 1990–1 Gulf War there was a falling-out with erstwhile comrades on the Left, some of whom were quick to suggest betrayal. Also as the 1990s progressed he sensed danger from another quarter. Although he had by now a more nuanced understanding of the strength of political Islam than he had shown in the 1980s, he remained a bitter and outspoken critic of Islamic extremism.[53] Against the background of his record of criticism of Islamic forces in Afghanistan and Iran in the 1980s, and the *fatwa* against Salman Rushdie in 1989, he had good reason to fear it.

[50] Halliday, *Cold War, Third World: an Essay on Soviet–US Relations* (London, 1989), p. 163. See also a similar statement on p. 8.
[51] Halliday, 'Revolutionary socialism is dead', *Workers' Liberty*, London, no. 16 (Feb. 1992), pp. 17 and 20.
[52] Halliday, *Arabia without Sultans*, p. 434.
[53] Halliday, *Islam and the Myth of Confrontation* (London, 1996), especially the chapter on 'The Iranian Revolution in Comparative Perspective', pp. 42–75.

Despite these pressures, in 1994 he managed to produce *Rethinking International Relations*, his most considered survey of the world after the Cold War. This was a 'a double response—to developments in political and social theory and in the academic study of International Relations, and to changes in the international system itself over the past years, most particularly the collapse of the Soviet bloc'.[54] It is a collection of essays (many of which were adapted from versions published elsewhere) rather than a fully developed coherent whole. Yet, as subtle and rich as anything in the field, it is proof of how in his LSE years he had matured into one of the most interesting and original thinkers anywhere on international relations.

Return to revolution

The end of the Cold War changed much for Fred, but not his interest in revolutions. In 1990 he published *Revolution and Foreign Policy: the Case of South Yemen, 1967–1987*, the updated version of his 1985 LSE doctoral thesis. The year of its publication, 1990, was the year in which the two Yemens (North and South) merged to form a single state. Its subject having, in a sense, ceased to exist, the book had diminished impact. Yet it is based on an intimate knowledge of the country and of the Yemeni dialect. As the Chair of the British-Yemeni Society stated in his obituary of Fred: 'Visiting Yemen in May 2010, I was astonished at how many people spoke of him with fondness and deep respect. He is remembered for the way he has helped explain Yemen to the world and for his long friendship with the country and its leaders in both the old north and south, and for his wonderful ability to tell jokes in the right Yemeni voice.'[55] Fred's book provides a subtle account of the politics of South Yemen in the twenty years following the British departure from Aden and the Protectorates in 1967. Not a particularly elevating story, it leaves the reader wondering just how much of Fred's early belief in revolution, already tempered by some of his difficult encounters with contemporary history—the defeat of the guerrillas in Oman, and the failure of the Iranian masses to take the path he and others had indicated—could survive in light of his frank account of developments in what at that time was called the People's Democratic

---

[54] Halliday, *Rethinking International Relations* (Basingstoke, 1994), p. ix.
[55] Noel Brehony, obituary published on the British-Yemeni Society website, <http://www.al-bab. com/bys/obits/halliday.htm>, accessed 7 Jan. 2011.

Republic of Yemen. Already in the acknowledgements, Fred noted with feeling: 'Neither before nor after independence has the nationalist and socialist movement in South Yemen been characterized by strategic unity, or by the ability to resolve conflicts in a democratic and responsible manner ...'[56] He is particularly interesting on the corrosive effects of the quest for the unity of North and South Yemen:

> For most Yemenis, it has, since the 1950s, been an article of nationalist faith that the two Yemeni states should unite and that this could be attained in the foreseeable future. No political leadership has been able overtly to contradict this, and all political parties have sought to mobilise the popular sentiment on unity, for their own purposes. At the same time, the issue of Yemeni unity, like that of Arab unity more generally, has been a cause of considerable friction between the Yemeni states, both because of disagreements on how this unity is to be achieved and because each has used the commitment to unity as a legitimation for interference in the internal affairs of the other.[57]

Fred saw South Yemen as a classic revolutionary state: hosting countless guerrilla and opposition groups from other states, the promoter of a radical new stand in international relations, and often in conflict with its neighbours and other states in the region. Yet he also notes the degree of accommodation that developed between the revolutionary state and its non-revolutionary neighbours. The book thus embodies a puzzle which was also evident in his earlier work on Ethiopia. How much was Fred a critical advocate of revolution, and how much a sympathetic but worried observer? The first seems gradually to yield to the second.

His 1999 book on *Revolution and World Politics* propounded a much more nuanced view of revolution than his earlier works. He asserts, powerfully, the continuing importance of revolutions, both in the domestic lives of states and in international politics. However, there is little echo of the idea—which had been reflected for example in his 1979 work on Iran—that there is a single 'international revolutionary movement' with common purposes that transcend borders. And he recognises that revolutionary states can fall as well as rise.[58] This is a book of extraordinary maturity and insight: the finest and most scholarly expression of Fred's enduring claim that neither revolutions nor international relations could be understood in isolation from each other.

---

[56] Halliday, *Revolution and Foreign Policy: the Case of South Yemen, 1967–1987* (Cambridge, 1990), pp. viii–ix.

[57] Ibid., p. 99.

[58] Halliday, *Revolution and World Politics: the Rise and Fall of the Sixth Great Power* (Basingstoke, 1999).

Last decade

It was while at LSE that Fred had a major mental breakdown. I can give neither a full description nor a full explanation. Early symptoms included renewed concerns for his safety after the terrorist attacks of 11 September 2001. In light of his experiences in the 1990s, when he had had some reason to fear Islamic extremism, these concerns were not without foundation. There was also a deep sense of frustration: he had warned the US not to support the Muslim fundamentalists in Afghanistan, and had not been heeded. And, quite simply, it had become almost impossible to be optimistic about the Middle East: this was itself enough to induce depression in one so deeply committed to progress in that region.

Under unremitting pressure to perform from the media as well as the academic world, he continued to function remarkably effectively. Indeed, in the changed landscape after 9/11 Fred was sometimes at his very best. A seminar he gave in Oxford in March 2002, entitled 'Travels in Badargumentstan', was a brilliant, witty and honest presentation on contemporary issues. It went well into injury time—and not one person in that crowded room would have wished it to stop. It was in 2002 that he was elected to the British Academy—a timely recognition of his many achievements, not least as a public intellectual.

All this was followed by Fred's collapse in 2002–3. It accompanied his efforts to complete the manuscript of his major book on the Middle East.[59] He later said that his collapse was 'a result above all of my own inability over many years, and against the advice of family and friends, to maintain a balanced life'.[60] The harsh pace he had set himself, and the self-imposed requirement to keep up with so many peoples, ideas, countries and realms of knowledge, must all have exacerbated the normal difficulties and strains of academic life. Constantly being expected not just to perform a range of different tasks, but to dazzle in them, had taken a toll. So too had grim turns of events in the past two decades in Afghanistan, Iran, Iraq and elsewhere. None of this was helped by the sense that governments, including his own, neither appreciated his insights nor heeded his advice. This sense, shared by many academics, was particularly strong in Fred's case and endured throughout his career. After Labour came to power in 1997,

---

[59] Halliday, *The Middle East in International Relations: Power, Politics and Ideology* (Cambridge, 2005). This was completed after he began to recover in late summer 2003.
[60] Halliday, 'Personalities, Events, Ideas', p. 6.

and having previously helped Robin Cook on Middle East issues, he had been disappointed not to have been consulted.

The collapse was the sombre background to a storm in a teacup at LSE. This concerned the seventy-fifth anniversary of the International Relations Department in 2003. A book had been compiled by two graduate students, Harry Bauer and Elisabetta Brighi, who had stepped into the breach for the department when a commissioned history had failed to materialise.[61] Fred had certain objections. According to Hill, Fred was concerned that the book 'did not do his role in the Department justice, nor the sets of interests which he cared most about'.[62] In his valedictory lecture five years later, he was more specific about the issues in this episode: 'We do not do enough to promote our claim, originally articulated by Justin Rosenberg in a *Millennium* article of the mid-90s, to be potentially the hegemonic discipline of the twenty-first century, and the most creative and open-minded department in the world devoted to it.' He recounted that the upshot of his discomfiture was that, in the spirit of fellow Dubliners, including Jonathan Swift, James Joyce and Oscar Wilde, he 'wrote a short anecdotal, rambling and satirical, history of our Department.... Luckily, wiser souls in the central administration prevailed and the text was never sent. Files were duly deleted. Indeed, I believe no copies now exist ...'[63]

Notwithstanding all these problems, in 2005 he was elected to the senior International Relations post at LSE, the Montague Burton Chair. This was a vindication of the controversial decision, taken twenty years earlier, to make him a professor. It coincided with his slow recovery from breakdown, and also with his turn towards a new outlet for his work, and new pastures.

From 2004 onwards he published about eighty columns on the openDemocracy website.[64] He said many times that this 'saved my life'. He now had a world outlet that he deserved, and the lack of which had gnawed away at him. Many of these columns are collected in a posthumously published book.[65] A further change came in 2005. From then until his death he was increasingly committed to work in Barcelona. For three years to

---

[61] Harry Bauer and Elisabetta Brighi (eds.), *International Relations at LSE: a History of 75 Years* (London, 2003).

[62] 'Tribute to Fred Halliday', LSE, 3 Nov. 2010, p. 2.

[63] Halliday, 'Personalities, Events, Ideas', p. 16.

[64] A selection of his columns is at <http://www.opendemocracy.net/author/fred-halliday>, accessed 13 March 2011.

[65] Halliday, *Political Journeys: the openDemocracy Essays* (London, 2011).

2008 he was part-time Visiting Professor at the Institut Barcelona d'Estudis Internacionals (IBEI), a newly established (2004) centre for postgraduate education and research in politics and international relations. In April 2008 he took up a Research Professorship at the Institució Catalana de Recerca I Estudis Avançats (ICREA) which enabled him to continue working closely with IBEI. In 2006 he and Maxine had separated: Fred moved out from their Highgate home to a flat in Bloomsbury that henceforth served as his London pied-à-terre.

In this period he was winding down but not ending his involvement in LSE. In 2008 he formally retired from his professorship, and began a three-year Research Associateship. In summer and autumn 2009 he urged the school to reconsider its decision to accept a donation of £1.5 million from an organisation closely connected with the Gadaffi regime, following this up in October with a strong memorandum warning of 'the reputational risk to LSE'.[66] His opposition to the LSE's dealings with the regime long predated 2009: he had also warned against, and actively opposed, the acceptance of Gadaffi's son, Saif al-Islam, as a doctoral student. His stance was amply justified. Following demonstrations in Libya in early 2011, and their violent repression by the authorities which initiated civil war, Sir Howard Davies, Director of the LSE, stated on 28 February 2011 that LSE's decision to accept this funding had 'backfired'; and on 3 March, amid continuing controversy about the LSE's extensive involvements with Libya, he resigned from the directorship.[67]

Fred's last few years of association with LSE are mainly remembered for occasional lectures there—none more memorable that the one in 2009 on the thirtieth anniversary of the Iranian revolution. Based on personal experience, extensive study and mature reflection, it evoked vividly the pathos of revolutions—the heroism and the cruelty, the aspiration and the decline. It received a standing ovation.[68]

Barcelona remained his main focus. Still recovering from his period of ill-health, he enjoyed the spirit of Barcelona: a great cosmopolitan city

---

[66] Halliday's memo 'LSE and the Qaddafi Foundation: A Dissenting Note', dated 4 Oct. 2009, was considered by the LSE Council on 20 Oct. 2009. The memo, and the minutes of the two LSE Council meetings that considered the donation, are available at <http://www.whatdotheyknow.com/request/63095/response/159233/attach/2/JeewaFOIBinder.pdf> accessed 10 April 2011.

[67] The text of Howard Davies' letter of resignation of 3 March 2011, and of the LSE Council's decisions of that date, are at <http://www2.lse.ac.uk/newsAndMedia/news/archives/2011/03/director_steps_down.aspx>, accessed 13 March 2011.

[68] Lecture on 'The Islamic Republic of Iran after 30 Years', 23 Feb. 2009. Available from: <http://www.lse.ac.uk/resources/podcasts/publicLecturesAndEvents.htm#generated-subheading24>, accessed 24 Jan. 2011.

where cultures meet, albeit one that remained in some respects intro-verted.[69] In Barcelona, as he explained in his 2008 retirement dinner speech at LSE, he sought 'to do what I can to promote IBEI as a new institution, with a staff and student body as lively and diverse as that of LSE, and … to make whatever contribution I can to Spanish and Catalan intellectual and academic life'.[70] He relished the chance to make Barcelona a centre for debate and academic reflection on international relations and politics. Alas, ill-health supervened, this time in the form of the cancer that was to kill him in a Barcelona hospital on 26 April 2010.

Fred's legacy

Fred's analysis of international problems became ever more profound. Like Isaac Deutscher, he may not have got all his predictions right, nor all of his analyses. His willingness to recognise this was one of his many strengths: not only did it make him a much more attractive and interest-ing writer than those who pretend never to have put a foot wrong, but also it took him on a journey of continuous and creative intellectual development. He had six notable qualities that were the basis of his achievements.

First, he was a public intellectual, of a kind of which we have too few in the UK. He had the essential characteristics of the public intellectual: a lively awareness of ideas, an engagement with the big issues of the day, and an ability to communicate with a range of audiences and in all forms of media. He clearly saw his mission as to overcome the narrow and suburban preoccupations and mental frameworks of the Western world, and especially of the English—whether of Left or Right. He always expressed himself pithily and comprehensibly: he was not the kind of public intellectual who hides behind a smokescreen of obfuscatory language.

Secondly, he could never be satisfied with abstract ideas that left human perception and volition out of the picture, nor with top-down views of order. He emphasised the simultaneity between the two realms of domestic and international. He believed that theory had to relate to the world, and to the ideas and aspirations of actual people. Therefore the most important research method was speaking with people at all

[69] Halliday, 'Barcelona o Catalunya: the real thing', written five months before he died, and posted on <www.opendemocracy.com> on 9 June 2010, accessed 3 Jan. 2011.
[70] Halliday, 'Personalities, Events, Ideas', p. 14.

levels, from heads of government to peasants, doctors and rebels in distant provinces.

Thirdly, he had extraordinary courage: not just the courage to visit dangerous places and people but also to change his mental framework, and to disagree with erstwhile friends and comrades. As Denis MacShane, MP, who had a been a junior minister in the Foreign and Commonwealth Office in the Blair Government, has said: 'Precisely because he came from a background of political solidarity with anti-imperialist and anti-authoritarian campaigns Fred had an empathy and understanding for the oppressed. Unlike the useless fools of crude anti-Americanism who excuse tyranny providing it is hostile to the West, Halliday dissected causes and effects and was as critical of Saddam Hussein and Iranian Ayatollahs as he was of the Shah and other undemocratic rulers.'[71]

Fourthly, he rescued internationalism from its besetting sin, namely an essentially chauvinistic approach which wants the entire world to be more like one's own society. Whether it comes from Right or Left, this kind of internationalism has led time and again to disaster. In Fred there was a permanent tension between a strong strand of universalism and a celebration of difference. That the tension was so strongly felt, and remained so unresolved, is what gave his work a particular, even unique, edge.

Fifthly, he had an unwavering belief in the necessity and possibility of change in the Middle East. From the publication of *Arabia without Sultans* in 1974 onwards, he and his writings were seen, in the region and beyond, as a focal point in debates about change. His principled rejection of the whole idea of a 'clash of civilizations' was based on a belief that political ideas are by nature international, and cross borders as easily as the wind and weather. His thoughts on how change might be achieved varied over time, and he was self-critical of some of his earlier pronouncements favouring armed revolution as *the* way. His underlying belief in change was to be vindicated—alas posthumously—in the 'people power' revolutions in the Middle East that started in Tunisia and Egypt in 2010 and 2011.

Finally, he did the most important thing that any teacher can do: to convey to successive generations of students, and to a wider public, his huge enthusiasm for, and belief in, the study of politics and international relations. Particularly in his lectures he displayed a dazzling combination of intimate knowledge of distant societies, mastery of many languages,

---

[71] Denis MacShane, in the collection of tributes to Fred Halliday on <http://www.opendemocracy.net>, accessed 3 Jan. 2011.

humour, hard facts, conceptual clarity, and above all independence and integrity. It is in this combination that his enduring legacy lies.

ADAM ROBERTS
President of the Academy

Note. I am grateful to Anthony Barnett, Edmund Fawcett, Jon Halliday and Maxine Molyneux for filling in gaps, especially regarding Fred's early years and education. Also to the many others who helped with their recollections and documentation.

ARTHUR HATTO

Arthur Thomas Hatto
1910–2010

ALTHOUGH ARTHUR HATTO would never have considered making such a claim himself, his passing on 6 January 2010, just five weeks short of his one hundredth birthday, assuredly marks the end of what justly may be called 'the heroic age' of German studies in the University of London. At best, he would have regarded himself as an epigone of that age which embraced such distinguished scholars as Robert Priebsch (1866–1935), John George Robertson (1867–1933), Leonard Ashley Willoughby (1885–1977), Edna Purdie (1894–1968), and Frederick Norman (1897–1968). In any case, as we shall see, although Hatto earned his crust as a professor of German Language and Literature, his abiding interests lay in a much broader field: he was a life-long student of texts composed in a dozen languages, spanning four continents (Europe, Asia, Africa, and America) and four millennia.

Arthur Thomas Hatto was born in London on 11 February 1910. His parents, Thomas Hatto, a solicitor's clerk (he later became Assistant Chief Solicitor in the British Transport Commission legal service), and his wife Alice, née Waters, a nurse, lived in Forest Hill and later in Clapham. Towards the end of the First World War their eight-year-old son spent an unforgettable year living with an aunt in the safety of the Sussex country-side, 'running wild', as he admitted, in and around the 'still semi-pagan' village of Barcombe, near Lewes. His head already full of exciting tales from the past, he was even at this early age deeply aware of his southern English roots, symbolised by his ancient West Germanic name, 'Hatto' (= 'fighter' < *χađ-). How a London solicitor's son could win the trust of his rustic contemporaries is something of a mystery, but win it he did. From them he learned the names and behaviour of the birds: 'I didn't feign

Proceedings of the British Academy, **172**, 173–198. © The British Academy 2011.

knowing anything, so everything I saw, I learned,' he recalled. There, too, he developed a lively awareness for what was important in seemingly strange human proceedings and in the time-honoured social patterns that structured Barcombe life. Here already, then, we may discern the making of a young man eager to learn and sensitive to the complexities of human society.

In 1923, with his imagination already well stocked with Greek and Far Eastern tales combining physical prowess and exquisite beauty, he won a scholarship to Dulwich College, an institution which—if we may judge from the success of the likes of P. G. Wodehouse, Raymond Chandler, Dennis Wheatley, and C. S. Forester—excelled at nurturing men with lively imaginations and a love of vivid turns of phrase. Entering on the Modern Side, he chose to study German, 'the most exotic language available'. His school record for 1926 and 1927 shows him to have been a pupil of modest achievement: he was placed barely above the middle rank of his contemporaries. He passed his School Certificate in 1926 taking Latin, French, German, Arithmetic and Elementary Mathematics, and achieving a distinction in English, which he attributed to his having written a brilliant essay on the subject of 'Roads', treating of roads in the Roman, Chinese and Inca Empires. He was a born cross-country runner and a keen rugby player; in later life he would display comparable energy, tenacity and commitment to the mental challenges he encountered in his chosen fields of study.

At the age of seventeen-and-a-half, at a time when he might have contemplated working for an Exhibition at Oxford or Cambridge, Hatto was sent by his father, unwilling to have his son 'loll on a Sixth Form bench', straight from the Remove to King's College London, a place renowned for its sobriety compared with the allegedly more licentious ambience of University College, 'the godless institution of Gower Street'. Nevertheless, thanks to the intercollegiate teaching arrangements at London University, he came under the influence of two eminent medievalists, the erudite but dour palaeographer Robert Priebsch, Professor of German at University College, and the colourful Frederick Norman, Reader in German at King's, whose extensive knowledge, wide reading, wit, and stimulating conversation captivated him. Forever afterwards Hatto referred to Norman in awe as 'my tutor'.[1] Although Hatto narrowly missed a First Class BA with

---

[1] Hatto's devotion and loyalty to Norman was manifested in his editing *Three Essays on the 'Hildebrandslied' by Frederick Norman; Reprinted and Edited in Honour of his Memory [...] by A. T. Hatto; together with a Letter by Andreas Heusler* (London, 1973).

Honours in German in 1931, having failed to achieve an Alpha mark on the German language paper, his teachers, Henry Gibson Atkins, Professor of German at King's, Priebsch and Norman, all clearly recognised that he was cut out for an academic career. It was Norman's wont, canny businessman that he was, to offer to buy up any books the students no longer needed at the end of their course. When Hatto offered his, Norman declined them, saying, 'No, not yours, Mr Hatto, you will be needing them in years to come!' At this point Hatto himself recognised where his future lay; the university was his true element and he never looked back.

It was important to improve his German, however, so in 1932 he was despatched to the University of Bern as Lektor for English, having meanwhile been given some coaching in the teaching of English to foreign students by J. R. Firth, later Professor of General Linguistics in the University of London, whose context-focused, ethnographic approach to language already appealed to him far more than the dry fare of the conventional Indo-European comparative philology in the Neo-grammarian mould. Immediately upon his arrival in Switzerland he set about trying to master the archaic local dialect of *Bärndütsch*, even participating in the ancient rustic team-game of *Hornussen* (so-called because the puck makes the sound of a hornet as it flies through the air at great speed). From 1932 to 1934 from his Swiss vantage point he was able to watch and weigh the collapse of German civilisation. Naturally, he also availed himself of the opportunity to further his studies by attending the seminars of the distinguished but (compared with Norman) dull medievalist Helmut de Boor (1891–1976) (whose daughters were reputed to sport swastikas under their lapels) and the modernist Fritz Strich (1882–1963) whose approach he considered too 'arty'.

Hatto enjoyed life in Bern so much that he had visions of becoming an octogenarian Lektor there. However, in 1934 his teachers summoned him back to London. At this time he had met in Switzerland a medical student from Düsseldorf, Rose Margot Feibelmann, whom he would marry in 1935. As she was from a Jewish family—her father, Max (b. 1874), was senior cantor of the main synagogue in Düsseldorf—their move to Britain probably saved her life and the lives of her parents also, for these would follow them to Britain in March 1939. The Hattos settled first at Radlett in Hertfordshire, later moving to Mill Hill. Margot Hatto, a lady whose firmness of character and deep sense of family he so much admired, fulfilled his ideal of an artistically and at the same time practically gifted partner. Eventually she set up a successful small printing business, specialising in greeting cards, and later became an accomplished silversmith, having studied the art at Sir John Cass College in London. She died on 7 July 2000.

The immediate cause of Hatto's return to London was that his teachers there, impressed with his academic promise, offered him an appointment as Assistant Lecturer in German at King's College. He had been awarded the London MA with Distinction in 1934, then a rare accolade (which Norman had also received under Priebsch) and one of which he always remained immensely proud—at that time, this was deemed the equivalent of a doctorate elsewhere.[2] As part of the degree requirements Hatto presented a thesis entitled 'A Middle German Apocalypse edited from the manuscript British Museum, Add. 15243', a topic that had been proposed to him by Priebsch. In this study, which he later published in German,[3] he showed that the manuscript was probably written between 1350 and 1370 in south-west Thuringia and was evidently closely related to MS Meiningen 57, dating from the first half of the fifteenth century.

After four congenial years at King's, Hatto's career took an unexpected turn. H. G. Atkins retired from the Chair in 1937 and Norman, who had held a Readership half-time at King's College and half-time at University College (receiving £350 p.a. from each college, which gave him more than if he had had a full-time post paying only £500 or so), had meanwhile been thwarted in his ambition to succeed Priebsch as Professor at the latter. L. A. Willoughby, though later renowned as a Goethe scholar, was appointed at University College—as a medievalist! Norman, no longer needed at University College, was obliged to become full-time at King's, succeeding Atkins as Professor. This in turn meant that Hatto's services as a medievalist were no longer required at King's. Fortunately, a vacancy had arisen at Newcastle, and Norman encouraged him to apply. As a young married couple, however, the Hattos were reluctant, not least for financial reasons, to leave their small, happy home near London. Norman, though incensed by this challenge to his authority—throughout his career he seemed to think that he had a divine right to decree who should teach German where—nevertheless recommended Hatto for a new position at Queen Mary College, London. Despite strong competition, he was appointed, not least, Hatto believed, thanks to his prowess at rugby. At the interview, the Principal, Sir Frederick Maurice (1871–1951), Field

[2] According to Norman, the university had introduced the Ph.D. degree in the humanities in 1917 as a means of luring wealthy Americans away from German universities—but without much success.

[3] As 'Eine deutsche Apokalypse des 14. Jahrhunderts', in Hans Vollmer's *Neue Texte zur Bibelverdeutschung des Mittelalters*, Bibel und deutsche Kultur, 6 (Potsdam, 1936), pp. 175–99.

Marshal Haig's former Quartermaster-General, asked him whether he had taken part 'in the famous match between Dulwich and St Paul's'—Maurice was himself a Pauline—to which Hatto replied, 'Yes, Sir, twice, and beat them twice!' When the candidate had left the room, Maurice said, 'That's the man I want!'[4] Hence, in 1938 Hatto became Head of the Department of German at Queen Mary College, an office he would hold with colourful distinction until his retirement in 1977.

Scarcely had he taken up his lectureship, however, than he was recruited on Norman's and Sir Frederick Maurice's recommendation in February 1939 to work in the cryptographic bureau in Admiral Hall's Room 40 at the Foreign Office, where two other professors of German, Walter Bruford and Leonard Willoughby, had already gained experience before 1918. Now, even before war was declared, Norman was steering able young linguists into war work of this kind. Hatto, in fact, found himself working under Norman in the Air Section. On 3 September 1939 they were seconded to the British monitoring and cryptographic centre at Bletchley Park to work under the cryptographic genius Captain (later Brigadier) John Tiltman (1894–1982). Hatto was thrilled when Tiltman succeeded in cracking the German 'stencil' cipher which no less a mathematician than Charles Lutwidge Dodgson, alias Lewis Carroll, had once declared to be unbreakable. George Steiner has opined, 'It looks as if Bletchley Park is the single greatest achievement of Britain during 1939–45, perhaps during this century as a whole.'[5] Whether or not that is so, 'BP' has been rightly called a 'nursery for Germanists', for among its denizens were many Germanists, several of whom would become professors after the war. Besides Hatto, they included Walter Bruford and Leonard Forster (both Fellows of the Academy), Kenneth Brooke, the lexicographer Trevor Jones, C. T. Carr, D. M. Mennie, R. V. Tymms, Dorothy Reich, William Rose, K. C. King, F. P. Pickering, and H. B. Willson (the last three distinguished medievalists).

But for the fall of France, Hatto might have been sent to the Continent to serve as a wireless operator in a cryptographic unit. As it was, he was set on decoding tasks at Bletchley Park, one of which was to produce the first report on the Luftwaffe's operations in France. He also worked successfully on Gestapo ciphers, German weather ciphers and others, and soon attracted attention—standing out from the largely Oxford-trained specialists in Classics, English, and Statistics—through his rare ability to

---

[4] This exchange was reported by Norman in a tape-recorded interview in June 1965, of which the author has a transcript. He had been the expert adviser at Hatto's interview.

[5] George Steiner's remark is cited in Robert Harris's novel *Enigma* (London, 1995), p. viii.

interpret even corrupted messages thanks to his philological training and his now excellent command of German. Unfortunately, his skill in such matters was regarded with envy by Oliver Strachey (the brother of Lytton[6]) who apparently believed that the war would and should be won without the help of London University, which did not make for a harmonious working relationship. However, Strachey had appointed the Classicist L. R. Palmer (1906–84), a man who, as a pupil of the legendary Ulrich von Wilamowitz-Moellendorf, had excellent German, and Denys Page (1908–78), later Regius Professor of Greek at Cambridge, to his section, and these recognised Hatto's considerable abilities. They gave him the task of trying to gather advance information on impending changes within existing ciphers, on the introduction of new ciphers, and on changes in German cipher personnel. In this role he had a major success, on the eve of the Allied landing in Sicily in July 1943. Despite being highly distrustful of their own cipher security and observing the strictest discipline in their communications, the Germans were let down by one of their own communications officers who broke the golden rule of not referring in a current cipher to any element of a new cipher it was proposed to introduce. Hatto discovered that, by foolishly revealing the three-letter call signs from the preamble to messages, this officer had inadvertently published the key to one of the Germans' most secret communication routes, and since the various networks were linked, this gave Bletchley Park access to communications to German land, sea and air forces before the Allied landings took place.

After the defeat of Germany, part of Hatto's section at Bletchley Park was to transfer to Ceylon en route for Tokyo. Although Denys Page invited Hatto to join his team there, he somewhat reluctantly declined since his wife had recently given birth to their daughter, Jane.

Hatto never spoke of the work at Bletchley Park, even after its importance became widely known following publication of F. W. Winterbotham's *The Ultra Secret* in 1974. According to one of his then colleagues, he was alarmed by this book (though he is not mentioned by name), fearing that he might be abducted by the Soviets to the Lubljanka, 'so far removed from the Reading Room of the British Museum'. Like Margaret Thatcher, he seems to have wished the secret had never been revealed.[7]

Though attached to Room 40 of the Foreign Office until 1945, he was able in 1944–5 to spend a weekly day of leave as a temporary lecturer

---

[6] Cf. also Hugh Trevor-Roper's experiences with Strachey, as related in Adam Sisman, *Hugh Trevor-Roper. The Biography* (London, 2010), p. 82.
[7] According to Sisman, *Trevor-Roper*, p. 465.

for Medieval German at bomb-damaged University College London. Returning to Queen Mary College in 1945, Hatto found himself with exiguous resources. In 1946-7 the whole College numbered no more than 783 students. Over the years he built up a flourishing German Department, starting with only one part-time colleague and ending with five permanent full-time staff and one-and-a-half language assistants. His own achievements, in scholarship and as a committed Head of Department, were soon rewarded with the conferment of the title of Reader in German on him by the University of London in 1946 and in 1953 by the title of Professor. An undated photograph of him from about this time, showing his sharp features and penetrating eyes, is reproduced in the college's official history.[8] He kept his staff on a light rein, trusting their maturity; he would, one feels, have had little sympathy with the modern obsession with teaching quality and research assessment exercises. To all he was unfailingly respectful, courteous and kind. His old-fashioned courtesy expressed itself for instance in the care he took always to address his seniors and even his junior colleagues by their formal academic titles, even long after the use of Christian names among colleagues began to be the custom (around 1970). And as an example of his sympathetic kindness one may cite the case of a colleague who lamented to him that the lecture he had just given had been poorly attended. Hatto consoled him with the words, 'Ah, Doctor [...], do not be downhearted. Who knows, the few who did attend your lecture may one day prove to be the most distinguished scholars,' words which the colleague concerned found to be most heartening and truly unforgettable. Yet, for all his kindness towards generations of students, Hatto never disguised his view that universities were for the elite and his belief that university education should never have been allowed to become an object of party politics.

Norman had a story of how, late one afternoon in 1935, he had encountered Hatto unexpectedly at a time when he should have been teaching. 'Hallo Hatto', he said, 'haven't you got your Science German class now?' With a puckish grin, he replied, 'Well, I should have, but when I went along last week there was nobody there, so I'm staying away this week to punish them!' Norman advised him not to punish them that way in future, lest he incur the wrath of the Professor.[9] In fact, though, Hatto

---

[8] G. P. Moss and M. V. Saville, *From Palace to College. An Illustrated Account of Queen Mary College (University of London)* (London, 1985). p. 113, ill. 240. Other photographs of him are found in *German Life and Letters*, NS 30 (1976-7), facing p. 91, and on the Special Forces Roll of Honour website <http:// www.specialforcesroh.com>.

[9] This incident was related by Norman in his interview in 1965.

was to become renowned as a committed and enthusiastic teacher, perhaps too enthusiastic for some of his students, one of whom recalled how when Hatto had been lecturing at some length on the symbolism of the lime-tree as a feature of the *locus amoenus* in medieval poetry the students one day covered the lectern with lime leaves: Hatto entered the room, sweeping the offending greenery aside without recognising it for what it was—a story which, however, is hard to credit in a man with such a keen eye for nature. His study of the lime appeared in the *Modern Language Review*.[10] When he gave a version of this paper to Hugo Kuhn's seminar at the University of Munich in 1961, the students were amazed at the way he put the symbol of the lime-tree into the context of global literature and archaic cultures, and by the verve with which he delivered the lecture. The vitality he displayed in lecturing was legendary: in teaching the ninth-century Old High German *Hildebrandslied* he would act out Hildebrand's and Hadubrand's parts on the lecturer's podium. Professor Ian Short, an undergraduate pupil of his at the time when Hatto was putting the finishing touches to his Penguin translation of the *Nibelungenlied*, remembers him as 'energetic, bubbly even, forever pacing around the room and talking nineteen to the dozen, [...] leaping onto the table to show either the agility or the sword-play of Siegfried, and darting nimbly over to the door to heave Gunther onto the coat peg in emulation of Brünhild. Never a dull moment ...!' He also remembers Hatto's many asides 'and the pleasure he took in interrupting himself and relating whatever it was that we were reading to a wider context, to folklore and to mythology, mostly, and to exotic literatures that none of us had even heard of'. In illuminating a particular textual detail by applying a comparative method Hatto was way ahead of his time. He outlined the aim of his approach in a letter he wrote to Daniel Prior: 'Without leaving the empirical level comparisons bring out individualities, help to illuminate, even decrypt obscurities, as though light, dancing round the vortex of specifics, were accelerated into an ever-intensifying brightness.'

Although Hatto was a fervent and loyal 'college man' he was also an ardent supporter of the federal University of London. He loathed administration and was never interested in power for its own sake, yet he was scrupulously conscientious in carrying out the duties of such offices as came his way. His entertaining aperçus enlivened many a meeting of the University's Board of Studies in Germanic Languages and Literatures.

---

[10] 'The lime-tree and early German, Goliard and English lyric poetry', *The Modern Language Review*, 49 (1954), 193–209.

He was a rigorous chairman of the Board of Staff Examiners for German, and a vociferous member of the Committee of Management of the University of London Institute of Germanic Studies whose fortunes he had followed with keen interest ever since Leonard Willoughby had proposed to the Senate in 1943 the establishment of such an institute to serve as a focus for German studies in London and 'a house of call' for visiting scholars from home and abroad. Nevertheless, there were really only two administrative appointments that he welcomed: that of representing the University's Faculty of Arts on the governing body of the School of Oriental and African Studies from 1960, an institution for which he cared very deeply and which gave him entrée to the world of professionals in the exotic and archaic cultures which so strongly attracted him and gave an added depth to his interpretation of much Germanic poetry; and his membership from 1969 of the committee of the University's Central Research Fund which he cherished because it furthered the careers of students.

From his earliest days at Queen Mary College and through the war and beyond he produced a stream of perceptive (and remarkably succinct) articles. The earliest appeared in *London Mediaeval Studies* (*LMS*), a short-lived journal founded by Frederick Norman and A. H. Smith at University College London. His essay there on 'Some Old High German vowels in the light of the phoneme theory'[11] appears to be his sole engagement with linguistic theory but also, it seems, the earliest known application of the phoneme theory to the earliest stage of German. Two further articles appeared in the same volume of *LMS*: 'Moriz von Craon' (pp. 285–304) and 'The elephants in the Strassburg Alexander' (pp. 399–429).[12] At about the same time he began a remarkable sequence of articles, published mostly in *The Modern Language Review* (*MLR*) and sometimes in *German Life and Letters* (*GLL*) and a number of leading German journals, mainly on aspects of medieval literature, notably on textual problems relating to Wolfram von Eschenbach and Walther von der Vogelweide, two of the leading poets of around 1200.[13] Nineteen of these pieces were later reprinted

---

[11] 'Some Old High German vowels in the light of the phoneme theory', *London Mediæval Studies*, 1 (1937–9), 65–76.

[12] The latter was reprinted in Peter Noble *et al.* (eds.), *The Medieval Alexander Legend and Romance Epic: Essays in Honour of David J. A. Ross* (Millwood, NY, 1982), pp. 85–105.

[13] They include: '*Minnesangs Frühling* 40, 19 ff.', *The Modern Language Review* (hereafter *MLR*), 33 (1938), 266–8; 'sînen dienest verliesen', *MLR*, 33 (1938), 416–22; 'vrouwen schouwen', *MLR*, 34 (1939), 40–9; 'Archery and chivalry: a noble prejudice', *MLR*, 35 (1940), 40–54; 'Were Walther and Wolfram once at the same court?', *MLR*, 35 (1940), 529–30; 'Gallantry in the mediaeval German lyric', *MLR*, 36 (1941), 480–7; 'The name of God in Gothic', *MLR*, 39 (1944), 247–51; '*Parzival* 183, 9 "… und arger schützen harte vil"', *MLR*, 40 (1945), 48–9; 'The name of God in

Germanic', *MLR*, 41 (1946), 67–8; 'Venus and Adonis—and the boar', *MLR*, 41 (1946), 353–61
(Hatto claimed that C. J. Sisson, one of the editors of the journal, offered him a Readership in
English at University College on the strength of this article alone!); 'Two notes on Chrétien and
Wolfram', *MLR*, 42 (1947), 243–6; 'On Wolfram's conception of the "Graal"', *MLR*, 43 (1948),
216–22 (a review of Konrad Burdach's *Der Gral. Forschungen über seinen Ursprung und seinen
Zusammenhang mit der Longinuslegende* (Stuttgart, 1938)); 'On Chrétien and Wolfram', *MLR*,
44 (1949), 380–5; ' "Revolution", an enquiry into the usefulness of a historical term', *Mind*, 58
(1949), 495–517 (this article was later anthologised in Rosemary H. T. O'Kane (ed.), *Revolution:
Critical Concepts in Political Science, Volume 1* (London, 2000), pp. 3–22; O'Kane calls Hatto a
'political philosopher', in her introduction (p. xl)—unintentional praise!); 'Walther von der
Vogelweide's Ottonian poems: a new interpretation', *Speculum*, 24 (1949), 542–53 (republished
in German translation as 'Die Ottonischen Gedichte Walthers von der Vogelweide', in Siegfried
Beyschlag (ed.), *Walther von der Vogelweide*, Wege der Forschung, 112 (Darmstadt, 1971),
pp. 230–50); 'Walther von der Vogelweide: A note on the poem "Madam, accept this garland" '.
German Life and Letters (hereafter *GLL*), NS 3 (1949/50), 141–5; 'On beauty of numbers in
Wolfram's dawn songs', *MLR*, 45 (1950), 181–8; 'An early *Tagelied*', *MLR*, 46 (1951), 66–9; (with
R. J. Taylor) 'Recent work on the arithmetical principle in medieval poetry', *MLR*, 46 (1951),
396–403; 'Zur Entstehung des Eingangs und der Bücher I und II des *Parzival*', *Zeitschrift für
deutsches Altertum*, 84 (1952/53), 232–40 (with a correction on p. 346); 'The lime-tree and early
German, Goliard and English lyric poetry', *MLR*, 49 (1954), 193–209; 'Snake-swords and boar-
helms in *Beowulf*', *English Studies*, 38 (1957), 145–60 and 257–9 (which ends with an illuminating
comparative reference to an Ainu epic); a review of Hermann J. Weigand's *Three Chapters on
Courtly Love in Arthurian France and Germany. 'Lancelot'—Andreas Capellanus—Wolfram von
Eschenbach's 'Parzival'* (Chapel Hill, NC, 1956), in *GLL*, NS 11 (1957/58), 57–60; 'Das Falkenlied
des Kürenbergers', *Euphorion*, 53 (1959), 20–23; 'Enid's best dress. A contribution to the
understanding of Chrétien's and Hartmann's *Erec* and the Welsh *Gereint*', *Euphorion*, 54 (1960),
437–41; '*Parzival* English', *GLL*, NS 15 (1961/62), 28–36; 'Das Tagelied in der Weltliteratur',
Deutsche Vierteljahrsschrift, 36 (1962), 489–506; 'Folk ritual and the Minnesang', *MLR*, 58
(1963), 196–209; (with D. Dalby) 'The historian of the hunt in Germany', *GLL*, NS 18 (1964/65),
189–93; 'Poetry and the hunt in medieval Germany', *Journal of the Australasian Universities
Modern Language Association*, 25 (1966), 33–56; 'Herzeloyde's Dragon-Dream', *GLL*, 22 (1968/69),
16–31; 'On the excellence of the *Hildebrandslied*: a comparative study in dynamics', *MLR*, 68
(1973), 820–38. Hatto also contributed essays to a number of Festschriften for Germanist
colleagues and conference proceedings. These include: ' "ine weiz …" Diplomatic Ignorance on
the Part of Medieval German Poets', in *German Studies Presented to Leonard Ashley Willoughby
by Pupils, Colleagues and Friends on His Retirement* (Oxford, 1952), pp. 98–107; 'Y a-t-il un roman
du Graal de Kyot le provençal?', in *Les romans du Graal aux XIIe et XIIIe siècles. IIIe Colloque:
Strasbourg, 29 mars—3 avril 1954*, Colloques internationaux du Centre National de la Recherche
Scientifique, 3 (Paris, 1956), pp. 167–84; ' "Der Aventiure meine" in Hartmann's Iwein', in A. T.
Hatto and M. O'C. Walshe (eds.), *Mediaeval German Studies. Presented to Frederick Norman by
his Students, Colleagues and Friends on the Occasion of his Retirement* (London, 1965), pp. 94–
103; 'The earliest extant Middle High German political songs: Friedrich von Hausen's "Si welnt
dem tode entrunnen sin" and "Ich gunde es guoten vrouwen niet" ', in P. Valentin and G. Zink
(eds.), *Mélanges pour Jean Fourquet* (Paris and Munich, 1969), pp. 137–45; 'Wolfram von
Eschenbach and the Chase', in Sigrid Schwenk *et al.* (eds), *Et multum et multa. Beiträge zur
Literatur, Geschichte und Kultur der Jagd. Festgabe für Kurt Lindner zum 27. November 1971*
(Berlin, 1971), pp. 101–12; 'Germanic and Kirgiz heroic poetry', in Brigitte Schludermann *et al.*
(eds.), *Deutung und Bedeutung: Studies in Germanic and Comparative Literature presented to
Karl-Werner Maurer* (The Hague and Paris, 1973), pp. 19–33 (Maurer had been a colleague at
University College London before the war); 'Die Höflichkeit des Herzens in der Dichtung der
mittelhochdeutschen Blütezeit', in Alfred Ebenbauer *et al.* (eds.), *Strukturen und Interpretationen.
Studien zur deutschen Philologie gewidmet Blanka Horacek zum 60. Geburtstag*, Philologica

in his *Essays on Medieval German and Other Poetry*, Anglica Germanica, 2 (Cambridge, 1980), arranged under the headings 'Love-poetry', 'Heroic poetry', 'Wolfram von Eschenbach' and 'Animal symbolism'. If one had to choose just a couple of essays to epitomise many of Hatto's outstanding qualities as an interpreter of literature, these might be 'Der minnen vederspil Isot',[14] and 'On the excellence of the *Hildebrandslied*: a comparative study in dynamics',[15] the latter appearing in the same year as he edited Frederick Norman's *Three Essays on the 'Hildebrandslied'*. In the former, dealing with a motif in Gottfried von Strassburg's *Tristan*, he brings to bear a wealth of knowledge, literary and practical, of falconry, parallels from other literary sources, study of the semantic field, and above all an appreciation of Gottfried's purposeful employment of metaphor to propose a solution to one of the most disputed interpretative issues in the work: he shows conclusively that it is the love potion that causes Tristan and Isolde to fall in love and not that they were already in love before they drank it. And in the essay on the *Hildebrandslied*, he demonstrates how the poet's presentation of the human drama of the deadly encounter between father and son displays far higher ethical and literary qualities than does treatment of the similar theme in Irish, Persian, and Russian heroic poetry.[16] This essay fruitfully brings together the two halves of Hatto's scholarly vision, as a Germanist and as a practitioner of comparative studies. Both essays represent philologically informed literary interpretation of the highest order—and all in the compass of a few pages! Virtually everything he wrote is characterised by unusual perspicacity and acuity, though his ingenuity was not always appreciated: for example, when he advanced his theory that the length of the strophes in the political songs of Walther von der Vogelweide reflected the social standing of the personage to whom they were addressed[17]—the twenty-four-line songs in

---

Germanica, 1 (Vienna, 1974), pp. 85–101; 'The secular foe and the *Nibelungenlied*', in Volker Honemann *et al.* (eds.), *German Narrative Literature of the Twelfth and Thirteenth Centuries. Studies presented to Roy Wisbey on his Sixty-fifth Birthday* (Tübingen, 1994), pp. 157–71.

[14] *Euphorion*, 51 (1957), 302–7; repr. in Alois Wolf (ed.), *Gottfried von Strassburg,* Wege der Forschung, 320 (Darmstadt, 1973), pp. 209–17.

[15] *MLR*, 68 (1973), 820–38.

[16] The article, reprinted in *Essays on Medieval German and other Poetry*, pp. 93–116, has, however, not met with universal admiration: see Jerome W. Clinton, 'The illusion of objectivity: A. T. Hatto on "The Story of Sohrāb" and the *Hildebranslied* [*sic*]', *Persica*, 17 (2001), 27–33, who declares that Hatto's piece is 'a caricature of what comparative literary studies should be—subjective and polemical where one looks for clarity and dispassion—and based on scholarship that is, at least with regard to the *Šāhnāme*, seriously deficient' (p. 29) and accuses him of western 'cultural bias' (p. 32).

[17] In *Speculum*, 24 (1949), 542–53.

the so-called 'Reichston' being directed to the Emperor, those in the shorter strophes to lesser princes—the experts were sceptical. In a letter of 16 May 1950 Carl von Kraus (1868–1952), the 'grand old man' of Walther studies, had indicated to Frederick Norman that he entertained doubts about the tenability of this thesis. Norman, replying on 23 May, wrote:

> [...] Hatto is extremely brilliant and extremely headstrong. He takes a great deal of convincing and he always prefers the difficult and abnormal if he can possibly find an excuse. Very stimulating and very dangerous. [...] I am, as you, most sceptical about the importance of patrons and the length of the strophes. This seems to me very fanciful and far too mechanistic. When I pointed out to Hatto that the mediaeval lyric was essentially a 'social' art and that the more social an art the less one could play esoteric tricks, he replied that he did not for a moment expect the audience to understand the references and that these references were merely meant for other poets. I fear I cannot agree [...].

And on 23 July, again to Norman, Kraus reinforced his doubts: 'Ihre Skepsis gegenüber der These Hattos, dass die Grösse der Strophen im Verhältnis zur Grösse der darin Besungenen stehe, teile ich durchaus. Die Rechnung geht auch nicht glatt auf.'[18]

As well as contributing numerous stimulating articles on several of the medieval German lyric poets—Kürenberg, Friedrich von Hausen, Walther von der Vogelweide, and Wolfram von Eschenbach, in particular—Hatto collaborated with his colleague Ronald Taylor (another pupil of Frederick Norman's) to publish a book on the thirteenth-century poet Neidhart: *The Songs of Neidhart von Reuental: 17 Summer and Winter Songs, set to their original melodies, with translations and a musical and metrical canon* (Manchester, 1958). This was the first fully critical edition of one of the most valuable groups of Minnesinger melodies to have survived.[19] A song by a Minnesinger, like one by a Troubadour or Trouvère, was a composite entity, blending literary and musical skills in a subtle interplay of conceptual and formal elements. Neidhart (*fl. c.* 1210–36), arguably the last great poet of the Middle Ages in Germany, injected a note of rustic exuberance into the increasingly sterile artificiality of the courtly Minnesang, but was criticised for this by Walther von der Vogelweide who lamented 'Alas,

---

[18] 'I entirely share your scepticism regarding Hatto's idea that the size of the strophes corresponds to the status of the persons to whom they are addressed. It just doesn't add up.' The correspondence between Norman and von Kraus is in the personal possession of the author.

[19] Despite its importance, the book received but a single review, by Norman, in *German Life and Letters*, NS 13 (1959), 155–7. Ronald Taylor, later to become Professor of German at the University of Sussex, made the music of the Minnesang one of his special fields, publishing *Die Melodien der weltlichen Lieder des Mittelalters* (Stuttgart, 1964) and *The Art of the Minnesinger* (Cardiff, 1968).

Courtly Song, that ever vulgar tones should have ousted you from court ...' In their study, Hatto and Taylor demonstrated that both musically and metrically the songs show a mathematical precision—Hatto's interest in such matters was surely a hang-over from his involvement with cryptography.[20] Neidhart's songs seem to have been dancing-songs; as such they held a particular fascination for Hatto in as much as the relevance of the seasonal, occasional, or ritual setting of poetic performances was so central to his enthusiasm for 'archaic' poetry.[21]

Hatto's publications discussed so far were addressed to a scholarly, mostly highly specialist audience. To the wider public, however, he is best known as a translator of medieval German narrative verse in the Penguin Classics series: Tristan,[22] Parzival,[23] and the Nibelungenlied.[24] How the Tristan translation came about is of interest. It was the result of a conversation between Hatto and E. V. Rieu, General Editor of the Penguin Classics series, over tea at a meeting of the London Medieval Society, of which Hatto was a co-founder. Rieu was there to hear a paper by Dorothy Sayers, who had translated the Chanson de Roland for Penguin. Hatto asked Rieu what he thought of the great medieval German poems. He replied that he had not really encountered them. Hatto persuaded him that the classic version of the Tristan story was that by Gottfried von Strassburg, and Rieu invited him to submit a specimen. This he did, and

[20] While Hatto was investigating 'the beauty of numbers' in medieval poetry around 1950, Norman had written to Carl von Kraus on 12 May 1950, as follows: 'Taylor is carrying on a furious intellectual battle with my old student A. T. Hatto, who is developing the most astonishing esoteric notions on numbers in mediaeval love poetry.' Kraus, for his part, was much more favourably impressed by the work of the Dutch scholar, Johannes Alphonsus Huisman, whose book *Neue Wege zur dichterischen und musikalischen Technik Walthers von der Vogelweide. Mit einem Exkurs über die symmetrische Zahlenkomposition im Mittelalter*, Studia litteraria Rheno-Traiectina, 1 (Utrecht, 1950), had just appeared.
[21] Witness also his article 'Stonehenge and midsummer: a new interpretation', *Man*, 151 (1953), 101–6, in which he advanced his view that the stones were a representation of a spring fertility dance. This theory was sharply debated in subsequent numbers of the journal. Interesting as it was, it has not stood the test of time, but Hatto himself treasured as high praise the archaeologist Stuart Piggott's reported comment on the idea: 'This is not mad.'
[22] *Gottfried von Strassburg: Tristan. Translated Entire for the First Time. With The Surviving Fragments of the Tristran of Thomas, Newly Translated* (Harmondsworth, 1960; rev. edn., 1967).
[23] *Wolfram von Eschenbach: Parzival* (Harmondsworth, 1980). One of his doctoral students, Linda B. Parshall, wrote a thesis on 'The art of narration in Wolfram's *Parzival* and Albrecht's *Jüngerer Titurel*' in 1974; this was published under the same title at Cambridge in 1980.
[24] *Nibelungenlied* (Harmondsworth, 1965, rev. 1969). The first half of this translation (Âventiuren 1–17 (i.e. down to and including 'How Siegfried was lamented and buried')) was reissued, bereft of context or commentary, in 2006 under the title *Siegfried's Murder,* as one of 'the greatest stories ever told' as volume 15 in the 'Penguin epics' series.

the deal was soon done. The translation includes also Hatto's rendering of the surviving fragment of the *Tristan* of Thomas (of Britain, or of Brittany[25]), which happily begins within a few lines of where Gottfried's text breaks off, and thus ensures that Penguin readers are not left guessing what fate overtook the lovers.

As Hatto wrote in the introduction to his *Tristan* translation (pp. 30–1),

> To place Gottfried's *Tristan* in its true perspective it must be stressed that it is but one of four great narrative poems in medieval German, the others being the *Parzival* and the *Willehalm* of Wolfram von Eschenbach, and the epic *Nibelungenlied*, all written within twenty years of one another at the beginning of the thirteenth century. Together with the songs of leading Minnesinger like Heinrich von Morungen, Walther von der Vogelweide, and Neidhart von Reuental, these longer poems make an age of great literature as yet unsuspected by readers of English at large. German genius has sometimes been over-cried in its native land, so that where there is a hindrance to its appreciation as here— only a discipline as exacting as that of classical studies will unlock the door to it—others have taken the line of least resistance and ignored the just claims to their attention of this fascinating poetry. Even that great master of medieval literatures, W. P. Ker, shows few signs of having savoured the poetry of the Hohenstauffen age of Germany. Here, then, is a lost world of the imagination awaiting discovery by the curious, and here, as a beginning, is Gottfried's *Tristan*, which, unless I have sadly betrayed it, should bring a shock of delight to those who were expecting an Arthurian romance, a Tennysonian idyll, or a Wagnerian melodrama; or who imagined that in the year AD 1210 Germany was still altogether in the Dark Ages.

Here, in essence, was Hatto's 'programme' for medieval German studies. Of the 'four great narrative poems' he himself tackled three.[26] Each of the translations is accompanied by supporting materials, introducing and contextualising the works and offering interpretative guidance. Hatto's colleague F. P. Pickering (1909–81), Professor of German at Reading and himself an eminent medievalist, is on record as saying that the introduction to *Tristan* was the best thing he had ever read on that work. Similarly, Alois Wolf considered it was Hatto's 'balanced judgement' that made the introduction to his 'masterly' (*meisterhaft*) and 'indispensable' (*unentbehrlich*) translation 'one of the most satisfying manifestations of recent Gottfried research'.[27] If one reads the introduction to Hatto's *Parzival*,

---

[25] For discussion of this problem see Hatto's 'Note on Thomas's Tristan' on pp. 355–63 of the translation.

[26] The fourth, Wolfram von Eschenbach's *Willehalm*, would be published in the same series by his pupil, Marion E. Gibbs (together with Sidney M. Johnson) in 1984.

[27] Wolf (ed.), *Gottfried von Strassburg* (see above, n. 14), p. IX: 'Hier wäre auch die Einleitung [...] zu erwähnen, die wegen ihres ausgewogenen Urteils zu den erfreulichsten Erscheinungen der neueren Gottfriedforschung gehört.'

one is struck by the boldness and assurance with which he writes on a range of critical issues that might nowadays be handled much more equivocally. His *Nibelungenlied* is particularly notable for the extensive ancillary material that it provides, including discussion of the possible processes by which historical events were transformed into legend, summaries of the most important cognate texts in Old Norse and other languages, and a detailed 'Introduction to a Second Reading' which still stands, even after almost half a century, as one of the best short overviews of the work in English or, indeed, in any language—in particular it provides a remarkably sane and lucid guide which will be appreciated by anyone who has had to struggle with the theories of Andreas Heusler, Friedrich Panzer, Gottfried Weber and others concerning the complexities of the subject. The three narratives are quite distinct in character, and each presents its own particular challenges to the translator in respect of form, language, and style. Hatto aimed for translations which would be eminently readable by his contemporaries, while maintaining the greatest possible fidelity to the sense and style of the originals—he was acutely aware that perfection was unattainable. He succeeded in producing stylish, non-archaising prose versions which mirror the high literary qualities of the three works and which display a sensitivity to the subtle distinctions of meaning which need to be teased out from the often polysemous medieval vocabulary, particularly in the area of ethical evaluation, in order to convey to the modern reader the precise nuances of words in their given contexts. This precision has meant that his renderings have sometimes been criticised for being somewhat mannered and precious, excessively coloured by the translator's own literariness—some of today's students find him quite a hard read!—but for the medieval German specialist who will be aware of the dangers of working mechanically with fixed renderings for particular items of vocabulary, the care taken in the latter regard makes Hatto's translations into sustained commentaries on the texts which are of inestimable value. His insistence on precise, where necessary specialised, language led him to encourage postgraduate students to undertake lexica of well-defined areas of medieval life, a notably successful example of such an undertaking being David Dalby's *Lexicon of the Mediæval German Hunt. A Lexicon of Middle High German Terms, 1050–1500, associated with the Chase, Hunting with Bows, Falconry, Trapping and Fowling* (Berlin, 1965).

The *Tristan* translation gave him especial pleasure, as is evident from his reported conversation with his father when it appeared. His father had offered him a belated apology for having entered him on the Modern Side at Dulwich some thirty-five years earlier, rather than on the Classical Side to read Greek. 'Not at all, Father', he replied. 'Having done German, I was eventually able to translate a world masterpiece, Gottfried's *Tristan*, for the first time anywhere, whereas had I read Classics I might have been tempted to translate Homer for the n-thousandth time!'

The success of his *Tristan* translation led to an invitation from John Asher (1921–96), Professor of German at Auckland and a pupil of Friedrich Ranke, a great-nephew of the historian Leopold von Ranke and editor of the then standard edition of *Tristan*, to visit New Zealand for several months in 1965. This took him to Istanbul, Delhi, Kathmandu, and Bangkok before reaching Auckland. At Wellington he was thrilled to make the acquaintance of John Cawte Beaglehole, editor of *The Journals of Captain James Cook* (Cambridge, 1955 ff.). After lecturing at all of New Zealand's universities, he returned via Fiji, Hawaii, California, the Grand Canyon, and New York where he was delighted to acquire a copy of K. K. Yudakhin's *Kirgizsko–Russkij slovar* (Moscow, 1965), a Kirghiz–Russian dictionary which would prove invaluable for his later scholarly endeavours.

Hatto was a scholar of prodigious energy. In the same year as his *Nibelungenlied* translation appeared he also published *Eos: an Enquiry into the Theme of Lovers' Meetings and Partings at Dawn in Poetry* (The Hague, 1965), the fruit of his first large-scale collaborative enterprise, involving over fifty specialists, which had occupied him since about 1952. He himself, as general editor, contributed the masterly 'general survey' (pp. 17–102), the chapter on Mediaeval German (pp. 428–72), and the appendix on imagery and symbolism (pp. 771–819). His interest in the dawn song can be traced back at least to the early 1950s when he published his short articles 'On beauty of numbers in Wolfram's dawn songs' and 'An early *Tagelied*' in *The Modern Language Review*. That the volume took so long to appear was principally due to the difficulty of finding a publisher for so large an enterprise; that it appeared at all was thanks to a substantial subvention from UNESCO, arranged through the good offices of Louis L. Hammerich, Professor of German at Copenhagen. This taught Hatto a painful lesson: that without patronage scholarship would inevitably wither.

Although Hatto was a professor of German and is undoubtedly best known to the general public as a translator of medieval German poetry, his real interests lay in a much broader field. Indeed he described himself as 'a student of archaic poetry masquerading as a Professor of German', and after his retirement from the Chair at Queen Mary College in 1977 he rarely published on medieval German literature again, in 1981 even declaring himself to be 'thoroughly out of touch with Mediaeval European studies'.[28] 'What has dominated my life of scholarship', he wrote in his own unpublished memoir, 'is a preoccupation with the Archaic Imagination, with its fresh, direct, compelling because profound traditional imagery of flora, fauna, luminaries, places and numina.' Already in *Eos* he had written pieces on Turkic and on the Dyak of Borneo, and from the later 1960s the proportion of his output devoted especially to Asian heroic narrative increased markedly—to the somewhat bemused admiration of the one-subject orthodoxy then prevailing in academe. His Asian interests were, in fact, of long standing, as is evident from his recollection of having given a paper on Yakut tales at Frederick Norman's folktale seminar at University College just before the war, the argument of which, he remembered, Anna Freud had summarily dismissed with (in Hatto's opinion) an appallingly inapt reduction of the tale's brother–sister protagonists to oedipal types.[29] Hatto's interest in the mythological and cultural aspects of the heroic poetry of the Yakuts, cattle-rearing Turks who had migrated to high northern latitudes, was long-lasting, as may be seen from several of his papers.[30] These essays represented the fruits of his having been awarded a Leverhulme Emeritus Fellowship following his retirement from Queen Mary College in 1977. This enabled him to devote himself single-mindedly to the study of heroic poetry in Central Asia and Siberia, especially that

---

[28] Letter to W. J. Jones, 5 June 1981. Nevertheless, in 1994 he did publish 'The secular foe and the *Nibelungenlied*', in the Festschrift for his colleague Roy Wisbey (Professor of German at King's College London, 1971–94), in which he showed that the key to the problem of the emergence of the 'friendly' image of Attila in German heroic poetry lies not in tribal history but in the dynamics of epic structure. This essay, he told the editors at the time, he believed was his best piece on the subject.

[29] This reminiscence is found in a revealing 'personal note' in 'Xara Kıırčıt—An enquiry into brother–sister relations in Yakut epic poetry', *Zentralasiatische Studien*, 14/1 (1980), 109–37, here p. 127. Norman had set up his Seminar on the Comparative Study of Folktales in 1936, not least, apparently, to enhance his bid to succeed Priebsch in the Chair of German but also because his young daughter had an insatiable appetite for fairytales and folktales. In particular it was concerned to investigate brother–sister relationships. While several of Norman's pupils, including Kenneth King, Peter Magill, and Maurice Walshe, were entrusted with the tales of European countries, Hatto was charged with gathering material from non-European areas. (Most of the material collected was later destroyed in an air raid on University College.) Reading in the library of the Folklore Society, housed at University College, Hatto revelled in the writings of Arthur Waley on Chinese and Japanese. Waley, along with Norman and Firth, Hatto regarded as the three most formative academic influences on his young life.

[30] For example, 'Zwei Beiträge zur oloŋχo-Forschung: I. Das Oloŋχo und die benachbarten Überlieferungen; II. Xān Jargistai—a Yakut epic trilogy', in W. Heissig (ed.), *Fragen der mongolischen Heldendichtung*, III, Asiatische Forschungen, 91 (Wiesbaden, 1985), pp. 446–529, 'Shamanism in the Yakut epic trilogy "Xan Jargistai"', *Ural-Altaische Jahrbücher*, NS 5 (1985), 146–67, and 'On some Siberian and other Copper-Crones', *Journal de la Société Finno-Ougrienne*, 85 (1994), 71–105.

of the Yakuts, for which he went to Helsinki to obtain material. He never ceased to be grateful to Lord Leverhulme who had had the imagination to perceive the needs of elderly scholars suddenly cut off from their privileges at their universities.

It is astonishing with what sureness but lightness of touch Hatto displays in his various writings his profound knowledge of the folklore of unfamiliar peoples such as the Selkups, the Ostyaks, the Kets, the Ewenki, indeed the whole of the wider Siberian and Far Eastern world down to the Orotschon and the Ainu on the edge of the Pacific Ocean. Already in the early 1950s Hatto appeared in a list of colleagues that includes leading figures in Oriental studies in the preface to Arthur Llewellyn Basham's monumental *The Wonder that was India: a Survey of the Culture of the Indian Sub-continent before the Coming of the Muslims* (London, 1954). Although it is not clear what Hatto had done to deserve this acknowledgement, it seems almost uncanny that Basham, the SOAS guru, should already be in this curious Germanist's debt. Clearly, he was already becoming noticed there—and indeed elsewhere. Papers he presented to the Mycenaean Seminar at the Institute of Classical Studies in 1959 and the African History Seminar at SOAS in 1960 would eventually form the basis of his foreword to Henry Francis Morris's *The Heroic Recitations of the Bahima of Ankole* (Oxford, 1964), in itself a *tour de force* as a wide-ranging disquisition on the cattle-raid as one of the most fertile themes of epic, from the Iliad to Wild West tales: he ranges over Greek myth, the Rig Veda, the Old Irish 'Cattle-raid of Cooley', and the legends of the Narts and Ossetes. Morris's book concerns the poetry in Runyankore (a Bantu language) devoted to the lifting and defence of the beautiful cattle of the Ankole district of Uganda, so greatly cherished by the aristocratic and warlike Bahima. What attracted Hatto about this material was 'the metrical boast of deeds done about the herds, in a language thick with kennings' (p. v).

Already during the war Hatto had taught himself Greek in order to be able to read Homer in the original. But what he regarded as 'the most important freely considered step' in the whole of his career was his resolve, at the age of about fifty, to teach himself Russian to overcome his frustration at his inability to access writings on ethnography and epic poetry written in that language. This would occupy him between the hours of 11 p.m. and 2 a.m., over a period of some two years, after his normal academic and domestic duties had been done. Having mastered Russian, he had then taught himself Kirghiz. These endeavours enabled him to expand enormously his knowledge of oral epic poetry. His efforts received support and encouragement from men like Arthur Waley, the Turkologist Sir Gerard

Clauson, the Mongolist Charles Bawden, his friend from his Bletchley days Bernard Lewis, and—from a distance—the Kazakh academician Älkey Margulan. He acquired an excellent reading knowledge of Kirghiz but, to his regret, was unable to speak it fluently—he was, as he himself admitted, essentially a deskbound ethnologist though he would have dearly loved to have carried out fieldwork in Asia. Nevertheless, it gave him much delight to try out what he called his 'Latin Kirghiz'—learned like a dead language—'after hours' at a conference at Turku in 1996.

He began publishing extensively on Kirghiz poetry, in a series of essays, all of them highly original, in the late 1960s. [31] Kirghiz material featured prominently in the Foundation Day Lecture he gave at the School of Oriental and African Studies in 1970, and in 1976 a lecture he gave to the Royal Asiatic Society was also devoted to it. For the SOAS lecture, later published, he chose as his subject *Shamanism and Epic Poetry in Northern Asia*—he had already tackled the subject of shamanism in an earlier essay exemplifying his organic approach to the art of archaic societies.[32] In the Foundation Day Lecture, he perspicaciously discerned links between shamans and bards as lying 'in the excitement bordering on ecstasy of

[31] They include: 'The Birth of Manas: a confrontation of two branches of heroic epic poetry in Kirgiz', *Asia Major*, NS 14 (1968–9), 217–41; 'Almambet, Er Kökcö and Ak Erkec', *Central Asiatic Journal*, 13 (1969), 161–98; '*Kukotay* and *Bok Murun*: a comparison of two related heroic poems of the Kirgiz', *Bulletin of the School of Oriental and African Studies*, 32 (1969), 344–78 and 541–70; 'Köz-Kaman', *Central Asiatic Journal*, 15 (1971), 81–101 and 241–83; 'The Kirgiz original of *Kukotay* found', *Bulletin of the School of Oriental and African Studies*, 34 (1971), 379–86; 'Semetey', *Asia Major*, 18 (1973), 154–80 and 19 (1974), 1–36; 'The catalogue of heroes and heroines in the Kirgiz *Joloi-kan*', in W. Heissig *et al.* (eds.), *Tractata Altaica* (Wiesbaden, 1976), pp. 237–60 (this volume was a Festschrift for the distinguished Hungarian-American Professor of Central Asian Studies at Indiana University); ' "Ak saraylap, kök saraylap" in Kirghiz epic poetry of the mid-nineteenth century', in R. Dor and M. Nicolas (eds.), *Quand le crible était dans la paille...: Hommage à Pertev Naili Boratav* (Paris, 1978), pp. 255–65; 'The attitude to nature in the mid-nineteenth-century Kirghiz epics', *Materialia Turcica*, 4 (1978), 22–7; 'Zyklische Anspielungen und Epitheta in der altkirgisischen Heldenepik', in W. Heissig (ed.), *Fragen der mongolischen Heldendichtung*, I, Asiatische Forschungen, 72 (Wiesbaden, 1979), 217–30; 'Das Pferd in der älteren kirghisischen Heldenepik und in der Ilias', in W. Heissig (ed.), *Fragen der mongolischen Heldendichtung*, II (Wiesbaden, 1980), 178–201; 'The marriage, death and return to life of Manas', *Turcica*, 12 (1980), 66–94 and 14 (1982), 7–38; 'Jantay. A Kirghiz lament for a chieftain, dated 1867–1869', in K. Sagaster and M. Weiers (eds.), *Documenta Barbarorum*, Veröffentlichungen der Societas Uralo-Altaica, 18 (Wiesbaden, 1983), pp. 186–95; 'Mongols in mid-nineteenth-century Kirghiz epic', in W. Heissig and K. Sagaster (eds.), *Gedanke und Wirkung. Festschrift zum 90. Geburtstag von Nikolaus Poppe*, Asiatische Forschungen, 108 (Wiesbaden, 1989), pp. 140–5; and 'Die Marschrouten in der älteren kirghisischen Heldenepik', in W. Heissig (ed.), *Fragen der mongolischen Heldendichtung*, V, Asiatische Forschungen, 120 (Wiesbaden, 1992), pp. 331–42.

[32] 'The Swan Maiden: a folk-tale of North Eurasian origin?', *Bulletin of the School of Oriental and African Studies*, 24 (1961), 326–52.

improvisation; in a dream- or trance-like style of first-personal narration; in a narrative content in the form of initiatory tests and heroic journeys to the Otherworld, marked by battle with spirits and monsters or by other encounters by land, air or water' (p. 3). His range of reference was breath-taking: the Sumerian poem 'Gilgamesh and the Huluppu Tree' (2000 BC), the Babylonian *Epic of Gilgamesh*, the Greek *Odyssey*, the Old English *Beowulf*, the twelfth-century Russian *Raid of Igor*, the Finnish *Kalevala*, the epic of the Ostyak and Vogul, the 'songs about giants' and the 'laments' of the Samoyed, the cosmos of the Yakut, Tungus heroic poetry, the Ainu of north Japan who referred to death as 'space for thought' and whose epic *Kutune Shirka* Hatto, 'in respectful disagreement with Arthur Waley', held to be partly shamanistic, and concluding with discussion of the Kirghiz oral heroic tradition, the most important living specimen of the genre. Of this he wrote, 'Desire for a national epic in the grand manner has led in the twentieth century to the triumph of cyclic tendencies already marked in the nineteenth. Highly gifted bards [...] have played their part in this decline with their vast inflation of motifs, with their Pan-Islamic moralisings or their class-conscious twists' (p. 17). The national hero Manas had all but engulfed Kirghiz folk-tradition—half a million lines of *Manas* were said to have been recorded.

Editing *Eos* had demonstrated what could be achieved by collaboration on themes and genres of international interest, and now, fired by his enthusiasm for heroic narrative, Hatto embarked on a still more ambitious project. In his view, Maurice Bowra's *Heroic Poetry* (London, 1952) had taken the subject as far as one person could: it was time to pool expertise. In 1964 the London Seminar on Epic was formed, a joint venture between Queen Mary College and SOAS, bringing together a hand-picked elite of some two dozen leading specialists. Whereas the dawn-song project had been conducted through correspondence between the contributors and the editor, the members of the Seminar on Epic, their numbers sometimes fortified by visits from distinguished guests from afar such as Viktor Zhirmunsky, met regularly about six times a year until 1972 and gave papers on their field, followed by mild conviviality (at Hatto's suggestion, the reader of the paper rewarding his listeners with liquor as near as feasible to that drunk by the audiences of the epic tradition in question) and intensely focused discussion. The result was the monumental two-volume *Traditions of Heroic and Epic Poetry,* issued under Hatto's general editorship.[33] To

---

[33] *Traditions of Heroic and Epic Poetry. Volume 1: The Traditions* and *Volume 2: Characteristics and Techniques*, Publications of the Modern Humanities Research Association, vols. 9 and 13

Volume 1 he contributed chapters on Medieval German (pp. 165–95) and Kirghiz (pp. 300–27), and to Volume 2 on epithets in Kirghiz epic poetry (pp. 71–93) and the enormously influential essay 'Towards an anatomy of heroic/epic poetry' (pp. 145–294), in which the context-sensitive programme foreshadowed in Bowra's best writing reached maturity as a many-sided conversation, markedly ethnographic in character, involving the bearers of the traditions themselves, the discerning scholar, and his expert interlocutors in the Seminar.

There is a consensus among specialists that Hatto's most important contribution to theory about heroic and epic poetry was his concept of 'epic moments', about which he wrote eloquently in his 'General introduction' to Volume 1 of *Traditions* and in his 1990 lecture *Eine allgemeine Theorie der Heldenepik*,[34] in both places acknowledging his indebtedness to his Munich colleague Hugo Kuhn (1909–78) for the kernel of the idea.[35] In his 'General introduction' Hatto observed that 'Epic poetry is apt to condense long-drawn tensions into brief scenes of dramatic power enhanced by visual magnificence, that is, "epic moments"' (p. 4) and, after two pages of illustrative examples, then adds: 'Epic moments are highly charged narrative ganglia, and it is suggested here as one of the fruits of comparative study that possession of them in memory confers power on the mature bard to build up an episode or even a string of episodes. In other words, it is suggested that epic moments, in addition to being great poetry are mnemonic elements of epic of an order altogether superior to that of "themes" or "formulae", now so well-discussed: and that they will therefore mark or help to mark the structures of epics' (p. 6).[36] We can follow Hatto working his way towards the concept of 'epic moments' when he writes: 'Such exciting epic-dramatic plots knitted into veritable ganglia of wills convey high points in the lives of a multiplicity of heroes with shared fates [...].'[37] And again, somewhat later: 'A tense ethos, however

---

(London, 1980–9). A sketch of the history of the Seminar is given by J. B. Hainsworth in *Traditions*, vol. 2, pp. 307–11.

[34] *Eine allgemeine Theorie der Heldenepik*, Rheinisch-Westfälische Akademie der Wissenschaften, Vorträge G, Heft 307 (Opladen, 1991).

[35] See Hugo Kuhn, 'Über nordische und deutsche Szenenregie in der Nibelungendichtung', in Hermann Schneider (ed.), *Edda, Skalden, Saga: Festschrift zum 70. Geburtstag von Felix Genzmer* (Heidelberg, 1952), pp. 279–306, and reprinted in Kuhn's *Dichtung und Welt im Mittelalter* (Stuttgart, 1959), pp. 196–219.

[36] It is characteristic of Hatto's modesty that this major theoretical innovation, which was certainly all his own work, was 'suggested here as one of the fruits of comparative study'.

[37] 'Plot and character in mid-nineteenth century Kirgiz epic', in W. Heissig (ed.), *Die mongolischen Epen. Bezüge, Sinndeutung und Überlieferung* (Wiesbaden), 1979, pp. 95–112, here p. 96. This

well heroes may disguise it with nonchalance and courtesy, surely breeds laconism and pregnant "moments" in which visual gestures condense much action?'[38] Hatto's concept of 'epic moments' has since been fruitfully taken up and developed by Daniel Prior who argues that epic moments can be used as diagnostic, diachronic indicators of the 'heroic' in an epic tradition.[39] Likewise, John D. Smith has demonstrated how a Rajasthani oral epic was structured in such a way that a series of 'epic moments' signalled the enactment and discharge of the narrative 'contracts' that constituted the plot.[40] Scholars such as Smith, Prior and Reichl[41] are not the only ones who regard the concept of 'epic moments' as the most significant contribution to theoretical writing on the topic since Milman Parry's work in the 1930s. Yet even so the idea has not yet gained the broad attention it deserves, partly no doubt because the comparative study of epic traditions is still strongly influenced by Albert Bates Lord (1912–91) and his book *The Singer of Tales* (Cambridge, MA, 1960). For his part, Hatto always distanced himself from the 'oral-formulaic theory', much in vogue when the London Seminar was operating but which he considered too mechanistic: his concern was rather with illuminating aesthetic and ritual peculiarities and their comparison.[42] Members of the London Seminar had already recognised that Lord's desire to impose his Serbo-Croat model on all traditions, not least the Homeric, was misguided if only because the Serbo-Croat tradition of heroic poetry took the form of ballads and lays, not epics. In any case, Hatto's own approach to the subject was developing

---

paper was largely based on the lecture he had given to the Royal Asiatic Society in June 1976. See also *Traditions*, vol. 2 (1989), pp. 145–306, here pp. 172, 178–80.

[38] 'What is a lay? Reflections on the Germanic, Serbo-Croat, and Fula', in M. Branch and C. Hawkesworth (eds.), *The Uses of Tradition: a Comparative Enquiry into the Nature, Uses and Functions of Oral Poetry in the Balkans, the Baltic, and Africa* (London, 1994), pp. 123–34, here p. 125.

[39] See D. Prior, *The Twilight Age of the Kirghiz Epic Tradition*. Ph.D. dissertation, Indiana University, Bloomington, 2002; and his essay, 'Sparks and embers of the Kirghiz epic tradition', *Fabula*, 51 (2010), 23–37. Prior also makes use of the concept in his edition of *The Semetey of Kenje Kara: A Kirghiz Epic Performance on Phonograph* (Wiesbaden, 2006).

[40] See J. D. Smith, 'Where the plot thickens: Epic moments in Pābūjī', *South Asian Studies*, 2 (1986), 53–64; also his 'How to sing a tale: Epic performance in the Pābūjī tradition', in *Traditions of Heroic and Epic Poetry*, vol. 2, pp. 29–41, and *The Epic of Pābūjī: a Study, Transcription and Translation* (Cambridge, 1991).

[41] See Karl Reichl, *Singing the Past: Turkic and Medieval Heroic Poetry* (Ithaca, NY, and London, 2000). For all that the importance of Hatto's work has been recognised in western scholarly circles, it has so far had little impact among native Kirghiz scholars, whose preoccupations are generally with the folklorised Manas versions of the twentieth century.

[42] For Hatto's views on Lord see his paper 'What is a lay?'.

before Lord's book appeared. Rather he took the work of scholars such as Sir Maurice Bowra (particularly his *Heroic Poetry* (London, 1952) and *Primitive Song* (London, 1962)) and Viktor Zhirmunsky and his book *Narodnij geroicheskiy epos* (Moscow, 1962) as his models.

The Kirghiz material became an abiding passion with him, from the 1960s through to the 1990s. He gave many lectures, chiefly at symposia organised by the Mongolist Walther Heissig (1913–2005) at Bonn, where together with like-minded colleagues (experts in Mongolian, Kazakh, Karakalpak, Buryat, Tibetan, and Sinologists with knowledge of the archaic minorities of China) he would engage in productive and enthrallingly fascinating debate. He came to be admired as above all a remarkably well-read, observant interpreter of texts, who always had something new and fresh to say. More significantly, he produced editions of Kirghiz material which were models of their kind, setting new standards and showing him to be a first-rate philologist. These were the *Memorial Feast for Kökötöy-khan* in 1977,[43] and in 1990 the *Manas* of Wilhelm Radloff (V. V. Radlov, 1837–1918), with its parallel Kirghiz text and English translation.[44] With them he had edited the entire corpus of mid-nineteenth-century Kirghiz epic poetry on Manas, the supra-tribal hero of the Kirghiz. Evaluating them, Daniel Prior has written: 'The editor's hand, steadied by long experience in the mature field of medieval textual criticism, reveals not only an original scholar, but also—in its assiduous mediation between predecessors' flawed efforts, the needs of his contemporaries, and the oral artistry of the bards—a scholar's scholar.'[45]

Altogether, with his many books and articles Hatto established himself firmly in the growing world of solidly language-based comparative study of poetry from archaic heroic cultures, a field to which he himself, following the inspiration of tutors and writers alike but against the mainstream of self-contained specialisation, had contributed so much by participation, encouragement, and example. Among his many essays, especially 'Towards an anatomy of heroic and epic poetry', *Eine allgemeine Theorie der Heldenepik*, and his 1993 Bonn symposium paper on the possibility of

---

[43] *The Memorial Feast for Kökötöy-khan (Kökötöydün ašı): a Kirghiz epic poem, edited for the first time from a photocopy of the unique manuscript with translation and commentary by A. T. Hatto*, London Oriental series, 33 (Oxford and New York, 1977). The original Kirghiz text is in the archive of the Oriental Institute of the Academy of Sciences at St Petersburg.
[44] *The Manas of Wilhelm Radloff, re-edited, newly translated and with a commentary by Arthur T. Hatto*, Asiatische Forschungen, 110 (Wiesbaden, 1990).
[45] Personal communication.

developing 'ethnopoetics',[46] are perhaps his finest: not only do they embody scholarship of the highest order but they are also extraordinarily stimulating in their breadth and depth.

In 1999, pioneering still towards the end of his ninth decade, he did the characteristically unexpected thing and published *The Mohave Heroic Epic of Inyo-kutavêre, reappraised and further interpreted by Arthur T. Hatto; on the basis of the edition of A. L. Kroeber and consultation of his field record,* (Helsinki, 1999), a study of an almost totally forgotten Native American epic on the basis of a record of a near-simultaneous English translation of a live performance, written down in the field by Alfred Louis Kroeber (1876–1960) in 1902. Kroeber, then twenty-six and teaching at the University of California, was determined to record as much as possible of the ways of life and languages of the Native Americans, including the Mohave, at the edge of Arizona. He found an informant, Inyo-kutavêre, who told him, however, that he had never told the story of his people from beginning to end. Kroeber and his interpreter listened to three or four hours of narration, and as many of translation and writing, over each of six days without reaching the end. Inyo-kutavêre thought one more day would suffice, but Kroeber was overdue at Berkeley. He promised to return by the next winter, and did, but by then Inyo-kutavêre had died. Kroeber did not bring the material to publication until 1951,[47] since when Inyo-kutavêre's narrative had lain largely unnoticed. Hatto had no doubt that it belonged to the genre of heroic epic. It had the high seriousness demanded by Aristotle, a firm structure, which Hatto believed to be inherited, not improvised, and an almost perfect purism as to time. It was a stirring story of leaving a valley promised by the source of the Mohaves' way of life, Mastamho, then fighting to regain it, first with failure, then with success. There are protagonists and antagonists, heroic warriors and fatal combats between equals. And here again there were 'epic moments'. Hatto's book is an important stimulus to thinking about the Mohave and neighbouring traditions, and to thinking about Native American narrative more generally.

The turn of the millennium saw Hatto immersed in the heroic epic poetry of a north-west Siberian people, the Obugrian Ostyaks (or Khanty), on whom he had already written in 1970. His last book, *The World of the Ostyak Epic Hero Princes*, is currently being edited for publication. The

[46] 'Ethnopoetik—Traum oder Möglichkeit?', in W. Heissig (ed.), *Formen und Funktionen mündlicher Tradition*, Abhandlungen der Nordrhein-Westfälischen Akademie der Wissenschaften, 9, 1995, pp. 11–25.
[47] A. L. Kroeber, *A Mohave Historical Epic* (Berkeley, CA, 1951).

monograph is based on eighteen epics, totalling some 22,000 long epic lines, recorded mostly in 1844 with the remainder from the end of the nineteenth century. Hatto regarded these epics as of unusually high quality. The singers were obviously intelligent and perceptive. Their epics are firmly existential and supported the ethos of communities which had mastered the harsh Ob-Irtysh environment and had courageously maintained their animistic beliefs under long persecution by the czar's servitors. To his mind, the corpus of Ostyak heroic epic poetry comes nearest of all the better known oral traditions to that of the Ionians, as one may imagine it at its still fully oral stage. Through the involvement of two different generations of singers one can even see how formulae and themes grow and are varied through time. The book, which is believed to be the very first attempt to open the way for Ostyak folklore traditions to reach international recognition, provides a meticulous analysis of the 'world' of the Ostyak Hero-Princes, which, like that of other heroes of epic, is a web of fact and fiction. No attempt is made to unravel that web, but often, where he scents useful data for archaeologists and other historians, Hatto marks them clearly in his footnotes and elucidates wherever he can.

To the very end of his long, uncommonly rich life Hatto thus remained intellectually active and buoyant. His life of study, as he put it, 'had been one long romp'. His zest for learning knew no boundaries, and he was ever generous in the help he offered to others. He had a breadth of interest, scholarly curiosity and sympathetic understanding that seemed to have an almost Victorian quality. Indeed, he had been born in the Edwardian era, but it was never easy to remember this when confronted with someone so mentally agile and so young at heart (for many years he drove a white sports car which, with his fondness for animal imagery, he called 'the white wolf' and referred to deprecatingly as 'a *boy's* car'). He was a scholar of massive erudition who wore his learning lightly and who was able, with the lightest of touches, to illuminate empirical thoroughness with gentle flashes of theory; an urbane gentleman with an impish sense of humour; a man who hated pretension and would always expose it with old-world politeness. He hoped that posterity would recognise, first, that, in *Eos* and *Traditions* he had laid the foundations of what he called 'ethnopoetics' and, secondly, that with his general theory of epic heroic poetry he had formulated an oral and universal approach, to be set beside Aristotle's textually enshrined and parochially Greek study.

Arthur Hatto was elected a Senior Fellow of the British Academy in 1991. He was also a Fellow or Honorary Fellow of three colleges of the University of London: King's (1971), the School of Oriental and African

Studies (1981), and Queen Mary (1992). In 1978 he had become a
Corresponding Member of the Finno-Ugrian Society and, in 1984, a
Foreign Member of the Seminar for Central Asian Languages and Cultures
in the University of Bonn. Though he gave up active research in 2005, he
developed a lively interest in the study of English social history, and was
still reading in Russian until early 2009. He died on 6 January 2010. A
service of thanksgiving for his life was held on 26 January 2010 at the
church of St Leonard at Flamstead, the Hertfordshire village where he had
made his home since moving from Mill Hill in 2004.

JOHN L. FLOOD
University of London

Note. This account owes much to Arthur Hatto's own 'Guidance for a sympathetic
Obituarist', a typescript he completed on his eighty-third birthday, the property of the
British Academy, which has been generously made available to me. Professor Hatto's
daughter, Mrs Jane Lutman, has also generously provided me with much personal
information about her father, and I have also benefited from the obituaries in *The
Times* (19 March 2010), by Dr Daniel Prior in *Fabula*, 51 (2010), 1–4, and by Dr Katalin
Uray-Kőhalmi in *Acta Orientalia Academiae Scientiarum Hungaricae*, 63 (2010), 383–6.
Mrs Lutman also very kindly supplied me with her father's own fairly full list of his
publications. A list of his publications (excluding his reviews[48]) from 1934 to 1976 was
published in the Special Number of *German Life and Letters*, ns 30, 2 (January 1977),
172–6, but as far as I am aware, no published list of his many writings from 1976 to
2010 has appeared, a deficiency I have attempted to make good in the foregoing pages.
I am grateful to Mrs Calista M. Lucy, Keeper of the Archives at Dulwich College, for
information about Arthur Hatto's schooldays. For personal reminiscences, expert
opinions, and additional information I am greatly indebted to the following: Dr Daniel
Prior (Columbus, Ohio), Professor Karl Reichl (Bonn), and Professor John D. Smith
(Cambridge), as well as to Dr Tony Grenville (London) and several former colleagues
in the University of London, especially Dr Rosemary Combridge, the late Professor
F. M. Fowler, Mr Martin Jones, Professor William Jervis Jones, Professor Silvia
Ranawake, Professor Ian Short, Dr Adrian Stevens, Professor David Wells, and Professor
David Yeandle.

---

[48] *German Life and Letters* alone carried thirteen reviews from his pen between 1957 and 1976.

LESZEK KOLAKOWSKI

Leszek Kolakowski
1927–2009

Leszek Kolakowski begins his magisterial three-volume history of Marxism with the sentence: 'Karl Marx was a German philosopher.' The sentence 'Leszek Kolakowski was a Polish philosopher' is, similarly, revealingly true while neglecting all that was distinctive and significant about his life and work. He was, indeed, author of many works on the history of philosophy and of numerous searching essays, often laced with irony and sharp wit, that reflect philosophically on central issues of our time: on Communism, under which he lived half his adult life, and on the Marxism that inspired it, which he called 'the greatest fantasy of our century … [which] began in a Promethean humanism and culminated in the monstrous tyranny of Stalin' and on the illusions of its true believers in the West; on the need for hope (as against hopelessness); on the dangers of utopianism; on evil ('the Devil', he wrote, 'is part of our experience' and evil 'a stubborn and unredeemable fact'); on original sin (to explain humanity's darker side); on the role of the sacred in culture; on 'God's unforgettableness' (hence his presence 'even in rejection') and the persistence of transcendence (the religious need, he argued, 'cannot be excommunicated from culture by rationalist incantation'); on arguments for and against God's existence; on philosophers, whom he divided into 'diggers', who 'neither sow nor harvest but only move the soil', and 'healers', who 'apply sceptical medicine' in order 'not to let us get carried away by wishful thinking'; and on the enterprise of philosophy itself, which, he thought, could never 'discover any universally admissible truths'. About philosophers he held a refreshingly and characteristically self-ironic view. 'A modern philosopher', he wrote, 'who has never experienced the feeling of being a

Proceedings of the British Academy, **172**, 201–211. © The British Academy 2011.

charlatan is such a shallow mind that his work is probably not worth reading.' Further, 'If a philosopher happened to have made a genuine contribution to science (one thinks, say, of mathematical works of Descartes, Leibnitz or Pascal), his discovery, perhaps by the very fact of being admitted as an ingredient of the established sciences, immediately ceased being a part of philosophy.'

But, arguably, his greatest achievement was not merely to write (and he wrote some thirty books over five decades) but to be heard. He was massively influential in his native Poland, above all during the Solidarity era, and, indeed, across central and Eastern Europe. After Kolakowski's enforced exile in 1968, first to North America and eventually to Oxford, the late Ernest Gellner told me that when he visited Poland people would ask 'How is he?' without needing to say whom they meant. On the liberation of Poland he was awarded the Order of the White Eagle. And Adam Michnik, editor of the newspaper *Gazeta Wyborcza* and leading activist and often-imprisoned resister under Communism, wrote of him after his death that for 'decades he has been the symbol and moral authority of a Poland that is spiritually sovereign, that defies enslavement, of a Poland of free thought and unbending soul'. At his death there was an outpouring of eulogies in Poland, where he was buried with military honours and a minute of silence in the national Parliament. He was also widely celebrated elsewhere, receiving accolades and prizes in France, Italy, Germany, Switzerland, Holland and Israel. In the United States he was awarded the first John W. Kluge Prize from the Library of Congress for lifetime achievement in those fields of scholarship (the humanities above all) for which there is no Nobel Prize. And yet in England, his adoptive home, he was, as Tony Judt has remarked, 'largely unknown' and 'curiously underappreciated',[1] although he was elected a Fellow of the British Academy (in 1980). He was also a Fellow of the Académie Universelle des Cultures, and of the American Academy of Arts and Sciences

He was born in Radom, Poland on 23 October 1927. His father, an economist and political writer, was killed by the Gestapo after the Germans invaded and the family was exiled to a primitive village in eastern Poland. There he found a library in the house of a minor aristocrat and set about educating himself with help from people in the neighbourhood and from teachers supplied by the Polish underground, who helped him pass exam-

[1] Tony Judt, 'Goodbye to all that? Leszek Kolakowski and the Marxist Legacy', repr. in Tony Judt, *Reappraisals: Reflections on the Forgotten Twentieth Century* (New York, 2008), pp, 129–46; this quotation, p. 129

inations. As the Russians drove the Germans out of Poland, he embraced Communism, partly in opposition to the anti-semitic and nationalist bigotry that he saw among Polish Catholics and partly (to use his own words in interviews) because he believed that 'radical, fundamental social changes were necessary' and because 'communism was for us the conqueror of Nazizm, a myth of a better world, ... of a kingdom of equality and freedom'.

After the war he joined the Communist youth organisation and the Communist Party and studied philosophy at the University of Lodz. He became junior assistant there to the Chair of Logic headed by Professor Tadeusz Kotarbinski. He had been studying for a doctorate in Warsaw since 1950 and was also teaching at the Party School of Social Studies. In 1952 he started teaching at the Department of Philosophy in Warsaw University and in 1959 was appointed to the Chair of the History of Philosophy. He joined the editorial boards of the weekly *Nowa Kultura* and the magazine *Po Postu* (*In Plain Words*), both run by young Communist intellectuals.

During this time he was moving away from Soviet-style Marxism and became increasingly influential upon the younger generation as a leading voice for democratisation and a spokesman for what came to be called 'revisionism'. After the Poznan riots in 1956 and the subsequent 'thaw' and accession to power of Gomulka in October of that year, it seemed that the hopes in a reformed Communism that Kolakowski encouraged might have a chance of realisation, but these were short-lived and he was attacked by the Party leadership: he was criticised by Gomulka for being 'the main ideologue of the so-called revisionist movement'. His writings were often seized by censors and his lectures attended by the secret police.

He nevertheless kept his Party card until 1966, when he was expelled for criticising the Government on the tenth anniversary of the Polish October. Two years later he was expelled from Warsaw University for 'forming the views of the youth in a manner contrary to the official tendency of the country' and left Poland, with Tamara, his wife, who is a psychiatrist and of Jewish origin. This was the time of a heightened anti-semitic and nationalist campaign against 'Zionists', but that was not, as sometimes suggested, the reason for their departure. The reason was that he could neither teach nor publish (by this time there was a total ban on his publications) and he was under constant police surveillance. He therefore accepted an invitation from Montreal, intending to leave for one year, thinking that it might perhaps be extended for two. Thereafter for the next twenty years his writings remained officially banned in Poland, though they circulated widely in samizdat form and were hugely influential in shaping the intellectual opposition which, in combination with the Solidarity movement, contributed greatly to the collapse of Communism in Poland.

Kolakowski meanwhile went first to teach at McGill University in Canada and then to the University of California at Berkeley, where he encountered the student radicalism of that time, about which he commented that 'there are better arguments in favour of democracy and freedom than the fact that Marx is not quite as hostile to them as he first appears'. In 1970 he was elected to a senior research fellowship at All Souls College, Oxford, combining that position with appointments first at Yale and then, from 1981 to 1994, the Committee on Social Thought at the University of Chicago. I was among the first to welcome him to Oxford and recall his very central-European reaction to the place. He had visited several colleges and was clearly impressed but curious about one thing: 'Where', he wanted to know, 'are the cafes?'

During this period of exile, he gave active support and advice to Solidarity in Poland. In fact his contacts with the Polish opposition long pre-dated Solidarity; he was a member of KOR (the Committee of Workers' Defence). He wrote articles, gave interviews and helped in fundraising. His writing focused on ethics, metaphysics and, increasingly, religion. And he became increasingly critical of Western Marxist and marxisant intellectuals and even of the very idea of socialism (see his contribution to *The Socialist Idea: a Reappraisal*, a collection which he co-edited with Stuart Hampshire: London, 1974), claiming that democratic socialism was as 'contradictory as a fried snowball'. This evolution was seriously disappointing to some left-wing intellectuals who had sympathised with his earlier revisionist Marxism. In 1973 the distinguished historian E. P. Thompson published 'An open letter to Leszek Kolakowski', in *The Socialist Register*, berating him for betraying the aspirations of the left. Kolakowski, unlike Thompson, held out no hope for the renovation of the Communist idea: 'This skull,' he wrote, 'will never smile again.' His response, 'My correct views on everything' (which appeared in *The Socialist Register* in 1974 and was republished in a collection of essays with that title: South Bend, IN, 2005) was an onslaught on thinking in terms of a 'system' and thereby purporting to solve 'all the problems of mankind in one stroke'—a theme succinctly restated in his essay entitled 'How to be a liberal-conservative socialist' (reprinted in *Modernity on Endless Trial*: Chicago, IL, and London, 1990).

Thereafter he lived quietly in Oxford, surrounded by his library of books in English, Polish, Russian, French and German—books of poetry, European novels, and books on art, on Christian theology, on the Jewish and other religions (he had a special interest in Buddhism), on the Bible, on witches and on the devil—and travelling from time to time, to give lectures and to receive prizes in his native Poland and across Europe. He was a member of the board of the Vienna-based Institute for the Human Sciences (Institut für die Wissenschaften von Menschen) and took part in regular meetings in Castel Gandolfo at which its members engaged in discussions, to which various other intellectuals were invited, with Pope John Paul II. Towards the end his eyes failed him, but his spirits, his wary scepticism and his irony, sometimes sardonic and always both sharp and subtle, never did. Back in 1959 he had launched his career as an essayist with an essay entitled 'The Priest and the Jester' (for which he received both the Veillon Foundation European Prize for the Essay and the Erasmus Prize in 1980), which counterposed the Priest, the guardian of tradition and accepted absolutes, to the sceptical Jester who 'doubts all that appears self-evident'. (This essay is reprinted in a collection of his essays published in translation in 1968 under the title *Towards a Marxist Humanism* in the United States and, less misleadingly, as *Marxism and Beyond* in the UK. The British edition includes an introduction explaining that he no longer held the views expressed in some of the essays.) He himself remained a jester to the end; one of his jests was to refer to his own essays as 'semi-philosophical sermons'.

* * *

In Britain his *Main Currents of Marxism* is his most widely known work. Its 1,200 pages, first published in English in three volumes (London and New York, 1978), and subsequently in one, is not a history of socialism and Communism; its focus is not on the social and political embodiments of Marxist ideas or their historical contexts but on their attractive power and dangers. His interpretation of these joins those of many other such twentieth-century diagnoses—such as those of Karl Popper, Jacob Talmon, Isaiah Berlin, Sidney Hook, Raymond Aron and many others—but it is more interesting than most, focusing, as Tony Judt has observed, on Marxism's fusion of 'Promethean Romantic illusion and uncompromising historical determinism'.[2] Kolakowski's view was that the Leninist version

---

[2] Judt, 'Goodbye to all that?', p. 133.

of Marxism, 'though not the only possible one, was quite plausible'. In support of his view that these features of Marxist thinking anticipated Communist tyranny, he cited many observers and critics, from Mikhail Bakunin to Rosa Luxemburg. And Judt is right to notice the 'unflagging efficiency and clarity' with which the arguments of the classical Marxist thinkers are expounded and placed within the overall story.[3] The second volume includes many European Marxists, including Poles, whose contributions have been little noticed in standard accounts. In the third volume, however, which treats of Marxism since 1917 and is entitled 'The Breakdown', the tone changes, as Judt comments, to one of 'almost unremitting contempt'.[4] (Interestingly, this third volume has never appeared in French translation.) Its last chapter, covering the period since Stalin's death, is perfunctory and the prospect of a further volume was renounced because, as its author remarked, 'I am not convinced that the subject is intrinsically worthy of treatment at such length.'

Regrettably less well known in Britain are Kolakowski's life-long achievements as philosopher and historian—one might say as philosophising historian—specialising in European intellectual history between 1500 and 1800, especially philosophical and religious ideas of the seventeenth century. Indeed his interpretations of European intellectual history between the Reformation and the Enlightenment are not only a major achievement in their own right but have a direct bearing upon his exposure of what he came to see as the leftist illusions of Marxism as well as his own philosophical reflections on religion, most succinctly expressed in *Religion: if there is no God* (Oxford, 1982) and in his analysis of the dilemmas of modern secular societies, as summarised in *Modernity on Endless Trial*.

He set out his methodological approach in an early book on Spinoza, available only in Polish, entitled *Individual and Infinity: Freedom and the Antinomies of Freedom in Spinoza's Philosophy* (Warsaw, 1958). His goal was to interpret classic problems of philosophy

> ... as problems of a moral nature, to translate metaphysical, anthropological and epistemological questions into a language suitable for expressing moral problems, to reveal their hidden human content: in other words, to present the problem of God as a problem of man, the problem of heaven and earth as a problem of human freedom, the problem of nature as a problem concerning the value of human life, and the problem of human nature as the problem of inter-human relationships.

---

[3] Judt, 'Goodbye to all that?', p. 131.
[4] Ibid., p. 132.

It was, however, in his most substantial philosophical-historical work, *Religious Consciousness and the Church: Studies in Seventeenth-Century Non-Denominational Christianity* (Warsaw, 1965), that his methodological views are most fully presented. This work was published in 1965 but he had been working on it since 1958. (It is available in French under the title *Chrétiens sans Église: La conscience religieuse et le lieu confessionel au XVIIe siècle*: Paris, 1969.) Here he made the case for the judicious use of conceptual constructs, or 'ideal types', subordinating the 'empirical elements of the historical world' to 'a central idea which manifests itself in a system of ideal constructions and through them confers meaning on each particular element of the emerging picture'. He sought to understand irreducible 'primary phenomena' through phenomenological insight, insisting that we seek to establish three distinct unities as our objects of inquiry: that of the author's personality, where we focus on his intention; that of his ideas viewed historically, where we focus on locating his ideas in the historical process; and that of the structure of his thought, where we focus on its autonomous logic. Adequate understanding requires identification with thinkers of the past in order to understand them from within, seeing their perspective as open, and viewing them from a distance, thus seeing their perspective as historically closed. We should avoid reducing meaningful structures to their historical determinants while realising that the interpretation of meaning, as reconstructed by us, is always open, liable to be changed by further historical developments, and thus dependent on the age in which we live, our place in it and the peculiarities of our cognitive perspective.

In that work Kolakowski applied these precepts consistently and impressively. Viewing religious faith, the experience of the sacred, as a 'primary phenomenon', he insisted that its various concrete manifestations could and should be explained historically. The book is a study of little-known thinkers from across Europe who embraced Christian ideas while rejecting affiliation with an existing Church. Thus its focus is upon non-denominational religious faith, that is, faith that involves resistance to the organised, institutionally controlled forms of religious life. He singles out mysticism as particularly important, as a special kind of religious subjectivism that is at once subjective, in concentrating on inner religious experience and denying the need for organised Christianity, and anti-individualist in its aim of direct union with the Absolute Being, thereby annihilating the individual self. The book covers the various conflicts between religious consciousness and ecclesiastical bonds, the attempts to abolish any organised mediation between the individual soul and God, the struggle against

religious subjectivism within the existing Churches, and the prudent policy of the Catholic Counter-Reformation of finding a place for it within
the Church, thereby giving it an outlet, while at the same time keeping it
under control. The book's message of distaste for institutionalised 'Truth'
was unmistakable. This theme, alongside Kolakowski's sceptical distrust
of claims to certainty, continued to inform all his subsequent writings. He
distrusted what Sir Isaiah Berlin, his sometime colleague at All Souls, whom
he admired, called 'monism': 'I do not believe', he wrote, 'that human culture can ever reach a perfect synthesis of its diversified and incompatible
components. Its very richness is supported by this very incompatibility of
its ingredients. And it is the conflict of values, rather than their harmony,
that keeps our culture alive.'

This early magnum opus can also be seen as linked to later works that
stress the irreducibly irrational components of spiritual life. In *The Presence
of Myth* (Polish 1972, English, Chicago, IL, 1989) he argues that the
mythopoeic layer of human existence is omnipresent and is the source of
meaning-creating energy, that a leap of faith underlies even our belief in
objective truth, which is itself a kind of myth, and that myths are necessary to render human existence meaningful since their disappearance
would lead to universal nihilism. *Religion: If there is no God ... On God,
the Devil, Sin and Other Worries of the so-called Philosophy of Religion*
(London and New York, 1982), focusing on religious myths, claims that
Dostoevsky's maxim 'If there is no God, everything is permissible' applies
not only to morality but to knowledge: abandoning God as an epistemological absolute leads to epistemological nihilism. And *Metaphysical
Horror* (Oxford, 1988; corrected edn. Harmondsworth, 2001) focuses on
the search for foundations—the 'elusive Grail of unshakeable certainty'—
'the quest for Truth and Reality—spelt with capital letters', an inescapable
pursuit of an endlessly recurring object of philosophical enquiry, which is
a 'structural part of culture or of human minds'. It 'cannot be satisfied
with anything less than the Absolute' and yet what it seeks is inaccessible,
just as God in the neoplatonic tradition in Christianity is ineffable. Claims
to know the Truth, in that sense, are illegitimate in both religion and science (and in political thought serve to justify totalitarian despotism). But
epistemological relativism is no less unwarranted and dangerous. No solution is offered other than the maxim that 'The search for the ultimate
foundation is as much an unremovable part of human culture as is the
denial of the legitimacy of this search.'

*God Owes Us Nothing: a Brief Remark on Pascal's Religion and on the
Spirit of Jansenism* (Chicago, IL, 1995) also explores the theme of inescap-

able conflict. Continuing the discussion of sixteenth and seventeenth-century religious thought from the earlier, major work, it also suggests parallels between the idea of a 'hidden God' beyond the reach of reason and dogmatic Marxism. Its topic is the 'world-shaking controversy about grace' between Augustianism, emphasising human dependency on divine grace, and Pelagianism, stressing the role of human freedom.

Jansenism represented the Augustinian position and was closer to the Lutheran and Calvinist Reformation than to Erasmus's Catholic humanism. The Jesuit Counter-Reformation, on the other hand, was engaged in the de-Augustinisation of the Church, modernising it, and was thus linked to the Pelagian view. In this respect, the Jesuits, in Kolakowski's words, represented 'the embryonic spirit of the Enlightenment and the common-sense belief in free will'. Thus the Jesuits, paradoxically, given their reputation, exhibited the spirit of modernism and Pascal reactionary Christian fundamentalism. But, Kolakowski argued, the situation was more complicated still, for in certain respects Pascal was more modern than the Jesuits, since, while disparaging the role of secular reason, he defended secular science against clerical authoritarianism and attacked scholastic reasoning in religious matters, thereby freeing faith from reason and reason from faith. And, in Kolakowski's view, his deep pessimism about the human condition remains a precious antidote against political utopianism which was a necessary by-product of the secularisation of Pelagianism. His opposition to Cartesian rationalism and his 'anti-Enlightennent thrust', he writes, 'makes Pascal our contemporary'.

These thoughts reappear in *Modernity on Endless Trial* (Chicago, IL, 1990), the main conclusion of which is that:

> ... while it is true that the Pelagian mentality; especially once it has 'secularized' itself and assumed the form of utopian politics, is deservedly discredited nowadays, it may well have played a liberating role in the history of modern Europe. It put into circulation a belief in human freedom conceived as an unconstrained ability to choose between good and evil, it made possible the habit of trusting in our spiritual prowess and our unlimited potential to better our lot, to create and to expand, to apply our curiosity to anything we can think of. If it brought disasters in our age, it also made possible the great achievements of modern European civilization in the arts, the sciences and social institutions. And so, let us accept, in the Pascalian manner, 'two contradictory truths'.

And indeed this embracing, even relishing, of the antinomies of human thought and existence, without seeking to resolve or synthesise them, is a distinctive feature of Kolakowski's style of reasoning and a trait he found intriguing and attractive in the thought of other thinkers. It is to be found, for instance, in his fine little study for the Past Masters series of Bergson (*Bergson*: Oxford and New York, 1985), which discerns two incompatible versions of 'Bergsonism': the idea that 'consciousness is a continuous self-creation ex nihilo' and the idea that the original direction of the entire process of evolution—though not its details—is divinely inspired. 'Starting with inner experience', he writes of Bergson, 'he discovered consciousness as an absolute creator and he made time its property; then he asserted it as a work of the divine artist. To have it both ways within the same discourse proved to be impossible.'

His other studies of European philosophers include *Positivist Philsosophy from Hume to the Vienna Circle* first published in Polish in 1966 (English translation as *The Alienation of Reason: a History of Positivist Thought*: New York, 1968, republished as *Positivist Philsosophy from Hume to the Vienna Circle*, Harmondsworth, 1972), *Husserl and the Search for Certitude* (South Bend, IN, 1975), and *The Two Eyes of Spinoza and Other Essays on Philosophers* (South Bend, IN, 2004), a collection which contains texts on the history of philosophy, mainly from the seventeenth century, not published before in English. There is also a little book *Why There Is Something Rather than Nothing. 23 Questions from Great Philosophers?* (New York, 2007; in the Polish edition there were thirty questions!)—his last book published in English. The last one written in Polish was *Fractions of Philosophy. The most widely known and most often quoted sentences of philosophers, with a commentary* (Warsaw, 2008). Apart from his many essays, appearing in various collections and ranging from the philosophical to the polemical to the whimsical, he was also the author of literary texts: several plays, (*Dr Faustus* among them), collections of fables entitled *Tales from the Kingdom of Lailonia* (published in Polish in 1963) and of biblical stories entitled *The Key to Heaven* (published in Polish in 1964) and his *Conversations with the Devil* (published in Polish in 1965). These have been republished in English as *Tales from the Kingdom of Lailonia and The Key to Heaven* (Chicago, IL, 1989) and *The Devil and Scripture* (London and New York, 1973).

Kolakowski expressed scepticism about the professed certainties of secular, atheistic liberalism and the prospects for reviving the Enlightenment. He was hostile to the stance of uncritical respect for other cultures, arguing that by failing to make critical judgements of other cultures and civilisations one diminishes the value of one's own. Yet he saw belief in scientific evidence as itself based on a kind of faith and held rational inquiry to be unable to settle religious questions or furnish a basis for morality, criticising those who 'try to assert our modernity, but escape from its effects by various intellectual devices, in order to convince ourselves that meaning can be restored or recovered apart from the traditional religious legacy of mankind'. He viewed the category of the 'sacred' as essential for culture but thought that it could not be grounded in secular ways, as 'godlessness desperately attempts to replace the lost God with something else'. Thus he offered reasons for the need for faith in a way that does not presuppose it, thereby risking offence to religious believers and thoroughgoing rationalists alike.

Leszek Kolakowski died on 17 July 2009.

STEVEN LUKES
Fellow of the Academy

Note. I am grateful to Tamara Kolakowska and Andrzej Walicki for their assistance in the preparation of this memoir.

HUGH LLOYD-JONES

Peter Hugh Jefferd Lloyd-Jones
1922–2009

HUGH LLOYD-JONES was born on 21 September 1922 at St Peter Port, Guernsey, the first child and only son of Brevet-Major William Lloyd-Jones and Norah Leila Jefferd. His parents had moved to the Channel Islands where it was then possible to live more economically than on the mainland, but soon returned. His father William belonged to a family from the Lleyn peninsula in North Wales; one of his distant relatives had been a Fellow of Jesus College, Oxford, which had strong Welsh connections. William was a regular army officer who had been posted to India in 1908. Since he found little satisfaction in soldiering there in peacetime he arranged a transfer to Africa; in his own words he chose to go there 'for experience and big-game shooting'. His tour of duty in the King's African Rifles, a regiment of which he wrote a history, is described in his other book *Havash! Frontier Adventures in Kenya* (London, 1925).[1] In 1913 in an engagement with brigands far out in the wilds he was seriously wounded in the leg, but managed to rally his men and complete the mission; however, gangrene and tetanus set in, and the journey back to a place where proper medical care was available was a terrifying ordeal lasting forty-three days, which left him white-haired at an early age. For his services he was awarded the DSO. When the First World War began he was fit enough for service, and for a time undertook the extremely dangerous duty of flying light aircraft to photograph enemy positions; most of the pilots fortified themselves with alcohol before taking off. After a while he was transferred

---

[1] The second book was *K.A.R.: being an Unofficial Account of the Origins and Activities of the King's African Rifles* (London, 1926).

Proceedings of the British Academy, **172**, 215–229. © The British Academy 2011.

to the post of Deputy Assistant Adjutant-General in the War Office with
the rank of major. There his duty was to liaise with French officers, whom
he found congenial because they were more intelligent and better educated
than most of their English counterparts. His war service was rewarded
with decorations from France, Italy, Romania and Serbia. But his injury
had taken its toll; he had to undergo an amputation and after a time further complications necessitated another operation. He was given ten
months leave, but because he took an extra month the army dismissed him
and he had to live on a very limited income. His fortunes improved in
1927, when thanks to influential friends he became Captain of Invalids, in
charge of the Royal Hospital Chelsea, in practice a sinecure with a stipend
of £600 a year and a magnificent apartment.

In 1921, after converting to Roman Catholicism, William had married
Norah Leila Jefferd. The ceremony took place in Westminster Cathedral.
His wife took the unusual step of refusing to bring up her children in that
faith. She came from a Devon family which at one time had been well off
but were no longer so, largely because of the incompetence of her father
in matters of finance. The youngest of eight children, she escaped from
her family at the age of 17, when she had already saved £60, and enrolled
at the Royal Academy of Music in 1913, taking lessons in piano and singing; she declined the offer of a career as a ballerina in Diaghilev's company
and became a singer in musical comedies. The initially happy marriage
began to go wrong, as her husband was always extravagant and wasted
money by drinking in clubs on Pall Mall; some of his debts eventually had
to be paid off by his wife. After a few years disaster struck, in the form of
a nurse engaged to look after the family. The marriage failed and divorce
followed in 1936, but this did not result in a generous settlement for Hugh's
mother, and with two children to look after and no more than a fraction
of her previous income Norah had to work very hard to make a living,
which she did by embroidering church vestments. The strain of these
events led to an attack of pernicious anaemia which was almost fatal, and
though she recovered from that she died at the relatively early age of 57.
Hugh, who had immediately taken a dislike to the nurse, avoided all contact with his father for many years and always retained the highest respect
for his mother, whose strength of character and financial prudence were
remarkable.

In view of his later career it is odd to discover that Hugh initially had
difficulty in learning to read, doubtless because the attempt to teach him
was made too soon; he is said to have exclaimed 'I shall never learn to read
or write. When I'm grown up I shall have a secretary.' In later years his

incompetent use of typewriters made many friends and colleagues wish that he could have a secretary. But he soon made up ground, and at the age of nine composed a short story set in the Balkans, which his mother showed to a journalist; the result was a long article in the *Evening Standard* for 5 October 1931 under the heading THRILLER WRITTEN BY BOY OF 9. The journalist enthusiastically asked his mother what he intended to be when he left school, to which the reply was 'He says he wants to be a pawnbroker.' Hugh had begun his schooling at the French Lycée in South Kensington, which ensured that he acquired great fluency in the language (in later life he had a useful command of other languages as well). But at the age of 8 he was sent to Stubbington, a boarding school near Portsmouth, which was most uncongenial; it was mainly for boys destined to enter the navy and not a place for any studious child, even if the boys were instructed to read the Bible in their spare time. The other boys were very unkind to Hugh, and he must have been acute enough to sense that the teaching was not of the best. His first letter home to his mother reported that they were trying to teach him a new thing called Latin, which he hated and would never learn, and his mother was to have it stopped; he concluded the letter with the formula 'Yours faithfully'. When his mother found him studying Greek by himself while the master supposed to be teaching him was playing tennis instead, she removed Hugh and sent him to a tutor in St John's Wood. Hugh subsequently conjectured that his father had sent him to Stubbington partly in the hope of paying little or nothing by way of fees and partly to reduce his opportunities for observing the misconduct of the nurse. With the help of the new tutor he came top of the list of King's Scholars at Westminster. Even with the benefit of the scholarship the fees came to £68 per year, a strain on the family's finances, whereas he could have gone to Eton for £7, but his mother refused to contemplate this alternative because she feared that Eton would prove to be a snobbish environment suitable only for the very rich. (She was subsequently assured by a friend that at the time her fear was justified.)

At Westminster Hugh was much influenced by the headmaster J. T. Christie, with whose family he enjoyed a lifelong friendship. One day Christie introduced the class to Sophocles' *Philoctetes* by telling them that a war was likely to break out soon, in which they would be officers and would have to face the kind of dilemma illustrated in the play. Hugh learned as much Greek as he could and his memory was so good that if he read a page twice he remembered the text; Christie had never come across anyone like him. He learned the texts by heart so as to be able to recite them to himself if he were unfortunate enough to be taken prisoner of war, as had happened to an uncle. He went up to Christ Church in 1940 and read the shortened course for Classical Honour Moderations. The tutors' reports show that he made an impression: 'Westminster's best classical product for a long time ... a nice man in spite of a cumbrous manner'; 'His scholarship, like his demeanour, is sometimes rugged and impulsive'; 'Has a definite impish charm'. Similarly when he returned after the war: 'something of a whale of a sponge; he reads and absorbs everything'; 'phenomenally receptive but more than that'.

After completing the first part of the course there was no point in waiting to be called up and he volunteered to join the army, being one of a group of Oxford classicists who had done well in recent examinations and were recommended to the authorities by A. D. (later Lord) Lindsay of Balliol (some others, less carefully selected, came from Cambridge). There was an urgent need to find people who were likely to be capable of learning Japanese quickly. They were sent to Bedford for an admirably organised course lasting four months, followed by a few weeks in London at the Foreign Office and the Ministry of Economic Warfare; nearly all of them were then assigned to work at Bletchley Park, but Hugh was one of three sent to India. Before leaving he had a lucky escape; he and his friend Walter Robinson, who after the war married Hugh's sister Barbara, arranged to collect their belongings from Bedford in two days time, but their landlady altered the plan and asked them to come one day earlier, which they did; the following day a bomb fell on the house, killing two children.

Hugh was to work at the Wireless Experimental Centre just outside Delhi, where the most important cryptographic operations were conducted, and for this purpose he had to be an officer. Until the commission came through he enlisted as a private, but soon after arrival in India was promoted sergeant. By Christmas 1942 his commission arrived; he had to be interviewed by a major-general in Rawalpindi, who asked him what he had been doing before he joined the army, and on hearing that he had been studying at Oxford asked 'What college?' To the reply 'Christ Church' the general merely said 'Ah, my father was there. Well, what regiment do you want to join?' That was the end of the interview.

This anecdote comes from a memoir Hugh composed recounting his wartime experiences. I quote a few key passages.

> In 1943 the pacific Gandhi tried to organise disorder in order to support the Japanese. For some time each bus going from our camp had to contain an officer with a rifle. A bus that I was on was threatened by a group of rioters just outside

the gate of our camp, and a woman seemed about to hurl a stone at it. I pointed the rifle at her, although if I had fired I should certainly have missed, and she dropped her stone and fled and the group rapidly dispersed. Gandhi's movement did not last long.

Early in 1945 I was concerned in one piece of work which had a definite, though a very limited military effect. Mainly owing to the work of Robinson, we were in a position to read messages in a code used by the enemy at corps level, and it was necessary to dispatch a party to the north of Burma so that messages should be handed without delay to those in action. About seven officers and fifteen other ranks were flown to the headquarters of 33rd Corps, then encamped at Yazagwo, just east of the native state of Manipur. Our camp was in the jungle. Not long before we arrived a soldier had gone out to relieve himself, and while doing so noticed an enormous tiger casually strolling down a path that led in his direction. Luckily he was too scared to move, and the tiger slowly walked past him, casting him a glance of unutterable contempt. In a miserable shack not far from our tents a Buddhist priest was intoning sutras with endless repetition; it was known that he had been there three weeks before, when fighting was going on not far away.

Another officer was supposed to share the work of translation with me, but I found that he was useless. Luckily I outranked him, being a captain and the second in command of our party, so that I was obliged to insist on doing all the work; this meant that I got very little sleep. But being excited I did not become exhausted. The enemy seemed to have no idea that their signals might be being read; from time to time a cipher clerk would forget his duty and send a message in clear. On one occasion a message indicated that a force whose number it conveniently gave was to move down a particular road at a particular time; the day after we had dealt with this, the Director of Intelligence came in person to thank us for having made possible an ambush by Gurkhas hiding in the bushes. The troops at corps headquarters, who called us 'the backroom boys', were friendly and helpful, and we were given 33rd Corps flashes.

At one stage the corps headquarters moved south from Yazagwo to Kalewa. Our forces were pursuing the Japanese down the road going southwards level with the coast; since the enemy had no aircraft left, their retreat down that road had been conducted under unremitting fire. We moved at night, and each vehicle had an officer with a rifle sitting next to the driver. The jungle came right up to the road, close to which lay numerous wrecked enemy vehicles and innumerable corpses of enemy soldiers. Since the flesh of their faces had been eaten by the vultures, their bones shone brightly in the moonlight.

Hugh's task had not been to break the codes but to translate the deciphered messages. At times there were not many messages coming in, and he had time to keep in touch with friends in England, especially his former headmaster's family. Frequent air mail letters were sent; on one occasion eleven arrived all at once. Unexpected and eccentric presents to the Christie daughters included a whole coconut with name, address and a stamp on the outer shell. One amusing moment in his office is on record. An Indian clerk when signing letters regularly added after his name the letters FBA. Hugh asked him 'Mr. X, may I inquire what the meaning of the letters FBA is?', to which the reply was 'Sir, they signify "Failed BA".' One more remark in his memoir is worth quoting: 'It seemed certain that after the war independence would not be long delayed, but I could not help doubting whether this would be for the good of the majority of people in the country.'

He was able to return to Oxford in the autumn of 1946 and took Final Honour Schools in 1948, having won the Chancellor's Latin Prose Prize and the Ireland Scholarship in 1947, besides being *proxime accessit* for the Hertford Scholarship. At the time competition for these prizes was greater than usual because of the large number of returning servicemen coming into residence alongside the freshers of normal age. Immediately after his final exams he was appointed to a Fellowship at Jesus College, Cambridge, where his pupils were to include John Gould, FBA, a distinguished holder of the chair of Greek at Bristol. In 1953 he married Frances Elisabeth Hedley, who had read classics at Newnham College. There were two sons and a daughter of the marriage. It was dissolved in 1981.

At the beginning of 1955 he went back to Oxford. His arrival had been delayed by tuberculosis, the initial cause of which may have been overwork towards the end of his military service. He had to spend a few months in hospital, which were followed by a longer period of convalescence, and as a result in later life his constitution was not as robust as it would otherwise have been. He took up the newly established post of E. P. Warren Praelector in Classics at Corpus Christi College. Warren was an eccentric American benefactor of the college. His donations included a fifteenth-century Greek manuscript of the *Iliad* (now MS 470); his eccentricities included stipulations that the Praelector should be available at all times to act as a mentor to junior members; that if he did not live in the main college buildings a tunnel should be dug under Merton Street in order to permit communication with the annex buildings; and that he should not teach women. The first of these conditions was not much advertised. The second was nullified when the college managed to obtain an engineer's certificate that the construction of the tunnel would be impossible. The third was evaded by arranging that his much respected colleague Tom Stinton of Wadham College should advertise classes at which Hugh was not officially present but contributed substantially. These classes gave opportunity for discussing a wider range of topics than was usual at that time in tutorials, since the syllabus for the first part of the course still ensured that many tutorials were devoted to prose or verse composition. But with Hugh these tutorials, conducted in the study of his home in Magpie Lane, were by no means always exercises in linguistic niceties, and they were never dull. One might suddenly be presented with the proofs of a forthcoming article on textual criticism of Greek tragedy and asked to comment on one of the difficult passages discussed. Pupils who found it hard to keep up with their tutor's incisive and demanding comments were sometimes rescued by the arrival of Hugh's semi-Persian cat. The cat would jump up onto the table and settle himself comfortably on the pupil's composition, at which point, since there was no question of asking the cat to move, the conversation between tutor and pupil became general. Sometimes it touched on cricket; he kept a set of the annual Wisden volumes and had an incredible memory for the scores made in famous matches. Cricketing terminology might be applied to scholarly matters, so that A. S. F. Gow's lengthy and detailed commentary on Theocritus was described as full of strokes with a defensive straight bat but with very few shots to the boundary. Conversation also turned often to politics and modern history, a subject which he had at one time considered reading at Oxford; his comments on many eminent figures in public life were notable for their severity, much of it thoroughly deserved.

In 1960 when E. R. Dodds retired from the Regius Chair the post was initially offered to Kenneth Dover, who declined it for family reasons. There was a good deal of support in the faculty for Spencer Barrett of Keble College, whose celebrated commentary on Euripides' *Hippolytos* was known to be well advanced but had yet to appear; but the outcome of consultations with the Prime Minister's office was that Hugh was elected at the age of 37. He had just published the Oxford Classical Text of the recently discovered *Dyscolus* of Menander, an edition in which he coordinated the work of a number of scholars and made a considerable contribution of his own. As professor he now had the chance to give lectures and seminars without resorting to subterfuge. The lectures attracted attention by their stimulating style; his slightly stooping figure and frequent jerky gestures of his right hand made an impression. But it was through his seminars that he achieved his greatest success. Continuing the tradition imported to Oxford from Germany by Eduard Fraenkel, the Corpus Professor of Latin, with whom his relations were sometimes tense (but he was not by any means alone in this), he conducted penetrating examinations of various Greek poetic texts; prose was of less interest to him, though he did once in retirement devote a term to Theophrastus' *Characters*. At first Menander was the preferred author; later he passed on to Hellenistic poetry, in conjunction with Peter Parsons, and tragedy, mainly Sophocles, for which he co-opted the present writer. The majority of those attending were graduate students, who were now much more numerous than they had been for most of Fraenkel's tenure of the Latin chair; promising undergraduates were readily admitted if their tutors recommended them, and it was common for one or more faculty colleagues or visiting academics to come. The fame of the seminars spread, and often there were foreign students helping to make up a group of twenty or more. No one, however well prepared, could fail to learn something. Beginners were struck not just by the professor's ability to quote Greek poetry verbatim, but by the assurance, sometimes acerbic (one German was described as a *Giftzwerg*), with which the work of many scholars they had supposed to be respectable was dismissed. The range of his knowledge and the speed with which he could identify the issue at stake were remarkable. Participants were naturally nervous when first called upon to discuss the passage that had been assigned to them, and occasionally an undergraduate did seem to have been treated with a severity that was not wholly deserved, but on the whole the seminars were an outstandingly successful institution with very few rivals. One participant who later had a successful career in a different field has put it on record that Hugh's trenchant criticism was extremely valuable to her. Several former graduate students have said that Hugh's daunting presence filled them with trepidation when they first had to go to consult with him about the choice of a subject for research. On arrival they were received with the utmost courtesy, and by the time they left they were in no doubt of the benefit they would gain from Hugh's supervision. He continued to take good care of them, reading their work promptly and offering stimulating advice; expressions of gratitude in their published work are not just formulaic.

In 1966 he was elected to the British Academy and shortly afterwards received an invitation to give the Sather Lectures at Berkeley in 1969; they appeared promptly in 1971 as the forty-first volume of the series with the title *The Justice of Zeus* (Berkeley, CA; second edn. 1983). It was an examination of a central concept of the early Greek religious outlook, 'written from a point of view markedly different from that of most writers of the intellectual history of the period in question'. Many expressions of disagreement with other scholars were inevitable, but Hugh went out of his way to stress that these should not be interpreted as lack of esteem for his predecessors. There is an acknowledgement of his debt to E. R. Dodds, whose work he had found a source of stimulus and inspiration ever since at the age sixteen he had been taken to hear Dodds lecture on Euripides'

Bacchae. Dodds in fact read the book in draft, offering suggestions and comments, one of which was: 'I stressed the element of change in Greek beliefs, you stress the element of continuity; we are both of us right, though both of us at times exaggerate the partial truth we are stressing.' One other remark in the preface deserves to be cited because it illustrates a principle which, as many of his later writings show, he never lost sight of: 'I ... chose a topic about which I felt eager to address the general reader, as well as my academic colleagues, and I have done my best to present the lectures in a way that he will understand.' They were an investigation of the relationship between religion and morality in Greek thought from Homer down to the fifth century. A long-standing question debated by scholars had been whether the gods as portrayed in Homer and later authors could be regarded as just. A quotation from the conclusions (p. 162) will give a good sense of arguments put forward:

> It is a gross misconception to suppose that the inherited religious thinking of the Greeks placed any barrier in the way of a rational explanation either of factual or of moral error. What happened in the world depended ultimately upon the gods, and their purpose was usually inscrutable to human minds; that did not mean that it was irrational, but that the reasons that governed it usually remained mysterious.

Other notable features of the book include an examination of the concepts of guilt-culture and shame-culture, which cannot be applied to classical Greek society as easily and simply as had previously been supposed by some enthusiastic supporters of an anthropological approach. And his grasp of the history of ideas is revealed by the reference to Nietzsche's *Birth of Tragedy* as marking a turning point in the understanding of Greek religious thought. One further remark that is worth quoting: 'One of the best reasons for studying the past is to protect oneself against that insularity in time which restricts the uneducated and those who write to please them.'

The book was dedicated to his life-long friends Marcelle and Anthony Quinton, and in the following years this friendship was in evidence again. In 1975 Hugh prepared a slim volume devoted to Semonides' satire on women which included illustrations of a number of sculptures by Marcelle (*Females of the Species: Semonides on Women*; London, 1975). Then in 1978 Marcelle made a set of sculptures of the signs of the zodiac, published with the title *Myths of the Zodiac* (New York, 1978). To accompany illustrations of them Hugh wrote an introduction about the history of the zodiac, together with notes about the myths associated with each of the signs. She had earlier made a striking bronze bust of Hugh, which was pictured on the cover of the Semonides book.

His two further major contributions to scholarship were both works of collaboration. In 1983 he and Peter Parsons issued *Supplementum Hellenisticum* (Berlin), a volume of almost 900 pages which presented the reader with the significant additions to our knowledge of Hellenistic poetry that had accrued in recent decades. Though they decided to exclude certain categories of text, principally dramatic and epigraphic, this was an enormous task, involving fresh collation of many papyri. The apparatus criticus is wonderfully learned and helpful; among its many virtues is the display of exemplary caution with regard to proposed supplements in fragmentary texts. The authoritative review in *Gnomon* by E. Livrea described the book as 'uno dei monumenti della filologia del nostro secolo'.[2]

The year 1990 saw the publication of the Oxford Classical Text of Sophocles, an author in whom he had taken a great interest from an early stage in his career. The edition was the product of a series of seminars held over a long period of years in conjunction with the present writer. The collaboration, as had been the case with *Supplementum Hellenisticum*, derived much benefit from the fact that each of us had his own specialism but was quite capable of understanding and commenting on the other's suggestions. With some hesitation, though we both had plenty of experience of writing Latin, we decided to compose the preface in English, a decision which greatly shocked some colleagues but which we felt was justified by the need to ensure that users of the edition would take the trouble to read carefully what we had to say. A second and less controversial innovation was the decision to write the monograph *Sophoclea*, in which we explained the reasoning behind many of our textual choices; it was followed in 1997 by a supplement *Sophocles: Second Thoughts* (Göttingen). In both volumes Hugh took the leading role in presenting the results of the seminar sessions and the almost daily meetings we held when preparing the copy to be sent to the printer. On completion of our task we were surprised to find that the number of our own conjectures, the majority of them due to Hugh, was much greater than we had anticipated at the outset, when we had determined that one of our two principal aims should be to offer an enlarged and improved selection of necessary or plausible conjectures, since other current editions seemed to us defective in this respect. We had not thought that we should find it necessary to make many interventions of our own. A perhaps less important surprise was that we had found many occasions to cite or adopt emendations by the Victorian

---

[2] *Gnomon*, 57 (1985), 601.

eccentric F. H. M. Blaydes, who had been pilloried or ignored by previous critics. Our secondary aim had been to provide a succinct but clear apparatus criticus, avoiding the need to burden it with a mass of potentially mystifying or unhelpful sigla for manuscripts which had very little individual value, but at the same time incorporating the results of a valuable palaeographical discovery. B. Zimmermann's verdict in *Gnomon* was: 'Die Ausgabe gibt Vers für Vers Zeugnis von dem methodischen Sachverstand, den hervorragenden Sprachkenntnisssen und der Gelehrsamkeit der Hrsgbb., der begleitende Band der Sophoclea liefert die erforderlichen Erläuterungen zur Textkritik und häufig auch—gerade in der Verbindung von Textkritik und Detailerklärung im Zusammenhang mit dem jeweiligen Stück und dem gesamten Werk des S.—interessante Perspektive der Interpretation.'[3]

This edition was followed by *Sophocles* for the Loeb Classical Library (Cambridge, MA, 1994–6), in the third volume of which he presented the fragments in an accessible format. The task of translating the plays was a task readily accepted (he had earlier translated Aeschylus' *Oresteia*—London, 1979—with short notes designed to help students). Though he says that his version has no literary pretensions, it very effectively meets the requirements of the series, the high quality of which in recent decades has been notable.

Being convinced that as the holder of one of the two leading chairs of Greek in Britain it was his duty to ensure as far as possible that the educated public continued to understand the interest and importance of the subject, he wrote many reviews and articles for a variety of journals. These, together with some lectures and obituary notices of distinguished colleagues, were eventually collected in three volumes. *Blood for the Ghosts* and *Classical Survivals* appeared in 1982, *Greek in a Cold Climate* in 1991, all published by his great friend Colin Haycraft, whose direction of the old-established London firm of Gerald Duckworth & Co. brought it into prominence as a publisher of books on the classics. Though some of the reviews are relatively slight pieces, the essays on eminent writers influenced by the classical tradition and on scholars such as Thomas Gaisford display an enviable grasp of the subject and an ability to convey to the general reader the significance of the themes discussed.

Concern with the classical tradition was displayed in another publication from 1982. A translation of Wilamowitz's short and brilliant *Geschichte der Philologie*, which had appeared as far back as 1921 but is still incomparably the best introduction to the subject, had been prepared by Alan

[3] *Gnomon*, 65 (1993), 109.

Harris and so at least became accessible to readers not confident of understanding with ease the original German text. It appeared under the Duckworth imprint as *History of Classical Scholarship*. Hugh added a preface of twenty-eight pages and over 600 footnotes, also correcting the occasional errors of fact. In seminars he would often tell students that they should learn something about the scholars of previous generations whose conjectures they were discussing, since knowledge of this kind might help in evaluating the contributions in question, and the first session of a seminar was usually devoted to an account of the textual transmission of the author in question followed by a sketch of the progress made by scholars since the Renaissance in their efforts to remove the numerous corruptions that had occurred in the course of many centuries of manuscript tradition. Though there are now other partial treatments of the subject on a larger scale, Wilamowitz's essay still deserves to be read in this convenient annotated version by every graduate student.

All these activities still left time for many visits to America and the maintenance of international relations, by which he set great store. It should perhaps be added that the income derived from these trips alleviated the burden of school fees for his children; Oxford professorial stipends were not generous and he did not have confidence in the free education provided by the state system. Apart from his term in California to give the Sather Lectures he had several spells of residence at Yale, where he was a Fellow of Morse College, and he was a well-known figure on other campuses. Among American colleagues he had a high regard for Bernard Knox, Robert Renehan and Zeph Stewart; in Europe his principal links were with Jean-Marie Jacques and Francis Vian in France, Rudolf Kassel in Germany, to whom he sent a number of pupils for a semester, Marcello Gigante and L. E. Rossi in Italy, and Walter Burkert in Switzerland.

Hugh did not have any ambition to distinguish himself in the administration of a college or a faculty, and he regarded attendance at committee meetings as a tiresome necessity reducing the time available for scholarship, but a necessity none the less because of a perceived need to defend certain positions. So he did go to meetings, often equipped with reading matter that clearly did not form part of the agenda papers. On one occasion at a governing body meeting in Christ Church there was discussion of the name to be given to a new building. The tutor in French, Alban Krailsheimer, prolonged the proceedings by a series of interventions which Hugh found irritating, and for the benefit of a like-minded colleague sitting next to him he jotted on a scrap of paper his own suggestion: *Der Sitz des heiligen Krails*. As a vigorous defender of the classics he did not shy away from controversy and there were occasions when his enthusiasm needed to be curbed; not all the letters that he addressed to the editors of the daily press or other periodicals reached their destination, because his wife Frances made sure that some of them disappeared before being posted. The enthusiasm with which he spoke on subjects dear to his heart was notable; once he was asked by the BBC to give a talk, which was tape recorded, and when he listened to the broadcast he thought someone else had been brought in to read his text, because he felt that he had not heard anyone speak with such passion since he had listened to Hitler; he wondered if the speaker would depart from the text and urge a crowd to go up to Boars Hill and uproot Gilbert Murray's rhododendrons.

His views on political and social issues were in most respects very conservative, and for someone with such a powerful intellect there was at times a curious lack of perception: he could not understand that many Oxford dons declined to award Margaret Thatcher an honorary degree because they believed her to be responsible for serious damage to the universities. He was also vehemently anti-clerical; yet this did not prevent him from being on the best of terms with some of the theology professors in Christ Church, in particular Robert Mortimer, later Bishop of Exeter, Henry Chadwick, James Barr and Rowan Williams. While occasionally referring with pride to his Welsh ancestry, he often expressed dislike for the Scots; a tutor in modern languages in one of the other Oxford colleges, notable for his dour insistence in matters of detail and his sometimes unpolished or even downright rude behaviour, was a very frequent target. Because of Hugh's strongly held opinions it was often necessary to find tactful ways of indicating that one did not agree with a view that he had just expressed; by this means friendship could be preserved, and he was a very loyal friend. He was also capable of revising an adverse judgement that he had formed of an individual; at one time he had been in the habit of making disobliging remarks about Constantine Trypanis, who at the time was the Bywater and Sotheby Professor of Medieval and Modern Greek at Exeter College, but he came to see that this was unfair and they enjoyed a very cordial relationship.

Any highly strung person has a tendency to be irritable if disturbed when trying to concentrate and Hugh was no exception. It is possible that certain childhood experiences had an unsettling effect; what is absolutely certain is that war service, even without the trauma of daily exposure to front-line combat, could not fail to leave its mark on a sensitive character, and those who found him difficult will not have made sufficient allowance for this fact. But as his life-long friend Catherine Porteous put it, he will be remembered for 'his erudition and scholarship, trenchant honesty and lack of humbug, and his sense of fun'.

On retirement in 1989 he received the honour of a knighthood. A year later appeared from Oxford University Press two volumes of his *Collected Academic Papers*, with a dedication *D.M. matris optimae*: their titles were, respectively, *Greek Epic, Lyric and Tragedy: the Academic Papers of Sir Hugh Lloyd-Jones* and *Greek Comedy, Hellenistic Literature, Greek Religion and Miscellanea: the Academic Papers of Sir Hugh Lloyd-Jones*. A third volume—*The Further Academic Papers of Sir Hugh Lloyd-Jones*—followed in 2005, in which the final item, originally published four years earlier, is a paper entitled 'Ancient Greek religion and modern ethics'. This he regarded as one of his most significant contributions to scholarship. Another important product of the same year was a supplement to *Supplementum Hellenisticum*.

In retirement he lived in Wellesley, Massachusetts, with his second wife Mary Lefkowitz, Mellon Professor of the Humanities at Wellesley College. They had married in 1982, having first met ten years earlier, thanks in large part to Eduard Fraenkel. He had read Mary's first article on Pindar, published in 1963, and had been kind enough to write to tell her that he found it convincing (a most welcome verdict from a demanding critic); at the same time he advised Hugh to read it. Mary continued to hold her chair at Wellesley until retirement in 2005. They retained a house in Oxford and made fairly frequent visits to Europe, since both were in demand as lecturers, often on cruises round the Aegean. Life in Wellesley had one drawback: Hugh was far removed from the world of cricket (in his entry in *Who's Who* he listed as his recreations 'cats, remembering past cricket'). On the other hand the household usually had a complement of three or more cats, mainly Siamese. And in the Boston area with its many universities there was plenty of opportunity for maintaining contact with colleagues.

The last years of his life were clouded by a series of illnesses. More than one operation was necessary; though they were carried out successfully the cumulative effect was to weaken his constitution and he died on 5 October 2009.

The recognition he received included honorary doctorates from the Universities of Chicago, Göttingen, Salonica and Tel-Aviv. He was also a member of the American Association of Arts and Sciences, the American Philosophical Society, the Academy of Athens, the Accademia di Archeologia Letteratura e Belle Arti of Naples, the Bayerische Akademie and the Nordrhein-Westfalische Akademie.

NIGEL WILSON
Fellow of the Academy

Note. Hugh left no autobiographical papers apart from the brief account of his war service, from which I have quoted above. I am therefore all the more grateful to the speakers at the memorial event held in Christ Church for their recollections, and I owe a special debt to his sister Barbara Robinson and to Mary Lefkowitz for help that only they could provide. I am also indebted to Dr Cristina Neagu for supplying me with a copy of the termly reports of Hugh's college tutors assessing his undergraduate performance.

DOUGLAS MACDOWELL

Douglas Maurice MacDowell
1931–2010

Douglas Maurice MacDowell, who died on 16 January 2010, was one of the most distinguished students of Greek oratory, law and comedy of the late twentieth and early twenty-first centuries.

He was born on 8 March 1931, the only child of Maurice Alfred MacDowell and his wife Dorothy Jean, née Allan. Both parents were of Scottish/Northern Irish extraction. His father worked for the London office of the Northern Assurance Company in Moorgate. His mother was a shorthand typist before giving up work on becoming a mother. One side benefit of his mother's previous occupation was that Douglas had learned to type (as well as to read and write) at the age of four.

His parents had no profound influence on his ultimate career choice. Neither parent had the opportunity to go to university and neither had ever studied Latin or Greek. His father, with whom he had a difficult and distant relationship throughout his life, had no sympathy with his intellectual interests, and indeed never attended school prize-giving or subsequent degree ceremonies. His mother, though always puzzled by Douglas's academic and professional activities, was invariably supportive and her visits with him to the theatre were later to pay dividends. He remained close to his mother and in adulthood continued to visit her until her death in 1990. His upbringing was secure and his childhood solitary and contented, disrupted only briefly at the age of eight by the war. He never developed a love of games and much preferred activities such as reading. This quietness remained with him throughout his life. In adult life he developed strong friendships but remained shy and was always more comfortable in his own company than with others.

Proceedings of the British Academy, **172**, 233–248. © The British Academy 2011.

He attended Keble Preparatory School for Boys, with an interval at Elgin Academy and Madras College St Andrews (when his father was sent by the RAF to Lossiemouth and Leuchars during the war), and then Highgate School. He later observed that he learned more English grammar at Elgin than anywhere else. His interest in Classics, as is often the case, was ultimately due to a good school teacher. His Classics master at Highgate School, the Revd C. H. Benson, was an ideal teacher for a bookish boy like Douglas. A poor disciplinarian but a good scholar, he was good at bringing on those students who were able and inclined to listen. It is at this point that the footprint for much of the later MacDowell is laid down. He particularly enjoyed the more technical and demanding aspects of the study of Classics. He enjoyed prose and verse composition in both languages but especially in Greek. He was particularly taken by the lyrics of Horace, not (he later said) for their literary quality but for the skill with which Horace was able to fit recalcitrant Latin words into complex and demanding alien metres. He also enjoyed ancient history, and especially fifth-century Athens. The other piece in the jigsaw is supplied by Aristophanes, whom (primed by his affection for Lewis Carroll and a fondness for Gilbert and Sullivan derived from his mother) he came to love, though (unlike most schoolboys) more for the wit than for the vulgarity; the editions through which he encountered Aristophanes were the expurgated ones at that stage (in the era before Kenneth Dover) considered fit for growing minds. At this time he also became interested in acting, an interest which continued into his university years. His most important parts were Mr Twigg in *Badger's Green* and Sir Andrew Aguecheek in *Twelfth Night*. Shy people frequently enjoy acting for the opportunity it gives to assume a role in public and Douglas felt later that his time on the stage had been of great benefit to him. It stimulated a performative side to his nature which he was later to let loose in lectures. And (with an irony which will not have been lost on a man who later came to love Demosthenes, who famously—at least in the later biographical tradition—struggled to bring on a weak voice) it taught him to develop and project a naturally quiet speaking voice.

In 1948 he was awarded a Domus Exhibition at Balliol College, Oxford (to which he had applied against the wishes of his school), and left school earlier than anticipated in March 1949 in order to complete his eighteen months of National Service (suddenly raised from twelve months) in time to commence his studies at Oxford in autumn 1950. He disliked National Service, though he was aware of the benefit alongside the tedium. Even the basic training, he felt, was not without value for a bookish young man from a sheltered and comfortable middle-class background, since it exposed him to kinds of people he would otherwise never have encountered. After his basic training he was made a sergeant instructor in the Army Apprentices School at Chepstow, and his duties consisted largely of teaching English to schoolboys. He felt that the experience was useful for his later career.

He found Oxford liberating. It gave him not just his own space but the opportunity to devote his time to the academic study he enjoyed, together with congenial intellectual company. His tutors included W. S. Watt, Kenneth Dover and Russell Meiggs. He learned more, he felt, from the Balliol tutors than from the Oxford lectures, which (at least in language and literature) he found 'dull' (Dodds) and (for the accent) 'largely unintelligible' (Fraenkel); on the whole he preferred the ancient history lectures (Andrewes, Brunt, Meiggs, Sherwin-White, Wade-Gery). Apart from stints as secretary, then chairman, of the Classical Society, his only other activity apart from study was drama. As the slave Xanthias in Aristophanes' *Frogs* he rode a thoroughbred pantomime donkey, one half of which was Robert Ogilvie, later Professor of Humanity at St Andrews. Though he saw himself (with typical modesty) as less gifted than some of his contemporaries (Ogilvie, Frederiksen), he took firsts in both Mods and Greats.

Despite this success, his progress into academic life was neither obvious nor inevitable. By the time he graduated he had begun to contemplate a career in the academy. Russell Meiggs was not encouraging and advised him to take the civil service exam, which he failed (he recalled later that he made a mess of the interview). Like many before and after him he then drifted into school teaching, first at Allhallows School, Rousdon, and then at Merchant Taylors'. He enjoyed teaching bright students at sixth form level but (again like many before and since) not the lower forms and by 1958 he had decided that this was not what he wanted out of life. He returned to the idea of university teaching, encouraged by his former classics teacher, Revd Benson. Early applications brought no interviews and he began to suspect that his referee, Meiggs, was not supportive, a suspicion reinforced when he substituted Dover for Meiggs and was successfully interviewed at Manchester in 1958. The feeling that Meiggs had been a lukewarm referee stayed with him, so that he never felt entirely comfortable with Meiggs afterward. But teaching now at a level more to his taste, he enjoyed life at Manchester and rose rapidly from assistant lecturer to lecturer (1961–8), then senior lecturer (1968–70) and reader.

He was appointed to the chair of Greek at Glasgow at the age of forty in 1971. Throughout his life he felt—sincerely—that this was a great

honour. He was conscious of the distinguished line of predecessors who
had occupied the chair, including Richard Jebb, Gilbert Murray and
A. W. Gomme. When he moved to Glasgow, it was to a separate department of Greek, though in 1988 the separate departments for ancient world
studies were merged into a single department of Classics. The world he
entered was a very traditional one and left undisturbed the subjects would
have slid quietly into obsolescence. He was (justly) proud of two innova-
tions he introduced. The first was the teaching of Greek language from
scratch, which (aware both of its importance and of its demands) unlike
some senior academics he taught personally rather than passing it off to
junior colleagues. The second was the class in Greek civilisation taught in
translation, of a kind he had taught in Manchester. Both teaching in
translation and *ab initio* language teaching have played a major role both
in reversing the decline in numbers studying Classics visible throughout
the UK from at least the late nineteenth century; they have also helped the
discipline not only to survive in a highly competitive higher education
environment but also to shrug off the elitist image which had plagued it
on its long retreat from its heyday as the basis for a gentlemanly education
and underpinning of empire. These were however the most radical changes
in the curriculum for a hundred years at Glasgow and (there as elsewhere
in the UK) met with resistance. They were however accepted and colleagues who worked with him both then and later recognise them as an
important step in the evolution of Classics teaching in its modern form
and an important part of his legacy to the department. His impact was
also felt in the revival of the Glasgow branch of the Classical Association
of Scotland. Though it never had the impact he wanted at high school
level (largely because of the decline in Classics in the state sector), it was
important not just for Classics in Glasgow but also for the larger Classics
community in Scotland. He was chairman of the Scottish Hellenic Society,
and of the Classical Association of Scotland and its Glasgow branch; he
was also secretary of the UK Council of University Classical Departments.
His commitment to Scotland, not just Glasgow, was shown in the publication series he instigated, Scottish Classical Studies, intended to raise the
profile of research in Classics in Scotland. In the area of what we now call
academic management he regarded himself as no more than a competent
organiser. Certainly administrative duties gave him no great pleasure and
he never sought them out. But he had an accurate sense of what needed to
be done and a capacity to make things happen which he underrated.

     If higher education is vulnerable to the financial climate, small depart-
ments are especially so. Classics departments throughout the UK felt

under threat during the 1980s (a threat partly alleviated but not removed by the amalgamations late in the decade in the wake of the Barron report) and MacDowell was anxious that Classics might be closed down. Aberdeen did in fact close their department in the 1970s, reducing university teaching and research in Classics in Scotland by 25 per cent at a stroke. The worst never happened at Glasgow, partly headed off by the merger of the departments of Greek and Humanity into Classics; but obtaining even senior replacements was a struggle. MacDowell's own post was one of the counters in the game. Under the terms of his appointment he had the right to retire at 70. Despite encouragement from the Principal, Graeme Davies, to retire earlier, he elected to stay on, unconvinced that he would be replaced, and finally retired in 2001 after 30 years in post (an achievement of which he was proud, and one not equalled since Lushington in 1875). His argument for staying on reflected not just his commitment to the chair and the department but his habitual modesty; acknowledging that a younger professor was more desirable, he reflected that 'even an elderly professor of Greek was better than none at all'. It was the same concern for the department that led him to apply for (and obtain) the Oxford D.Litt. in 1992; in an age when the doctorate had become the norm for anyone entering an academic career, he felt that it would add in a small way to the department's HR statistics (which as the then Head of Department he had to compile). In the same way, part of his pleasure in being admitted to the Royal Society of Edinburgh in 1991 and the British Academy in 1993 was the boost it might give to the standing of the department in the eyes of the university.

He was in the end proved right about the chair. He was not replaced on retirement. The strength of his own commitment was underlined by a remarkable gesture in his will; he left Glasgow University £2m, the bulk of his estate, to support the chair of Greek. He evidently (astutely) held off to the last in the hope that against all the signs the university might still invest its own money; despite the frustration and profound disappointment, it must have given him consolation to be in a position to do something to rescue a chair which he was proud to have occupied. At the time of writing I understand that the university has agreed to accept the bequest and to establish a MacDowell Chair in Greek.

He brought to his teaching the gifts which made his research so accessible, a serious commitment to getting it right and a rare capacity for making complex problems intelligible without superficiality. Lecturing also allowed an outlet for his histrionic side. He had discovered in the 1960s (at a time when lecturing was a dry business) a talent for presenting

Aristophanes in a theatrical way, acting out the parts in a range of voices; this had proved popular in public lectures and he used it to good effect in his lectures on comedy at Glasgow. Both for colleagues and for students he maintained an open door policy. He is remembered by former students as a generous teacher in every sense. A remorselessly rigorous researcher himself, who could be unforgiving with inaccuracies, inconsistencies or superficiality from professionals, he was patient with students struggling to find their way, though unsympathetic to mere show. One of his former students recalls a seminar in which MacDowell asked a question and a student gave an answer which was not just wrong but also totally irrelevant to the question. To the amusement of a visiting academic who was present Douglas patiently replied 'not quite', before proceeding to steer the discussion in the right direction. He was passionate about the value of a classical education and went to extraordinary lengths to support promising students. A member of the Senior Honours class of 1982 recalled that he bought everyone in the class ('and I'm pretty sure all Senior Honours students every year') a subscription to *Journal of Hellenic Studies*. He was equally generous with time. Douglas Cairns, now Professor of Greek at Edinburgh, recalls: 'When I was in my first year, on the grounds that I needed to read more Greek than was read in the Ordinary syllabus, we met once a week in his room to read the *Acharnians* together.' When the department started to recruit postgraduate students in the late 1980s and after, he made a point of holding a weekly reading class on Aristophanes with them. Graduate students in financial difficulties would find that an anonymous donor had been found to assist with their costs. Only the most perceptive guessed that the donor was MacDowell himself. This was part of a large pattern of quiet philanthropy.

At the time of his first appointment at Manchester he had undertaken no research at all. Immediately on taking up the job he set about making good the lacuna. The direction he took was in part—but only in part—a matter of chance. Both at school and at university he had always been interested in Greek history. While teaching at Merchant Taylors' he had picked up a copy of the selection of texts from the Athenian orators which Sir Richard Jebb had produced for school use in 1880 (a book ironically, as MacDowell later noted, dedicated to 'the Greek class at the University of Glasgow'). He had never studied the orators in any depth and he immediately recognised both the potential of the corpus as a way into the social and political history of ancient Athens from a direction distinct from and complementary to the historians and the lacuna in twentieth-century British scholarship. So he decided to write a commentary on an oratorical text. He was encouraged in the enterprise by Dover, whose own interests included Greek prose of the classical period. The nineteenth and early twentieth centuries had seen some very good commentary work on Greek oratory in the UK (including a clutch of commentaries from J. E. Sandys) but interest had largely fizzled out. The lack of interest was reinforced by a tendency to think in discipline terms, with Plato left largely to the philosophers and orators and historiographers to the ancient historians. The orators had effectively become subsidiary material in larger works on political history, or, worse, models of style for Greek prose composition. The blight did not affect Continental and American scholarship. The Budé series in France and the Loeb series in the USA patiently plugged the gaps in the works of the orators. MacDowell's interest in the orators was ahead of its time in British classical scholarship. But though he can claim the credit for stimulating a resurgence of interest in the Greek orators in the United Kingdom, there was no rush to follow. In fact it was not until the eighties (two decades after his first book) that MacDowell's commentary work found successors in the UK, with the appearance of Edwards–Usher, *Antiphon and Lysias*,[1] and *Demosthenes: Selected Private Speeches* by Carey–Reid.[2] From then on interest in the Greek orators has burgeoned to the point that it is difficult to recollect a time when MacDowell was almost alone (apart from Stephen Usher at Royal Holloway) in the field in the UK.

The author and text he chose for his first book, Andokides *On the Mysteries* (Oxford, 1962), reflected his sense of the potential of the orators as a complement to historiography. *On the Mysteries* deals at one remove with the notorious incident of the mutilation of the herms (stone tetragonal columns with a human head and genitals) which took place overnight not long before the sailing of the Athenian expedition against the city of Syracuse in Sicily in 415 BC. The atrocity (both because it had the potential to blight the expedition as a bad omen and because it smacked of conspiracy) triggered a witch hunt which had a convulsive effect on Athenian political life and probably doomed the expedition by removing the talented and mercurial Alkibiades from command. The incident is told briefly in the sixth book of Thucydides' history. Andokides was a whistleblower who revealed the names of some of the perpetrators and his speech *On the Mysteries* (which was written not at the time of the original

---

[1] M. Edwards and S. Usher, *Greek Orators I. Antiphon and Lysias* (Warminster, 1985).
[2] C. Carey and R. A. Reid, *Demosthenes: Selected Private Speeches* (Cambridge, 1985).

affair but for a subsequent political trial fifteen years or so later) both complements and disagrees with Thucydides on some key points.

MacDowell's work on Andokides led by a (retrospectively) natural route to his second project, which added a complementary strand to his research. While working on his commentary, he was reading the speeches of Andokides' contemporary, Antiphon (the Robespierre of Athenian politics), one of the key instigators of the coup which overthrew the Athenian democracy in 411. Antiphon was a professional writer of speeches for the courts and the corpus which survives is devoted to homicide cases. His reading alerted MacDowell to a gap both in the scholarship and in his own knowledge. He reflected that there was no book available to explain the intricacies of Athenian homicide law, a fascinating blend of religious and legal ritual remarkable for its complexity in a system which was characterised both by its relative simplicity and by its efficiency. The result was his second book, *Athenian Homicide Law in the Age of the Orators* (Manchester, 1963). The combination of oratory and law in MacDowell's interests bridges a perceptible divide in the scholarship. Though the orators are our most important source for the reconstruction of the Athenian legal system both in principle and in practice, there is a tendency for people to opt for oratory (often with rhetoric) or law as the primary focus of their study. MacDowell unusually was interested in and equally strong in both.

Of both these volumes, produced in a period of four years, he was later to recall with pride and amusement that they had been typed on a portable typewriter balanced on a coffee table (there was no desk) in his lodgings in Manchester. He subsequently felt that they had been written too hastily. Certainly by the standards of his later commentaries the Andokides volume is slim. It remains however the standard English language commentary after almost five decades (though Edwards's Aris and Phillips commentary has appeared in the interval to update the discussion and to make the text available to a wider audience[3]). And it is marked by MacDowell's careful attention to detail and his strong sense of historical context. The book on Athenian homicide law is tiny compared with the larger word counts in subsequent books on the subject. It is however a gem of a book, still read, still cited and an invaluable work to place in the hands of students. MacDowell always had a gift for presenting challenging subjects in lucid English which makes his work accessible to the novice without surrendering either grasp of detail or rigour of argument. It also inadvertently opened up a debate which was to run for decades, about the

---

[3] M. Edwards, *Andocides* (Warminster, 1995).

right to prosecute in Athenian homicide cases. The wisdom was, and is, that this right was confined to blood relatives of the victim (or masters in the case of slaves). MacDowell argued that while the obligation to prose-cute was confined to blood relatives, the right was open to anyone. His view has stimulated a number of refutations (and some very good research) over four decades or so, including a monograph devoted to the subject.[4] The difficulty of delivering a single knock-down blow to MacDowell's suggestion serves as a useful reminder of the slender base for even (per-haps especially) our most confident and persistent statements about the ancient world. The debate also illustrates two aspects of MacDowell's character. The first is a willingness to grasp nettles. The second is a good-humoured acceptance of the provisionality of research (more rare than it should be); he was later to decide that the early MacDowell was wrong.

The homicide book was important in a more fundamental sense than its contribution to the study of a particular aspect of Athenian law. When MacDowell wrote, there was scarcely anyone writing on ancient Greek law in the UK, except for A. R. W. Harrison and (from a constitutional angle) Peter Rhodes. There is a long and distinguished tradition in mainland Europe. The towering works are in German (Lipsius, Ruschenbusch, Wolff), Italian (Paoli) or French (Gernet). All—and this is significant—were operating in an environment informed by the European systems of civil law. The USA had produced excellent researchers in the field of ancient law, particularly Bonner and Calhoun; but these were in the early decades of the twentieth century. The UK had had scholars working on the orators from a legal background (like Charles Rann Kennedy) but interest in law in itself was largely absent. In the past two decades scholars working in the Anglo-American common law system have established a distinct place in the discipline. MacDowell did not create this trend. But he did blaze a trail in recognising and demonstrating the intrinsic interest of Athenian law as a subject worthy of study for itself. And it is difficult to imagine the current level of interest in Athenian law without his intervention.

The book on homicide law was followed after a long interval by a more widely focused book which confirmed his lasting place in the study of Greek law. The first volume of A. R. W. Harrison's *The Law of Athens* had appeared in 1968.[5] This book, which deals with property, is magnifi-cent. The second volume on procedure was incomplete on his death in 1969. MacDowell had agreed to write a book on Greek law for Scullard's

[4] A. Tulin, *Dike phonou: the Right of Prosecution and Attic Homicide Procedure* (Stuttgart, 1996).
[5] A. R. W. Harrison, *The Law of Athens*, 2 vols (Oxford, 1968, 1971).

Aspects of Greek and Roman Life series and was due to spend a term as Visiting Fellow at Merton College, which would offer an opportunity to discuss his ideas with Harrison, who was Warden there. Harrison's death ruled this out and MacDowell spent his time at Merton assembling Harrison's papers for publication as Volume 2 of *The Law of Athens*, which appeared in 1971. He was offered but declined the opportunity to complete the book as Harrison's co-author. He found Harrison's approach (derived from Roman law) uncongenial and old-fashioned and he preferred to continue with his own book as an independent project. The decision to go it alone was the right one. MacDowell's *The Law in Classical Athens* (London, 1978) is still three decades later the first port of call for anyone wishing to get a grip on the basics of the Athenian legal system. The book itself however is anything but basic. It is deeply grounded in the evidence (as the rich endnotes demonstrate) and covers the whole gamut of procedure and substance. But it wears its learning unostentatiously. MacDowell preferred lucidity to adornment. Though it goes unnoticed by the reader, this was a difficult book to write, far harder than it would be today, when anglophone scholarship on Athenian law has mushroomed. There was little available in English and MacDowell had to work though a substantial bibliography in German, a language for which he professed no great facility. The book on Athenian law was followed after a long interval by a volume on Spartan law in the Scottish Classical Studies series which MacDowell had instigated.[6] Reliable sources for Sparta are few (far fewer than Athens, our best—but still inadequately—documented state for the classical period) and reviews of the book were more mixed. MacDowell felt afterwards that his judgement had been correct but he did not return either to Spartan history or to Spartan law. The decades after the book on Athenian law saw a steady stream of articles and chapters on law. But his lasting monument in this field is the 1978 book, which still offers a no-nonsense introduction to the beginner or non-specialist while also remaining an essential point of reference for the expert. He was disappointed that the UK publisher did not opt for a paperback reprint. But it was published in paperback in the USA (Ithaca, NY, 1986), which has ensured its availability as a coursebook and its place on reading lists. His eminence in the field of ancient Greek law was recognised in invitations from Hans Julius Wolff from the 1970s to participate in the triennial (subsequently biennial) international colloquia on ancient law (published as

---

[6] *Spartan Law (Scottish Classical Studies No. 1)* (Edinburgh, 1986).

the *Symposion* series) which he initiated and which MacDowell attended frequently from 1982.

Among the papers on Athenian law, one in particular is worth singling out as showing the calm nettle-grasping side of MacDowell. It is a piece produced while he was preparing the Athenian law book.[7] It was destined to have a long and controversial shelf-life. For most readers of ancient Greek texts, *hybris* was (often still is) predominantly a theological notion, the pride which comes from excessive prosperity, prompting a man to misprise his own significance and offend against the gods. The notion has entered the collective consciousness and is now ineradicable. But it is derived largely from tragedy and is actually applicable only to a small minority of surviving plays. And it is not the way the word works in most contexts, especially but not exclusively lawcourt speeches. The reference is usually secular and relates to dealings between humans; it generally covers abusive, frequently but not inevitably physical (especially violent), mistreatment (including sexual abuse). In classical Athens it was a crime, but notoriously one which the law left to common-sense definition by the juries (the law said: 'If someone commits *hybris* …'). MacDowell's 1976 paper in *Greece and Rome* sought to revise this picture and relocate *hybris* within inter-human conduct and within the legal system. Nick Fisher, who had independently been working on a monograph on *hybris*,[8] also published on it in the same volume of *Greece and Rome*,[9] offering an alternative interpretation. As Stephen Todd has memorably observed,[10] where MacDowell located *hybris* in the psychology of the perpetrator (excessive behaviour caused by surfeit—of money, drink, energy), Fisher located it in the sociology of the victim (loss of face in an honour-sensitive society). As well as good evidentiary support, both positions have their limitations (especially when one tries to turn fine differences into substantive law in a legal system where precise definitions play only a very circumscribed role) and subsequent writers have tended to look for a middle ground. But these papers continue to form the frame within which the debate takes place.

As with law, Athenian oratory (especially Demosthenes) remained a passionate interest. In 1990 he published a commentary on the speech against Meidias (*Demosthenes, Against Meidias (Oration 21)*) with Oxford

[7] '"*Hybris*" in Athens', *Greece and Rome*, 23 (1976), 14–31.
[8] N. R. E. Fisher, *Hybris: a Study in the Values of Honour and Shame in Ancient Greece* (Warminster, 1992).
[9] N. R. E. Fisher, '*Hybris* and dishonour I', *Greece and Rome*, 23 (1976), 177–93.
[10] S. C. Todd, *A Commentary on Lysias, Speeches 1–11, Part 1* (Oxford, 2007), p. 92, n. 8.

University Press (subsequently reprinted by Bristol Classical Press in 2002). Like his other work this commentary blends meticulous scholarship with accessibility. Unusually for its day (but almost obligatory now) it included a translation facing the Greek text. As well as allowing the commentary to do its work more efficiently (since translation is often the best comment on linguistic minutiae), this move also acknowledged that the work would be used by readers with limited Greek or even with no Greek at all. The scholarship is visible not only in the detailed comments on matters of language, style, text, law and history but also in the care devoted to producing the text. Collations of manuscripts in previous editions had been limited. Acknowledging that it was not feasible to collate all, MacDowell still consulted forty-seven of the medieval manuscripts. He also devoted part of the introduction to the still contentious issue of the authenticity of the evidentiary documents (laws, depositions etc.) which survive in the medieval manuscripts of some Demosthenic forensic speeches (and intermittently in the manuscripts of other orators). The topic had received no serious attention since the nineteenth century. MacDowell revisited the subject of the line numbering which survives in some manuscripts to conclude (as had others) that the documents were added to the text after the stichometric edition was completed. The documents (which were read out by the clerk during the hearing, not by the litigant) appeared to have been introduced from another (possibly archive) source. His further conclusion (typically sensible) echoed that of Drerup at the end of the nineteenth century that there is no single answer to the question of authenticity; each document has to be taken on its merits. A second and equally impressive commentary on Demosthenes, *On the False Embassy*, was published (again with Oxford University Press) in 2000. The commentary covers the speech delivered by Demosthenes in 343 BC in his prosecution of his enemy Aischines for (allegedly) betraying Athens' interests as envoy to Philip II of Macedon in 346. Here as often before MacDowell was drawn to the gaps in the research; he selected the speech because it receives less attention than the later *On the Crown* (considered since antiquity to be Demosthenes' masterpiece). The book shares the strengths of its predecessor, including both a chalcenteric engagement with and a magisterial treatment of the medieval manuscripts. A smaller commentary (again with translation) on the *Encomium of Helen* by Gorgias of Leontinoi was published by Bristol Classical Press in 1982. Though on a more modest scale than his other commentaries, the work reflects both his capacity to reach different audiences and his continuing concern to provide for teaching needs (it arose from a course on oratory

which he taught at Glasgow). He also found time to contribute two volumes to the series of annotated translations of the Greek orators edited
by Michael Gagarin and published through University of Texas Press, the
first volume with Gagarin in 1998 (on Antiphon and Andokides,[11] of which
he contributed the Andokides section, revisiting his first research project),
and a further volume on speeches 27–38 of the modern editions of
Demosthenes (devoted to the cases relating to his own inheritance and a
number of private actions for which he acted as professional speechwriter),
which appeared in 2004.[12]

His final work was again on oratory and was devoted to Demosthenes.[13]
It was produced at a time when his health was already poor and he was
often tired, a testimony (as a former student observes) to his 'inner steel'.
Two recent anglophone books have addressed the corpus of fifth- and
fourth-century oratory in its entirety.[14] But Demosthenes certainly merits
a dedicated volume. He has of course attracted a great deal of interest
from the direction of political history. But the only recent monograph on
the speeches was devoted to style.[15] In depth MacDowell's *Demosthenes*
sits in the tradition of the monumental *Die attische Beredsamkeit* of
Friedrich Blass. The book eschews the option of following Demosthenes'
career as a simple chronological narrative, though introductory chapters
deal both with Athenian oratory in general and Demosthenes' life and
work in particular. The bulk of the volume is organised thematically by
type of case/occasion, offering background information, summary and
comments on the argument of each speech. Part of Demosthenes' career
was spent as a hired speechwriter (*logographos*) for the courts; this trade
(though popular with litigants, as the number of surviving examples suggests) was subject to a degree of disapproval in a system which viewed
legal professionalism with suspicion and aspired to equality before the law
(whatever the reality) and the speeches were generally written anonymously. As a result the Demosthenic corpus contains a number of speeches
whose authorship is contentious, some of which are probably or certainly
spurious. MacDowell's book addresses the whole corpus, including contentious speeches whose authenticity he accepts (such as the funeral oration allegedly delivered for the dead in the battle of Chaironeia), those on

[11] M. Gagarin and D. M. MacDowell, *Antiphon and Andocides* (Austin, TX, 1998).
[12] *Demosthenes, Speeches 27–38* (Austin, TX, 2004).
[13] *Demosthenes* (Oxford, 2009).
[14] S. Usher, *Greek Oratory: Tradition and Originality* (Oxford, 1999) and M. Edwards, *The Attic Orators* (London, 1994).
[15] L. Pearson, *The Art of Demosthenes* (Meisenheim am Glan, 1976).

which he is agnostic or suspicious (as the *Erotikos* which appears as the sixty-first speech in modern editions) and even those where he accepts modern arguments for misattribution (especially the set of speeches certainly or probably delivered—and written—by Apollodoros the son of Pasion). It is a fitting last work, since it distils his reading of and on Demosthenes, who had established himself as MacDowell's favourite orator (as he was for most readers in antiquity); like all of his preceding work, it is written with the reader and not the writer in mind and is designed to offer an introduction in each case to aid the reading of the text. It is destined to remain the gateway to Demosthenes' oratory (as distinct from his politics) for anglophone students for the next three decades or more.

The third strand of his research reflected his early interests at school and university. In 1971 he published a commentary on Aristophanes' *Wasps* in a series for which Kenneth Dover was general editor.[16] Fifth-century comedy is so inseparably embedded in its context that it cannot be read without constant recourse to its social and political environment. So Aristophanes also appealed to MacDowell's interest in Athenian history. There had been some uncertainty whether his project would be *Wasps* or *Lysistrata*. The outcome was the right one. Editing and annotating *Wasps* with its plot focus on the Athenian legal system played to MacDowell's established research strengths; the sexual theme of *Lysistrata* was less to his taste. Good commentaries have a long life and the *Wasps* commentary, now forty years old, has weathered handsomely. It deals lucidly and succinctly with text, staging, humour, style, historical and legal *Realia*. Here as in his work on the orators the textual judgements show the hallmark MacDowell style as an editor and textual critic. His approach is essentially common-sense conservatism, marked by a readiness to accept the manuscript tradition in defiance of dogma where it can be made to yield sense, neither cavalier nor credulous. As with oratory and law, the love of Aristophanes stayed with him throughout his career. It continued in a steady stream of articles and reviews over the years, to culminate in a monograph, *Aristophanes and Athens* (Oxford, 1995). The volume offers (after a chapter on the early lost plays, elusive but important both for our sense of Aristophanes' development and for our understanding of the evolution of fifth-century comedy), a reading of each of the surviving plays in chronological order. The title reflects his interests—not just Aristophanes but Aristophanes in his historical context. Comic scholarship is prolific. But there are very few books like this which one can place in the hands of

---

[16] *Aristophanes, Wasps, Edited with Introduction and Commentary* (Oxford, 1971).

students to take them into the text and context in a readable and approachable way without either superficiality or flash.

Many would be satisfied to have made the mark he did in any one of the fields which he researched. To achieve the scale and quality of Douglas MacDowell's output in three distinct fields of classical scholarship is a remarkable achievement. The long shelf-life of his early research and the guaranteed longevity of his subsequent scholarship is a legacy which speaks for itself.

The love of theatre fostered by his mother remained with him throughout his life and he would regularly visit the London theatres. In his youth he had travelled little: a family holiday with his parents to Norway in 1948, a three-week holiday in Gibraltar as a prize for an essay competition run by the Overseas League in 1950, a trip to Greece while still an undergraduate with Martin Frederiksen in 1953. He made up for this in later life. Apart from travel on academic business, one of his favourite pastimes was to visit museums and art-galleries and (importantly) opera houses in the major cultural centres of Europe—Rome, Florence, Venice, Vienna, Verona, Paris, as well as Covent Garden in London—especially in the company of his close friend and colleague, Costas Panayotakis. He remained firmly European in focus, with visits to the USA confined to academic conferences and otherwise a trip to Tangier from Gibraltar in 1950 his only ventures beyond.

Though his early shyness never left him, he was a generous friend and a kind and courteous host. The word 'gentleman' recurs in comments from those who encountered him. Though he was both aware and justifiably proud of his achievements, he was always (unduly) modest about his abilities, despite his eminence. He was (without affectation) both surprised by and appreciative of the evidence of esteem he received, not only the election to the Royal Society of Edinburgh and to the British Academy but also and especially—and more personally—the conference held in his honour on his retirement (whose proceedings were subsequently published[17]), which was attended by colleagues from around the world, including to his great pleasure his former research students and his teacher of fifty years previously, Sir Kenneth Dover. He remained to the end a private man who knew how to keep his counsel. A researcher who interviewed him toward the end of his life was struck by the contrast between the discreet MacDowell and the brutal honesty of Kenneth Dover, observing: 'When I

[17] D. L. Cairns and R. Knox (eds.), *Law, Rhetoric and Comedy in Classical Athens: Essays in Honour of Douglas M. MacDowell* (Cardiff, 2004).

talked to MacDowell I felt I was facing Alec Guinness/George Smiley: I was telling him everything, he was telling me nothing.' I think Douglas would have been both amused and pleased.

Douglas Maurice MacDowell, MA, D.Litt., FBA, FRSE. Born 8 March 1931; died 16 January 2010.

CHRIS CAREY
University College London

Note. I wish to express my thanks to Douglas Cairns, Mike Edwards, Alex Garvie, Roger Green, Kostas Kapparis, Elizabeth Moignard, Mick Morris, Costas Panayotakis and Dimos Spatharas for valuable information and advice.

MICHAEL PODRO

Michael Podro
1931–2008

MICHAEL PODRO was a scholar of real note and a genuine intellectual, and also a significant public presence in British cultural life. What mattered to him above all was serious thinking about art, thinking that took place in the gallery in front of actual works of art as well as in the study. His scholarship had a broad reach and integrated the larger concerns of philosophical aesthetics, art history and art criticism. The distinctive combination of rigorous analytic thinking and close viewing he cultivated made him particularly attentive to the complexities of response elicited by works of art. Significantly, the impetus for his election as a Fellow of the British Academy in 1992 came both from philosophers and art historians.

The impact he had extended well beyond his accomplishments as an original and creative scholar. He took education very seriously, exerting a considerable influence on the study of art history, not only as director (1970–4, 1977–80) of the programme in art history and theory he was instrumental in developing at the University of Essex, but also as a leading intellectual presence throughout his time there, first as Reader (1969–73) and then as Professor (1973–97). An inspirational figure, he enlivened the discipline of art history through the generosity with which he engaged those who like him valued the life of the mind. He was a member of the editorial boards of the *British Journal of Aesthetics*, *Word and Image* and the *Zeitschrift für Ästhetik und Allgemeine Kunstwissenschaft*. He was a significant presence in the museum world, playing an active role as a trustee of the Victoria and Albert Museum (1987–96). His services to the academic community and the art world were recognised with the award of CBE in 2001.

Proceedings of the British Academy, **172**, 251–272. © The British Academy 2011.

Intellectual project

Podro's outstanding achievements as a scholar—he was undoubtedly one of the most important figures of his generation writing on the history and theory of art—had a lot to do with the sustained nature of his intellectual project. He thought harder and more fruitfully than anyone in the field about the value of a close critical engagement with works of art, exploring the complex interplay of visual perceptiveness and cognitive and ethical awareness such engagement entailed. As he wrote in the conclusion to his first book, *The Manifold in Perception: Theories of Art from Kant to Hildebrand* (1972), any genuinely productive 'critical discussion of the arts' necessarily brought to bear larger assumptions about 'the nature of the mind and the location of the arts within the over-all context of our human purposes and perceptions'.[1]

What particularly fascinated him was the paradox central to Kantian aesthetics—that an aesthetic response to a phenomenon was categorically different from a conceptual and moral or ethical understanding of it, but brought into play a capacity for such understanding. The disinterestedness entailed by the aesthetic, he was at pains to stress, should not be confused with indifference to knowledge or ethical or political considerations. He was as opposed to narrowly formalist conceptions of the aesthetic as he was to the anti-aesthetic stances that became fashionable in artistic and academic circles. While he insisted that the terms in which one apprehended a work of art were categorically different from those operating in one's everyday visual engagement with things, an aesthetic response had for him a significant vernacular dimension. He made frequent recourse to a parallel between literature and art to clarify this point: just as poetry and literature use as their basic materials the language deployed by people in their ordinary social commerce with one another, so picturing deals in the visual vernacular of perceptions and images that form the fabric of people's everyday commerce with the phenomenal world.

Podro's explorations into art and the aesthetic fall into three broadly defined categories. First, there is his philosophical examination of the aesthetic attitude, and in particular understandings of the aesthetic that developed out of the critical thinking of the late European Enlightenment. Kant functioned as his leading point of reference, supplemented by the more political understanding of the aesthetic later developed by Schiller.

---

[1] M. Podro, *The Manifold in Perception: Theories of Art from Kant to Hildebrand* (Oxford, 1972), pp. 125–6.

These concerns formed the substance of his first book and he returned to them in the publication on which he was working at the very end of his life.[2]

A second major concern was the intellectual basis of art historical analysis. In his most widely known and frequently cited study, *The Critical Historians of Art* (1982), he examined the tradition of German art historical scholarship that emerged in Germany in the nineteenth century and culminated in the work of Heinrich Wöllflin, Erwin Panofsky and Aby Warburg, a tradition that was instrumental in establishing art history as a serious academic study. This was no ordinary historiography of the discipline, but something much more interesting and valuable. He focused on the theoretical commitments that had informed the more successful attempts by scholars working in this tradition to fashion a genuinely critical history of art. For Podro, such critical history needed to be both serious historical enquiry and theoretical exploration of the nature of art as a cultural phenomenon. In other words, it was a study that involved constant negotiation between historical reconstruction and critical thinking about art. His philosophical background meant that he was able to do justice, in a way that other scholars at the time examining the intellectual basis of modern art history could not, to the complexities of the neo-Kantian thought informing nineteenth- and early twentieth-century German critical study of the visual arts.

Forming the third area of enquiry in his larger project was a sustained examination of the nature of pictorial depiction that eventually gave rise to his very fine book *Depiction* (1998). He posed the fundamental question as to how seeing subject matter or a motif in a picture or cognate form of art such as low relief differed from while also bringing into play everyday perceptual engagements with the world. Throughout his career, Podro insisted that viewing and creating pictures involved a complex imaginative interplay between one's apprehension of features and structures internal to processes of picture making, and one's perceptions of things and situations and images in the outside world that these evoked or depicted.

In making this point, Podro was not so much offering a defence of artistic figuration against the widely held assumption that the more vital forms of modern art were necessarily those that had abandoned traditional pictorial representation. Rather he was critiquing the oversimplified models of viewing presupposed by the formalist conceptions of art

---

[2] Aspects of this work have been published as articles—see below, n. 31.

informing such assumptions—models in which seeing a painting as a representation or depiction of a motif or subject was assumed to be categorically distinct from seeing a painting as a material phenomenon in its own right. Podro broadly agreed with Richard Wollheim's conception of the 'twofoldedness' of viewing paintings—a process of 'seeing in' that involved being visually aware of the marked and coloured surfaces of the painting at the same time as discerning in these a recognisable phenomenon existing in its own space rather than on the painting's flat surface.[3] This for Podro was not just a technical issue about perceptual processes, but had to do with the way in which the mind was activated in the close viewing of a work of art. The mind's imaginative processing of the visual particularities of a painting and their interconnections, he insisted, brought into play larger understandings of the world we live in—understandings involving ethics and politics as well as knowledge.[4]

Formation—literature, philosophy and art

Podro was born in North London to Jewish parents on 13 March 1931. His early home life there introduced him to an intellectual and cultural milieu that later was to prove important for him. His father Joshua Podro, a Jewish immigrant from Austria of Russian origin who had settled in London, was a biblical scholar of some note—he developed these interests in his spare time while running a successful press-cutting agency. As a young man he had been involved in a Yiddish circle that included figures such as the poet Isaac Rosenberg and the painter David Bomberg. Michael Podro's aunt, Clara Klinghoffer (1900–70), was an artist who had enjoyed a considerable reputation in the British art world of the 1920s, known for her portraits and figure studies—she is represented by a painting, *The Old Troubadour* (1923), in the Tate collection.[5]

   Podro's education after he finished school and completed his National Service with the RAF in 1951 was somewhat unconventional and unusually broad. It began with his reading English at Cambridge as an undergraduate. This was important, not so much for developing his interest in literature as for laying the basis of his life-long preoccupation with critical

[3] R. Wollheim, *Painting as an Art* (London, 1987), pp. 46–7.
[4] M. Podro, *Depiction* (New Haven, CT, and London, 1998), p. 8. Some of the ideas developed in this book were sketched out in an earlier article, 'Depiction and the Golden Calf', in A. Harrison (ed.), *Philosophy and the Visual Arts* (Dordrecht, 1987), pp. 3–28.
[5] Several of these details are taken from Podro's obituary in *The Times* (3 April 2008).

responsiveness to works of art. F. R. Leavis was a major inspiration, giving him (as to so many others of Podro's generation) a sense of the abiding significance of close critical engagement with literature and, by implication, with visual art too. Particularly important was Leavis's sense of the ethical and intellectual stakes involved in this critical engagement, having to do not with the content of a work as such but with the nature of the aesthetic response it activated and of the imaginative world it conjured up. William Empson, another key figure in British literary criticism at the time, was also important for Podro, though he was not teaching at Cambridge. Like Leavis, he conveyed a sense that critical analysis involved something much more than mere professional or academic expertise, and had a deeper intellectual rigour to it.

Podro summed up what he had gained from his early involvement with critical writing on literature by asking 'how can the procedures of literary criticism be transferred to the criticism of painting?' 'This', he maintained, 'has remained for me central.'[6] It remained central partly because studies of language and literature played a more significant role in British intellectual life than studies concerned with visual art and representation, and so constituted a somewhat richer field of enquiry. It also did so because the art-critical analysis with which he was familiar for the most part drew on somewhat inflexible models of formal structuring and signifying procedure—this being true both of an earlier modernist, purely visual formalism and its later more sophisticated semiotic iterations. Podro sought to bring the resources of close reading to bear on close looking, defying the rigid divide between the literary and the pictorial, or between the linguistic and the visual, often found in modern theorising about visual art.

After finishing his degree in English in 1954, Podro's career took a new turn when he registered as a part-time student at the Slade School of Art in London. It was there that he met his future wife, Charlotte Booth, a fellow student who later became a conservator in the Royal Institute of British Architects' collection of architectural drawings. Married in 1961, the close companionship they formed was to play a central role in both their lives, as did that with the two daughters they had, Natasha and Sarah. Michael Podro is survived by his wife, Charlotte Podro, and both daughters.

During Podro's year at the Slade in 1955–6, Ernst Gombrich was offering seminars in art history that Slade students could attend. His encounter with Gombrich set him on a new trajectory. Gombrich was then working

---

[6] M. Podro, 'Brief outline of a biography', undated typescript, after 2001.

on the book, *Art and Illusion: a Study in the Psychology of Visual Represen-tation*, that when it came out in 1959 became the single most important and certainly the most widely read and influential study in the history of art to appear in the post-war years. The issues Gombrich was working through, having to do with pictorial representation and the perceptual processes involved in viewing paintings and other forms of visual depic-tion, were to become foundational for Podro's engagement with art history. Podro took from Gombrich two key ideas, the first being that the percep-tion of a visual representation was not a purely visual or optical process, but also involved a mental conceptualising. The second was that the recog-nition of a motif in a painting, while it developed in part out of a familiar-ity with representational conventions particular to painting, also brought into play habits of viewing deployed in the everyday perceptions of things in the world around us.

Put simply, Gombrich's central argument was as follows—what happens when we see a picture of a horse is not the same as what happens when we see a horse, yet the former perception depends on visual memories of the latter. There was one aspect of Gombrich's perceptual psychology of art that Podro was to find increasingly problematic, however, namely his assumption that at the moment when we see a horse in the picture of a horse, we no longer see the picture's representational devices. For Gombrich it was as if we had a momentary illusion of perceiving a horse in the visual effects generated by the painted representation. On his understanding, we adjust our perceptual framing so that we compensate for the disparities between the look of the painting and the look of an actual horse, and for a moment only see what these perceptions share. In this way a work that initially seems unnaturalistic can, when we adjust our expectations, give rise to a vivid visual impression of the motif it depicts.

Richard Wollheim's review of *Depiction*, the book by Podro that was his eventual answer to Gombrich's *Art and Illusion*, nicely sums up what was at stake in Podro's debt to and departure from Gombrich's phenom-enology of viewing. Gombrich, Wollheim explained, developed two theses from his explorations in perceptual psychology that were to preoccupy Podro, one negatively and one positively. The first was 'that we cannot simultaneously be aware of what is represented (the subject) and of the representing support (the surface)'—with the latter seen as including the literal markings and texturings created by the artist. The second was 'that there is, in our experience, no observable boundary between subject and surface; as we scrutinize a painting, subject turns into surface, surface into subject'. And he concluded: 'Podro claims what is evidently correct: that it is only by rejecting Gombrich's first thesis that we can do full justice to his second.'[7]

Podro came to the conclusion that the close viewing of a painting precluded making any clear separation between seeing the painted surface and seeing what was represented—a viewer did not alternate between these two ways of seeing, but was drawn into the painter's way of imagining and depicting things to the point that the what and how of representation become inextricably bound up with one another. An awareness of painterly effects and structuring made the image or motif discerned in the former all the more imaginatively compelling. This both built on and contradicted Gombrich's understanding of how we apprehend a painting.

Podro's encounter with Gombrich had a further dimension of productive give and take. Through Gombrich, Podro was made aware of a rich tradition of German art historical analysis that had not yet been assimilated within the study of art history in the UK—such study being limited largely to formal stylistic analysis, connoisseurial attribution, and archival research into artistic practices, patronage, and historical and cultural 'background', without any overarching critical framing that would make larger sense of art as a cultural or even a distinctively visual phenomenon. Gombrich, while offering rich insights into the strengths and limitations of the analysis developed by the major figures of German art history such as Wöfflin and Panofsky, was deeply sceptical of the critical philosophical thinking underpinning the more speculative aspects of their work. More specifically, he refused to engage with the Kantian and neo-Kantian ways of conceptualising art and artistic culture that were foundational for the intellectual tradition within which they were working. It was this gap that Podro went on to fill. Podro also distanced himself from the crude anti-Hegelianism that became marked in Gombrich's later pronouncements on art history and cultural history as he became ever more reliant on Karl Popper's positivistic critique of Continental thought.[8]

During his year at the Slade, Podro began working under Gombrich's guidance on the theoretical concerns shaping the tradition of German art historical analysis to which Gombrich had introduced him. Gombrich advised him to strengthen his background in philosophy, and he spent the next year, 1956–7, studying in the Philosophy Department at University College London, working towards his Ph.D. qualifying examination.

[7] Richard Wollheim, 'Depiction. Michael Podro', Times Literary Supplement (April 23 1999).
[8] Podro offers a very illuminating account of Hegel's ideas on art and of the role these played in nineteenth-century conceptions of the history of art in his book The Critical Historians of Art (New Haven, CT, and London, 1982), particularly pp. 17–30.

Gombrich put him in touch with Richard Wollheim who was teaching philosophy at University College at the time. This proved to be another crucially important encounter for Podro, leading him to embark on a Ph.D. dissertation jointly supervised by Gombrich and Wollheim. The dissertation was on the late nineteenth-century German art theorist Konrad Fiedler. Fiedler's neo-Kantian conception of art's autonomy and understanding of the mental processing of visual form played a significant role in the new systematic analysis of artistic style that developed in German and Austrian art historical scholarship at the turn of the century—best known nowadays from the still widely read publications of Heinrich Wölfflin.

Characteristic of Podro's independence of mind and critical acuity was his willingness to act on the dawning realisation that Fiedler's theoretical analysis, far from being a key to understanding what the neo-Kantian tradition that interested him might offer in the way of a richer critical understanding of art, in fact marked something of a dead end—a dead end resulting from a mode of thinking that fundamentally misconstrued the more radical implications of Kant's philosophical aesthetics. In the book, *The Manifold in Perception: Theories of Art from Kant to Hildebrand*,[9] that eventually developed out of his doctoral dissertation, he concluded: 'In the writings of Fiedler the image of human personality has become so limited, and so little detailed experience of works of art or anything else is called upon, that it is hard not to see him as the end of a tradition.'[10]

Career—art historian, educator and public personality

While working on his Ph.D., Podro was based at the Warburg Institute in London, where Gombrich held a position first as Reader and from 1959 onwards as Professor of the History of the Classical Tradition and Director. It was during his years studying at the Warburg in the late 1950s that Podro met Michael Baxandall, a fellow student of Gombrich's, and the two of them became close friends. They formed a discussion group which met to tease out the implications of the new ideas Gombrich was developing on the mental processing of visual and pictorial representa-

---

[9] Adolf von Hildebrand was an artist friend of Fiedler's. His book, *The Problem of Form in the Visual Arts* (published in German 1893), one of the foundational texts of modern formal analysis, drew heavily on Fiedler's theoretical ideas.
[10] Podro, *Manifold*, p. 120.

tions with his explorations in the psychology of perception. The upshot was not just the important work of two of the foremost art historians to make their mark in Britain in the following few decades, Podro and Baxandall.[11] There also emerged a distinctive understanding of art historical study, rather different from Gombrich's positivistic one, that brought to bear British analytic thinking on the larger concerns and intellectual ambitions of nineteenth- and early twentieth-century German scholarship. As different as Podro's and Baxandall's approaches were, with Baxandall much more concerned with specificities of historical circumstance and particularities of the languages of art critical and art theoretical discourse, and Podro with examining the philosophical underpinnings of visual aesthetics, they shared certain very important commitments. For both, a close and attentive viewing of works of art and a preoccupation with the subtleties of the perceptual and intellectual processes such viewing set in train were absolutely central.

Podro's first teaching job was as Head of Art History at Camberwell School of Art and Crafts in South London, a position he took up in 1961 after completing his Ph.D. This might seem an unconventional move for someone with Podro's theoretical and philosophical bent. However, it gave him a freedom to devise an innovative programme of historical and theoretical study of art that a more conventional base in a university philosophy department, or in one of the few university art history departments, would not have allowed. Here he developed his talents as an innovative educator committed to a study of art history that gave students a theoretical understanding of art as well as familiarising them with key aspects of its history. The practice of studio teaching involving close examination and discussion of students' work dovetailed with his commitment to enhancing academic historical study with practical criticism conducted in front of original works of art.

Teaching at Camberwell brought him into contact again with contemporary art practice. It was there that he developed a close friendship with the artist Frank Auerbach whose approach to painting proved important for the ideas on artistic depiction he was developing at the time.[12] That Auerbach was working in a semi-figurative rather than purely abstract mode was less important than the larger question his densely worked over paintings seemed to pose—was compelling artistic depiction still possible

---

[11] On Baxandall, see J. Onians, 'Michael David Kighley Baxandall 1933–2008', *Proceedings of the British Academy*, 166, 2010, 27–46.
[12] Auerbach did a number of portrait studies of Michael Podro.

in present-day circumstances?[13] Auerbach's response, as Podro characterised it in an article he published some years later, was a hard won and
precarious yes. The almost indecipherable overlay of mark making in
Auerbach's depictions, Podro explained,

> ... keeps one particularly aware of the way in which the artist transforms and
> reconstitutes the subject. For the artist who does not simply try to mirror, mimic,
> or map, the initial subject has to be given up, every obvious hold on it sacrificed
> in order for it to be remade, with all the uncertainty of whether it will be
> retrieved, whether it will re-emerge or re-emerge in any adequate way in the
> materials and rhythms of the medium.[14]

Podro hinted here at a contemporary problematic of depiction that rarely
surfaces elsewhere in his writing—namely that immersion in processes of
painterly mark making might remain simply that and the resulting work
never come alive as an image of something. Podro usually emphasised the
mutually enhancing relay between processes of painting and delineating a
motif, seeing these as fusing in successful depiction to produce a vivid
sense of something seen or felt that seemed to emerge out of the paint work.
At times his response to Auerbach's work came closer to this harmoni-
ously integrative conception of painterly depiction, as in this comment he
made about the 'play of real and fictive salience' in a thickly worked head
by Auerbach: 'It is as if, through a leap of the imagination, the rich
complications of Auerbach's paint reveal the intricacies of live tissue
around and inside the skull of the sitter.'[15]

Podro also developed a friendship with another major figure in the
contemporary British art world, Ron Kitaj. Podro features in one of
Kitaj's better known paintings, *The Jewish Rider* (1984–5), a work whose
complex overlay of associations would have been particularly appealing
to Podro—the famous *Polish Rider* by Rembrandt, one of Podro's favourite artists; the train journeys Podro regularly took to Colchester travelling
from his home in London to the University of Essex where he started
teaching after leaving Camberwell; and specifically Jewish associations
with train travel—the Holocaust on the one hand and the image of the
displaced, itinerant Jewish intellectual on the other. The latter suggestions
are implicit in a way that Podro would have appreciated, and not too serious

---

[13] The paintings and drawings from life Giacometti was producing at the time posed a similar
question.
[14] M. Podro, *Frank Auerbach. The Complete Etchings 1954–1990* (London, 1990), unpaginated.
[15] M. Podro, 'Frank Auerbach. Paintings and drawings, 1954–2001', *Times Literary Supplement*
(21 Sept. 2001).

or insistent—the Podro figure is contemplative, but also a bit of a dandy in his white shoes, echoing Podro's warmly performative persona.

Kitaj's appeal for Podro is slightly puzzling. While it is easy to see why Kitaj's intellectual approach and the alternative he offered to abstract formalism would have appealed to Podro, his approach to painting—in particular his somewhat collage-like juxtaposition of motifs, his disregard for the formal niceties of painterly depiction, and his cultivation of a slightly edgy discrepancy and heterogeneity—is at odds with what Podro generally responded to in the art he most admired. In a review Podro wrote some years later of Kitaj's work, he suggested as much when commenting on the paintings Kitaj had shown in his first 1963 London exhibition:

> When, in a painting, we recognize a scene or a figure or a still life we assume that the painted surface will offer us ways of imagining the subject more fully: analogies between shapes, the pressure of the brush, relative opacity and transparency of medium may be absorbed into imaging the subject. But the paintings shown ... did not make their effect this way, despite the fact that this was something at which he was immensely accomplished.

Podro went on to comment on the apparent arbitrariness of the montaging of motifs in Kitaj's paintings and the absence of underlying visual or semantic connectivity: 'Implicit connexions are not in the service of realizing a scene but of intimating an event by texts, confused imaginings, oblique reminders ... If one asks what legitimizes these connexions the answer must first acknowledge the disparateness of areas of reference which have been yoked together.'[16] 'Yoked together' is an apposite term for describing the disarticulated montaging of elements characteristic of much pop and assemblage art of the period. Podro's deploying of the term testifies to his openness to new developments taking place in art and critical thinking about art to which he was constitutionally unsympathetic. In Kitaj's case, one suspects, friendship and shared intellectual concerns trumped aesthetic sensibility, as they often do.

In 1967, Podro left Camberwell to take up a temporary position as Lecturer in the Philosophy of Art at the Warburg Institute, returning to his intellectual home. However, it was with his move to the University of Essex as Reader two years later that he began to play a much more public role in the British art historical world. He was to remain at Essex until his retirement in 1997, and during his early years there played a key role building up the new Department of Art History and Theory. He set in place a

---

[16] M. Podro, *The Burlington Magazine*, 317, No. 1105 (April, 1995), 242–7 (see particularly pp. 242–3, 244).

distinctive curriculum very different from that offered at other universities. Traditional art history was complemented by programmes of study in art theory, philosophical aesthetics, critical theory and historiography of art-historical enquiry, and practical criticism of works of art. For him, disseminating his ideas through educational initiatives and interaction with students, and through his highly performative lectures at Essex and elsewhere, was as if not more important than the scholarly production of monographs and articles. He had a keen sense of mission and was an agitator and reformer as much as he was a scholar. It is a matter of some regret that he never had a real opportunity to deploy his intellectual energy and initiative at the institution that formed him, the Warburg Institute.

Podro's breadth is clearly evident from the range of people whom he knew from different walks of life—philosophers, painters, art historians, psychoanalysts, and museum curators. As a trustee of the Victoria and Albert Museum for almost ten years (1987–96) he became actively involved with difficult policy issues that had to be negotiated in these somewhat turbulent times for the Museum. His enthusiasms were not just intellectual and educational. He was fascinated too by the intricacies of political manoeuvre, both as an observer of this curious form of human sociability and as a participant, making effective interventions, whether at his home institution the University of Essex, or as a trustee at the Victorian and Albert Museum, or as a forceful voice in the ideologically charged debates that took place at academic conferences in the 1980s.

Psychoanalytic explorations

Podro also played a role in the world of British psychoanalysis. He was a chair and trustee of the Squiggle Foundation, an organisation devoted to the study and dissemination of the ideas of the analyst and writer D. W. Winnicott, a leading figure in the object relations school. Winnicott's studies on the role of play in child development were particularly attractive to Podro, given Podro's abiding interest in Schiller's conception of the imaginatively charged play characterising an aesthetic engagement with things.[17] Podro became a close friend of Marion Milner, a prominent

---

[17] Podro devoted almost as much space to Schiller as he did to Kant in his book, *The Manifold in Perception* (pp. 36–60) and the book on which he was working just before he died included an as yet unpublished article on Schiller. Podro saw Schiller as particularly important for having recast Kant's understanding of aesthetic judgement in a such a way that a more active role was played in it by the ethical and moral dimensions to mental life.

writer and analyst sympathetic to Winnicott's way of thinking. She was also an amateur painter, who published a fascinating book, *On Not Being Able to Paint* (1950), analysing her experiences trying to create paintings that convincingly conveyed aspects of her inner life and sense of things.[18] In his fine memorial tribute to Milner, Podro reflected on something for which he in a way was striving in his own writing, namely her 'ideal of aesthetic education, where thought was to be continually tested for how it resonated with what was most intimate and personal. In her own writing there are no gaps between the personal voice and the general argument, between, we might say, a lyric and a philosophical register.'[19]

Psychoanalysis plays a curious role in Podro's writing. It hovers on the margins as an insistent presence, but only rarely is it explicitly addressed. It is as if he felt a compulsion to take on board the disruptive intrusions of the unconscious in conscious life central to modern psychoanalytic ways of thinking, but equally felt compelled to keep these considerations at one remove. Is this perhaps a case of his being true to his injunction that in our apprehensions of things 'we cannot make fully focal what emerges most powerfully'?[20] The concluding section of his book *Depiction* includes an excursus touching briefly on what psychoanalytic theory might offer in the way of understanding the irrational and violent phantasies activated by works we find particularly compelling. Characteristically for him, the work cited there is a still life by Chardin,[21] where the violence is quite muted, suggested by a large eviscerated fish featured in an array of sea food and kitchen utensils.

Up to this point his analysis has been concerned with the expansive and constructive dynamics of an aesthetic response. It is for the most part envisaged as a freely engaged, integrating process of making sense of the perpetually shifting perceptual, mental and affective responses activated by a work of art—with the proviso that it is of the essence of the aesthetic that this intuitive sense will never quite conform to any conceptual defini-tion one might attribute to the work. But this still leaves open the question of how 'the productive or aesthetic stance' as Podro called it 'would accommodate the sense of potential extremity of feeling, including terror

---

[18] *On Not Being Able to Paint* (London, 1950) was first published under the pseudonym, Joanna Field.
[19] M. Podro, 'A tribute to Marion Milner', *British Journal of Psychotherapy*, 15 (1998), 252–3.
[20] Podro, *Depiction*, p. 176.
[21] Jean Baptiste Siméon Chardin, *La Raie (The Skate)*, 1726, Musée du Louvre, Paris. Interestingly he does not refer to the hostile presence of the kitten hissing with its back tensely arched.

and pity, that seems bound to our conception of art'. How 'might our
account of the complexity of painting and the viewer's engagement with
it be thought of as more than fortuitously related to such extremity?'[22]
This question is never answered. What Podro subsequently offers is a discussion of how compelling works of art that draw on strongly affective
unconscious material, material deriving from formative childhood phantasies and traumas, do so by distancing us from the potentially unmanageable resonances of such material—redeploying it within a conceptually
and perceptually satisfying artistic structure that brings its resonances
within the purview of our rational purposes and interests. But the real
question is never answered—namely how the irrational substratum of
psychic life endows aesthetic engagement with a work with real urgency it
would not otherwise have, and does not simply furnish material on which
such engagement draws. Nevertheless Podro had the intellectual insight
and integrity to realise that he needed to pose the question, even if he was
unable to follow through on it in the sustained way he pursued over avenues
of thought.

The problems Podro faced incorporating the insights of psychoanalytic theory into his Kantian analysis of the aesthetic emerge early on in
an intriguing essay 'Art and Freud's displacement of aesthetics', published
in a volume of essays on Freud edited by Jonathan Miller that came out
in 1972. Here he makes a suggestive analogy between the intuitive sense of
something coherent but inarticulable that emerges from the multiplicity
of perceptions in an aesthetic response, and the sense of there being an
unconscious impulse underlying the apparently senseless concatenation
of thoughts and images in a dream. Podro develops this analogy with an
intriguing parallel between Kant's notion of an aesthetic idea and Freud's
of an unconscious idea. He argues that in each case conceptually elusive
features of mental or psychic life are hinted at through constellations of
ideas and images and perceptions that, apprehended in their totality, elude
rational definition. Podro describes as follows the mental processes at
work in the formation of Kantian aesthetic and Freudian unconscious
ideas:

> For Kant it was a matter of the profusion of interconnected imagery being a
> suitable exercise of our minds for hinting at the realm of the supersensible. For
> Freud that profusion was a means by which ideas readily available to us could
> be organized in such a way as to allow associated thoughts, otherwise too dis-
> turbing for us to consider, into consciousness; and these thoughts in turn, were

[22] Podro, *Depiction*, p. 171.

indicative of something which was within and not outside us: not a reality to which our knowledge aspired, but a reality from which our urgencies derived.[23]

The passage hints suggestively at the ways in which the disruptive imperatives of the unconscious addressed in psychoanalytic understandings of psychic phenomena are radically different from the integrative imperatives of the rational impulses operating in his Kantian understanding of the aesthetic. However, he does not go on to consider whether this might call for some modification of his understanding of the affective dimensions to an aesthetic response. He at most hints at the problems involved by making a distinction between the ways in which the irrational imperatives of unconscious impulse are negotiated and brought to consciousness in therapeutic diagnosis, with a view to uncoupling their hold on the patient's psychic life, and the ways in which such impulses are mediated and creatively reworked in works of art, so that they then enliven and give resonance to one's mental life.[24]

Interventions

Podro's guarded, if also critically self-aware, engagement with psychoanalytic theory highlights his deep commitment to a positively engaged and poised rationality of the kind he admired in Kant's thinking. The scepticism regarding the conscious capabilities of the mind, and the negative assessments of the reach of rational understandings of the self articulated by Freud, were temperamentally as well as intellectually at odds with Podro's outlook, even as he recognised how compelling at some level Freud's insights—and those of his less humanist successors—were.

   Both living and thinking for Podro were at their best open-ended, explorative processes, involving constant give and take and negotiation. This cast of mind sets him clearly apart from recent deconstructive and poststructuralist ways of thinking. One could say he was utterly unfashionable and, after the postmodern turn in academic studies of art and culture gained ascendancy in the 1980s, possibly even a little rearguard, despite his earlier having been at the forefront of the move to a more theoretically aware and critically self-conscious approach to the study of art history. But there is a lot to this unfashionability that is not just admirable,

[23] M. Podro, 'Art and Freud's displacement of aesthetics', in J. Miller (ed.), *Freud. The Man, his World, his Influence* (London, 1972), p. 129.
[24] Podro, *Depiction*, pp. 170–1.

but also very necessary. He offers an intellectually rigorous and ethically grounded alternative to the disintegrative logic and relentless negation so often found in recent critical thinking about art and culture—whether this takes the form of theoretically inclined postmodern melancholy, or bolshie anti-theoretical scepticism.

At the same time, Podro was very attentive to recent trends in intellectual life and in his own understated way actively engaged with and responded to these. He wrote a very incisive, and far from unsympathetic assessment of Jacques Derrida's *The Truth in Painting* soon after the English edition appeared in 1987.[25] Each of his major books, while developing long-standing preoccupations of his—of which thinking through the broader implications of Kant's theory of aesthetic judgement for a critical understanding of art was the most central—focused on issues and problems that were very much in the air. In each case, Podro would indicate how his analysis addressed certain limitations in the theorising about art current in recent scholarly literature. He refused to engage in extended critique, and his interventions were short and to the point, almost afterthoughts. He thereby made it clear that the burden of what he had to offer was not an admonishing of tendencies he found ill-advised, but rather a rigorously critical exploration of material that he believed merited careful consideration because of the positive insights it had to offer.

In the conclusion to his first book, *Manifold in Perception*, Podro indicated that his examination of post-Kantian thinking about the aesthetics of visual art was in part directed against the narrow definitions of the aesthetic found in recent writing about art, that in turn had given rise to a narrowly sceptical take on aesthetics by Anglo-Saxon philosophers. Podro had in mind those theories of art that singled out a particular aesthetic quality or aesthetic attitude as defining the essence of art—such as say the narrow formalism associated with Roger Fry or the crude expressive theory of Croce.[26] Revisiting Kant and the more critically aware post-Kantian thinking about art, he believed, would make evident the complexity of the aesthetic attitude and give the lie to such misunderstandings. Podro was also at pains to correct a misconception of Kantian notions of aesthetic disinterestedness that equated this with an insistence on the autonomy of artistic form and the complete separation of the apprehension of artistic phenomena from the perception of phenomena in the world at large.

[25] M. Podro, 'Derrida on Kant and Heidegger', *Art History*, 11 (1988), 433–8.
[26] Clement Greenberg's neo-Kantian formalism would have been another case in point.

The analysis Podro offered in *The Critical Historians* had to do with the role aesthetic theory played in critical art history, rather than with aesthetics as such. The book came out at a moment in the early 1980s when there was considerable interest in and debate about the theoretical basis of art history as a discipline. The historiography of art historical study was attracting a great deal of scholarly attention, and a number of studies began to appear on major figures in the German tradition of art historical scholarship such as Erwin Panofsky.[27] At the same time, traditional approaches to art historical study, in particular the focus on stylistic analysis, were being intensively critiqued. Something of a schematic divide opened up between proponents of an approach that gave precedence to the political, social and cultural circumstances of artistic production, and those who believed that art historical study needed to concern itself with the distinctive visual qualities of works of art. This roughly panned out as a conflict between a social historical approach that envisaged art as shaped by external factors and a formal approach concerned with factors internal to art. There always had been something of a divide in art historical study along these lines but it became particularly acute in the late 1970s and early 1980s and also overtly politicised.

Podro's study intervened in this debate by offering a picture of a critical history of art that threw into question the exclusive claims being made on either side of the debate. In a terse formulation, he pointed out how a critical history of art that had any broader ambitions was necessarily one which required 'us to see how the products of art sustain purposes and interests which are both *irreducible* to the conditions of their emergence as well as *inextricable* from them'.[28] In so much as he defended artistic autonomy, this had to do with ethical integrity of purpose, and not some exclusive concern with style and the formal characteristics of art. In addition, he argued against the narrow historicism prevalent at the time, in which it was assumed that present-day understandings of art had to be excluded from any properly historical study of the art of past cultures. In Podro's view, 'Two central concerns gave direction to the writing of critical history: first, to show the way in which art exhibited a freedom of mind, like that experienced in discursive thought or in composed, self-possessed behaviour; and second, to show how the art of alien or past culture could

[27] Michael Ann Holly, *Panofsky and the Foundations of Art History* (Ithaca, NY, and London, 1984).
[28] Podro, *Critical Historians*, p. xvii.

become part of the mental life of the present.'[29] His central point was that
a critical history was characterised by an ongoing give and take between
broad, theoretically informed exploration of the nature of art and close
examination of particular works of art and the particular material, social
and cultural conditions instrumental in their formation.

Depiction, Podro's most readable and immediately engaging book,
includes some brilliant discussions of performativity in Rembrandt's por-
traiture and the complex orientation of viewpoint in his work. It came out
in 1998 in a rather different context from *The Critical Historians*. Podro's
concern was now with an aspect of artistic practice that previously had
been central to understandings of art, particularly painting, but that had
been increasingly marginalised both in art education and in theoretical
discussions of art during the course of the twentieth century—first as a
modernist privileging of formal abstraction gained ascendancy, and then
as various conceptual, semiotic and poststructuralist modes of theorising
took over. The latter have been instrumental in shaping not just understandings of modern and contemporary work but also broader attitudes
towards the aesthetics of the visual arts. By depiction, Podro did not just
have in mind mimesis or visual representation, or the making of recognisable naturalistic images. At issue rather was the artistic practice defined by
a give and take between the artist's apprehension of a motif or visual effect
(which could be remembered rather than directly seen) and the material
process of rendering it in a vivid and compelling way. A viewer's apprehension of such work in turn involved a sustained, constantly shifting
interplay between recognition of aspects of things or images previously
seen that the work conjured up and material particularities of the artist's
paint work or sculpting.

Podro made the point that, as depiction had become displaced as a
central concern in twentieth-century art, general understandings of art
were being impoverished by the theoretical polarity that resulted between
traditional representational and recent non-representational ways of conceptualising art.[30] With his analysis of 'the imaginative potential' of painterly depiction, he was effectively arguing against the widespread dismissal
of depiction as a phenomenon unworthy of serious theoretical consideration, a dismissal that failed to take account of the fact that most discussion of art still had to do with work in which depiction played a central
role. Though he preferred to put his case implicitly rather than explicitly,

---

[29] Podro, *Critical Historians*, p. xxii.
[30] Podro, *Depiction*, pp. 23–7.

the position he took effectively challenged widely held, often quite unreflective, assumptions that the claims of realistic or naturalistic representation were largely mythic, that naturalistic looking depictions were in the final analysis as conventionalised as abstract ones. Podro's *Depiction* presented an intellectually sophisticated and principled alternative to this reigning semiotic orthodoxy. It was a semiotics which took the view that the motifs in a work of art largely gained their significance as signs defined by artistic and cultural convention, and that recognition of visual resemblances between a motif and a phenomenon seen in the world had no significant role to play in a critically engaged response to a work of art, particularly when this was a work of modern art. Podro's brief statement positioning himself in relation to current assumptions about the insignificance of artistic depiction was directed for the most part at recent Anglo-American philosophical thinking about the nature of artistic representation.[31] However, it applied equally well to the less rigorously argued unease about depiction and iconic resemblance in discussions of modern and contemporary art: 'There is an incompatibility between the interest of depiction as it has been characterized [in my discussion] so far and what we might call, broadly, semiotic or nominalist accounts.'[32]

Epilogue—the aesthetic attitude

Podro was working on a further book at the very end of his life. This final intervention only reached publication in fragmentary and incomplete form in several articles, the most recent of which, 'Literalism and truthfulness in painting', appeared in 2010.[33] Here he was in a way returning to the

---

[31] Podro (*Depiction*, p. 182, n. 15) particularly had in mind Nelson Goodman. Goodman's *Languages of Art* (London, 1969) had a significant impact in the art world. The case he made there for the sign-like as distinct from iconic nature of visual representation helped prepare the way for the take-up of French semiotic theory by British and American writers on art in the late 1970s and early 1980s.

[32] Podro, *Depiction*, p. 27.

[33] M. Podro, 'Literalism and truthfulness in painting', *British Journal of Aesthetics*, 50 (2010), 457–68. This was probably intended as a concluding chapter of the book. Other chapters have appeared in preliminary or partial form as follows—the chapter on Diderot as 'Les limites de la peinture: Diderot et Herder', *Revue germanique internationale*, 13 (2000), 87–96; the one on Herder as 'Herder's *Plastik*', in J. Onians (ed.), *Sight and Insight. Essays on Art and Culture in Honour of E. H. Gombrich* (London, 1994), pp. 341–54; and the one on Kant as 'Kant and the aesthetic imagination', in D. Arnold and M. Iversen (eds.), *Art and Thought* (Malden, MA, and Oxford, 2003), pp. 51–70. The chapter on Schiller, that is substantially different from the section on

concerns he had addressed in his first book, *The Manifold in Perception*, taking the philosophically grounded aesthetic theory developed in the late Enlightenment as a basis for a developing a fuller understanding of what was at stake in a properly critical engagement with works of art.

He was addressing two central claims. First, he was concerned with how in the late Enlightenment the shift from art theory to what we call aesthetics brought with it a new understanding of the critical engagement with art as an exercise of mental faculties that had value in its own right, and did not require justification in terms of higher religious or metaphysical values. For Podro this aesthetic theory was particularly important in laying the foundations for modern critical conceptions of art and a viewer's engagement with art. Secondly, he saw this late Enlightenment speculation as throwing into relief a key feature of the specificity of the aesthetic, namely, the value placed 'on aspects of experience that eluded clarity and therefore did not constitute knowledge or serve as the basis of knowledge'. He went on to relate this elusiveness to his first point by putting it in historical perspective:

> Earlier, such elusiveness had been valued either as part of mystical or religious experience, itself conceived of a special part of knowledge, or it was associated with the delicacy of perception, alertness and wit in responding to others, an aspect of courtesy, a moral quality. It was when it became valued as an exercise of sensibility in its own right beyond serving knowledge, sociability or morals —and this is what happened in the thought of Diderot and Kant—that our conception of art and aesthetics took on its modern cast.[34]

A passage in his unpublished introduction to the book illuminates the particular context in which he was setting his re-examination of the aesthetic. With the stress on elusiveness, not as a sceptical assertion of undecidability, nor as an anti-rationalist positing of some ineffable real that eludes conceptual definition, but as something integral to rational processes of thinking that the aesthetic threw into sharp relief, he saw himself as positing an approach that got beyond a debilitating divide between formalist and anti-formalist approaches in modern critical analysis of art. Both in his view were caught up in reductive understandings by seeking determinate explanations of what constituted a work of art. The point of the aesthetic attitude, he argued, was that it involved the mind in a closely engaged yet open exploration of the interplay between a work's signifi-

---

Schiller in *Manifold of Perception*, is unpublished. The book manuscript is cited here under the title *The Aesthetic Attitude.* Chapters are paginated separately.

[34] M. Podro, *The Aesthetic Attitude*, Introduction, pp. 3–4.

cance and formal structuring, which of its nature could never be fixed or stabilised. Formalist criticism, while calling attention to features one might otherwise not notice, can

> have the debilitating effect of narrowing attention, so that the reader/viewer looks at the painting [or work of literature] just for these features ... The problem of such formalism (sometimes wrongly attributed to Kant) is not with what it points to but what it eliminates. Correspondingly, what is wrong with the arguments of the anti-formalists is what they, on their part, ignore or deny: those relations by which the mind is engaged in its exploration of the work. Reductive formalist is simply one kind of reduction, like literalism or narrowly social and psychoanalytic reading ...[35]

This final study also addressed the ethical imperatives informing a fully engaged aesthetic responsiveness. In part Podro sought to do this by re-examining the case Schiller made for the ethical significance of the aesthetic attitude in his *Letters on the Aesthetic Education of Mankind*.[36] Schiller's understanding of the aesthetic was certainly crucial for later modern constructions of the aesthetic as pointing to utopian possibilities radically at odds with, but also nevertheless to some degree latent in, the realities of human social and political interactions in the modern world. Interestingly, Jacques Rancière, from a political perspective very different from Podro's, but one equally at odds with easy postmodern pessimism, has also made a strong case for clarifying what is at stake in modern understandings, and misunderstandings, of the relation between the political and the aesthetic by returning to Schiller.[37]

Podro's most compelling claim for the ethical significance of the aesthetic comes in his discussion of 'Literalism and truthfulness in painting'. This has to do with a particular kind of truthfulness, and commitment to truthfulness, we attribute to the art we take seriously. At issue is not literal truthfulness, the truthfulness of the subject matter, or truthfulness to visual appearance of the representations the work of art offers up, though, as Podro explains, artistic truthfulness is not entirely disassociated from such truthfulness either. His point is that the truthfulness of what one recognises in a work—a situation, a phenomenon, a human presence, an understanding of or attitude towards things—is sustained by the compelling nature of the internal, artistic relations and effects the work creates.

[35] Podro, *Aesthetic Attitude*, Introduction, pp. 6–7.
[36] As before, Podro was at pains to trace how Schiller developed his political and ethical understanding of the aesthetic from ideas about ethical values latent in the structuring of aesthetic judgement that Kant never explicitly articulated (*Aesthetic Attitude*, Kant, pp. 16–7).
[37] Jacques Rancière, 'The aesthetic revolution and its outcomes', *New Left Review*, 14, second series (March–April 2002), 133–7.

Such truthfulness, Podro argues, emerges most strongly when the ordering of the art work allows no easy resolution, positing difficulties that can only be overcome through sustained attention and extended negotiation of the conflicting possibilities being suggested. There is then a double effect of truthfulness, produced by the 'sustainability and fertility' of the 'correspondences' and interrelations the work articulates on the one hand, and the 'sense of difficulty' these create, the blocking of easy resolution, on the other. Such truthfulness, involving as it does 'the sense of sustainable analogy and conflict' kept in play as one attends to a work closely, is true to life, but in a way that of its very nature cannot be equated with the work's literal truth.[38] This in turn suggests a truthfulness operating at the level of a 'more extensive sense of significance: the sense that what is told or depicted stands as exemplary of some wider fabric or relation of ideas'. This is a claim often made for the truthfulness of realist art and literature—as fiction that conveys a sense of something real whose truthfulness, not found in unprocessed reality, has a depth and resonance extending beyond the particularities of what is literally represented.

Podro is less concerned with such claims than he is with the ethical basis of the open, expansive nature of the mental processes at work in an aesthetic response, and with the commitment to truthfulness this entails. What Podro has to say on the subject sums up what is possibly the most important single imperative driving his life-long preoccupation with the complexities of an aesthetic response to art, and it makes an appropriate note on which to end. The truthfulness of a work of art, he explains,

> ... lies in its capacity to prompt in the audience the widest mobilization of its own thought, bringing latent and difficult thought to consciousness. It elicits, we might say, truthfulness in the audience. What is involved is that the work demands we become aware of the relevant level of importance, placing the subject against as wide a horizon of values as can be made relevant, looking for what can be revelatory.[39]

What mattered to Podro above all was the commitment to sustaining a freshness of response to whatever was engaging him, whether this be ideas, people or works of art. Even when he was critically ill with cancer at the end of his life (he died on 28 March 2008), this urge to respond openly and creatively and intently remained with him.

ALEXANDER POTTS

University of Michigan

[38] Podro, 'Literalism', 460–2.
[39] Ibid., 462.

PETER RUSSELL

Peter Edward Lionel Russell
1913–2006

PROFESSOR SIR PETER RUSSELL will be remembered as one of the great British scholars of the twentieth century.[1] Russell, who was King Alfonso XIII Professor of Spanish Studies at the University of Oxford from 1953 until his retirement in 1981, belongs to those who not only moved with equal facility between history and literature but also made lasting contributions to each both as scholar and teacher. In a career spanning over seventy years he produced seminal work in the fields of Spanish Medieval, Renaissance and Golden Age literature and culture, of the political and dynastic history of the Iberian Peninsula during the late fourteenth century, and of the Portuguese discovery of the African Atlantic together with the cultural and economic dimensions that attended it. To all of these he brought an intensely human and logical approach, the product not only of a vast and questing intellect but of a wealth of personal experience which made him very much more than a scholar and man of letters.

Though he rarely referred to it more than obliquely, Russell's service to his country both before and during the Second World War stands comparison with his academic career. Recruited into the secret service in the

[1] For this account use has been made of: (i) the four-page typescript memoir of his life up to 1953 (titled 'Peter Edward Lionel Russell', hereinafter 'PELR') which Russell deposited with the Academy in November 1992; (ii) Ian Michael, 'Sir Peter Russell (1913–2006)', *Bulletin of Spanish Studies*, 83 (2006), 1133–44; (iii) obituaries in *The Independent* (by Alan Deyermond, 5 July 2006), *The Daily Telegraph* (by Jeremy Lawrance, 10 July 2006) and *The Guardian* (by Nigel Griffin, 22 August 2006); that in *The Times* (14 July 2006) was an abridgement of one written by the author; and (iv) items from Russell's papers in the author's care together with the author's memories and knowledge.

mid-1930s, Russell was sent to Spain during the Civil War where tours with parties of undergraduates and research in local archives provided excellent cover for monitoring, among other things, the movements of Nationalist warships which had on several occasions interfered with the passage of British goods into Republican ports. This assignment almost cost him his life in August 1938 when he was arrested by the Guardia Civil photographing the cruiser *Canarias* from the Islas de Cíes in the Ría de Vigo. Russell's position was made the more precarious by the discovery that he was sharing the Hotel Atlántico in Vigo with officers of the German military whose presence in Spain was then officially denied—officers with whom he had dined on at least one occasion. Though facing execution following an interrogation with the Falange, he was released on the orders of Franco himself and after some difficulty obtaining exit papers made for the border town of Túy from where he gratefully crossed the Minho into Portugal. Russell would recall his march across the bridge with machine guns at his back as the longest of his life, but thereafter when the subject of Franco arose in conversation he was wont to recall how he owed his life to the Caudillo.

Russell returned to Oxford where the outbreak of the Second World War brought him into Military Intelligence, though it was not until the summer of 1940 that his service began in earnest. During July and August of that year Russell was involved in ushering the Duke and Duchess of Windsor from Estoril to the Bahamas where the former was installed as Governor for the duration. There were rumours, which Russell did little to dispel, that he was under orders to shoot them if they threatened to fall into German hands during their nightly visits to the casino at Estoril, though he enjoyed cordial relations with the Windsors and in later years would not brook too much criticism of them. Russell was subsequently involved in preparing the British occupation of the Canary Islands in the event that Franco allowed the Germans safe passage across Spain to capture Gibraltar, though it amused him to note that the plans were drawn up using outdated Admiralty charts from the late eighteenth century. After a few months kicking his heels in Oxford Russell was commissioned into the Intelligence Corps (IC) in December 1940 and began training with MI5, mainly at Oriel College where the IC had its wartime headquarters. This came to an abrupt halt in March 1941 when the car in which he was a passenger ran into a parked lorry in the blackout. Rushed to Oxford, Russell nearly died on the operating table in the Radcliffe Infirmary before spending four or five days unconscious. Reconstructive surgery in Basingstoke under the great New Zealand plastic surgeon Archibald McIndoe was followed by convalescence at Harewood House, though Russell's injuries left him permanently scarred and thereafter required the use of a denture. No sooner had he been discharged in August than he was sent to Lochailort, the Commando and secret operations training centre on the west coast of Scotland. Still recuperating, he was severely beaten by former officers of the Shanghai Police during the part of his training intended to prepare him for the possibility of an enemy interrogation. Russell secured his return to Oxford within a week.

In late 1941 Russell was taken on by the Overseas Division of the Security Service (MI5) and in March 1942 appointed Security Coordination Officer in Jamaica, after which he practically never wore uniform. His duties ranged from examining the holds of ships calling at Kingston to the identification of possible German agents through interrogation. Many refugees from occupied Europe were passing through the Caribbean on their way to safety in Latin America or the United States and on one occasion Russell found himself interviewing a man who weeks earlier had been conversing with Goering in Berlin, the *Reichsmarschall* being susceptible to bribery in return for safe-conduct out of Germany. Russell's service also involved contact with Sir William Stephenson, the Canadian director of British Security Coordination (BSC) better known as 'the Man called Intrepid'. BSC was the umbrella organisation for the entire British intelligence effort in the Western Hemisphere, but Stephenson's zeal to eliminate certain individuals suspected of spying for the Axis brought him into conflict with station officers such as Russell who had to remind him that liquidation was not within MI5's remit. Promoted major, in 1943 Russell was sent to the Gold Coast where MI5 was engaged in security and counter-espionage activities against the Vichy French and German agents who were tracking convoys carrying minerals and foodstuffs from West Africa to Britain. Although based in Accra, Russell's beat included all the then British colonies in West Africa and entailed visits to the French colonies and the Belgian Congo, through many of which he made prolonged journeys by car. The posting was of value to his subsequent research and in his last major work Russell paid tribute to the RAF pilots who had flown him to and over many of the places which loomed large in the Portuguese reconnaissance of Guinea during the fifteenth century.[2]

Russell's final assignment was to the Far East in 1944 and it was in Ceylon that he performed the most important service of his military career. As a result of the breaking of Japanese cyphers MI5 learnt of the existence

[2] *Prince Henry 'the Navigator': a Life* (New Haven, CT, 2000), p. xv.

of an Indian nationalist agent to whom the British gave the codename CARBUNCLE. CARBUNCLE had been recruited to operate in Ceylon by the Japanese in Singapore but was picked up and handed over for Russell to 'turn' him using the 'Double-Cross' system perfected with German agents in Europe. Against the threat of execution, the would-be agent agreed to transmit whatever intelligence the British saw fit to provide his controllers. Although this initially consisted of 'chicken feed'—accurate data of limited value or past importance—the opportunity was eventually taken for a major exercise in disinformation which in CARBUNCLE's case was an attempt to lure a Japanese cruiser out of Singapore against reports that an Allied supply convoy had sailed from Trincomalee. The bait was duly taken and though Russell was evasive on the subject the vessel in question may have been the heavy cruiser *Haguro* which was intercepted and sunk off Penang by a flotilla of British destroyers in May 1945.

The end of the war found Russell in Trincomalee in the rank of Acting Lieutenant-Colonel. Not long after he was invited as ranking officer to command a landing on an island off Sumatra whose garrison had yet to learn of the Japanese surrender. The offer was declined but the incident was one Russell always had great amusement in recounting. Another episode he recalled, though with rather less pleasure, was his interrogation of the Japanese commander in the Andaman Islands which had been under military occupation since 1942. Asking the officer why he had herded a large proportion of the native population into barges and then had them sunk by gunfire in deep water, he received the indignant reply that this had of course been necessary to ensure sufficient food for the garrison, the Andamans being small and relatively infertile.

Russell was by now anxious to resume his academic career in the austerities of post-war Oxford but there remained one final duty: disposing of CARBUNCLE. According to Russell, he was instructed to settle with CARBUNCLE in whatever way he thought fit. Boarding a ship bound for Singapore, it was suggested to him that CARBUNCLE might find a watery grave *en route*, something the latter evidently expected as well. In the event, Russell couldn't bring himself to any such action and when the ship made Singapore he disembarked with CARBUNCLE attached to his wrist by means of a pair of handcuffs. Producing a key, Russell unfettered them both and, to CARBUNCLE's astonishment, told him to 'Fuck off!' CARBUNCLE duly took to his heels and was last seen disappearing into the crowd. Although offered a permanent career in MI5, Russell had no hesitation in turning it down. Nonetheless, one can't help speculating that the many university committees over which he subsequently presided together with the waspish discourse of academic life and politics must often have seemed trivial in comparison with the harsh realities of wartime intelligence, of death and survival, tragedy and brutality, incompetence and genius. As Russell recalled

> I am one of those academics of the 1930s who, not without a certain unease of conscience, look back on the Second World War as one of the most positive and creative periods of their lives since it gave them a great variety of new experiences as well as opportunities to discover in themselves talents which would have remained hidden had they not been hauled out of academia.[3]

* * *

Peter Edward Lionel Russell was born in Christchurch, New Zealand on 24 October 1913. His father Bernard Wheeler of Halifax, Nova Scotia was a retired captain in the Royal West Kent Regiment, his mother Rita the youngest daughter of Thomas Russell who had made his fortune as a barrister, businessman and newspaper proprietor in New Zealand. A second son, Hugh (later a distinguished epidemiologist) was born in 1916, but the marriage was by then in trouble and, following an acrimonious divorce, Wheeler's sons adopted their mother's maiden name by deed poll in 1929, which in Peter's case meant that he took his fourth given name as his last. Wheeler, meanwhile, played no further part in their lives, even to the extent of leaving the boys' letters unanswered. As Russell put it, he 'dropped dead' in a pharmacy in Sydney one day in 1935. Russell's boyhood was divided between England and New Zealand where the family lived comfortably in the shadow of Knowlescourt, his grandfather's Tudor revival mansion in Christchurch. All his life he retained the fondest memories of this house, his grandfather playing the organ after dinner, his Uncle Gerald tuning in to the United States on his crystal radio set and Russell himself beginning a lifetime of voracious reading in its many passages and recesses. From 1901 Russell Senior had provided a base for officers of Scott's expeditions to the Antarctic while their ships were moored at nearby Lyttelton. With three attractive young ladies in residence it was not long before Captain Scott's men found even more to engage their interest than Mr Russell's generous hospitality and both Peter's mother and his aunt Hilda became engaged to members of the expedition. The former eventually broke off her engagement to Lt Michael Barne but Hilda was married in 1904 to the then Lt Edward Evans, Second Officer of the relief ship *Morning*. Scott and Evans (now second in command) came south again

[3] 'PELR', p. 3.

with the *Terra Nova* in 1910 but the expedition ended in disaster when Scott and his party perished after reaching the Pole on 17 January 1912, thirty-three days after Amundsen planted the Norwegian flag over the uncharted desolation. A year later, Amundsen came to lunch at Knowlescourt. As Peter's mother recalled, 'He asked Teddy [Evans] why Scott did not make more use of his dogs. Amundsen said his dogs did all the work, and pulled all the stores, now and then he killed and ate one, and fed the dogs too.'[4] It is a question that has exercised historians of the heroic era of polar exploration ever since. Tragically Aunt Hilda succumbed to complications during pregnancy while traversing the Mediterranean in 1913, but Evans remained close to the family and went on to find fame as 'Evans of the *Broke*' for his exploits during the Great War, eventually becoming Admiral Lord Mountevans. Uncle Teddy, vain and ebullient, was one of the characters of Russell's youth, and it was through him that Russell once danced to jazz with Queen Maud of Norway, Evans's second marriage being to one of her ladies-in-waiting.

Russell's first formal education came in the muscular environment of St Andrew's College, Christchurch, but in 1926 the decision was made for Rita to accompany her sons to England so that they could complete their schooling in the old country, the boys' grandfather having by now made himself financially responsible for their education. Russell lasted a term at Sedbergh before being sent to Cheltenham College, which he detested. Decades later he explained why:

> In those days it was a school which specialized in training boys for the Indian Army or the British Army and for the Indian and Colonial Civil Services and the emphasis was all on producing conformist types preconditioned for such careers. Though I did quite well scholastically at Cheltenham I was never at home with the demand to conform to a new set of class-bound English social values whose rationale I never succeeded in understanding.[5]

These formative perceptions and the geographical and cultural displacements that marked his youth bring us to some of the defining characteristics of Russell the scholar, at once fascinated by the interplay of societies and ever ready to take up the cudgels against received ideas and conventional wisdom with devastating critiques made from the inside.

However much he loathed Cheltenham, it was here too that Russell first came into contact with Spanish and took the first steps on what became his professional career:

[4] Rita Muriel Russell, unpublished memoirs (typescript copy in author's collection), p. 17.
[5] 'PELR', p. 1.

I am often asked how I came to be interested in Spanish. The answer is wholly prosaic. I did not wish to repeat another year working at French and German for the Higher School certificate, which I had already obtained. Taking up Spanish, rather surprisingly then an optional subject at Cheltenham College, offered a way out and also gave me the satisfaction of doing something rather out of the ordinary.[6]

Not only that, but Cheltenham had a closed scholarship in Spanish to Oxford, the award of which brought Russell up to read French and Spanish at The Queen's College in October 1931, to which Portuguese was added in 1934 when this subject first became available in the university. In the months since leaving Cheltenham that spring Russell had taken the opportunity to visit Spain for the first time. His arrival in Madrid on 14 April was inauspicious, it being the day Spain was declared a Republic and King Alfonso XIII went into exile. A few weeks later Russell witnessed the burning by Anarchists of the Jesuit residence on the Calle Flor together with its priceless library, archive and artworks. Stopping to question one of the perpetrators as to his motive, Russell was informed 'Porque los Jesuitas son dueños de los tranvías' ('Because the Jesuits own the trams'). It was the beginning of a lifetime's observation of the passions and quirks of Hispanic society. Russell completed a memorable first visit to the Peninsula by signing on as the cabin boy of a British steamer at Barcelona. By the time it reached the Port of London three weeks and a dozen Iberian ports later, Russell was fluent in Spanish.

In 1934 the award of the De Osma Studentship brought him back to Madrid and to the famous Residencia de Estudiantes where he encountered many of the luminaries of the Second Republic, including Américo Castro, Ramón Menéndez Pidal, Luis Buñuel and Federico García Lorca whose impromptu piano recitals in the common room were a feature of life there. The following reminiscence, shared by Russell when he was 'well into his anecdotage', not only gives a flavour of his dry humour and critical eye, but also of the air of controlled demolition that was never far from his work:

I had first met don Ramón [Menéndez Pidal] in 1933 or 34 in the poetically famous garden of the Residencia de Estudiantes in Madrid. It was, I recall, not the happiest of social occasions. Also with me was another Oxford undergraduate who used to cause us considerable annoyance here in Oxford by his unwanted propensity to correct our spoken Spanish. On this particular afternoon the eminent President of the Residencia, Alberto Jiménez Fraud, a devoted anglophile known personally in later years to a few of us still around, told us that there

[6] Ibid.

were three distinguished Spanish scholars chatting together in the garden and that he would like to present us to them. The group consisted of Ramón Menéndez Pidal, Américo Castro, and Fernando de los Ríos, a prominent Republican politician. These three scholarly *grandezas*, as I recall, acknowledged our presence with a fairly perfunctory nod after which we stood politely by while don Ramón continued speaking to his friends. Suddenly my companion from Oxford, a tall man, leaned forward and, extending his finger in the direction of don Ramón's nose, declared à propos of something the latter had just said, 'En castellano eso no se dice.' I rather hoped that this clanger would earn my companion his long-awaited comeuppance but don Ramón, as I recall, paid not the slightest attention to this uncivil interruption nor did his friends and it was left to the distraught don Alberto, always a model of good manners, to apologize for his protégé's behaviour and, no doubt, to wonder whether his decision to offer Oxford students *becas* and accommodation in the residencia had been a wise one.[7]

In 1997 Russell presented his 'Recollections of the Spanish Second Republic' at a graduate seminar in Oxford. During it he reaffirmed one of his indelible impressions from the years between 1931 and 1936, namely that Spaniards of all political colours were agreed on one point and one point only: that their country's problems would only be resolved through bloodshed. So it turned out.

Meanwhile, Russell had greatly taken to Oxford where he recalled his undergraduate years as 'totally happy ones' and college life 'like Liberty Hall' after the privations of an English boarding school. A member of the *jeunesse dorée* of the 1930s, he moved in the circle of Maurice Bowra and George Kolkhorst (known as 'the Colonel'), which included John Betjeman and John Sparrow. In later years Russell would smile at the memory of lively parties held at Yarnton Manor, Kolkhorst's residence outside Oxford with its Gobelins and collections of Oriental porcelain and jade of which he gained an abiding affection. Russell was also associated with the circle of W. H. Auden and Christopher Isherwood which extended to the deserted beach at Maspalomas at the southern tip of Gran Canaria that later became known as Playa del Inglés. These and other social contacts honed an already powerful mind into a formidable tool of perception, intuition and expression which was never blunted. Taking a First in French, Spanish and Portuguese in 1935, Russell turned to history with the encouragement of the then King Alfonso XIII professor, W. J. Entwistle, a decision which much disappointed his grandfather who wanted him to read law and take

---

[7] 'Reinventing an epic poet: 1952 in context', in Alan Deyermond, David G. Pattison and Eric Southworth (eds.), *'Mio Cid' Studies. 'Some Problems of Diplomatic' Fifty Years On* (London, 2002), pp. 63–71 at 67–8.

over his practice in New Zealand. Nor was Russell Senior the only party dismayed at this turn of events, which offended the better part of the Modern Languages Board and brought a good deal of opprobrium down on Entwistle's head. As Russell recalled, the Board 'in those days suffered from a collective paranoia which led them to imagine that the historians were constantly plotting to do their subject down and to kidnap the best graduates from their Faculty'.[8] It was the sort of absurdity which Russell, never one to conform for conformity's sake, delighted in skewering.

Undeterred, Russell began research on a doctorate on the Plantagenet involvement in the Iberian Peninsula under the somewhat erratic supervision of Sir Maurice Powicke, Regius Professor of Modern History, and particularly with the Balliol medievalist V. H. Galbraith. Deprived by the outbreak of the Civil War of any opportunity to pursue his research in the great archives of Spain, Russell instead concentrated on the rolls and other documentary holdings of the Public Record Office. While acknowledging the grounding Powicke, Galbraith and others had given him in diplomatic, Russell never shared the confidence of the traditional historian in the implicit veracity of original documentation. If there was one dominating theme in his work it was the debunking not only of spurious claims by contemporaneous figures and their apologists, but of the efforts by subsequent scholarship and vested interests to recast history and literature in the service of a regime or ideology. The result was an *œuvre* which, lying at the interstices of history and literature, was always broad-ranging, often sceptical and frequently iconoclastic. In the early 1930s Russell completed a novel which was never published. Though any ambition he may have harboured to become a writer had eventually to be set aside, Russell brought a many-layered style to his scholarly prose which was not only as complex as the man but also perfectly suited to his chosen approach.

Appointed to a graduate scholarship at Queen's in 1935 and to lectureships at St John's College and then Queen's in 1937, Russell's early research resulted in *As Fontes de Fernão Lopes*, a study of the fourteenth-century chronicler which appeared in Portuguese translation in 1941.[9] Russell did not learn of its publication until a volume on the subject caught his eye in a bookshop in wartime Lisbon—his own, as it turned out, published (albeit in Russell's name) by a colleague to whom he had supplied a prewar typescript. The book was a first exercise in what came to be recognised as the Russell style, demonstrating as it did that the Lopes manuscripts

---

[8] 'PELR', p. 2.
[9] Trans. António Gonçalves Rodrigues (Coimbra, 1941).

in the Arquivo da Torre do Tombo in Lisbon were not holograph originals as then believed but unreliable sixteenth-century copies. His doctorate was interrupted by the war and not completed as such but research continued after demobilisation and in 1955 Russell published his first major work, *The English Intervention in Spain and Portugal in the Time of Edward III and Richard II*, an exquisitely crafted account of the political and dynastic upheavals which beset the Peninsula in the late fourteenth century.[10] Already in 1945 he had while still languishing in the tropics been elected to the Laming Fellowship in Modern Languages at Queen's and appointed to a University Lectureship in Spanish. Then in 1953 he gained the King Alfonso XIII Chair of Spanish Studies which, together with the office of Director of Portuguese Studies (until 1976), he held with increasing distinction for the next twenty-eight years. As Russell recalled, he had only put his name forward at the urging of Maurice Bowra, chairman of the Electors and now Vice-Chancellor of the university, who was unimpressed at the strength of the field. The election of a scholar not yet forty and with only one slender volume in print was not without controversy; two years later the appearance of *The English Intervention* settled any remaining doubts. 'The rest', as Russell later put it, 'is on public record.'[11]

By the end of the 1950s Russell had begun to show the scholarly range and dynamism for which he became famous. In 1951 he stunned an audience by demonstrating through diplomatic that the *Cantar de Mio Cid*, the great epic of Spanish medieval poetry, had been composed not by a minstrel but by a poet with legal training writing a century later than was universally accepted.[12] These conclusions were interpreted in some quarters as an act of *lèse-majesté* against the great medievalist and doyen of Spanish scholarly orthodoxy, don Ramón Menéndez Pidal, and feathers were ruffled both in Britain and Spain, but the application of historical and diplomatic analysis was a turning point in the study of European epic poetry. The legacy of 'Some problems of Diplomatic in the *Cantar de Mio Cid* and their implications' was explored in a conference held in Oxford to celebrate the fiftieth anniversary of its publication, to which Russell added his own wry perspective.[13] In 1953 came two articles demonstrating that literary relations between Catholic Spain and Protestant England in the

---

[10] Oxford, 1955.

[11] 'PELR', p. 4.

[12] 'Some problems of Diplomatic in the *Cantar de Mio Cid* and their implications', *Modern Language Review*, 47 (1952), 340–9.

[13] See above, n. 7.

seventeenth century were closer than had ever been imagined.[14] A few years later work started on a full-length biography of Prince Henry the Navigator, to whose soubriquet Russell added apostrophes once he established that the Infante's seafaring credentials consisted of a few trips between the Algarve and Morocco. In 1960 Russell began his assault on the personality cult assiduously propagated by the Infante himself and remodelled by successive generations of the Portuguese ruling élite. The result, a lecture delivered at Canning House in London, so incensed the Portuguese Embassy that strenuous though unsuccessful efforts were made to block its publication.[15] The demolition was completed in a valedictory lecture delivered at Oxford in 1983 and published under the apt title of 'Prince Henry the Navigator: the rise and fall of a culture hero'.[16] The biography itself was finished in the 1960s but Russell was dissatisfied with the result and set it aside for thirty years. Though essentially complete, the project was burdensome to him and for many years Russell mordantly referred to it as 'the Alligator'.

Meanwhile, Russell moved into the literature of the Spanish Renaissance and in 1957 produced the first in a series of essays on the tragicomedy known as *La Celestina*, which among other things exploded a succession of native myths on Spanish fifteenth-century humanism and resulted in a near-definitive edition which appeared in 1991.[17] Next Russell turned to Cervantes and in 1969 brought his penetrating insight to bear in another of his seminal articles, '*Don Quixote* as a funny book', in which he attacked the Romantic notion of Cervantes' hero as a purely tragic figure.[18] His work on Cervantes culminated in a magisterial survey in the Oxford Past Masters series published in 1985.[19] Between whiles he found time to produce a volume on translation and translators in Spain and Portugal (1985) as well as gathering the leading lights in the field to produce *Spain: a Companion to Spanish Studies* (1973) which has provided a matchless

---

[14] 'English seventeenth-century interpretations of Spanish literature', *Atlante*, 1 (1953), 65–77, and 'A Stuart Hispanist: James Mabbe', *Bulletin of Hispanic Studies*, 30 (1953), 78–84.
[15] 'Prince Henry the Navigator' [Canning House Seventh Annual Lecture] (London, 1960).
[16] Oxford, 1984.
[17] The essays are 'The art of Fernando de Rojas', *Bulletin of Hispanic Studies*, 34 (1957), 160–7, and especially 'Literary tradition and social reality in *La Celestina*', *Bulletin of Hispanic Studies*, 41 (1964), 230–46, and 'Arms versus letters: towards a definition of Spanish humanism', in A. R. Lewis (ed.), *Aspects of the Renaissance: a Symposium* (Austin, TX, 1967), pp. 45–58. For the edition, see Fernando de Rojas, *Comedia o Tragicomedia de Calisto y Melibea* (Madrid, 1991; rev. 1993 and 2001).
[18] '*Don Quixote* as a funny book', *Modern Language Review*, 64 (1969), 312–26.
[19] *Cervantes* (Oxford, 1985).

primer to the subject for students in both the English- and Spanish-speaking worlds.[20] His essays on Spanish literature were collected in 1978 and those on Portugal, Spain and the African Atlantic in 1995.[21] By now well into his eighties, Russell turned once more to the Infante and in 2000 produced the long-awaited *Prince Henry 'the Navigator': a Life*.[22] It was the crowning achievement of a brilliant career, a work of immense subtlety, breadth and authority half a century in the making.

Russell's contribution as a scholar was matched by his stature as the pre-eminent teacher of Hispanic studies in the United Kingdom. He was a notable lecturer, clear, coherent, engaging and always grounded in wide reading and deep thought, the material delivered in an elegant Oxford drawl. His tutorials, usually given at home, were conceived as a meeting of minds. Undergraduates found themselves at ease and on first-name terms with a scholar who wore his learning very lightly and never talked shop any more than was necessary. Not for him the intellectual conceit or rebarbative put-down that blighted many student–tutor relationships. Graduate students, meanwhile, were treated as friends and colleagues, their tutorials frequently shifted to a fine restaurant or reconfigured as part of a lengthy excursion at home or abroad. Beginning in the 1970s his students began to fill an increasing number of university chairs in Hispanic studies and history in Britain and abroad, while the Cambridge Iberian and Latin American Studies series became under his editorship the premier forum for new research in the field. Yet for all his massive erudition Russell never lost sight of scholarship as a civilising human endeavour that had necessarily rather more to do with life than with the subject at hand. It was a conviction which, as he admitted, eventually took on a somewhat pessimistic tincture:

> I have always taken what some have thought the unnecessarily pessimistic view that most literary criticism of whatever kind is by its nature a fruit destined to fall ripe from the bough. Or, to recall a Persian proverb [...], the caravan always moves on leaving behind it dogs that go on barking at the site where it previously stood because change has passed them by.[23]

---

[20] *Traducciones y traductores en la Península Ibérica, 1400–1550* (Barcelona, 1985) and *Spain: a Companion to Spanish Studies* (London, 1973; rev. 1977); Spanish trans. *Introducción a la cultura hispánica*, 2 vols. (Barcelona, 1982).

[21] *Temas de "La Celestina" y otros estudios (del "Cid" al "Quijote")* (Barcelona, 1978) and *Portugal, Spain and the African Atlantic, 1343–1490* (Aldershot, 1995).

[22] New Haven, CT, 2000.

[23] 'Reinventing an epic poet: 1952 in context', p. 63.

Although Russell always found the protocol attaching to the King Alfonso XIII chair something of a burden, in 1962 he hosted the inaugural conference of the International Association of Hispanists at Oxford and took the opportunity to curate a memorable exhibition of *Hispanic Manuscripts and Books before 1700*.[24] From 1962 to 1964 he served on the influential University Grants Committee for Latin American Studies, and was a member of the editorial board of the *Bulletin of Hispanic Studies* between 1959 and 1996. In Oxford he established the regular weekly research seminar for graduate students, which continues to meet on Tuesdays at 5 p.m. in the Taylorian Institution. Not himself an ardent conference-goer, Russell was in many respects a shy man who preferred the life of a solitary scholar. His practice was to work quietly and send his manuscripts to press with little or no input from his colleagues before sitting back to watch the *frisson* produced by his findings. This while fending off occasional invitations to take up the headship of colleges both in Oxford and Cambridge.

There were few regrets from a great career which was recognised with election to the Portuguese Academy of History (1956), the Real Academia de Buenas Letras of Barcelona (1972) and this Academy (1977). He received a D.Litt. from the University of Oxford on his retirement in 1981 and in 1989 became the first recipient of the Nebrija Prize conferred by the University of Salamanca. In 1989 he was made a Commander of the Spanish Order of Isabel la Católica, receiving the same dignity in the Portuguese Order of the Infante Dom Henrique in 1993 which Russell was amused to learn conferred the right to use a portable altar. He was knighted in 1995. After his retirement a succession of visiting professorships at the universities of Virginia, Texas, Johns Hopkins and Vanderbilt between 1982 and 1987 brought the Russell style to a generation of graduate students in America. By the end of his life Russell had been the subject of four Festschriften from friends and former students on both sides of the Atlantic and achieved literary immortality by being written into several novels by the noted Spanish author Javier Marías, including the trilogy *Tu rostro mañana* (2002–7) of which he was a dedicatee.[25] He knew, as his

---

[24] P. E. Russell, D. M. Rogers and O. N. V. Glendinning, *A Catalogue of Hispanic Manuscripts and Books before 1700 from the Bodleian Library and Oxford College Libraries Exhibited at the Taylor Institution, 6–11 September* (Oxford, privately, 1962).
[25] The Festschriften were: (i) F. W. Hodcroft, D. G. Pattison, R. D. F. Pring-Mill and R. W. Truman (eds.), *Medieval and Renaissance Studies on Spain and Portugal in Honour of P. E. Russell* (Oxford, 1981); (ii) Alan Deyermond and Jeremy Lawrance (eds.), *Letters and Society in Fifteenth-Century Spain: Studies Presented to P. E. Russell on His Eightieth Birthday* (Llangrannog, 1993);

students knew, that he had lived in a golden age for Hispanic studies as for academic life generally in the English-speaking world. That he was one of its chief adornments had long been acknowledged.

If these remarks capture Russell's achievements as an officer, scholar and teacher, they do not encompass the qualities of mind and personality that yielded success in practically every endeavour to which he turned his hand, often one suspects in the face of great mental torment. Nor do they capture the immense presence of the man, the imposing figure unbent by age, the huge lion-like head and inscrutable eyes, the person from whom not a word or thought was wasted when things really mattered. Russell had style and throughout his life preserved both his physical stature and much of what in his youth had been devastating good looks. From his extensive flat in North Oxford, opulently furnished and always replete with fine food and wine, Russell presided over a wide circle of scholars and friends that to his last years ranged from college tutees of the 1930s to literary and intellectual luminaries on both sides of the Atlantic. Among them were three friends from Queen's: John Ochs of *The New York Times*, the economist Charles Kennedy, and Lord Franks. His generosity to those of scarcer financial means was legendary and there can have been few people he cared for who were not favoured with his largesse in one form or another, often on the least pretext. Though never in any doubt as to his powers, Russell was an exceedingly charismatic man who delighted in the rare gift of being able to hit it off with anyone. As in his research, he had no time for humbug of any sort—'bogus' was a word that fell often from his lips—and his friends knew that exposure to his gentle but penetrating wit was to be paid his highest compliment. Nor, of course, were those who crossed him likely to forget it. Russell took it all in his stride, always master of the situation, always a model of self-control, never losing his composure. Beyond a flair for language, his secret was a breathtaking command of the art of communication in its fullest sense, and to spend time in Peter's company was to witness a subtle concert of head and hand gestures which conveyed more than words ever could.

In his last years, though much preoccupied with his own mortality, he never lost his sense of humour or boyish glee at the absurdities of life. Asked how he was, he would sometimes reply 'Awaiting a visit from the

(iii) Julian Weiss (ed.), *Studies in Honour of Peter E. Russell on His 80th Birthday*, published as a special number of *Celestinesca*, 17, no. 2 (Fall 1993); and (iv) Alan Deyermond, David G. Pattison and Eric Southworth (eds.), *'Mio Cid' Studies. 'Some Problems of Diplomatic' Fifty Years On* (London, 2002).

Reaper', or just 'Surviving', his voice lowered an octave before issuing a guffaw. However, neither his mental faculties nor his flexibility of mind were impaired by the passage of time. He had the ability to cast aside the tastes and convictions of a lifetime if a better alternative recommended itself. The IT revolution was early and enthusiastically embraced and his home was always filled with the latest gadgets and conveniences which he delighted in showing off, sometimes with alarming results. He was addicted to the Antipodean soap operas that began appearing on British television in the 1980s and at the time of his death at home on 22 June 2006 was plotting the purchase of high-definition TV to watch the World Cup in Germany. To that extent Peter Russell was much the youngest of his circle.

To know Peter Russell was to be admitted to a world—many worlds—to which one would otherwise never have gained access. Whether they were of his discovering such as the Portuguese Atlantic or of his own experience such as wartime counter-espionage, those who shared them always knew that something special was being vouchsafed, just as they appreciated the innate depth and elegance in which they were lived and revealed. For those of us who were his friends Peter Russell was a prince whose passing marks the close of an era more refined and assured than our own.

BRUCE TAYLOR
Los Angeles, California

Note.   My sincere thanks to Ian Michael for much information and encouragement in the preparation of this obituary, generously given as always.

MAURICE SCOTT

Maurice FitzGerald Scott
1924–2009

AN OBITUARY FOR MAURICE SCOTT can only be a poor substitute for his own excellent account of his life (*My Life*, Parchments of Oxford, 2008). If an outsider's view of that life has anything to recommend it, the reason is perhaps that the writer may offer a more objective assessment of some of Maurice Scott's scientific contributions than the author himself provides. A self-critical tendency reveals itself when he writes of his own work. On the opinion of Christopher Dow concerning his first book, *A Study of United Kingdom Imports* (Cambridge, 1963), that it was very boring, he writes: 'This angered me at the time, but I am afraid it was true.' Why either Dow or Scott himself should have thought that a book about UK imports should be impossible to put down remains mysterious. In fact, however unexciting, this is an outstanding study, looking at UK imports in a detailed and analytical way that is no longer replicated today.

Maurice FitzGerald Scott was born on the 6 December 1924 in Dun Laoghaire (then Kingstown) near Dublin. He did not remain in his place of birth for long. His father's military employment soon took him to India where he remained until he was 3 or 4, before returning to Ireland. Maurice's parents moved to the Isle of Man in 1931. He was home-educated by his mother until 1935, after which he attended The Craig Windermere Prep school from 1935 to 1938. His secondary education was completed at Campbell College, Belfast, in 1943.

Maurice Scott's parents were distinctly different. His father was a soldier interested in shooting, walking, and golf; he also practised bee-keeping. His mother came from a more intellectual background. Her great-grandfather was a Bishop of Cork, Cloyne and Ross. Maurice's maternal

Proceedings of the British Academy, **172**, 293–300. © The British Academy 2011.

grandfather was George Francis FitzGerald, a physicist most famous for the Lorenz–FitzGerald contraction; the shortening of moving objects in the direction of their motion, a key feature of the relativistic dynamics from which Einstein built his Special Theory. It is perhaps easier to see the influence of maternal genes in Maurice's career. However he surely owed a dedication to golf and walking to his father.

Maurice Scott joined the Royal Engineers in 1943, starting with a six-month course in engineering at Cambridge. He writes of being under-whelmed by Provost Sheppard of King's College. In October 1943 an infantry training course was followed by further training until he passed out as a Second Lieutenant. By the time he was ready to fight, the war in Europe had ended. He travelled by ship to Burma, arriving too late to catch the war there, as the atom bombs had forced Japan to surrender. Nonetheless, the reoccupation of Burma demanded military skills, and Scott used his to help move a West African division across the Irrawaddy. Put in charge of the Officers' Mess, Maurice had to organise Christmas Dinner. The local market was useless when turkeys were required, but peacocks turned out to be a good substitute. The intensely practical side of Maurice's character was already evident.

In the summer of 1946 came demobilisation so that Maurice Scott could attend Wadham College, Oxford. As an ex-serviceman he was allowed to complete his degree in two years. He chose PPE with the emphasis on Economics. However Philosophy had long interested him. He was told to read Kant, but found Kantian ethics absurd, on the ground that general ethical rules could not possibly be derived from one simple principle. Late in his life the philosophical interest of the young Maurice Scott re-asserted itself with his publication *Peter's Journey: a Search for the True Purpose of Life* (London, 1998).

Scott's economics tutor was Donald MacDougall, the beginning of a huge enduring influence on his life. He graduated with a First, yet felt that he had much more Economics to learn. A studentship at Nuffield College followed, devoted to writing a thesis on the efficiency of nationalised industries, supervised by Norman Chester, of whom he writes: 'I don't believe that he understood my thesis and gave me little useful comment.'

When MacDougall became the first Director of Economics at the OEEC in Paris (later the OECD) he offered Scott his first paid position. The Paris organisation prepared annual reports on all member countries, with the aim on one interpretation of keeping US aid money flowing. In this unexciting number-crunching one can detect a large influence on Maurice Scott's life-long thinking. He had to bury himself in national income accounts. He was later to express regret that students today bypass that discipline, because concepts such as income, and particularly depreciation, are not at all straightforward, a point that theoretical discussions frequently ignore.

In 1951 the Conservatives returned to power in Britain, with Churchill as Prime Minister. He appointed his war-time scientific advisor Lord Cherwell (the Prof) as Paymaster General, and he in turn appointed MacDougall as his Chief of Staff. Scott in Paris received the message: 'The Prof wants you in Whitehall,' and so began for Maurice Scott three years in London as a civil servant working on economic affairs. These were hard times for the British economy, but boring they were not to be. During these years MacDougall was involved in countering the so-called ROBOT affair. The idea was to freeze most sterling balances with the aim of protecting the UK balance of payments. The Prof was briefed to resist the scheme in Cabinet on the grounds that such a desperate measure was not needed and would do great harm if implemented. These arguments won the day and the ROBOT affair is now largely forgotten. Great secrecy meant that Scott was only marginally involved in these machinations. More important for him in this period is his meeting with his future wife Eleanor.

Maurice Scott's marriage to Eleanor was transparently a success. She was a wife of a kind no longer fashionable, or in many cases even feasible. She was the homemaker, mother to Maurice's daughters, and his ideal companion. More than this, her lively mind, and unfailing humour, made it always a pleasure to meet her, on her own, or with Maurice.

In 1954 Scott went to Cambridge to work as research assistant to Christopher Dow on a National Institute of Economic and Social Research (NIESR) study of the British economy. Dow favoured a cost–push theory of inflation, unfashionable at the time. When he argued that the quantity of money was unimportant, Scott asked him why in that case the government should not cut the cost of financing its deficit by issuing money instead of selling bonds. In 1956 Scott applied for positions in Oxford and chose the tutorial fellowship at Christ Church. At that time the college often preferred aristocracy to merit when choosing which students to admit, and there were many closed scholarships for top public schools. Scott fought a battle in favour of meritocracy that was eventually successful. Two leaves of absence from Christ Church took Scott to the National Economic and Development Office (NEDO) to work with MacDougall, and on visits to Asia to work with Ian Little and Tibor Scitovsky on the project that produced *Industry and Trade in Some Developing Countries* (Oxford, 1970).

This last was the beginning of Maurice Scott's intensive engagement with the study of industrial policy in developing countries, especially in connection with the effects of bureaucratic controls and tariff protection. He travelled widely, observing what he encountered sharply and precisely. The contrast between stagnant India and Pakistan, disabled by heavy bureaucracy and high tariffs, and dynamic Taiwan, made a strong impression.

In 1970 Maurice Scott was elected an Official Fellow of Nuffield College, Oxford. Although this is a research position with small teaching obligations, it allowed Scott to supervise the training and research of some of the outstanding students that were members of the college. These include Nicholas (now Lord) Stern, Vijay Joshi, Deepak Lal, Martin Wolf and Sudhir Mulji. Nuffield College brought Scott into close contact with Ian Little and James Mirrlees, who were engaged in their pioneering work on social cost–benefit analysis (SCBA). More travel followed, including a visit to Kenya, where Scott undertook detailed estimates of shadow prices that engaged him for four years.

These were times when SCBA was high fashion, in particular at the World Bank. Today that is no longer the case. One reason is that tariffs today are far lower than was the case then. Equally important may be the realisation that complex formulae, such as those that SCBA requires, are open to endless manipulation to obtain a desired result.

In 1975 Scott was involved in a controversy concerning the management of the British economy in a period of crisis and growing unemployment. Wynne Godley, then at the Department of Applied Economics at Cambridge, proposed the reflation of the British economy by means of high import protection. In conjunction with Ian Little and Max Corden, Scott produced a paper, published later in 1980 as *The Case Against General Import Restriction* by the Trade Policy Research Centre, arguing that the tariffs required by the Godley policy would be huge and increasing, and that they would not solve the problem of the inflationary tendency of the British economy close to full employment.

As early as the 1970s Scott was publishing papers concerning the productivity of investment. This was the beginning of a big research programme that was to yield nearly twenty years later *A New View of Economic Growth* (Oxford, 1989). It is best to take a backward-looking view of this enterprise, because the book pulls everything together, and integrates several different lines of thought. Scott's main ideas may be summarised as follows:

1. Physical depreciation of capital equipment before it is really old is relatively unimportant. Depreciation is mainly a relative price change. Profits from investment gradually fall over time as real wages rise. Therefore depreciation does not reduce the total output or income of an economy and should not be subtracted from gross investment when measuring investment's contribution to growth.
2. If gross investment is used in growth accounting there is no residual to be attributed to technical progress.
3. A much wider view of investment should be taken than is standard. It should be defined as the cost of changing economic arrangements. It also includes things such as new ways of marketing as well as more conventional spending on machines etc.
4. Scott's model of economic growth eschews a production function. The proximate causes of economic growth are the rate of investment and the growth in quality-adjusted employment.
5. Some of the above is evocative of the vintage models of economic growth that were fashionable in the 1960s. However those models included their own version of exogenous technical change, although this was delivered via new investment. In Scott's model technical progress is an integral part of investment. By changing things, investment creates new opportunities for future investment. After a one-year investment holiday new investment would be less productive than it would be had investment continued.

In *A New View of Economic Growth* Scott uses the above ideas to construct an empirical model of growth with no production function that performs at least as well as received models. Maurice Scott started his consideration of economic growth from the ground up, with nothing taken for granted. People who write like that sometimes suffer from an insufficient awareness of the literature that they have chosen not to follow. Not so Scott. The earlier work is all there; described in detail; rigorously criticised; built on, or discarded for clear reasons.

The year of publication of *A New View*, 1989, produces the curious effect that the names that many people today would associate with the concept of endogenous growth (Romer, Aghion and Howitt) do not even appear in the index. Later on Maurice Scott did comment on Romer's work, as in his paper in the Winter 1992 edition of the *Oxford Review of Economic Policy*, and also in *My Life*.[1]

---

[1] A full list of Scott's writings forms an appendix to *My Life*.

Scott was especially proud of the fact that he tested his model on actual data and that he constructed his own data set in accordance with some of his economic accounting principles. Almost half his book is then concerned with applying his model to explain a range of issues including stylised growth 'facts', and the difference between social and private returns to investment.

A New View did not receive the reception that it merited. A hostile review article by Edward Denison only made things worse.[2] Sadly the profession is not sympathetic to big wide-ranging re-examinations of major fields when they do not take the form of papers in top journals. Even more significant, and to no credit to the economics profession, is the cool reception that Scott received at seminar presentations, in the US and elsewhere, and the indifference to various later articles. The likely explanation is the strong attachment of the relevant specialists to the neoclassical production function. That Maurice Scott's achievements were not entirely unappreciated was indicated by his election to a Fellowship of the British Academy in 1990. This might have happened without the publication of *A New View*, but the time of the election suggests otherwise.

Although he continued to travel, Nuffield College was his workplace and the beneficiary of his outstanding administrative skills. As one of the college investment bursars he was highly innovative and influential in establishing principles on the basis of which the college could decide how much to spend in any financial year. It is plain that simply spending dividends and rents is an arbitrary rule, and one that in a world with inflation would lead to a decline in the real endowment. Maurice Scott's rule for computing what he called notional income is typical of him in that it combines the sophisticated and the practical. That similar exercises are now routine across the University of Oxford owes not a little to the felicitous example of Nuffield College in the management of its financial affairs.

In the second part of his life he was quintessentially the Oxford don. Yet he was never parochial; communicating widely and effectively with scholars in Oxford and elsewhere. In tune with his work early in life Scott never ceased to be a numbers man. He wanted his questions answered by numerical estimates. From his writing, however, his commitment to basing numerical estimates on the right conceptual framework is always evident.

[2] Edward Denison, 'Scott's *A New View of Economic Growth*: a review article', *Oxford Economic Papers*, 43 (1991), 224–36; see also Maurice Scott, 'A reply to Denison', *Oxford Economic Papers*, 43 (1991), 237–44.

It is always difficult to know what a scholar will be remembered for, or if he will be remembered at all. It must be hoped that future historians of economic thought will not fail to record the revolution of the 1960s and 1970s that may be called paradoxically 'the economic approach to economic development'. Where previously economic development was often treated as an esoteric branch of anthropology, it was reunited with standard economic analysis, in which prices matter. Several economists can be associated with that intellectual revolution, none more than Maurice Scott and his colleagues at Nuffield College.

An example of the new approach is provided by the recognition of the crushing burden that high tariffs imposed on economic development in developing countries. The big insight here is the point that partial equilibrium measures miss a crucial effect. The inflated costs of inputs created by protection impose a heavy burden on all sectors, including those supposedly unprotected. It frequently happens in economics that an idea goes through two stages as follows. The first response is that people say: this is wrong. Then later they say: this is correct but so obvious as to be trivial. That is pretty much what happened with the pro-trade philosophy for which Scott deserves a big share of the credit, and for which he deserves to be long remembered.

Economics is inevitably a dry technical discipline, and few economists leave behind written work that projects their inner characters and personalities. Here Maurice Scott is notably exceptional. His autobiography *My Life* is extraordinarily open and honest. He does not shrink for instance from writing about his difficulties in his quest for sexual initiation. His *Peter's Journey: a Search for the True Purpose of Life* (London, 1998) is a brave enterprise. To write about the true purpose of life, whether as a professional philosopher or as an amateur, is to invite ridicule. After reading this unique and engaging work very few readers will consider it laughable.

Peter's Journey tells the story of a young man who travels through a sometimes dream-like landscape in search of life's meaning. While it is entirely different from John Bunyan's *A Pilgrim's Progress*, one is inevitably reminded of that classic travelogue. Where Bunyan's Christian encounters obstacles and temptations, Maurice Scott's Peter meets a variety of competing philosophies and counter-philosophies. These are voiced sometimes by colourful invented characters, who seem to have emerged from the pages of Iris Murdoch novels; and at other times by real, if dead, individuals. So Peter meets Beatrice Webb and Leo Tolstoy. He does not encounter Charles Darwin in person, but the author of *The Descent of Man* is the nearest the book has to a hero. Also greatly respected is Adam

Smith, not for his *The Wealth of Nations*, but as the author of *The Theory of Moral Sentiments*.

The young Maurice Scott's robustly common-sense approach to philosophy is again in evidence here. He takes revealed religion seriously enough to give it a turn on his stage while he plainly finds it impossible to credit. The leading problem discussed is the old one: how can an all-powerful and benign deity be reconciled with the terrible suffering of mankind. Peter on his travels might have met Dostoyevsky as well as Tolstoy. A theme that is visited and revisited during Peter's journey is how selfish should selfish human beings be, and how can we reconcile a good life with our rightful and unavoidable selfishness?

Peter eventually arrives at a position which is much the same as that of David Hume and Adam Smith:

> 'Will you therefore seek to love everyone?'
> 'No. I don't think love can be spread around very widely and still remain genuine—unless you're a real saint that is. You can feel real sympathy widely enough to want to help relieve suffering by people in far-away places, especially if you're vividly made aware of it on television, for example. But that isn't a very strong and enduring feeling for most people, nor will it be a very important guide to their conduct.... I remember Mrs Jellyby in *Bleak House*, who was busy promoting a scheme to have 250 healthy families cultivating coffee and educating the natives of Boorioboola-Gha, on the left bank of the Niger, while her own many children run about dirty and neglected ...'

Eleanor Scott died in January 1989 leaving a large hole in Maurice Scott's life. He continued to be active and optimistic, with friends of both sexes. Deafness became a growing burden, one that is difficult to appreciate for those who have never experienced it. In a characteristic fashion Maurice made no secret of his problem, but discussed it openly with friends and colleagues, and never allowed it to isolate him. Hearing aids transformed one-to-one interactions for him, and this mattered more than the frustration of group situations.

Maurice Scott was equally open and forthcoming after he was diagnosed with the prostate cancer that eventually ended his life. His daughters did a great deal to make his life as rich as possible. Yet he remained self-sufficient, and he took up new activities. These included painting, for which he had a distinct talent. He leaves behind three daughters and nine grandchildren. He died on 2 March 2009.

CHRISTOPHER BLISS
Fellow of the Academy

PETER TOWNSEND

Peter Brereton Townsend
1928–2009

PETER TOWNSEND was a towering figure in the intellectual history of social policy in the twentieth century. He made his contribution both as a sociologist who changed the way poverty was thought about and as a passionate campaigner for poor and disabled people. He opened up more aspects of society to rigorous study than most scholars ever succeed in doing. He did so with a passion that did not always make him popular and certainly made him enemies. But his contributions will last and he inspired a generation of young scholars who are continuing his legacy. He died on 8 June 2009 aged 81. The British Academy, to which he was elected in 2004, is commemorating him with a named prize to encourage research and writing in the fields he made his own.

He challenged and then overturned what had become the accepted ways of conceptualising and measuring poverty—beginning with his seminal contributions in the early 1950s on which he continued to build throughout his career. He made the lives of elderly people, at home with their families, a legitimate topic for sociologists. He studied the life of old people in the vast old poor law institutions of the time and in scandalously run private 'homes'. He made the financial circumstances of old people and of poor families a national issue at a time when the public had been lulled into thinking these problems had been solved. Then, in the 1960s, he opened up to public scrutiny the lives and financial circumstances of people with disabilities. He helped to open up the debate on health inequality as a key member of the Black Review in the late 1970s and publicised its findings. He moved on to study the role of international organisations like the World Bank, arguing they were often the cause of poverty not the solution. Social policy had to be international in its reach. Finally, he turned, in his seventies, to making human rights his new intellectual lever for change. In every case these topics were not just studied. His academic work became the starting point for practical and political action. As a result of his inspiration and involvement, each strand of inquiry left institutional legacies that would continue to maintain the political pressure to act.

Beginnings

Just over a year before he died Townsend began an unfinished autobiography. He had ten years earlier given a series of taped interviews about his early life that is lodged at the University of Essex and the British Library Sound Archive, on which I have drawn. The following extract from his draft autobiography shows how he viewed his own origins (he was born on 6 April 1928).

> I was the only child of a separated, and later divorced, mother. I was brought up by my widowed maternal grandmother, while my mother earned our living. My mother's father Thomas was, like his father Charlie, listed on his marriage certificate as a bookie's 'agent', but in the 1901 Census he was 28—a shipyard labourer. My father's father was a judge of rabbits, and more prosaically was listed as a master printer.

His great-great-grandfather had been a musician and dramatist, a friend of Charles Dickens. He married Sarah Brereton—her surname being Townsend's second forename. His father had been proud of that lineage evidently. It could be traced back to one who came with William the Conqueror and whose descendants gained a knighthood and became Sherriff of Staffordshire—or so his father told him.

Despite that Peter's early life was tough. His mother was a singer in local opera and operetta. After his father left she moved in with her mother and all eventually moved to London where she earned her living singing in local clubs and then in musicals where she became modestly well known and toured entertaining the troops. That ended with the war and she took a series of jobs, suffering from depression for a period. Townsend saw his father occasionally—a commercial traveller by this time. His grandmother, who effectively brought him up, was the rock in his early life and source of his moral compass.

He attended local elementary schools but his long hours of reading alone helped him gain a scholarship to University College School. He did well there. The Head Teacher C. S. Walton was a particular inspiration—

open minded and liberal. Peter was Captain of the School for two years. He was influential in abolishing the Cadet Corps and setting up charitable activities to replace it. He spanned the arts–science divide, being good at maths, art and literature as well as geography. It was for that subject that he was offered a scholarship to Cambridge. Before going up he did his National Service without any enthusiasm. At Cambridge he switched to Moral Sciences. He took his degree in two years as was allowed under the post-war regulations. He was not greatly impressed with that part of his teaching and thought of his future lying in journalism and began writing for student magazines. But then he discovered anthropology and took a further postgraduate year in that subject specialising in the anthropology of what were then the 'West Indies'. It was not the anthropology of far away people that attracted him, however, but close observation of the lives around him. He began writing about the slum area in which he was living with Ruth, who became his first wife. They had met in Hampstead, he from the bottom of the hill, she from the top, the daughter of a leading dentist.

After graduating he gained a scholarship to the Free University in West Berlin where they both lived, returning for Ruth to have their first child in 1952. He took a job as a research assistant in what we would today call a think tank, Political and Economic Planning (PEP), from 1952 to 1954. It once had a major influence in the 1930s, but by the 1950s it had become a rather unimaginative and conventional organisation—so Townsend would conclude. It did give him the opportunity to produce his first influential publication on poverty.[1] In it he fundamentally rejected the findings of the third survey of poverty in York which Rowntree had just published with Lavers, suggesting that the welfare state had largely elim-inated poverty.[2] A debate was organised between the authors of these two conflicting accounts. The young research assistant was generally deemed to have won the argument. A special meeting of the British Sociological Association followed at which Townsend met Brian Abel-Smith, then working at the National Institute for Economic and Social Research. They had both been at Cambridge at the same time but had met little. Now there began a lifetime of collaboration.

Townsend left PEP to work as part of Michael Young's Institute of Community Studies from 1954 to 1957 doing the kind of 'anthropologic-al' work he had discovered at Cambridge. He studied the lives of the

---

[1] P. Townsend, 'Poverty ten years after Beveridge', *Planning*, 344 (1952), 21–40.
[2] B. S. Rowntree and R. G. Lavers, *Poverty and the Welfare State* (London, 1951).

unemployed in one community in the North of England,[3] but it was his study of the *Family Life of Old People* in the East End of London that became a classic.[4] He put these individuals' lives into their social context and let them speak. This art of listening to his subjects, telling their story and putting it into a wider sociological frame, was to inspire a generation of young followers. Townsend said he owed a lot to Peter Willmott for his apprenticeship in this kind of study.

Townsend became dissatisfied with Young's restless shifts from one topic to another and agreed to join Abel-Smith in Richard Titmuss's Social Administration Department at the London School of Economics (LSE). His appointment was as a Research Fellow, funded by the Nuffield Foundation, to study life in old people's homes. He was later appointed as lecturer. He was to stay until 1963 when he became Professor of Sociology at Essex. In his diary for 1 August 1956 he noted, after spending an evening with Titmuss and his wife Kay:

> We all like to think we can be critical of our own society. Richard asks questions about things everybody else accepts. It is this and his integrity, rather than mental brilliance and dexterity, which make him the one surgeon under whom I want to practice.

This says as much about Townsend as it does about Titmuss.

Challenging poverty orthodoxy

It is difficult at this distance to grasp the intellectual courage it must have taken for a young man, recently down from Cambridge with no publication record, to challenge nearly a half century of work on the measurement of poverty by one of the pioneers of such research—Seebohm Rowntree. But that is what he did in a series of papers[5] that culminated in his *magnum opus*, *Poverty in the United Kingdom.*[6] Rowntree had been aware of the social determinants of the spending patterns of the poor, hence his notions of 'squalid living' and 'secondary poverty'.[7] But in seeking to convince a wider public that there were significant numbers of people liv-

---

[3] P. Townsend, 'Social security and unemployment in Lancashire', *Planning*, 349 (1952), 113–36.
[4] P. Townsend, *The Family Life of Old People* (London, Penguin edn., with a 'Postcript', 1963).
[5] P. Townsend, 'Measuring poverty', *British Journal of Sociology*, 5 (1954), 130–7; P. Townsend, 'The meaning of poverty', *British Journal of Sociology*, 13 (1962), 210–27.
[6] P. Townsend, *Poverty in the United Kingdom: a Survey of Household Resources and Standards of Living* (Harmondsworth, 1979).
[7] B. S. Rowntree, *Poverty: a Study of Town Life* (London, 1901).

ing below a minimally 'efficient' or socially acceptable level of income he took as his central measuring rod the cost to a family of feeding itself to a 'scientifically' determined minimum dietary standard. To this were added other judgements about minimal spending needs. It was this supposedly 'hard' core approach to measuring poverty that appealed to a succession of later investigators in the 1920s and 1930s, including leading social statisticians like Bowley and Llewellyn Smith. Rowntree had published a second survey of York using a wider range of more generous poverty lines.[8] But in the third, less thorough, study of poverty in post-war York, Rowntree and Lavers had kept to the idea of primary poverty to give them a measure that they believed could be compared over time.[9] Their conclusion that, viewed in this way, poverty had all but disappeared, outraged Townsend. It did not square with his observations of the poor. He began to put together a sociological refutation. Families' spending patterns and notions of 'necessity' are not grounded in dietary expert lists but in individuals' everyday experience of the social norms of behaviour—what your child is 'expected' to be able to do, eat and wear, for example, or the need to engage in social contacts. Occupations have different expectations of clothing, travel, and socialising. They may well have first call on family budgets despite the priorities set by dietary experts. As these social norms changed so should society's notion of a minimum acceptable life style and the cost of sustaining it.

His was the first challenge to the widely accepted view that the post-war reforms to the welfare state amounted to 'a job done'—a view I found remarkably widely accepted even on the left after 1951 in the archive work I have been doing recently. His central achievement was to define poverty in a way that has become an international point of reference.

> Individuals, families and groups in the population can be said to be in poverty when they lack the resources to obtain the types of diet, participate in the activities and have the living conditions and amenities which are customary, or at least widely approved, in the society to which they belong. Their resources are so seriously below those commanded by the average individual or family that they are in effect, excluded from ordinary living patterns, customs and activities.[10]

What should be put in the place of an absolutist dietary logic for poverty measurement? Here disagreements were to break out between colleagues who accepted Townsend's basic premise and Townsend himself. He explored

---

[8] B. S. Rowntree, *Poverty and Progress: a Second Social Survey* (London, 1941).
[9] Rowntree and Lavers, *Poverty and the Welfare State.*
[10] *Poverty in the United Kingdom*, p. 31.

varied ways to interpret and give statistical meaning to the concept. How did people from different social backgrounds actually perceive poverty? How had the state, in its various forms, interpreted 'a minimum acceptable standard of living' and how had that varied over time? Was it possible to discern an income standard, relative to other incomes, at which families were disproportionately denied access to commonly accepted social norms of living? This last was clearly Townsend's preferred idea and he worked hard to produce evidence of such a turning point.[11] He concluded that there was a significant increase in deprivation, key social activities not engaged in, once income had fallen to a level of 60–70 per cent of the mean income.

It was a highly controversial conclusion. His own figures and discussion showed how difficult it was to establish such a turning point. Later analysis by econometricians produced more sophisticated means of doing so but never fully convinced. What were commonly accepted norms? Which norms? How common? Which groups in society share them? What happens if they do not? What happens as they change?

This was, some concluded, just an attempt to dress up the goal of equality in the morally loaded term 'poverty'. The term 'poverty' carried with it an implication and a moral imperative that something should be done about it. That was a value judgement. Social scientists had no business trying to pre-empt such judgements with 'scientific' prescriptions.

Others wanted to stick closer to Rowntree's original strategy, working out explicit budget standard minima that could be openly debated and would change with costs and expenditure patterns. Socially 'necessary' items could be deduced by asking samples of the population to assess their centrality and changes over time. Yet others argued that Rowntree had not been as blind to the essentially relative meaning of poverty as Townsend implied.

Despite these differences, however, there was widespread acceptance that poverty was a relative concept and that some basis for adopting an acceptable measure of relativity had to be devised. Much poverty analysis has addressed that issue and refined Townsend's insight over the past fifty years.

Townsend went on working with colleagues at Bristol, where he took up a chair in 1981 and became Director of the School of Applied Social Studies. Here he developed with colleagues like David Gordon more sophisticated measures of deprivation and social exclusion and extended

---

[11] Chapter Six of *Poverty in the United Kingdom*.

their use internationally. They helped produce a statement by seventy leading social scientists calling for more agreed common measures of poverty. He worked with others at the Townsend Centre for International Poverty Research at Bristol on a series of seminars with international experts and published the results in 2000.

Even in the United States, which continued to employ a historically based absolute measure as its official poverty line, Townsend's arguments were seriously considered in a major report by the National Research Council in 1995 and some adjustments to the official methodology recommended.[12]

Many who accepted that a relative view of poverty was a legitimate one also argued that to include other perspectives gave a more rounded view. It was important to know how far absolute measures of living standards had changed, especially for the poor in times of rapid economic change. In poorer societies there was something morally different about absolute minima below which lay death or starvation as distinct from other less central aspects of social life. These kinds of consideration led to an interchange between Amartya Sen and Townsend in *Oxford Economic Papers* during the 1980s. It is one of the very few detailed debates between those adopting economic and sociologically driven interpretations of the same phenomenon. It was characteristic of Townsend that he felt both equipped, and morally required, to conduct a long debate with one of the leading economists in the world in a major economics journal.

Creating a new way to measure income distribution

Changing the balance of theoretical debate about poverty was, thus, Townsend's first major contribution to sociology. In the course of this process he made a related but distinct contribution to the way we measure income distribution that holds to this day. He did so in collaboration with his LSE colleague Brian Abel-Smith.

If Townsend could be a stickler for good sociological grounding for his arguments he could also be a political pragmatist, spurred on, no doubt, by his intensely pragmatic colleague. Let us not worry about the theory, or at the very least confine it to chapter one. Let us get on to derive a number that will be difficult to argue with politically—one can almost

---

[12] C. F. Citro and R. T. Michael (eds.), *Measuring Poverty: a New Approach* (Washington, DC, 1995).

hear Abel-Smith arguing. That was precisely the strategy they jointly employed in the most famous Occasional Paper in Social Administration of all time, *The Poor and the Poorest*.[13]

The state, the argument ran, sets its own implicit poverty line by agreeing that those below a certain income will be given support if they are sick or unemployed, retired, or unable to work. This was undertaken by the National Assistance Board. From time to time Parliament approved a new 'basic scale rate' and various extras were added at the discretion of local officers for defined special circumstances. The result was, therefore, a politically determined level on which such people were expected to live. It was a kind of implicit poverty line. How many families who were in work were living below that level? How many were living below that income and not drawing benefit if they were not in work? How many children were in families affected? How many were poor on that definition?

The answers were that no one knew. There were no comprehensive national surveys of the distribution of income that included non-tax-payers. Well, there was, but no one was using it for that purpose. Every year the Ministry of Labour undertook a Survey of Family Expenditure to set the weights for the basket of goods that were to be used in calculating the retail price index. To check its respondents' accuracy they were asked questions about their income. The results were used for verification purposes but never analysed and published in full. The pair persuaded the Ministry to enable them to use the income returns to measure the number of households whose income fell below the National Assistance Board benefit levels. They were not permitted to simply undertake another run of the punched cards but had to go to the original paper returns and transcribe them. Their research assistant, Caroline Woodroffe, recalls several weeks of work in a gloomy old workhouse in Watford where the original questionnaires were stored. However, in the end, this process produced the first estimates of the poverty of the working poor since Rowntree's contested ones.

Their publication, deliberately timed to come out just before Christmas 1965, created a political storm and effectively launched the Child Poverty Action Group. Townsend went on to chair that organisation for twenty years until he became President in 1989. But the approach used in that study became established as the UK's official means of tracking income distribution among lower income households. The use of the National

---

[13] B. Abel-Smith and P. Townsend, *The Poor and the Poorest*, Occasional Papers in Social Administration No. 17 (London, 1965).

Assistance rate as a poverty line had its deficiencies but that was replaced. Later official surveys became more detailed, the sample extended and the precise measure of the poverty line changed but the essential approach remained. More, it set a tradition of using official large-scale surveys for secondary analysis, a very important development in its own right.

Studying the lives of older people

The second important focus of study that lasted a lifetime was Townsend's work on older people—'the elderly' as he called them, in common with most other authors at the time. There had been work on the demography of ageing, and some on the financial, health and social circumstances of old age but nothing that rigorously examined older people's social lives, took their accounts as legitimate evidence and combined them with other sources to produce policy relevant conclusions. I think it is fair to see him as the founder of our modern sociology of old age.

It all began with a project to interview just over two hundred elderly people in Bethnal Green as part of research undertaken at the Institute for Community Studies. His rapport with those he interviewed and his capacity to let them tell their story shines out from the book and is a model for those entering the field today.[14] The strong connections individuals had across the generations in that community, the importance of grand-parenting and the tensions of retirement are sensitively portrayed. They are as relevant today. But so, too, were older people's relationship with the state, then the National Assistance Board, and their reluctance to apply for financial help. Out of these whole life studies began to emerge national policy questions not just about pension levels but also how public institutions interacted with vulnerable individuals, about housing allocation, redevelopment policy and much else.

This work led on to a complementary one studying those living in institutions. It was Townsend's idea, not supported by Michael Young, probably because it was not seen as a 'community' study and so it was undertaken on his move to the LSE. It led to probably his finest work, *The Last Refuge*.[15] It was based on a national sample of homes—the large old poor law institutions housing over a thousand people in many cases,

---

[14] *The Family Life of Old People.*
[15] P. Townsend, *The Last Refuge: a Survey of Residential Homes for the Aged in England and Wales* (London, 1962).

smaller local authority homes, voluntary, often religious foundations, and varied privately run homes. No such comprehensive study of this sector had ever been undertaken. It involved not just visits and interviews with staff and 'residents' but observation, discussion with local authority and care staff, analysing records, by hand, some gained with considerable effort and negotiation.

The interviewing was done mostly by two people supplemented by three others, including Townsend's wife. He took two temporary jobs as a bathing attendant, bathing elderly men, to get some feel of life on the inside. The result was a book that must rank as the near-perfect example of the social administration tradition. It began with a history of the state's involvement in the care of elderly people and the varied range of public, private and family care that existed in the late 1950s. This was then followed by a series of brilliant, closely observed sociologies of institutional life within the old workhouses, the newer local authority homes, the varied voluntary homes, and a range of private homes. A long chapter was devoted to each. In them he described and discussed the interacting effects of buildings, administrative and professional rules, methods of control, the nature of daily living and the lack of outside contacts, staffing ratios and the assessments of 'residents'. Such structural factors and their impact on residents' daily lives were illustrated with their own moving accounts. The regimes in each sector were contrasted, drawing on the then new literature of institutionalisation to which this was a major contribution. Past work had been primarily devoted to psychiatric institutions. This study was one of the first to observe and discuss institutional neurosis and the rules and practices that gave rise to it, leading him to draw the crucial distinction between isolation and loneliness.

Townsend did not leave it there. He contrasted institutional life with the home and family lives he had already studied. He went on to discuss practical policy alternatives. How many of these 'inmates' could be looked after at home with proper community services? What would that cost to achieve over a reasonable period? Should the state permit unregulated provision of very vulnerable people for profit with no regulation of standards? In a subsequent pamphlet he spelt out how the sector could be regulated. Here we have the classic Townsend—breaking new sociological ground but using it to inform detailed practical policy suggestions. That was then followed up with the regular harassment and embarrassment of politicians until they took notice.

A year before *The Last Refuge* he had published the results of a national sample survey of private nursing homes undertaken with Caroline

Woodroffe.[16] Why did people find their way there? What external oversight was there of the highly varied and often dreadful conditions? The report ended, as always, with recommendations, this time for inspection and regulation. Both these studies put the spotlight on some of the darkest corners of British society and demanded action. He had also embarked upon, partly written-up and then abandoned, a parallel study of geriatric wards in hospitals. This abandoned study was something he was regretful of later in life, not least because of the damage it had done to the researcher involved—Sheila Benson. She felt let down with little of her own work published: 'I sometimes took on too much', he admitted.

Action followed this stream of work, if less fully and more slowly than he would have wished, but come it did. In 1963 central government required local councils in England and Wales to produce ten-year plans to expand community care services, to build smaller old people's homes and close the old workhouses. Regulation of old people's residential homes and nursing homes, private and public, followed later. But here was major policy change that can be clearly traced back to Townsend's research. Academically the idea that these institutions were somehow beyond the legitimate scope of study and public scrutiny was destroyed by Townsend's accounts.

He went on to participate in a study of *Old People in Three Industrial Societies*.[17] It began a new tradition of comparative work in this field and, even if not widely noticed at the time, set a marker for the future.

His concern with older people's circumstances did not end there. Simultaneously he was working with Titmuss and Abel-Smith charting their financial circumstances. He was a member of a Labour Party subcommittee that set out a detailed blueprint for a completely new graduated pension scheme—National Superannuation. It rejected the old Beveridge flat rate model and was based, instead, on a combination of the Swedish, German and US Federal social security pension schemes.[18] The plan was to take nearly another two decades to be implemented in a watered down version as the State Earnings Related Pension Scheme. That was subsequently undermined by later legislation in Mrs Thatcher's time. But the principle that state action is necessary to ensure all individuals,

[16] C. Woodroffe and P. Townsend, *Nursing Homes in England and Wales: a Study of Public Responsibility* (London, 1961).
[17] E. Shanas, P. Townsend, D. Wedderburn, H. Friis, P. Milhoj and J. Stehouwer, *Old People in Three Industrial Societies* (London and New York, 1968).
[18] Labour Party *National Superannuation: Labour's Policy for Security in Old Age* (London, 1957).

and not just the poor, make adequate provision for their old age has been underpinned by modern behavioural economics. It is reflected in the policies and analysis advanced by the Turner Commission.[19]

Townsend had, over his lifetime, contributed to changing the lives of older people in major ways—their financial circumstances, their chances of being cared for at home or in a civilised way in institutions. That would surely have been enough for most people in any one career. But no, he next turned his attention to people with disabilities.

Understanding and improving the lives of those with disabilities

When Townsend began his career there was nothing that could be called the 'sociology of disability'. By the time of his death it was a flourishing field internationally. This was largely the result of his pioneering work, the inspiration and support he gave to young colleagues, and to his political drive. His approach was inclusive. It embraced those with mental as well as physical disabilities. It showed that the attitudinal and structural exclusions they suffered had common origins as well as differences which only a sensitive understanding of their lives could reveal to a wider public.

His initial work on disability had grown out of the *Last Refuge* study of older people in residential homes. How far were residents incapable of looking after themselves and for what reasons?

> It is one of the fundamental questions we have to answer if we are to rationalise our rather muddy definitions of 'disability' and 'incapacity', decide what role institutional care should play in modern society, and devise fair methods of compensating individuals for injury or disability.   (p. 257)

This led Townsend to devise a survey instrument that would measure residents' 'incapacity for self care'. It graded individuals' capacity for mobility and self care, getting in and out of bed, washing, dressing and so forth, and their capacity to communicate, together with activities necessary to overcome special handicaps. This survey instrument was built up from his team's observations of daily living and from studies undertaken by others in various specialist settings and some instruments used by staff in some hospitals. All this is set out in an appendix to *The Last Refuge*. This survey approach is now such a standard element in studies of people's need for

---

[19] Turner Commission, *A New Pension Settlement for the Twenty-First Century* (London, 2005).

care that it comes as a shock to see his team inventing such an instrument almost from scratch. Throughout, Townsend emphasised the need to define and measure disability in terms of people's capacities or incapacities not their specific labelled condition.

Clearly, if the scale of the problem was to be assessed, similar measures were needed and applied to those living in the community and their circumstances understood. The next stage in this strand of work was a survey carried out at the University of Essex shortly after he moved there in 1963. It involved disabled people living in Essex, Middlesex and in parts of London. Sally Sainsbury was his research officer and went on to make disability her life's study. In an account of this work in a lecture to the Royal College of Surgeons Townsend outlined what was to become a classic definition of disability that included, but cut across, the normal highly specific medical conditions.

> Irrespective of a disabled individual's *specific* behaviour or condition he attracts certain kinds of attention from the rest of the population by virtue of the 'position' that the disabled, when recognised as such, occupy in that particular society.[20]

From then on, Townsend writes over several decades about the lives of those suffering from a range of disabling conditions, the service inadequacies they encounter and the uncertain, messy and inadequate financial support they and their carers received. There were also the barriers to employment. Disabled children, those with learning handicaps, those in long-stay hospitals for the 'mentally handicapped', the frail elderly, the long term sick—all came under the spotlight.

He was not content, as always, to draw attention to failings in government policy and to point a finger at those in the professions and in politics whom he saw standing in the way of reform. In 1965 he helped found and sustain a movement to change things; the Disablement Income Group (DIG) campaigned for a common, as of right, income for those unable to work because of disability.

In the early 1970s he began working towards a much wider organisation bringing together a wide range of groups who supported those with particular disabilities. With Alan Walker and others he eventually founded the Disability Alliance in 1973. He was to chair that organisation for many years, as he had the Child Poverty Action Group. It was remarkably successful especially in its early years. With Alan Walker he devised and was

---

[20] The Policy Press (eds.), *The Peter Townsend Reader* (Bristol, 2010), p. 479.

the co-author of the *Disability Rights Handbook* and a survey of the lives of disabled people.[21]

The organisation campaigned not just for those suffering from disability but also for those who were the main carers, and he threw himself into the campaign to get government to provide payment for those who made financial sacrifices to care for kin—the Attendance Allowance.

These new benefits established in the 1970s at a time of economic crisis were sustained through Mrs Thatcher's era and survived subsequent attacks on their universal nature as 'welfare extravagance'. It is a tribute to the careful practical and moral case Townsend and colleagues mounted that they have been sustained.

Inequalities in health

While his colleagues Abel-Smith and Titmuss had concentrated much of their work on the finance of and open access to health *services* throughout the world Townsend had always focused on the impact structural inequalities in society had on individuals' healthy *life chances*. The coming of the National Health Service may have removed many financial barriers to health care but he questioned whether it had made any impact on the underlying causes of unequal health.

It was a point Townsend had made in his appreciation of Titmuss's life in an essay written for the *Lancet* in 1974.[22] In 1977 just before the thirtieth birthday of the NHS, David Ennals, the Secretary of State for Health and Social Security, set up a small committee to consider what had happened to differences in health status between the social classes. Prompted by his advisor Abel-Smith, Ennals appointed as members not only Townsend but also Titmuss's co-author from the 1930s, and friend, Professor Jerry Morris—an epidemiologist. The other members were the Secretary of the then Social Science Research Council and Sir Douglas Black, a Chief Scientist at the DHSS and President of the Royal College of Physicians. He was to chair the committee but it was Townsend and Morris who drove the committee's work and Townsend who emerged as its champion.

The review was completed in 1980 just after a new Conservative Government had come to power—the result was the Black Report, as it came to be known.[23] In an attempt to hide its controversial findings it was

[21] A. Walker and P. Townsend (eds.), *Disability in Britain: a Manifesto of Rights* (Oxford, 1981).
[22] P. Townsend, 'Inequality in the Health Service', *The Lancet*, 15 June 1974, 1179–90.
[23] Black Report, *Inequalities in Health: Report of a Research Working Group* (London, 1980).

released in very small numbers (250), in cyclostyled format only and on the Friday before an August Bank Holiday! There was a dismissive introduction by the Secretary of State.

The government had not reckoned with Townsend, who publicised it, talked to journalists, wrote widely about it and in the end got it published by Penguin Books with a foreword to which he contributed.[24] It became a best-seller and is still cited world wide to an astonishing degree. There have been successor reviews that have elaborated but not contradicted its main conclusions.

This is not to say that there have not been disputes about the Black Report's conclusions. For instance, was social class applied to males the most helpful way to consider trends in differential health status, given the changes in social class structure over time? But Black's primary finding, and it was Townsend's major contribution, was to locate differences in health status and life expectancy in the structural constraints and inequalities within which individuals live. It may be true that poor people smoke more and have less healthy diets, but why is that? They may take less exercise but how far is this a reflection of the physical limitations of the areas in which they live and the strains and expectations with which they live? These were much more subtle explanations than any simple relationship between 'inequalities' in income and health outcomes. They emphasised the contexts within which people spent their lives at work, at home, in poor neighbourhoods and over the life course. These insights have been confirmed and extended in later work

Hence Black's recommendations went far beyond giving advice on smoking or diet. They recommended improvements to social services and benefits. This, of course, upset the government machine. What were these medics and sociologists doing poking their noses into other ministries' affairs and suggesting big public spending beyond their remit? Their set of recommendations fell upon deaf government ears, as have more recent reports, but the report changed the nature of public debate, gained widespread academic notice internationally and began gradually to affect policy.

Townsend was in demand to undertake surveys of local health inequalities and to advise the newly devolved Welsh Assembly on tackling health inequalities. He led an inquiry which, perhaps predictably, came to different conclusions to those of the committee advising the English Secretary of State. Instead of measuring differences in the demands that people from different demographic groups made on health services, information

---

[24] P. Townsend, M. Whitehead and N. Davidson, *Inequalities in Health: the Black Report and the Health Divide* (Harmondsworth, 1992).

should begin with individuals' own perceptions of their poor health, he argued and suggested how this could be done.

International dimensions to poverty and human rights

All the way through his career Townsend made use of international literature and examples of policy practice. He moved to the University of Bristol as Professor of Social Policy and Director of the School of Applied Social Studies in 1983. There his research emphasis became more international in focus, both European but global too. It was, however, being appointed to the Michael Harrington Chair at the City University in New York in 1992 that led to his book analysing the international aspects of poverty.[25] He retired, formally, in 1993 taking up a Centennial Professorship in International Social Policy at the LSE in the same year.

He became increasingly critical of the way international agencies were, in his view, exacerbating world poverty not alleviating it. This was occurring as a result of insensitive and unrealistic structural adjustment policies imposed on developing countries by 'Washington' institutions—the IMF and the World Bank. In this he was reflecting other writers' diagnoses but he was able to link the frame of thought that drove many of these policies to similar, as he saw it, mistaken directions in domestic policy, notably by the US and UK governments.

What we needed, he argued, was a set of institutional reforms to those agencies that would set us in the direction of an international welfare state with poverty relief at its heart. This was a utopian goal but, as ever, he spelled out the first steps on the way. Mobilise and gain collaboration between existing national organisations. Develop a critique of existing policy trends. Develop common policy principles and common measuring tools for poverty and social exclusion. Develop strategies for international agreements on international taxation, company law to control global corporations. Get agreement on improvements to social security world wide. Develop strategies for social policy in the developing nations and make poverty central to aid policy. Reform the international agencies that were doing so much damage.

He moved, for one last time, into a new framework of analysis. The human rights literature seemed to offer a new way into conceptualising and campaigning for some old goals. He discovered that under the United

---

[25] P. Townsend, *The International Analysis of Poverty* (Hemel Hempstead, 1992).

Nations' International Covenant on Economic, Cultural and Social Rights there was a right to Social Security. This informed much of his human rights work. He and colleagues had a powerful influence on UNICEF and their revised definition and survey of child poverty in the developing world.[26]

Not long after returning to the LSE he was approached by those in the Law Department who wanted to start a new Masters programme on human rights. Would he perhaps teach a paper on children's rights? He seized the chance and threw himself into the design of the degree, helping to get it through the politics of the LSE system and then teaching with all the old fire. The degree became one of the School's most popular new offerings and the law students loved it.

A remarkable life

Looking back over these more than fifty years of hyperactive academic and political life it is difficult not to ask how did he do it? There were, of course, costs and life changes to contend with too.

He was a Founding Professor at the University of Essex, helping to set up the new university and the study of sociology and social policy there. The early years, especially during and after 1968, were not easy. He became a Pro-Vice-Chancellor between 1975 and 1978 with all the administrative worry that entailed. He would work at Essex in the week having only the weekend with his family in London, often interrupted with speaking engagements. Looking back, as he did in his interviews, he regretted this. His passionately held views also led him to fall out with some old friends and colleagues he had once admired and worked with closely. On his own admission he sometimes took on too much which had its impact on colleagues.

There were life changes too. He had met his first wife, Ruth, when he was fifteen, and they both grew and grew apart in mid-life. The break caused pain but they remained good friends to the end. There was a second marriage, to Joy Skegg, a health economist interested in social inequalities, and then, in the last decades of his life, he met someone with whom he fell, and remained, deeply in love. Jean Corston was Labour Party Regional Organiser for the South West whom he met at a Labour Party Conference

---

[26] D. Gordon, C. Pantazis and P. Townsend, *Child Rights and Child Poverty in Developing Countries: First Report to UNICEF* (Bristol, 2002).

in 1980. They married in 1985. She later became MP for the Bristol East
constituency (1992–2005), Chair of the Parliamentary Labour Party and
then entered the House of Lords.

Freed from the demands of running a department and other organisations, returning to teach as much as he wanted, driven by the sheer joy of
teaching, Peter relaxed. Some old wounds were healed. With his wife in
Parliament he spent much of the week in London and returned to the
LSE. He was generous with his time, amazing students with whom he
would go to have tea or lunch after a lecture and seemed to have endless
time for them. Here was this international figure willing to spend time in
the refectory until all the queries had been properly answered.

He was not an outstanding public speaker but he wrote brilliantly and
never clouded his work with academic jargon. He was not an abstract
theoretician or a statistician. He took the constraints imposed by social
structures as his starting point. He did not believe they were immutable.
Indeed, he spent most of his life trying to change them. But he saw how
they could constrain and shape people's lives in demeaning ways.

In 1958 he published an essay in a collection edited by Norman
McKenzie called *Conviction*.[27] It was an attempt by a younger generation
to rethink what socialism meant. Entitled 'A society for people', his essay
contains the essence of Townsend's creed. It set out at the age of thirty
what his life's work was to be and what motivated it.

> I work as a sociologist. I should like this to mean that I explore, and write about,
> present-day society so that others may understand it better. I should like it to
> mean that I spend a good deal of time observing and interviewing small cross-
> sections of the population before writing detailed reports which aim to keep
> human beings at the forefront. Above all, I should like it to mean studying
> very carefully the life of the poorest and most handicapped members of
> society.   (p. 103)

I read that in my second year as an undergraduate at Oxford and decided,
like others I suspect, that yes, that was what I wanted to do, too.

He might have called himself a socialist but he was a relentless critic of
Labour Governments which in his view failed to rise sufficiently effectively or vigorously to the task of confronting poverty. He jointly edited
two Fabian critiques of Labour's two periods in office in the 1960s and the
1970s.[28] He was critical of the Blair Labour Government, too, but he never
gave up on or left the Labour Party.

[27] N. Mackenzie, *Conviction* (London, 1958).
[28] P. Townsend and N. Bosanquet (eds.), *Labour and Inequality* (London, 1972); *Labour and
Equality* (London, 1980).

'Knowledge for its own sake' was not a notion Townsend could embrace. Knowledge was pursued relentlessly for what it could achieve in illuminating practical action to help the disadvantaged. It began with understanding ordinary people's lives. Once understood it had to be communicated. Top journals and RAE assessments were diversions. If a top journal was the best way to convince and communicate so be it. If a Fabian pamphlet, a book or a *Guardian* article would do it better, that is where he must write. But for all the political campaigning his contribution to the sociology of poverty, of old age and to understanding health inequalities will remain monuments to an outstanding academician. I share with John Hills the view that the last sentence of *The Last Refuge* sums up Townsend:

> It may be worth reflecting, if indeed a little sadly, that possibly the ultimate test of the quality of a free, democratic and prosperous society is to be found in the standards of freedom, democracy and prosperity enjoyed by its weakest members.   (p. 438)

HOWARD GLENNERSTER
Fellow of the Academy

Note.   In writing this I have drawn on Townsend's own life story given as a series of interviews with Paul Thompson 1997–9 and lodged both on the University of Essex website and in the British Library Sound Archive. I have also talked with friends and ex-colleagues. I have been generously given material and reflections by them.

An invaluable source of his writings for those without easy access to a university library is the edited volume produced shortly after his death and edited by Alan Walker and other colleagues: *The Peter Townsend Reader* (Bristol, 2010). A full list of his life's publications is available from the University of Bristol website at <http://www.bristol.ac.uk/poverty/Background_files/townsend%20publications%2048-08.pdf>.

FRANK WALBANK

Frank William Walbank
1909–2008

I

FRANK WALBANK was born on 10 December 1909 into a family of trades-
men, schoolteachers and millworkers in Bingley, a small industrial town in
the West Riding of Yorkshire which nearly fifty years afterwards provided
the background for John Braine's novel *Room at the Top*. His father,
Albert Walbank (1879–1967), was an elementary school teacher and his
mother was Clarice, née Fletcher (1880–1965); Albert was a cobbler's son
who won a scholarship to Yorkshire College (later the University of Leeds)
but a serious train accident put an end to his university career. The auto-
biographical memoir which Frank compiled in much later life,[1] showing
an enviable capacity for detailed recall, contains lengthy and entertaining
descriptions of family members, some of whom (like his father) were elementary school teachers. It portrays their network as 'a kind of lower middle
class provincial version of Galsworthy's Forsytes' but also describes a
wider milieu which allowed a degree of social and geographical mobility
within the region and had some opportunities for self-education beyond
the very basic levels. In part that was provided by the Workers' Educational
Association (WEA), in which his father was active and to which he was

---

[1] Details of source-material, information, and acknowledgements are set out in the *Note on
sources* at the end. Abbreviations used are: *CP* for his *Collected Papers* (Cambridge, 1985), *HCP*
I–III for the three volumes of his *Historical Commentary on Polybius* (Oxford, 1967), and *PRHW*
for Walbank's *Polybius, Rome and the Hellenistic World* (Cambridge, 2002). For reviewed
publications, I have listed reviews known to me, at first or second hand: others may still lurk
unreported, and a few which are known but are incomplete or unlocated have been omitted.

Proceedings of the British Academy, **172**, 325–351. © The British Academy 2011.

later to devote much effort and commitment himself. In part, too, there were routes which a clever boy might be able to follow, as when his primary school headmaster encouraged him at the age of ten to apply for admission to Bradford Grammar School (BGS) and when he was awarded one of the few scholarships which were available to boys living outside the city.

His years at BGS (1920–8) were the first and crucial stage in his social and intellectual transformation. Even before he took up his scholarship he was conscious of 'living simultaneously in several different worlds', a sense which exposure to the much larger and wider society of Bradford served to intensify. He records, for example, how through a socially better placed school-friend he encountered that friend's sister Barbara Betts, then a schoolgirl at Bradford Grammar School for Girls, who as Barbara Castle was to have a distinguished career in Labour Party politics and governments. Even more significant was the choice which he faced, after a year in the school, between 'the classical side' and 'the modern side'. He and his parents, persuaded (quite wrongly) that the modern side was an academic dead-end, and also over-persuaded by a domineering head of classics, chose the classical side, a decision with life-long consequences. Though, as he acknowledged, 'I do not regret at all that my parents' ignorance turned me into a classical scholar,' it was not the only decision of his life which was taken on wholly inadequate grounds.

A second decision was also not his, namely a sudden remove, instigated by a teacher who spotted his exceptional ability, half-way through the school year in February 1924, up into the cohort which was preparing for the School Certificate in five months' time. The expenditure of much unexpected and unwelcome effort enabled him to pass with credit and to 'fit into the BGS pattern of pressurised promotion into the scholarship machinery'. A whole chapter of his *Hypomnemata* (see the *Note on sources*, below) is devoted to his years in the Sixth Form, to the tuition in classics which he received, and to the personalities of his teachers. It was intensive, barely relieved by anything which lay outwith the purview of a university's Faculty of Arts, and yet from his account enjoyable. Three consequences followed. One was that 'when we went up to the university we had already read far more than classics students today have read even when they take their final degree examinations'. A second was to be asked by one of his teachers to translate, précis, and duplicate for the class 'a small, rather grubby German school edition' of Polybios: from such casual seeds can great oaks grow. The third was the efficacy of the 'scholarship machinery' in training him well enough to apply to both Oxford and Cambridge and to gain a Minor Scholarship at Peterhouse, a college which he had chosen himself simply because he knew from his collection of cigarette cards that it was the oldest Cambridge college but which proved to be a true *alma mater* in later life. Together with grants from other sources, he had the necessary resources (about £220 a year) to enter Cambridge.

His transformation now entered its second stage. Though initially locked into the language-and-literature grind of Part I of the Tripos, and though gladly taking some of the wider cultural opportunities which Cambridge offered, he had seen himself as a historian from the outset, and began to shape his life accordingly, by choosing the Second Punic War option in Part II, by learning enough Italian to read De Sanctis' *Storia dei Romani*, by attending a course in modern Greek, and crucially by responding when the Hellenic Travellers' Club offered a prize for an essay on 'Federalism in the Greek world'. Winning the prize, as he did, gave him a free place on a three-week Club cruise round Greece and Eastern Sicily in 1930: his first trip abroad, and 'very important for me'. Initial plans to become a schoolmaster were trumped by gaining a clear First in Part II in 1931 and by a consequential invitation to stay on for a year of research. Stimulated by his earlier essay on federalism, a rapid decision to focus on Aratos, coupled with the need to learn German, took him to Jena for two months in summer 1931, an experience which gave him an impressively fluent command of the language throughout his life. Back in Cambridge as a 'post-graduate' before such beings were properly recognised, he worked intensively enough to complete a 50,000-word essay before he had the good fortune to be appointed to a teaching post in north Manchester in September 1932. However, the award of the Thirlwall Prize soon afterwards for that essay, and its publication by Cambridge University Press in September 1933 as *Aratos of Sicyon*, helped to take him to the University of Liverpool as an Assistant Lecturer in Latin from January 1934.

Aratos is a remarkable book: an apprentice work of a 24-year-old (which occasionally shows), but already displaying the maturity of a lucid unadorned prose style of which he was to remain a master for the next seventy-five years. Stylistically, it is a hybrid. On the one hand it reflects an older historiographical fashion by offering a largely unreferenced narrative while presenting the sources in an initial chapter and confining discussion of the intractable chronological problems to a lengthy Appendix and chronological table. On the other hand, as reviewers influenced by Croce noted with some puzzlement,[2] it eluded convention by eschewing all

[2] Major reviews: W. H. P[orter], *Hermathena*, 48 (1933), 266–71; P. Treves, *Athenaeum*, 12 (1934), 324–9. Others: B. S. P., *Journal of Hellenic Studies*, 54 (1934), 99; M. Cary, *Classical Review*, 48

identification of Aratos as the figurehead of this or that programmatic but nebulous ideal, seeing him instead as a pragmatic conservative diplomat whose actions came to be driven primarily by fear of Spartan populism. Moreover, it provides a core analytical clue to understanding mainland Greek affairs in the 240s, 230s, and 220s BCE by portraying seemingly arbitrary Achaian, Aitolian, and Spartan military movements within Peloponnese as rational attempts to split real or potential opposing alliances: as reviewers said, more maps were needed.

II

The various threads of the next period of his life are best traced separately. Scholarly work and publication in the 1930s present the easiest task, for apart from the start of a lifetime's energetic activity as a reliable, judicious and punctual reviewer they were dominated by work on what became his second book, *Philip V of Macedon*.[3] Like *Aratos*, it was written to be submitted for a Cambridge prize, the Hare Prize, which it was awarded in 1939, and like *Aratos* it continued the unplanned but convergent twentieth-century process, in which many European scholars have participated, of providing accessible scholarly biographies of the major political figures of the Hellenistic period. Like *Aratos*, too, it segregated narrative and analysis from Appendices which reviewed sources, chronological problems, and dates. There the similarities end, for it represented a huge advance, revealing Walbank's third transformation into a scholar of maturity and international authority: as I write, seventy years later, even though our knowledge of Hellenistic Macedonia has improved greatly since 1940, his book has dated very little and is still the standard work, recognised as such from the start even though there were many disagreements on details.[4] That advance is visible not just at the level of

---

(1934), 36–7; J. Hatzfeld, *Revue des Études Grecques*, 48 (1935), 331; M. Segre, *Mondo Classico*, 5 (1935), 33–4; T. A. Brady, *Classical Journal*, 31 (1936), 513–14. Here and in the following footnotes, reviews are listed in chronological order of publication.

[3] Cambridge, 1940: repr. with a new foreword, Hamden, CT, 1967.

[4] Major reviews: J. A. O. Larsen, *Classical Philology*, 38 (1943), 56–8; P. Treves, *Journal of Hellenic Studies*, 63 (1943), 117–20; J. V. A. Fine, *American Journal of Philology*, 64 (1943), 461–5; A. Aymard, *Revue des Études Anciennes*, 48 (1946), 107–14. Others: M. Cary, *History*, 26 (1941), 141; P. Treves, *Contemporary Review*, 159 (March 1941), 357–8; W. W. Tarn, *Journal of Roman Studies*, 31 (1941), 172–3; D. E. W. Wormell, *Hermathena*, 57 (1941), 141–2; C. Edson, *American Historical Review*, 47 (1942), 826–7; A. H. McDonald, *Classical Review*, 56 (1942), 123–5; A. Momigliano, *Oxford Magazine*, 12 Feb. 1942, 188–9 (bibliography no. 220: not repr. in

presentation, with ten maps and full footnotes, or even because he adopted a style which 'shows his working' outwards from the primary evidence, but fundamentally in two kinds of independence. One was unavoidable, for he could not depict the elusive and contradictory personality of Philip himself without confronting Polybios head-on and going against the grain of the latter's prejudiced and simplistic portrayal. The other was a matter of choice: whether to follow widespread convention by depicting Philip's life in inevitablist terms of Greek disunity and Roman expansion (which was to abuse the historian's knowledge of the future), or to trace the complex interactions of power within Greece, within the eastern Mediterranean, and with Rome during Philip's lifetime in purely contingent year-by-year terms. Walbank chose the latter, and by avoiding simplicity provided clarity and (in his 'Conclusion') a balanced final judgement.

Productive scholarship notwithstanding, personal and political matters dominate his account of the 1930s. Fundamental was the progress of his relationship with Mary Woodward Fox, some three years his junior and herself from near Bingley, elder daughter of a businessman in the textile industry, Oswald Charles Fox. They first met in summer 1931 and married in July 1935, setting up house in rented accommodation in Liverpool. Both being liberal-radical by temperament in any case, they came to be heavily caught up in the contemporary politics of the Left, not just by being influenced by much left-wing literature (not least the Left Book Club) or of reacting to the Nazification of Germany, seen at first hand during holidays, but in terms of much dedicated activity for the Communist Party, the Labour Party, and various action groups. To describe and contextualise that activity in detail would cut across the tenor of this memoir, but four consequences are highly relevant.

The first stemmed from their work on behalf of refugees, since in August 1938 they felt themselves morally obliged to give house-room to a Sudeten German who had fought with the International Brigade in Spain and was now an illegal immigrant in Britain. Not only did this cause much domestic stress, but after rather over a year, in October–November 1939, those who had harboured and supported him until war was declared were prosecuted. Strong moral support from university colleagues helped to

his *Contributi*); J. W. Swain, *Classical Journal*, 38 (1942), 175 (the only sour note); P. N. Tarkov, *Vestnik Drevnej Istorii*, 4 (1947), 97–101; J. H. Thiel, *Tijdschrift voor Geschiedenis*, 62 (1949), 281. Reviews of the 1967 repr.: S. I. Oost, *Gnomon*, 40 (1968), 314–15; E. R. A. Sewter, *Greece and Rome*, 15 (1968), 99.

confine the penalty to a fine of £5 on Walbank (Mary was not indicted).[5] However, in conjunction with his then membership of the Communist Party it caused him to be told to resign from the Home Guard, which he had joined, and probably influenced the *repulsae* which he encountered on applying for work with the Ministry of Trade or (even after a positive interview) at Bletchley Park. Thereafter it was agreed with the university that he would remain in his post, would be registered as being in a reserved occupation, and would continue in the National Fire Service. In consequence he saw the horrors of the Liverpool Blitz (even more lethal in proportion to population than London's) at first hand from his observation post at the top of the Victoria Tower.

The second consequence affected Mary directly and him indirectly but substantially, for the birth of their first child, Dorothy Joan, in May 1939 combined with the stresses of the time to trigger a bipolar affliction which remained with her thereafter and periodically became acute. That, plus a frightening near miss on the house during the Blitz, led them to seek the comparative safety of Lytham St Anne's on the Fylde coast, to which her parents had moved on retirement: commuting the forty-five miles to and from Liverpool in wartime conditions was no fun. Two further children were born there, Elizabeth Mary ('Mitzi') in June 1942 and Christopher John in June 1944. The family did not move back to Liverpool until after the war. By then Walbank, now acting head of department for 1945/46, was seeking election to a chair. He had no initial success, but was elected in May 1946 to fill the Liverpool Chair of Latin: his long, detailed, and learned paper of 1940 explicating a much misunderstood passage of Virgil on the technicalities of weaving had evidently helped to reassure the committee that he was not just a historian.[6]

The third consequence was the composition of his third book, *The Decline of the Roman Empire in the West*.[7] Commissioned as a volume for a Marxist series, brief (92 pp.), virtually unannotated, and very stridently a Tract for the Times, it paints the entire trajectory of the Roman state over some 1,200 years with a very broad and very red brush, following Gibbon in seeking a naturalistic explanation but tracing its decay to the stagnation which was intrinsic to a class society dominated by a minority

---

[5] Press reports of the court case, published in the *Liverpool Daily Post* for 28 and 30 Nov. and 19 Dec. 1939, are held in the university's Special Collections and Archives (see *Note on sources*, below).

[6] 'Licia telae addere (Virgil, *Georg.* 1.284–6)', *Classical Quarterly*, 34 (1940), 93–104. Its creation owed much to Mary's family background in the textile industry.

[7] London, 1946; repr. New York, 1953. Expanded version in Japanese, Tokyo, 1963.

culture. To put it plainly, it was not a good book: though reviewers were courteous, they made their reservations very clear indeed.[8] Even so, Walbank records that it made his name in non-Classical scholarly fields as no other of his books did. Moreover, it has an unexpected historiographical interest, precisely because it derives so transparently from Rostovtzeff, Heichelheim, and Oertel's chapters in Volumes X and XII of the *Cambridge Ancient History*, but uses 'straight' the Marxist language of class and bourgeoisie which Rostovtzeff had used but inverted. Detailed assessment of it attaches more appropriately to the second edition of 1969 (see below), but it is right to record the surmise (it is no more) that its content and thrust to some degree reflected the lectures which he gave throughout the war to serving soldiers, more on current affairs of all kinds than on professional themes.

Linked in subject-matter to that third book, but very different in tone and purview, was another major publication which also had its roots in the 1930s.[9] This, a long chapter on trade and industry during the Later Roman Empire,[10] passes unmentioned in his memoirs, perhaps because the unfortunate publication history of *The Cambridge Economic History of Europe* allowed its appearance only in 1952. Though he revised it in 1966 and added a few later amendments in the 1970s, it was so far out-of-date by the time that that revision itself emerged in 1987, in the equally unfortunate second edition,[11] that it is more appropriately reported here. Clearly planned editorially to complement both C. E. Stevens's chapter in volume I,[12] and V. G. Childe's chapter on trade and industry in barbarian Europe in volume II, it offered a very summary reading of the theme as a

[8] Reviews: A. Aymard, *Revue des Études Anciennes*, 49 (1947), 345–8; Forbes, *Archives Internationales d'Histoire des Sciences*, 2 (1948), 215–18; A. H. M. Jones, *Journal of Roman Studies*, 38 (1948), 149–50; E. A. Thompson, *Classical Review*, 63 (1949), 65–6; A. Momigliano, *Rivista Storica Italiana*, 62 (1950), 112–17 at 114, repr. in *6º Contributo* (Roma 1980), II. 716–22; D. Atkinson, *History*, 36 (1951), 251; R. Goossens, *Latomus*, 10 (1951), 106–7; Asaka, *Journal of Classical Studies*, 2 (1954), 139–44; G. Faider-Feytmans, *L'Antiquité Classique*, 23 (1954), 239; C. D. Gordon, *Phoenix*, 8 (1954), 74; A. Balil, *Zephyrus*, 6 (1955), 325; W. den Boer, *Mnemosyne*, 11 (1958), 90.

[9] I do not know how and when he came to be approached for this major chapter when his track record did not suggest expertise in the economic history of the Later Roman Empire.

[10] 'Trade and industry under the Later Roman Empire in the West', in M. M. Postan and E. E. Rich (eds.), *The Cambridge Economic History of Europe*, II: *Trade and Industry in the Middle Ages* (Cambridge, 1952), pp. 33–85.

[11] M. M. Postan and E. Miller, with C. Postan (eds.), *The Cambridge Economic History of Europe*, II: *Trade and Industry in the Middle Ages*, second edn. (Cambridge, 1987), pp. 71–131.

[12] 'Agriculture and rural life in the Later Roman Empire', in J. Clapham and E. Power (eds.), *The Cambridge Economic History of Europe*, I: *the Agrarian Life of the Middle Ages* (Cambridge, 1941), pp. 89–117 (pp. 92–124 in the second edn.).

three-act drama, where at first 'The prosperity of the early Empire was a triumph for the principles of economic *laissez-faire*' in 'a single economic system' (pp. 49, 48). Thereafter the obscure and calamitous third century CE showed currency debasement, loss of population, and the disintegration of the large inter-provincial trading blocs. Finally, the transformation of the *collegia* into 'a hybrid form of controlled private enterprise', together with the partial encroachment of domain-economy and of taxes levied in kind onto a monetary economy, yielded a 'semi-planned economy' (pp. 62, 63). That this portrayal too derived directly and uncritically from the same scholarship as *Decline* is patent, and for that and other reasons has to be seen as wholly superseded by more recent work. Yet it is also fair to remember the unhelpful constraints within which Walbank was working. An evidently enforced footnote-free format made direct connection between evidence and argument impracticable, while the split between agrarian and non-agrarian activity made it impossible to follow the processes of production and transformation of primary materials as a continuum. Worst of all was the inability, forced on him by the concentration on 'Europe', to take the activities of the eastern Mediterranean into his purview *pari passu* with Italy and the west. For the Roman Empire that was an absurdity, at once descriptive, intellectual, and cultural, which the volume shared with another more recent compilation,[13] and which contributors could counter only marginally. That is not of course to deny the reality of the core component of his argument, the 'third century crisis' (though it is now seen in far more complex and nuanced terms),[14] and at least one reviewer called Walbank's contribution 'one of the best chapters in the volume, very concrete, balanced and careful'.[15]

It remains to return to the 1930s and to record a much happier fourth consequence of contact and collaboration with refugees. A trip to Greece and Albania in 1936 began an involvement with Albania and with Albanian refugees which continued thereafter, making Walbank one of the few 'Western' scholars who were *persona grata* there during the Hoxha regime and stimulating a number of reviews, letters to newspapers, and published papers on the history and topography of the region. Besides other scholar-refugee friends—his memoirs cite Victor Ehrenberg and the

---

[13] F. Vittinghoff (ed.), *Europäische Wirtschafts- und Sozialgeschichte in der römischen Kaiserzeit* (Stuttgart, 1990).

[14] For example, in W. Scheidel, I. Morris and R. Saller (eds.), *The Cambridge Economic History of the Greco-Roman World* (Cambridge, 2007), especially its final chapter, 'The transition to late antiquity'.

[15] E. B. Fryde, *History*, 40 (1955), 327–8 at 327.

brothers Paolo and Piero Treves—there was also collaboration, as with Momigliano on a stupefyingly detailed assemblage of references to work on Greek history during the war,[16] with Isobel F. Brash on a parallel assemblage with a much wider remit,[17] and later with his Liverpool colleague Charles Brink on the construction of Polybios' Book VI.[18]

III

For Walbank, now at 37 a professor and head of department, and once more fully resident (in Birkenhead) as a householder with a growing family, 1946 was a turning point, offering him a stable base on which to build largely as he wished. His achievement was indeed a tribute both to his energy, intelligence, and dedication and to Mary's support, but it is right also to note the contribution of two *patroni*. The first was Bertrand Hallward,[19] his mentor and tutor in Peterhouse, who had made possible that first crucial postgraduate year of research and had himself published in Hellenistic history: their combined longevity allowed Hallward to attend Walbank's ninetieth birthday party and Walbank to attend Hallward's hundredth. The second, much more influential, was J. F. (colloquially 'Fred', later Sir James) Mountford, Professor of Latin at Liverpool 1932–45 and Vice-Chancellor 1945–63.[20] Reading between the lines of Walbank's memoir, one senses clearly that Mountford viewed him with much favour from early on, giving him not merely much scholarly help (as various footnotes gratefully acknowledge) but also much valuable career advice and assistance. In return, Walbank clearly respected him, admired

---

[16] *Year's Work in Classical Studies*, 33 (1939–45 [1948]), 43–75, with p. 69. Momigliano also contributed to a follow-up report of publications in 1945–7 (*Year's Work in Classical Studies*, 34 (1950), 43–59, with p. 56).

[17] 'Les études classiques en Grande-Bretagne pendant la guerre', *Bulletin Association Guillaume Budé*, 1 (1946), 73–110. His co-author was a notable local headmistress from 1941 till 1963: S. Harrop, *The Merchant Taylors' School for Girls, Crosby: One Hundred Years of Achievement, 1888–1988* (Liverpool, 1988), pp. 114–39.

[18] However, a paper on the origins of the Second Macedonian War (*Journal of Roman Studies*, 27 (1937), 180–207), published as a collaboration, was an end-to-end join of two independently written papers.

[19] Later a notable Vice-Chancellor of the University of Nottingham. He survived, remarkably, until the age of 102, and received an affectionate obituary from Owen Chadwick (*The Independent*, 20 Nov. 2003). As with Walbank himself, Hallward's exceptionally long life precluded entries for them in R. B. Todd (ed.), *The Dictionary of British Classicists*, I–III (Bristol, 2004).

[20] For whom see *The Dictionary of British Classicists*, II. 683–4, and T. Kelly, *For Advancement of Learning: The University of Liverpool 1881–1981* (Liverpool, 1981), *passim*, esp. pp. 290–3.

his diplomatic and administrative skills, and in those and other respects took after him throughout his career.

Indeed, but for Mountford Walbank might never have become 'Mr Polybios'. When in 1943 Walbank began to ponder his next major project, Mountford suggested a commentary on Tacitus' *Histories*, a suggestion which got some way with colleagues but encountered the news, from correspondence with Oxford University Press, that the project was already bespoken for Ronald Syme. The invitation to consider something else instead prompted recall both of Walbank's work at BGS on Polybios and of the intense engagement with him which his biographies of Aratos and Philip V had already required. He therefore offered the Press the project of a commentary on Polybios, and though eventually Syme (then in Turkey) relinquished the *Histories* project, by then (April 1944) Walbank was immersed in his second choice and was soon to have a letter of encouragement from the Press (June 1944)—though even so he seriously underestimated the magnitude of what he was taking on.

It may help the non-specialist reader of this memoir if I explain why. Basically, he had to surmount five distinct challenges.[21] The first was that which Polybios himself had encountered when, as a Greek politician held as a respected internee in Rome after 167 BCE, he set himself to narrate and to explain to the Greek-reading audience of the eastern Mediterranean how the Roman Republic had come so rapidly to dominate the Mediterranean. His initial plan was to cover the core period of that transformation, the 'not quite fifty-three years' (1. 1. 5) from 220 to 167 BCE, but a later enlargement of the design brought the narrative down to 146, the year of the destructions of Corinth and of Carthage. Polybios had argued forcefully that from *c*.220 onwards the affairs of the various powers of the Hellenistic eastern Mediterranean had become so intertwined with each other that narratives centred on a single polity or single region were no longer adequate: in order to accomplish such a task one had to weave together a number of separate but interacting narratives focused on varying theatres. His solution was two-fold: first, to emulate, or rather to surpass, his fourth-century predecessors Ephoros and Theopompos by embracing a geographically gigantic purview of activity and interaction, ranging as need arose from the Iranian plateau to Portugal; and secondly, to keep track of events by adopting a rigid annalistic format, using Olympiads and Olympiad years as his framework and offering within each year-block a

---

[21] 'Commentary theory' (for which see below, n. 44) would have been a sixth, but was not yet on the horizon in the 1940s.

number of regional narratives, short or long according to the material he could acquire and the importance he felt it merited. So far so good: indeed, as the format of many a modern book reveals, his view of the late 220s BCE as a crucial *Wende* in the history of the Mediterranean is recognised to be as valid now as when he formulated it. However, the consequence for the potential commentator is that he or she has both to follow and to assess the accuracy and appropriateness of all the components of so polycentric a narrative, and in order to do that needs to know everything relevant which can be known not just about one region (as with Greece and Macedonia for Philip V) but about the entire Mediterranean and its deep hinterland, including the whole Nile valley, the Balkans, the Alps, Mesopotamia and Afghanistan—and not just the geography: the preface to *HCP* III thanks a Liverpool colleague 'for dispelling a little of my almost total ignorance about seaweeds'. The task needs a polymath, even a panmath: and that is before one tackles the actual operational task of deciding what it is that the reader of Polybios needs to know.

That is just the start. The second challenge was that Polybios was writing within a mature and quarrelsome Greek historiographical tradition, wherein one began where a predecessor had left off,[22] criticised him and other predecessors and competitors *eundo*, and interspersed the narrative with cadenzas which showed off one's erudition, personal experience, rhetorical skills, and specialist knowledge. True, his critiques and cadenzas are skilfully placed so as to rest and to contrast with the narrative,[23] but they also impose upon the commentator the necessity of explaining who he is criticising and why. That is no easy matter, when the writings of the victims are themselves known only from fragments. However, that necessity paid off in the longer term, for it gave Walbank an unrivalled knowledge of the lost Hellenistic historians, on which he was able to build in paper after paper in later life.

The third challenge is presented by the state of the text. Of Polybios' forty books, we have a complete text for books I–V, and most of VI. The rest is a mass of fragments: mostly excerpts (some very lengthy) on various themes made by Byzantine compilers, together with paraphrases and summaries of varying reliability surviving from later authors such as Strabo and Plutarch, and citations of words or geographical names in

---

[22] As Polybios himself did by beginning his narrative in 264/3, where Timaios had left off (Plb. 1. 5. 1 and 39. 8. 4–5).

[23] Three are entire books (VI on constitutions; XII, a critique of his predecessors; XXXIV on geography). For a systematic review of his critiques, see K. Meister, *Historische Kritik bei Polybios* (*Palingenesia*, IX) (Wiesbaden, 1972).

lexicographers. Though much work was done long ago on putting the pieces of the jigsaw puzzle together in the right order, there was still some work for Walbank to do, as his *Commentary* attests,[24] and in any case there remain large sections of narrative which we know existed but are now wholly unrepresented: Books XVII and XL, indeed, have no extant fragments at all. Since the question how far one should try to fill the gaps by reconstructing Polybios' narrative from derivative sources is deeply intractable, for the reader's sake a balance had to be offered between unhelpful taciturnity and unreliable guesses.

Previous scholarship presented a fourth challenge. For the Greek text itself Theodore Büttner-Wobst's five-volume Teubner edition, though old-fashioned in its layout, provided an acceptable text, and Mauersberger's *Polybios-Lexikon* had begun to appear in 1956. Commentary was another matter. Only once before had a genuine commentary on the text been attempted, by Johannes Schweighaüser of Strasbourg in 1789–95, and though exemplary for its time, and saluted with warm appreciation for 'its thoroughness and sound common sense' by Walbank himself in the Preface to *HCP* I, editorial notes were on a strictly limited scale, were largely philological, and in any case had been rendered wholly out of date by the accretion of knowledge. In consequence, when Walbank began work scholarship on Polybios largely comprised a shelf-full of specialised monographs, mostly in German or Italian. Consistently enough, Guy Griffith, who provided a useful list of them in 1954 in anticipation of the publication of *HCP*, summed up what was probably a current consensus—a mixture of respect and exasperation—by reporting that '[h]is work became authoritative in a way which recalls the authority of Thucydides for the history of his age.... The one thing which no interpretation yet ... has been able to supply for Polybius is one single spark of genius. With all his virtues, worthy, diligent, shrewd and comprehending as he was, he has remained *par excellence* the scholar's historian, because he lacked the skill or the touch to set the mind alight in the common reader.'[25]

Lurking within that judgement, debatable though it is, lay the final challenge: how could 'the scholar's historian' be brought out of the back-

---

[24] For full exposition, see *HCP*, II. 1–28 (for books VII–XVIII) and *HCP*, III. 1–50 for books XIX–XL, with a summary table for books VII–XXXIX at *HCP*, III. 51–62.

[25] G. T. Griffith, 'The Greek historians', in M. Platnauer (ed.), *Fifty Years of Classical Scholarship* (Oxford, 1954), pp. 150–92: quotation on p. 171; bibliographical references in notes 87–100. In the rev. version, *Fifty Years (and Twelve) of Classical Scholarship* (Oxford, 1968), an Appendix to Griffith's chapter adds much new material on Polybios (pp. 235–6) but merely cites *HCP* I in a footnote (p. 240, n. 1).

waters of scholarship into the mainstream? By good fortune, a solution was available, in the form of the 'historical commentary'. Naturalised in Britain from German scholarship by the 1880s at latest, first for Latin texts and then for Greek texts, not least with Frazer's giant edition of Pausanias of 1896, it has been predominantly an Anglophone art-form for over a century, for reasons which would bear further investigation. The first canonical 'historical' model, How and Wells's commentary on Herodotos, emerged in 1912.[26] This was overwhelmingly 'historical' rather than 'literary' in its contents, and was targeted at undergraduates (as the Preface announces), no doubt primarily those reading Greats at Oxford or congener courses. Both because it treated the entire text of Herodotos, and because it valiantly attempted to use current archaeological and anthropological research in order to contextualise the text within the polities and cultures which Herodotos touched on, it represented a major generic advance for its time. It was itself followed, in 1945, by the first volume of what became the second canonical 'historical commentary' on a Classical author, that of A. W. Gomme on Thucydides. This was much larger than that of How and Wells, having been planned as three volumes (though it eventually became five) and emerging in crown octavo format rather than octavo. It too paid attention overwhelmingly to the events narrated rather than to text or style, and though such has been the intensity of subsequent work on Thucydides and the period he covers that Gomme's commentary has itself now in large measure been replaced by a worthy successor, it set the standard by which subsequent work in the genre would be judged.

Walbank's own *Commentary* unquestionably met that test.[27] By the date of the publication of volume I in 1957, he had already published some sixteen papers on aspects of Polybios and his period, so that review editors of periodicals knew what to expect and trained their heavy guns on it accordingly.[28] From that bombardment Walbank emerged not merely

---

[26] W. W. How and J. Wells, *A Commentary on Herodotus, with Introduction and Appendixes*, I–II (Oxford, 1912).

[27] *A Historical Commentary on Polybius*, I *(Commentary on Books I–VI)* (Oxford, 1957, corr. repr. 1970): II *(Commentary on Books VII–XVIII)* (Oxford, 1967): III *(Commentary on Books XIX–XL)* (Oxford, 1979).

[28] Major reviews: Anon., *Times Literary Supplement*, 19 July 1957, 440; M. Gelzer, *Gnomon*, 29 (1957), 401–11, repr. in his *Kleine Schriften*, III (Wiesbaden, 1964), 201–15; J. A. O. Larsen, *Classical Philology*, 53 (1958), 246–51; A. H. McDonald, *Journal of Roman Studies*, 48 (1958), 179–83; P. Pédech, *Revue des Études Grecques*, 71 (1958), 438–43; H. H. Scullard, *Classical Review*, NS 8 (1958), 243–5; E. T. Salmon, *American Journal of Philology*, 79 (1958), 191–4; K.-E. Petzold, *Historia*, 9 (1960), 247–54. Other reviews: M. Chambers, *Classical World*, 51 (1957), 80;

intact but with his reputation significantly enhanced. Though of course many individual points of dispute and disagreement were raised, the general but not quite universal reaction was to salute it as a magnificent piece of scholarship (Salmon, p. 191) and to express grateful relief that after over 150 years scholars had 'a worthy successor to Schweighaeuser' (McDonald) and 'the foundation of a new approach to Polybian studies' (Cole), a set of judgements which the three other *pezzi grossi* of such studies in the 1950s, Matthias Gelzer, Paul Pédech, and Karl-Ernst Petzold, clearly endorsed: its detailed scholarship, balanced judgements, and avoidance of extreme interpretative positions were widely admired. However, a dissenting note is worth recording. It came anonymously in the *Times Literary Supplement*,[29] where the reviewer lamented that 'its aims no less than its achievement are conditioned by the old, limited view of what such a work should be', in particular because, notwithstanding the appearance of von Fritz's *The Theory of the Mixed Constitution in Antiquity* three years before in 1954, 'students of political theory or the philosophy of history will find it somewhat barren sustenance'. The point was fair, but was out of generic focus: history as observed, the concatenation of events and processes, is not history as created and shaped.

Rather, one is minded to offer a very different criticism, for despite its quality and admirable lucidity, it is not an easy read: to move from Gomme on Thucydides to Walbank on Polybios, as I did as an undergraduate in the late 1950s, was to move from the discursive to the distilled—from Telemann to Brahms. After a brief preface and fifteen pages of abbreviations, comes an Introduction which sketches Polybios' life and journeys, his views on history, his use of the term for 'chance' (*Tyche*), his sources, and his chronology, all in thirty-seven pages, and then we are straight into the dense forest of notes, references, corrections to the Loeb translation, citations of other relevant texts in Greek or Latin, geography, historiography, and general *explications du texte*, for over 700 pages. And even then, long though it is, it could have been longer with advantage. Yet it is

---

P. Pédech, *Erasmus*, 10 (1957), 301–2; E. J. Bickerman, *American Historical Review*, 63 (1957–8), 167–8; J. H. Thiel, *Tijdschrift voor Geschiedenis*, 70 (1957), 393; J. F. Gilliam, *Philosophical Quarterly*, 38 (1958), 511–12; R. M. Haywood, *American Journal of Archaeology*, 62 (1958), 242–3; J. H. Thiel, *Mnemosyne*, 11 (1958), 366–8; R. Till, *Historische Zeitschrift*, 185 (1958), 367; J. W. Cole, *Phoenix*, 13 (1959), 83–5; T. B. Jones, *Classical Journal*, 54 (1959), 331; I. Matos, *Romanitas*, 2 (1959), 260; F. Hampl, *Anzeiger für die Alterumswissenschaft*, 13 (1960), 31–4; W. Schmitthenner, *Gymnasium*, 67 (1960), 245. Most surprisingly, I can find no review in an Italian periodical.

[29] See above, n. 28: it is not recorded in *L'Année Philologique*, but made known to me via the dry comment which it provoked in Larsen's review (p. 247).

all carefully composed, with breathers in the form of excursuses of three to five pages at appropriate points, which describe topography or sketch the structure of certain intractable problems and controversies. The larger examples of these excursuses are invaluable summaries, terse, judicious, and impartial, which nearly always give the reader what s/he needs to know and have been the core of many a lecture or essay: Hellenistic history in its landscape, from Alps to Caucasus, was at last becoming accessible.

IV

HCP I was far from being his only activity in the 1940s and 1950s. Very soon after taking up his appointment at Liverpool, and throughout his career thereafter, he was continuously active in outside work and administration. To focus on such matters in a memoir of scholarly achievement would not normally warrant extended notice, but for Walbank they came to be an integral and important part of his life. Various reasons converged. Initially, indeed, his work as examiner in the Higher School Certificate for the Joint Matriculation Board and later for the Oxford and Cambridge Board was simply a means of earning extra income to pay for holidays, but already by 1943 he was also acting as a scrutineer for the JMB, visiting schools during examinations to ensure that they were being properly conducted.[30] By 1951–2 he had graduated to awarding for the Oxford and Cambridge Board, a role which continued till at least 1957–8, and also served as an examiner for the Civil Service in 1960–1. Lecturing to non-academic audiences and occasions also began in the 1930s, first on a course for the unemployed in County Durham and then widely in wartime to groups of troops—an experience which he vouched for as 'good practice for lecturing anywhere'—and to Rotary Clubs, army courses, and WEA classes all over north Lancashire and beyond, until the family returned to the Liverpool area: involvement with the WEA centre at Langdale in the Lake District continued for years thereafter. To this list, and in anticipation, one must add active participation in the local Association of University Teachers' branch, of which he later became president, service on the Liverpool Playhouse Committee in 1961–2, and even involvement with the Oxton Leaseholders' Association.

---

[30] One of his last published utterances *in vivo*, a brief letter in *The Independent* (29 March 2005), recalls a conversation with a Liverpool headmaster on one such occasion.

However, long before then, university administration had claimed his attention. That he became acting head of department in 1945–6, instead of his formally senior colleague Stanley Bonner, must have reflected an observed aptitude, one which blossomed greatly thereafter. A trivial role on a hall of residence subcommittee in 1946–7 led to service on the much heavier-weight Staffing Committee from November 1947 and on the Birkenhead Education Committee in and long after 1948–9, presumably as university nominee. From then on he became one of the pillars of university administration, while from 1951 onwards, on Ormerod's retirement, occupying a far more appropriate chair as Rathbone Professor of Ancient History and Classical Archaeology. Then 1956–7 saw him on the Institute of Education, on the Halls Committee, on Staffing Committee, on a building committee for a student residence, on the Extra-Mural Finance Policy Committee, on the City's Museums Committee, on the Education Studies Committee, and on the Development Committee; the following year Finance Committee and the Governing Body of the Technical College joined the portfolio. And so it went on, for 1962–3 saw him on Council, on Committees for the Arts Building, for the appointment of the Vice-Chancellor, Chairs, the Institute of Education, Layout, Extra-mural work, Development, the Chair of Spanish, Staff House, Education Studies, and the City Museum. Though the annual list tapered off a little in the 1970s, to it one must add the chairmanship of several of these committees (and of others), five years as Public Orator (1955–60), and his three years as Dean of Faculty (1974–7), a final major administrative task which he much enjoyed and wherein he left behind golden opinions.

This was to go far beyond the necessary minimum expected of a professor, even beyond a high norm: for years he seems to have been First Pro-Vice-Chancellor in all but name. There may have been a strong element of patronage by Mountford; there certainly came to be a certain zest in shaping decisions via discussion round a table and via close working relationships with administrative colleagues; but there was also a personal and darker reason. His younger daughter's memoir reveals how chaotic and disruptive domestic life could be during Mary's frequent bouts of illness and spells in hospital, and portrays Walbank as a loving and caring husband and parent indeed, but also as a male of his generation, with his generation's view of priorities and of differentiated gender roles.[31] Just as at home, if the study door was shut, he was not to be disturbed, so too, to a degree which it is hard now to estimate justly, the acceptance of such

---

[31] Full reference in *Note on sources*, below.

extra external activity served as an escape from situations and from strains which on occasion were intolerable.

Nor was Walbank's activity confined to Liverpool. Even aside from the normal round of external examining for BA and Ph.D. degrees, wherein he was continuously active until his retirement at least, his diary summaries are full of references to external lectures at this or that university, to Classical Association or Triennial meetings, and to the annual meetings of selected male British ancient historians at Wellingborough. By 1947–8 he was on the Classical Journals Board, and by 1958–9 on the Council of the Roman Society. Well before then he had already attracted national recognition and preferment: elected FBA in 1953, by invitation he delivered the Gray Lectures in Cambridge in March 1957, the J. L. Myres Memorial Lecture in Oxford in 1965, and the Sather Lectures in Berkeley in 1970–1,[32] having served as Reviews Editor of the *Journal of Roman Studies* from 1959 till 1969, as President of the Roman Society in 1961–5, and as President of the Classical Association in 1970. The further recognition which followed after retirement is noted below.

V

Ten years after *HCP* I, its successor appeared. It was not, as originally intended, the second of two volumes, but the second of three, containing the commentary for books VII–XVIII.[33] Walbank's letter of April 1962 to the Press, setting out the detailed case for three volumes, is quoted and discussed by John Henderson elsewhere.[34] It was clearly an inescapable

---

[32] See below, nn. 40–2. The Gray lectures seem not to have been published, for unknown reasons.

[33] Major reviews: A. H. McDonald, *Journal of Roman Studies*, 58 (1968), 232–5; P. Pédech, *Gnomon*, 40 (1968), 829–31; P. Pédech, *Revue des Études Grecques*, 81 (1968), 617–19; J. A. O. Larsen, *Classical Philology*, 64 (1969), 42–7; J. E. A. Crake, *Phoenix*, 23 (1969), 213–20; R. M. Errington, *Classical Review*, NS 19 (1969), 165–8; W. Peremans, *Revue Belge de Philologie*, 47 (1969), 1051–3. Other reviews: Anon., *Bibliotheca Orientalis*, 25 (1968), 277–8; R. Foray, *Latomus*, 27 (1968), 975–6; F. Hampl, *Anzeiger für die Altertumswissenschaft*, 21 (1968), 230–2; J.-C. Richard, *Revue des Études Latines*, 46 (1968), 464; A. E. Astin, *Journal of Hellenic Studies*, 89 (1969), 136–7; A. Díaz Tejera, *Emerita*, 37 (1969), 418; A. H. McDonald, *Antiquaries' Journal*, 49 (1969), 151; H. W. Parke, *Hermathena*, 109 (1969), 68; P. Pédech, *Les Études Classiques*, 37 (1969), 78–9; R. Till, *Historische Zeitschrift*, 209 (1969), 641–2; É. Will, *Revue Historique*, 95/246 (1971), 91–2.

[34] In ' "A piece of work which would occupy some years …"': Oxford University Press archive files 814152, 814173, 814011', forthcoming in Gibson and Harrison (see *Note on sources*, below). See also Henderson's earlier essays: (a) 'Polybius/Walbank', in J. Birchall and S. Harrison (eds.), *Texts, Ideas, and the Classics: Scholarship, Theory and Classical Literature* (Oxford, 2001), pp. 220–41: (b) 'From Megalopolis to Cosmopolis: Polybius, or there and back again', in S. Goldhill (ed.),

change, for the commentary is no less dense and meaty, the excursuses are if anything on a smaller scale and more linearly attached to the text, and no attempt was made to turn a commentary on disjointed fragments into an intelligible stand-alone overview of events. Two reviewers, Pédech and Díaz Tejera, did indeed lament the absence of those passages of Livy which derive from Polybios, but Walbank's decision to focus only on those passages which are directly attested as Polybios' was the only way of avoiding discussion of the credentials of attributions and indirect attestations, discussion which more properly belongs in commentaries on Livy, Plutarch, or Appian or in a specific monograph. Indeed, it might well be said that only with the volumes of *HCP* ready to hand can such a monograph be contemplated.

Disjointed though the fragments are, Walbank was still able to offer unitary studies of major issues and events such as the reasons for assigning fragments to their books and positions (1–28), the treaty of 215 between Philip V and Hannibal (42–56), the character of Scipio Africanus (191–6), the topography of New Carthage (205–20), the battle of Zama in 202 (445–63), or the battle of Kynoskephalai in 197 (572–92). Equally salient and admirable was his clear-eyed view of Polybios' inaccuracies, for example by showing how he was poor on geography but good on topography, and he had no illusions about the dismal impression created by Polybios' tetchy portrayal of his predecessor historians in book XII: as Walbank commented all too justly on 12. 17–22, 'this criticism of Callisthenes shows P. at his worst' (364). In contrast Walbank was himself ready to revisit his own earlier views and arguments, as on the date of the Roman-Aitolian alliance,[35] on the date of the death of Ptolemaios Philopator (434–7) or on the chronology of Aegean events in 201 (497–500), not to mention the extensive Addenda and Corrigenda (628–50). The denseness of the *Commentary* did arouse some resistance, Paul Pédech in his *Revue des Études Grecques* review commenting that with the accumulation of detail the trees were hiding the forest, but one may prefer to agree with Malcolm Errington's judgement that '[w]hat matters ultimately is that the reader seeking information is given discussion and direction to the literature, from which he will be able to make up his own mind—even though in practice, with Polybius, he will usually end up agreeing with Walbank's own discreetly presented view'.

Being Greek under Rome: Cultural Identity, the Second Sophistic and the Development of Empire (Cambridge, 2001), pp. 29–49.
[35] pp. 162–80, with a lengthy critique in Crake's review in *Phoenix*.

Two other stand-alone publications of the decade need notice. The lesser one, his Myres lecture in Oxford in 1965,[36] employing a wide-ranging title but focusing very largely on Polybios and on the debt which Walbank claimed (not altogether convincingly) he owed to Thucydides, exemplified what became a pattern, that of using lecture or article format to expand on themes which arose from the *Commentary* but required a greater length of exposition and argument than could be accommodated within it. The larger one was a new version of his 1946 book *Decline* (see above, pp. 330–1), retitled (in homage to Gibbon) as *The Awful Revolution*.[37] It was considerably enlarged, with two additional chapters which reviewed the cultural background of the Late Empire more fully, and the strident immediacy of the original gave way to a more scholarly tone. Its most important feature, however, was unchanged, viz. its status as a serious essay in historiographical theory, offering a fully worked-out Marxist analysis of the 'Decline and Fall'. Though translations into Swedish and Spanish followed, and though its interim enlarged version of 1963 in Japanese sold—astonishingly—over 13,000 copies, retrospect suggests that interpretative success eluded it. The two main questions (neither of which was really addressed either by Walbank or by reviewers) were, first, whether a Marxist analysis couched in terms of a stasis of internal political and economic forces could adequately acknowledge and accommodate the sheer impact of invasion, on the part of peoples who had benefitted for several centuries from the unplanned transfer of military technology, without marginalising the importance of such a stasis; and secondly, whether the survival of the eastern Empire, at least until the 620s CE if not until 1204, did not fatally undermine any Empire-wide explanation. Subsequent scholarship has more and more inclined to the view that 'it is no longer possible to maintain a simple and unitary explanation of expansion and decline which will apply to the whole of the Mediterranean world under Roman rule'.[38]

---

[36] Published as *Speeches in Greek Historians* (Oxford, 1965). Reviews: P. Pédech, *Revue des Études Anciennes*, 68 (1966), 421–3; S. Usher, *Journal of Hellenic Studies*, 87 (1967), 216; S. I. Oost, *Classical Philology*, 62 (1967), 139.

[37] *The Awful Revolution: the Decline of the Roman Empire in the West* (Liverpool, 1969). Reviews: Anon., *Times Literary Supplement*, 69 (1970), 38; R. Browning, *Classical Review*, NS 21 (1971), 101–3; A. Chastagnol, *Revue de Philologie*, 45 (1971), 186; G. Clemente, *Rivista di Filologia e Instruzione Classica*, 99 (1971), 99–104; L. Cracco Ruggini, *Athenaeum*, 49 (1971), 196–9; É. Demougeot, *Revue des Études Anciennes*, 42 (1970), 229–34; W. Frend, *History*, 55 (1970), 96; D. Kagan, *Classical World*, 64 (1970), 30; O. Murray, *Journal of Roman Studies*, 60 (1970), 264; E. R. A. Sewter, *Greece and Rome*, 16 (1969), 229. Translations into Japanese (1963), Swedish (1973), and Spanish (1978, repr. 1981, 1984, 1987, 1993, 1997).

[38] I thank Alan Bowman for permission to cite this summary formulation of the current Oxford Roman Economy Project.

VI

As Walbank entered his sixties, in December 1969, an invitation to deliver the Sather Lectures at Berkeley in winter 1971 released him temporarily from the 'straitjacket' (his own word) of commentary by offering the opportunity to present Polybios in a single connected exposition. The six lectures, published with commendable speed in late 1972,[39] became at once the basic book on the historian, and have remained so ever since.[40] A detailed sketch of the man and his work comes first, followed by chapter 2, a review of the historiographical traditions within which Polybios was working, and, by chapter 3, an explanation of Polybios' own term '*Pragmatike historia*' as a description of his would-be dispassionate, didactic, and factual history of his own times. Chapter 4 reviews the architectural structure of the *Histories* and the degree of change of attitude and approach which can be detected. The two final chapters focus more specifically on Polybios' response to Rome as a politico-military entity, chapter 5 analysing his flawed but fascinating attempt in Book VI to use the terminology of Greek political theory in order to describe the society and polity of Rome, and chapter 6 attempting to assess the impact on Polybios of living within (but not a part of) that society while detained at Rome after 167.

Reviewers gave the book a warm and grateful welcome, noting its lucidity and caution, its common sense and insight, its lack of special pleading, its brevity, and its command of specialist scholarship.[41] True, there were pleas for a more descriptive account (Pearson), for more on Polybios' style and use of Greek (Wormell), or for more on his strengths and less on his failures (Oates). However, I single out two of the major reviews because the responses which they encapsulate reflect two very different tendencies

---

[39] *Polybius* (Berkeley and Los Angeles, CA, and London, 1972). Unchanged pb. repr. 1990.

[40] Though B. McGing, *Polybius' Histories* (Oxford, 2010), now offers an alternative reading for the English-reading student

[41] Major reviews: J. de Romilly, *History & Theory*, 14 (1975), 226–33; P. S. Derow, *Phoenix*, 30 (1976), 308–11; K.-E. Petzold, *Gnomon*, 50 (1978), 37–78. Other reviews: Anon., *Times Literary Supplement*, 3723 (13 July 1973), 812; M. Delaunois, *Les Études Classiques*, 25 (1973), 464; Landberg, *Lychnos* (1973–4), 341; F. Lasserre, *Erasmus*, 25 (1973), 885–6; D. E. W. Wormell, *Hermathena*, 115 (1973), 118; A. E. Astin, *History*, 59 (1974), 447–8; M. Errington, *Journal of Roman Studies*, 64 (1974), 262–3; E. Gabba, *Athenaeum*, 52 (1974), 371–3; A. Momigliano, *New York Review of Books*, 21/12 (18 July 1974), 33–5, repr. in his *6° Contributo* (Roma 1980), II. 77–85; D. Musti, *Journal of Hellenic Studies*, 94 (1974), 195–6; L. Pearson, *American Historical Review*, 79 (1974), 121–2; D. Roussel, *Revue des Études Grecques*, 87 (1974), 468; O. Taplin, *Greece and Rome*, 21 (1974), 88; R. Till, *Historische Zeitschrift*, 218 (1974), 649–51; A. H. Bernstein, *Classical World*, 68 (1975), 447–8; J. F. Oates, *American Journal of Philology*, 96 (1975), 77–8; Orosio, *Augustinus*, 20 (1975), 204; S. I. Oost, *Classical Philology*, 71 (1976), 194–5.

in the modern reception of ancient historiography. Petzold's immensely detailed, scrupulous, and sympathetic scrutiny of each chapter seeks to elucidate Polybios through Polybios, arguing that his thought was more consistent than Walbank allowed. In contrast, de Romilly's luminous essay (for it is that) showed how Polybios derived his interpretative categories of reality from the Greek historiographical tradition, whether Thucydidean format and approach or Isocratean precepts on the legitimation of power, but by that token also showed how he could neither fully grasp the bold originality (*sc.* ruthlessness) of Roman policy nor apply Greek political theory seamlessly to a polity which it did not fit.

The third wave remained, in the form of the final volume of *HCT*. The task took longer than Walbank intended, achieving publication only in 1979.[42] Format, size, and style were unchanged, and again a massive Introduction (1–62) reviewed in detail the case for assigning fragments to Books XIX–XL. Since those twenty-two Books covered Mediterranean-wide events over the fifty years from 196 till 146, there was less scope for excursuses,[43] though the geographical Book XXXIV on its own required some seventy-six pages (563–639) which are a *tour de force* of encyclopaedic information. Again, too, reviews were warmly appreciative, though, since all concerned knew by now what to expect, the focus lay largely on minutiae and Walbank's partial re-ordering to the fragments rather than on the history of the second century BCE as a whole. Yet, behind the comments lay the recognition of the exceptional excellence of the *Commentary* as a whole, a recognition best and most sensitively expressed by Domenico Musti:

> Il sentimento fondamentale del lettore di questo commento è di gratitudine: l'opera di Polibio è diventata ormai, per merito della piú che ventannale fatica di Walbank, accessibile e leggibile per intero; il commento ne illumina tutti i *Realien* e ne scandiglia tutti i problemi; l'interpretazione dell'autore non prevarica mai; introdotta con mano leggera, lascia sempre libero il lettore; talvolta poi, con l'umiltà del vero atteggiamento scientifico, lo mette addirittura a confronto con un onesto ripensamento. In quest'opera c'è piú che una lezione mirabile di tecnica espositiva e organizzativa (che non è l'ultima delle qualità di un commento); vi spira un senso di etica professionale, che suscita il rispetto e costituisce un modello.[44]

---

[42] He had submitted the MS timeously for a 1977 publication, but the typesetters, faced with what was literally a *manu scriptum*, and a not very legible one at that, needed it to be either typed or recopied: in the event much of it had to be 'carefully written over' (information from Dorothy Thompson). His 1932 Olivetti portable presumably did not do Greek.

[43] The major one revisited the problem of the Achaian assemblies (406–14); later republished as chapter 10 in *PRHW*.

[44] 'The reader's basic reaction to this *Commentary* is one of gratitude: thanks to Walbank's labours of over twenty years, the work of Polybios has now become accessible and readable in its

VII

The publication of *HCP* III saw the Walbanks already well established in Cambridge, where they had moved on his retirement in 1977. Release from administration, Mary's much improved health, closer proximity to their daughters, an enviable level of health and energy, and access to college and university facilities all combined to bestow upon him a spectacularly active and productive retirement. Contact with students was not lost, for he taught for the University of the Third Age in Cambridge and continued to participate (as he had done for years) in Barry Dobson's annual course on the Roman army in Durham. Work on Polybios continued too, not least with a thirty-page 'Introduction' to Ian Scott-Kilvert's translation of the bulk of the text in the Penguin Classics series in 1979,[45] but release from the straitjacket of commentary offered new and wider opportunities. One, his first 'normal' book for forty years, was *The Hellenistic World*,[46] published in 1981 as his contribution to the Fontana History of the Ancient World. This had been a formidable assignment, for it needed to weave together at least four narratives. One was that of the post-Alexander reversion of the macro-region previously controlled by the Achaemenid Persian Empire to its earlier format as a competitive concert of regional powers. A second was that of the shifting multidimensional balance of power among them. A third was that of the intricate cross-penetration and development of cultural practices, institutions, and beliefs across a huge landscape extending from the Western Mediterranean to the Persian Gulf and beyond. A fourth was that of the step-by-step encroach-

---

entirety. The *Commentary* throws light on all its Realien and measures the depth of all its problems: the author's interpretation, delicately introduced, never equivocates and always leaves the reader at liberty: sometimes, even, with the modesty of a truly scholarly attitude, he actually confronts the reader with his own second thoughts. Within this work there is more than just a marvellous exemplar of explanatory and organisational skill (which is not the least of the qualities of a Commentary): there breathes in it a sense of professional integrity, which arouses our respect and offers a model.' *Rivista di Filologia e Istruzione Classica*, 109 (1981), 322. 'Modello' indeed, so that it comes as a surprise to find no reference to Walbank or to the *HCP* in the literature about 'commentary theory' which has emerged in recent years: for example, G. W. Most (ed.), *Commentaries—Kommentare* (*Aporemata*, 4) (Göttingen, 1999); R. K. Gibson and C. S. Kraus (eds.), *The Classical Commentary. Histories, Practices, Theory* (*Mnemosyne*, Suppl. 232) (Leiden-Boston-Köln, 2002).

[45] *Polybius: the Rise of the Roman Empire* (Harmondsworth, 1979, and reprs.).

[46] London (hb. version Brighton and Atlantic Highlands, NJ, 1981). Second imp. with amendments, 1986; third imp. with further amendments, 1992. Translations into Italian (1983, new rev. edn. 1996), German (1983), Spanish (1985), Japanese (1988), Greek (1993), Korean (2002), Polish (2002), and Arabic (2009). Folio Society edn. with new illustrations as *The Hellenistic Age* (2002).

ment of Roman hard power at the expense of that dynamic balance, growing even as Graeco-Levantine soft power gradually enveloped Italy and began to extend further. Worse, the creation of any overarching meta-narrative had to compensate for the fact that written evidence survives largely from Egypt (thereby posing the problem of how far *sui generis* its culture and polity were) or from Greece and western Asia Minor. The latter regions were tangential to events unfolding in the core areas of the Levant and Mesopotamia, but were central to the processes of partial convergence and assimilation which created the 'Classical World'. Though the book was largely welcomed at the time for its lucid style and clear organisation, and though it has enjoyed wider translation than its stable mates, it did not satisfy everyone, some critics seeing it as dry, over-focused on Greece itself, thin on the physical evidence, and silent or inadequate on many salient themes.[47]

Fortunately, Walbank could also address the task on a much larger scale, for he became the senior editor of three volumes of the new edition of the *Cambridge Ancient History*. The first to emerge, VII[2] 1, *The Hellenistic World,* achieved publication in 1984, the two others, VII[2] 2, *The Rise of Rome to 220 B.C.,* and VIII[2], *Rome and the Mediterranean to 133 B.C.,* in 1989. Here, though he contributed four excellent chapters himself to volume VII[2] 1, it was primarily efficient planning and the collaboration of numerous contributors from Britain, mainland Europe, and North America that allowed a far more detailed and wide-ranging approach to the meta-narrative. Yet in many ways the reception of these volumes (of which VII[2] 1 attracted the most attention[48]) was more important than their contents. Though individual chapters naturally prompted comments of very various kinds, evaluation and criticism (some of it quite fierce) mainly comprised a debate about objective, format, and method, which had as its target not so much the 'Hellenistic World' in general *qua* interpretative

---

[47] Major reviews: S. M. Burstein, *Classical Journal*, 78 (1983), 262–4; H. I. MacAdam, *Berytus*, 30 (1982), 117–21 (strongly critical); G. Casanova, *Aegyptus*, 65 (1985), 235–40. Others: N. R. E. Fisher, *Greece and Rome*, 29 (1982), 94; P. Green, *Times Literary Supplement*, 81 (1982), 206; P. M. Fraser, *History*, 67 (1982), 299–300; D. S. Potter, *Classical Review*, NS 33 (1983), 347–8; R. S. Bagnall, *Classical Outlook*, 61 (1983), 28; W. Huss, *Historische Zeitschrift*, 237 (1983), 667–8; A. Basson, *Apollonia*, 2 (1983), 88–91; P. Oliva, *Eirene*, 21 (1984), 130–1; H. Leclercq, *Les Études Classiques*, 54 (1986), 424–5. Of the Italian translation: C. Bearzot, *Aevum*, 58 (1984), 122–3. Of the German translation: M. Clauss, *Historisches Jahrbuch*, 105 (1985), 227–8.

[48] P. Green, *Times Literary Supplement*, 84 (1985), 891–3; N. R. E. Fisher, *Greece and Rome*, 32 (1985), 216–17; M. Errington, *Historische Zeitschrift*, 241 (1985), 659–61; S. Hornblower, *Classical Review*, NS 36 (1986), 85–9; F. G. B. Millar, *Antiquaries' Journal*, 66 (1986), 163–4; K. J. Sacks, *American Journal of Archaeology*, 90 (1986), 118–20; R. J. Rowland, *Classical World*, 79 (1986), 351; H. Leclercq, *Les Études Classiques*, 54 (1986), 424–5.

concept as the pros and cons of using multi-author collaboration and of concentrating on diachronic, politico-militarily defined components. Especially now with the availability of alternative formats, whether magisterial monographs[49] or multi-volume productions planned on wholly different lines,[50] that debate needs to be pursued—but not here.

Though by now well into his seventies, Walbank was not done yet. His *Selected Papers* of 1985 republished twenty-one of his earlier publications with minimal changes.[51] Nearly all were Hellenistic, and nine carried the name 'Polybius' in their titles, but their range—Greek, Roman, and historiographical—was far wider. Even then, and over and above a continuing flow of papers and reviews which continued until his death and beyond, two substantial original publications were yet to come—both from well within his comfort zone of scholarship, it is true, but containing much new material nonetheless. The first was his collaboration, after Guy Griffith's withdrawal, with Nicholas Hammond on the third volume of the Oxford *History of Macedonia* (Oxford, 1988). Walbank's 165-page contribution, narrating Macedonian history and its interaction with the Greek states from 301 to 221 BCE, was, as always, lucid, balanced, and fully documented, gratefully using the advances in epigraphic and archaeological knowledge which Greek scholarship had achieved in the previous forty years. Being almost wholly politico-military, and being written from (as it were) within the kingdom, it provided an invaluable, because consistently oriented, narrative of guidance: hardly surprisingly, reviewers fell upon it with gratitude and relief.[52]

The second major piece was a twenty-seven-page report on Polybian studies from *c.*1970 till *c.*2000, which carried on a format established by Musti[53] and showed how closely and systematically Walbank continued to pursue all relevant publications that related to 'his' author. He gave it the place of honour as the first chapter in a second volume of collected papers which appeared in 2002.[54] That volume reflected an even more concen-

---

[49] For example, M. Sartre, *D'Alexandre à Zénobie. Histoire du Levant antique, IVᵉ siècle av. J.-C.—IIIᵉ siècle ap. J.-C.* (Paris, 2001).

[50] For example, Salvatore Settis (ed.), *I Greci*, I–IV (Torino, 1996–2002).

[51] Reviews: J. L. Ferrary, *Revue des Études Latines*, 63 (1985), 447; J. Briscoe, *Classical Review*, NS 37 (1987), 123; E. Gabba, *Athenaeum*, 65 (1987), 252; K. Kinzl, *Gymnasium*, 95 (1986), 87–8.

[52] Reviews: H.-J. Gehrke, *Historische Zeitschrift*, 252 (1991), 669–70; A. M. Devine, *Classical Bulletin*, 66 (1990), 129–34; D. Engels, *American Historical Review*, 96 (1991), 1172–3; M. Zahrnt, *Gnomon*, 65 (1993), 307–12; P. Cabanes, *Revue des Études Grecques*, 106 (1993), 238–9.

[53] *Aufstieg und Niedergang der Römische Welt*, I. 2 (1972), 1114–81.

[54] *Polybius, Rome and the Hellenistic World* (Cambridge, 2002). Reviews: B. Rochette, *L'Antiquité Classique*, 72 (2003), 364–5; D. W. Baronowski, *Bryn Mawr Classical Review*, 2003.03.07;

trated focus on Polybios than the first, only five of the twenty papers not having the word 'Polybius' in their titles; even more, too, they explored historical, geographical, or historiographical themes which ran throughout Polybios' text and did not readily lend themselves to appropriate full-scale treatment in the *Commentary*. Though most were therefore 'traditional' in theme and approach, the two final papers joined the fashion for reception studies by exploring the readings of Polybios offered by John Dryden and Gaetano de Sanctis. That a paper written in 2001, a copy of which he sent to me in January 2006 as 'probably my last offprint', could appear in a volume on intertextuality admirably illustrated how new bottles could accommodate his vintage wine.[55]

By then, however, as his handwriting revealed, health and energy were beginning to falter. The death of Mary in 1987 lay nearly twenty years in the past, and the flood of public and academic honours which he had received had mostly come in the 1990s.[56] To his and to general regret, he felt unable to attend in person a colloquium held on Polybios in his honour in Liverpool in July 2007—though happily a video which he made to serve as a brief introductory discourse survives as a visual record, the text of which will appear in *Polybius and his World* (see *Note on Sources*). Yet his spirit survived to the end: a mere twenty days before his death on 23 October 2008, as an email sent by his daughter Dorothy reports, he spent 'a most enjoyable morning' being interviewed as part of a project to do with organ donation for clinical research.

Three achievements stand out. First, of course, though at considerable human cost, *HCP* I–III, for few scholars have been so closely associated with a single predecessor as he came to be with Polybios. Just as Nadia Boulanger did much to restore Monteverdi to his rightful stature in the history of music, so too Walbank, by bringing Polybios out of the specialist

---

R. M. Errington, *Historische Zeitschrift*, 277 (2003), 157–8; J.-C. Richard, *Revue des Études Latines*, 81 (2003), 419–20; A. Erskine, *Classical Review*, NS 54 (2004), 166–7; R. J. Penella, *New England Classical Journal*, 31 (2004), 56–8; É. Foulon, *Phoenix*, 59 (2005), 179–81; M. Dubuisson, *Latomus*, 65 (2006), 831.

[55] 'The two-way shadow: Polybius among the fragments', in G. Schepens and Jan Bollansée (eds.), *The Shadow of Polybius: Intertextuality as a Research Tool in Greek Historiography. Proceedings of the International Colloquium, Leuven, 21–22 September 2001* (Leuven, 2006), pp. 1–18.

[56] Silver Jubilee Medal, British Academy, 1977; Corresponding Member, Deutsche Archäologische Institut, 1987; Honorary Fellow, Peterhouse, Cambridge, 1984; Honorary D.Litt., University of Exeter, 1988; Kenyon Medal, British Academy, 1989; CBE 1993; Honorary Member, Israel Society for the Promotion of Classical Studies, 1994; Commissioned as a Kentucky Colonel, 1995 (an unexpected accolade which gave him great pleasure); Honorary D.H.L., University of Louisville, KY, 1996; Honorary Foreign Member, American Academy of Arts and Sciences, 2002; Corresponding Member, Royal Netherlands Academy.

side-channels into the mainstream of historiography, helped to make his theme and period, the rapid rise of Rome to Mediterranean predomin-ance, into one of the central stories of Classical Antiquity, and simulta-neously set the gold standard for a historical commentary on a Classical text. Secondly, one should cite his work on Polybios' wider milieu, for Walbank knew the text so well that he could use it as a window through which to obtain a much clearer vision, repeatedly and lucidly brought to scholarly notice, of Hellenistic history, historiography, geography, and society: a technique which others now imitate. Thirdly, and crucially, he was the last surviving member of a small group of outstanding scholars —Finley, Fraser, Jones, Momigliano, Syme, and others—which crystal-lised in the 1940s and 1950s and raised the standard of British-based Graeco-Roman history from respectability to the top level of international distinction. His death ends an era which the Academy, and scholarship in general, can look back on with admiration and gratitude.

JOHN DAVIES
Fellow of the Academy

Note on sources. Walbank's life and work are unusually well documented, to the point indeed where a book-length portrayal of the scholar in his epoch and contexts would be both practicable and valuable. For that circumstance he himself is primarily responsible, first and foremost by having composed by 1992 a 195-page memoir of his life up to his appointment to the Liverpool Chair of Latin in 1946. This memoir, en-titled *Hypomnemata* as homage to the title of the memoirs of Aratos, was intended for private family circulation, as it remains. Twenty-five pages of detailed notes, scribbled down in three sequences in a barely decipherable holograph, summarise his diary for the years 1945/6 until 1978, and were clearly intended at one stage to form the basis of a second instalment of *Hypomnemata*, which was never written. In addition, an almost complete list of his publications up to 1984 was published in 1985 in *Selected Papers*, pp. 344–60: an emended and updated list, including posthumously published titles, has been compiled. I am most grateful to his daughter, Dorothy Thompson, FBA, for making these materials available at an early stage. In addition, he lodged an extensive archive (33 boxes) of scholarly and administrative papers with the Special Collections and Archives section of the Sydney Jones Library at the University of Liverpool (refer-ence number D 1037). They include diaries, lecture notes, personal and professional papers, MSS of publications, reports and photographs: detailed cataloguing is currently (spring 2011) in progress. Other papers remain with Dorothy Thompson as literary executor.

Obituaries were published in *The Guardian*, 19 Nov. 2008 (R. J. Seager), *The Independent*, 28 Oct. 2008 (P. D. Garnsey), *The Times*, 13 Nov. 2008 ([JKD]), *Scripta Classica Israelitica*, 28 (2009) 182–3 (G. Herman), *Levensberichten en Herdenkingen*

FRANK WILLIAM WALBANK 351

(Nederlandse Akademie van Wetenschappen, Amsterdam, 2010), pp. 120–3 (H. W. Pleket), and *Gnomon* (P. Franke). The *Journal of Roman Studies*, 74 (1984), a volume inscribed in honour of his seventy-fifth birthday, was prefaced by an appreciation of him by Arnaldo Momigliano (reprinted in *8° Contributo* (Roma 1981) pp. 424–6: bibliography no. 671). The papers from a colloquium held at Liverpool on Polybios in July 2007, ed. B. Gibson and T. Harrison as *Polybius and his World. Essays in Memory of F. W. Walbank* (Oxford, forthcoming, 2012), include a personal portrayal 'Growing up with Polybius: a daughter's memoir', by Mitzi Walbank, and a detailed account by John Henderson, based on Oxford University Press archives, of the gestation of *HCP.* The papers of a second colloquium, held in Athens on 18–20 September 2009, will include a short memoir by Chr. Habicht: publication details are not yet firm. A third colloquium to mark what would have been Walbank's centenary was held at Kazan in December 2009. A number of Russian evaluations of his work are listed by V. I. Kascheev in *Vestnik Drevnej Istorii* (2010), 3, 225–33 at 233. A draft entry for him for the *Dictionary of National Biography* has been prepared by Peter Garnsey: publication or access details are not yet known.

For information and documentation I am most grateful to Anna Blumenthal, Doreen Bowsher, Peter Brown, Herbert Burchnall, Peter Garnsey, Tom Harrison, Robin Seager, Peter Urquhart, Maureen Watry, and above all Dorothy Thompson.

MICHAEL WILLIAMS

Michael Williams
1935–2009

A South Wales beginning

MICHAEL WILLIAMS was an historical geographer and environmental historian who received international acclaim for his work on mankind's use and misuse of the world's wetlands, forests and other fragile resources. He was born in Swansea on 24 June 1935, the son of Benjamin Williams, who was a trade representative, and Ethel (née Marshell) who came from Yorkshire.[1] Michael was the youngest of three children, with an older brother and sister. His paternal grandfather had been a coal miner and family members of that generation had been Welsh-speakers. Michael attended secondary schools in Swansea, first Emmanuel Grammar School in suburban Derwen Fawr and then Dynevor Grammar School in the city centre. His mother encouraged him in his academic interests, and a very inspiring teacher at Dynevor kindled his early fascination for Geography.

Having passed his school leaving examinations (advanced levels in English, History, and Geography), Michael entered the University College of Wales, Swansea in 1953 to read Geography, with some ancillary lectures in Economics, English and Political Institutions.[2] At that time Geography was taught by only two members of staff within the wider frame of

---

[1] H. Clout, 'Michael Williams, 1935–2009', *Geographical Journal*, 176 (2010), 111–14; R. L. Heathcote, 'Obituary: Michael Williams, 1935–2009', *Geographical Research* (*Australian Geographical Studies*), 48 (2010), 215–17; E. Baigent, 'Michael Williams', *Journal of Historical Geography*, 36 (2010), 466–72.
[2] In 1996 this would be renamed the University of Wales Swansea.

Proceedings of the British Academy, **172**, 355–375. © The British Academy 2011.

Geology.[3] However, that situation was about to change when an independent department was set up in 1954 and a Professor of Geography was appointed, in the person of Dr William G. V. Balchin (1916–2007), a Cambridge graduate, who had taught at King's College London (KCL) since 1945.[4] Along with Professor Sidney W. Wooldridge, FRS, Balchin had transformed the teaching of geography at KCL from being a subset of geology to become an independent discipline. This was accomplished with the collaboration of geographers at the London School of Economics, just a short walk away. At Swansea, Balchin had to go it alone; however the University College had embarked upon a major programme of expansion and funding for new departments, staff and buildings.

At the beginning of his studies Michael met a fellow student, Eleanore (Loré) Lerch, who became his regular partner at Saturday night 'hops'. With typical gusto, Michael would lead her around the dance floor with such determination and enthusiasm that she had to overcome her natural reluctance. They married in 1955, and Loré's combination of degree subjects (History, German and English) would come to support Michael's later work. After having been taught by a couple of geographers and staff from other departments in his first year, Michael encountered some newly arrived academics during the remainder of his undergraduate programme and the quality of his performance improved rapidly. As he entered his final year, the geography department moved into spacious new facilities, designed by the ambitious new professor, in the Natural Sciences block on the Singleton Park campus.

Among his lecturers was Frank Emery, a young Oxford graduate and fellow Welshman, who had a fascination for historical geography and a particular interest in the cultural landscape of the Gower peninsula. He proved to be a real source of inspiration for Michael, who would write in 1988:

> It is clear, looking back over old lecture notes, that the landscape and its makers were paramount in his thinking and interest. W. G. Hoskins' *Making of the English Landscape* [volume], Clifford Darby's 'The changing English landscape',

---

[3] The geographers were geomorphologist Gillian Groom and climatologist John Oliver, both of whom had joined the University College in 1948. Prior to their appointment, D. Trevor Williams had taught geography in the department of geology from 1931 to 1946, being followed for two years by B. H. Farmer. From 1927, students could achieve a Certificate in Geography linked to either Geology or Engineering Survey. Geology (with Geography) was housed until 1956 in Singleton Abbey, a Victorian structure and now the central administrative building.
[4] W. G. V. Balchin, *Concern for Geography* (Swansea, 1981), pp. 9–27; A. Coleman, 'Obituary: Professor W. G. V. Balchin', *Geography*, 93 (2008), 62–3.

and E. G. Bowen's *Settlement of the Celtic Saints in Wales* were a triad of inspirational works from which much else flowed ... His personal kindness in helping in the archive and reading room were other pleasant memories. Nothing seemed to please him more, however, than to take students into the field and explore the landscape of Gower and its surroundings.[5]

Michael delighted in this kind of geography and Frank Emery had an enduring influence on him. However, Emery was only a junior lecturer and he left Swansea in January 1957 when a lectureship became vacant at Oxford. Twenty years later, he would re-enter Michael's life as a colleague in the School of Geography there.

Michael had graduated with a first class BA degree in the summer of 1956 and was encouraged to undertake research for a higher qualification. He held a college postgraduate scholarship and, as was the custom at the time, was employed as a demonstrator in the department just as Balchin had been employed at Cambridge. In this capacity, Michael supported full-time staff in practical classes, map work exercises, field classes, occasional tutorials and other activities. This arrangement was to last for a maximum of three years. After a chance visit earlier in 1956, Michael and Loré had become fascinated by the strange, flat landscape of the Somerset Levels and Michael decided to focus his research on determining how that stretch of former marshland had been drained and converted into rich pastures and productive farmland. In selecting this topic he was following the example of Emery and also that of Balchin who had combined his training in physical and historical geography to trace how the cultural landscape of Cornwall had been fashioned from prehistoric times to the twentieth century.[6] Balchin's book appeared in 1954 as the second volume in *The Making of the English Landscape* series edited by the historian, Hoskins.[7] However, it was the lectures delivered by Dr Clifford Darby, FBA (1909–92) at Cambridge in the 1930s that had made Balchin aware of historical geography, demonstrated how the humanised landscape might be interpreted, and introduced him to some of the source materials that might be employed in such an enterprise.

After important work with the Naval Intelligence Division during the war, Darby had been appointed to the John Rankin Chair of Geography at Liverpool and then in 1949 moved to head the Department of Geography

[5] M. Williams, 'Frank Vivian Emery, 1930–1987: an appreciation', *Journal of Historical Geography*, 14 (1988), 451–4.
[6] W. G. V. Balchin, 'Contributions on the geomorphology of south-west England', Ph.D. thesis in Geography (London, 1952).
[7] W. G. V. Balchin, *Cornwall: an Illustrated Essay on the History of the Landscape* (London, 1952).

at University College London (UCL).[8] Through his writings and personal contact, he would come to exercise a powerful intellectual influence on Michael. Despite the affinity between Michael's research topic and Balchin's recent book, it was John Oliver, who had known Michael throughout his undergraduate career and of whom Michael thought very highly, who supervised the work on the Somerset Levels. The initial spark probably came from Emery's teaching. Further support came right at the end of the project from Stuart H. Cousens, the department's young lecturer in historical geography. Combining archival work with investigations in the field, Michael made good progress on his thesis and completion was in sight when his scholarship and fixed-term demonstratorship came to an end in the summer of 1959. University posts were still few and far between and, like many young researchers at this time, Michael thought that his future might lie with secondary school teaching. To that end, he studied for a diploma in education in 1959–60, being resident at St Catharine's College, Cambridge, where Darby and Balchin had studied as undergraduates.

During that year, Michael completed his doctorate for the University of Wales, for which Darby, by then head of the largest geography department in the United Kingdom, was appointed external examiner. His books on the English Fenlands, which had developed from his doctoral work, made him ideally qualified to determine the quality of Michael's work.[9] Of course, Darby was more than satisfied with the thesis, which he regarded as not only a fine piece of historical geography but also an exemplar of 'the draining of the marsh' and of 'agricultural improvement', two of his favoured themes in his lecture course on 'The changing English landscape' at UCL. Whilst approving of Michael's use of sources, the flow of his argument, and the quality of his cartography that had been refined under the careful eye of Balchin, he was perplexed by Michael's use of quartiles to determine class intervals on quantitative maps. Michael once told me that he tried to explain the impeccable logic behind this statistical convention but Darby remained unmoved, and insisted that quartiles had no place in historical geography. As the viva drew to a close, he lobbed a bombshell by posing the question: 'Mr. Williams, if you had to cut out a

---

[8] H. Clout and C. Gosme, 'The Naval Intelligence Handbooks: a monument in geographical writing', *Progress in Human Geography*, 27 (2003), 153–73; H. Clout, 'Henry Clifford Darby, 1909–1992', *Geographers: Biobibliographical Studies*, 24 (2005), 79–97; P. J. Perry, 'H. C. Darby and historical geography: a survey and review', *Geographische Zeitschrift*, 57 (1969), 161–77; H. Clout, *Geography at University College London: a Brief History* (London, 2003).
[9] H. C. Darby, *The Medieval Fenland* (Cambridge, 1940); *The Draining of the Fens* (Cambridge, 1940); 'The role of the Fenland in English history', Ph.D. thesis in Geography (Cambridge, 1931).

chapter from your thesis, which one would it be?' Michael knew that he had prepared himself thoroughly but he had not anticipated this. He remained speechless, and then Darby exclaimed: 'Only joking.' This painful pleasantry brought the ordeal to an end. Michael had his doctorate (the first in Geography to be awarded at Swansea), and he had earned the respect of Darby, a fellow historical geographer from South Wales, but now he was in need of a job.

The Australian interlude

At this time, British higher education had not entered the phase of rapid expansion that would characterise the second half of the 1960s, however there were openings for new academic staff in the Commonwealth and the United States. Michael responded to an advertisement for a lectureship in human geography at the University of Adelaide, South Australia, and was offered the position. For the next seventeen years, this would be home for Michael and Loré, whose daughters Cathy and Tess were born there in 1962 and 1965 respectively. Although small, the geography department at Adelaide was flourishing and friendly, under the benign leadership of Professor Graham Lawton who sought to operate through consensus rather than imposing a clear vision from the chair.[10] The department was a happy place in which to work, with the academic programme being organised and refined with a fair amount of agreement. Differences were resolved through discussion and the department thrived and expanded to accommodate the large 'baby-boom' generation that was passing through higher education. Geography teachers were in demand in Australia and many students went through the bonding system, financed by the education department, in return for an undertaking to teach for at least three years in the state school system, wherever they were required. In the first two years of the undergraduate programme, students had a balanced diet of physical, human and regional courses, which displayed geography as an holistic discipline that sought to understand the differentiation of the earth's surface. Some specialisation was possible in the final undergraduate year, which enabled teaching staff to present their specific interests to the students. Demand was so great that some introductory lectures were repeated in evening classes, aimed mainly at prospective teachers.

[10] P. J. Smailes and T. L. C. Griffin, 'Geography at the University of Adelaide, 1960–1991', *South Australian Geographical Journal*, 102 (2004), 62–81.

Michael developed an impressive portfolio of lectures in human, historical and settlement geography, published several papers from his doctoral work, and revised his thesis, which would appear in 1970 as *The Draining of the Somerset Levels*, from the Cambridge University Press, the same publisher that had brought out Darby's Fenland books three decades earlier.[11] Darby checked through the revised manuscript and, not surprisingly, no mention of quartiles was to be found. Michael had taken advantage of the University of Adelaide's rather generous arrangement for sabbatical leave to bring his account up to date through further fieldwork in Somerset and other enquiries during 1966.[12] He spent some months at UCL, where the geography department was now headed by Professor W. R. Mead, FBA, since Darby had returned to Cambridge to occupy the established chair there. Michael found the UCL Department,

> a stimulating place, intellectually and socially. There was a galaxy of stars, every one a name to be conjured with as a well-known expert in some branch or regional emphasis in geography. The weekly seminars on historical geography, guest speakers and a flow of overseas visitors ... added to the excitement.[13]

In London, Michael delivered a set of lectures on Australasia, in place of R. Leslie Heathcote and R. Gerard Ward who had moved to university posts in Australia and Papua New Guinea respectively. His presentations were well received by the undergraduates, and Mead described him as 'Immensely enthusiastic about his work, fertile in ideas, much enjoyed by students, and completely integrated in our company.'[14] He regretted that funds were not available to offer him a permanent position in London.

Back in Adelaide, Michael's new research was organised in two interwoven strands. The first involved historical research into the impact of European settlers in South Australia and the subsequent shaping of the

[11] M. Williams, 'The draining and reclamation of the Somerset Levels, 1770–1833', *Transactions of the Institute of British Geographers*, 33 (1963), 163–79; 'Drainage activity in the Somerset Levels since 1939', *Geography*, 49 (1964), 387–99.
[12] M. Williams, 'The enclosure and reclamation of waste land in England and Wales in the eighteenth and nineteenth centuries', *Transactions of the Institute of British Geographers*, 51 (1970), 55–69; 'The enclosure and reclamation of the Mendip Hills', *Agricultural History Review*, 19 (1971), 65–81; 'The enclosure of waste land in Somerset, 1700–1900', *Transactions of the Institute of British Geographers*, 57 (1972), 99–123.
[13] M. Williams, 'Henry Clifford Darby, 1909–1992', *Proceedings of the British Academy*, 87 (1995), 289–306.
[14] Letter from W. R. Mead to the Academic Registrar of the Australian National University, dated 18 Oct. 1971; Archives of the Geography Department, UCL.

cultural landscape, whilst the second focused on the creation and functioning of contemporary rural settlements.[15] Each of these themes gave
rise to articles in learned journals, and they were complemented by a couple
of papers on suburban processes around Adelaide and the impact of the
city upon its hinterland.[16] In 1969, Michael had edited a short book on the
occasion of the forty-first meeting of the Australian and New Zealand
Association for the Advancement of Science at Adelaide.[17] This was
described by Les Heathcote as a 'masterly combination of aerial photog-
raphy keyed to cadastral plans with an associated analytical commentary'.[18] For the fiftieth ANZAAS Jubilee Congress in Adelaide in 1980,
the same theme would be chosen but the state would be depicted from
space rather than from aircraft. In 1975, Michael joined J. M. Powell,
FBA—another British expatriate historical geographer—in editing a volume that brought together seven thematic essays on the economic impact
of European settlers on rather small sections of the vast territorial extent
of Australia.[19] Not surprisingly, Michael's contribution focused on rural
settlements and offered an interpretation of the ultimate aim of colonial

[15] A pioneering study in this area was: D. W. Meinig, *On the Margins of the Good Earth: the South
Australian Wheat Frontier, 1869–1884* (Chicago, IL, 1962). This book and Don Meinig's many
books on the historical geography of North America would have an important influence on
Michael.
[16] For example, M. Williams, 'The historical geography of an artificial drainage system: the
Lower South East of South Australia', *Australian Geographical Studies*, 2 (1964), 87–102;
'Gawler: the changing geography of a South Australian country town', *Australian Geographer*,
9 (1964), 195–206; 'A note on the influence of Adelaide on rural shopping habits', *Australian
Geographer*, 9 (1965), 312–15; 'Delimiting the spread of settlements: an examination of evidence
in South Australia', *Economic Geography*, 42 (1966), 336–55; 'The parkland towns of Australia
and New Zealand', *Geographical Review*, 56 (1966), 67–89; *Adelaide* (Melbourne, 1966); 'Two
studies in the historical geography of South Australia', in G. H. Dury and M. Logan (eds.),
Studies in Australian Geography (Melbourne, 1968), pp. 71–98; 'The spread of settlement in
South Australia', in F. Gale and G. H. Lawton (eds.), *Settlement and Encounter: Geographical
Studies presented to Sir Grenfell Price* (Melbourne, 1969), 1–50; 'Town farming in the Mallee
Lands of South Australia and Victoria, *Australian Geographical Studies*, 8 (1970), 173–91;
'Periods, places and themes, a review and prospect for Australian historical geography', *Australian
Geographer*, 4 (1971), 403–16; 'Simplicity and stability in rural areas: the example of the Pinnaroo
district of South Australia', *Geografiska Annaler*, 54B (1972), 117–35; 'Planned and unplanned
changes in the marginal lands of South Australia', *Australian Geographer*, 13 (1976), 271–81;
'Settlements in rural areas: planned landscapes and unplanned changes in South Australia',
Landscape Planning, 4 (1977), 29–51; and later, 'The clearing of the woods', in R. L. Heathcote
(ed.), *The Australian Experience: Essays in Australian Land Settlement and Resource Management*
(Melbourne, 1988), pp. 115–26.
[17] M. Williams (ed.), *South Australia from the Air* (Adelaide, 1969).
[18] Heathcote, 'Obituary: Michael Williams'.
[19] J. M. Powell and M. Williams (eds.), *Australian Space, Australian Time* (Melbourne, 1975).

policies between 1788 and 1914, namely to create more and smaller settler landholdings, which largely failed.[20]

However, a much larger project on South Australia was in progress, which would appear in a new historical geography series launched by Academic Press.[21] Drawing on a decade and half of research, this 542-page monograph adopted the 'vertical theme' approach advocated by Darby, who favoured archives and libraries, and by Hoskins, who enjoyed work in the field, to explaining how and why particular sections of the earth's surface have their distinctive appearance. The title was a precise reflection of Hoskins's best seller, *The Making of the English Landscape* (1955). Michael began by describing the view from his office on the ninth floor of the Napier Building of the university, looking first at the city and its suburbs, then the surrounding farmlands, and finally at the country towns on the far horizon. Chapters on clearing woodland and on draining swamps echoed Darby's favourite themes, but discussions of nineteenth-century surveys, of irrigation schemes, and building the agricultural townships were emphatically new world messages. The book appeared to critical acclaim, although one reviewer stressed that it focused only on the 'settled area' of the state, namely those districts that were surveyed for agricultural settlement, and did not consider the arid pastoral country that made up most of South Australia. It was followed by a shorter, revised version in 1979.[22] In that year, Michael received the John Lewis Gold Medal from the Royal Geographical Society of South Australia for his contribution to historical geography.

In addition to teaching and undertaking research, Michael had served as Secretary of the Institute of Australian Geographers from 1969 to 1972, and then spent a sabbatical year (1973–4) at the University of Wisconsin-Madison where new research challenges would start to unfold. Despite having been promoted to Reader in 1972, upon his return to Adelaide he found the department to be rather less congenial than it had been in the 1960s. Interdepartmental competition for resources had become intense, and the introduction of anthropology in 1974 captured some of the student demand that had previously looked toward geography.[23] In addition, there was local competition for undergraduates from the geography

[20] M. Williams, 'More and smaller is better: Australian rural settlement, 1788–1914', in Powell and Williams (eds.), *Australian Space*, pp. 61–103.
[21] M. Williams, *The Making of the South Australian Landscape* (London, 1976).
[22] M. Williams, *The Changing Rural Landscape of South Australia* (London, 1977, repr. in Adelaide by the South Australian State Government Printer in 1991).
[23] Smailes and Griffin, 'Geography at the University of Adelaide'.

department of the new Flinders University at suburban Bedford Park. In 1977, Graham Lawton was on the point of retiring, there was no obvious successor, and the University of Adelaide found itself in financial straits. A general 'freeze' on appointments was imposed, which affected the chair and a vacant lectureship in geography. The period of consensus was over, morale was low, and the student intake for geography plummeted in 1978. Without doubt, prospects at the University of Adelaide looked unappealing. In addition, Michael and Loré had to decide whether their daughters' higher education would be in Australia or elsewhere. On both of these grounds, returning to England seemed to be the wise choice, especially since Frank Emery had let Michael know that there was a vacant lectureship in the School of Geography at Oxford. Michael found it difficult to make the decision to apply and delayed again when he was offered the post. However, having made the decision, he never regretted it.

The Oxford years

In 1978, the Williams family left Adelaide, Michael having accepted a University Lectureship in geography at the University of Oxford, made vacant by the retirement of A. F. ('Freddie') Martin. His new academic base was at Oriel College where he became director of studies in geography, Sir Walter Raleigh Fellow (1993–2002), and Vice-Provost (2000–2). Concurrently, he was director of studies in geography at St Anne's College (1978–1997). In 1990 Michael acquired a University Readership which was followed six years later by the personal title of Professor of Geography. In 2002, he became professor emeritus. Michael brought a wide range of teaching experience and made various contributions on aspects of human geography in the first year of undergraduate study. Along with Frank Emery, his former lecturer from Swansea days, and Jack Langton he gave lectures and seminars in the historical geography of England, c.1650–c.1800 Honour Special Subject.[24] Spanning two years of study, this involved one year of empirical material and a subsequent year of methodology, theory and fieldwork. Michael's methodological seminars focused on the ideas

[24] Emery wrote *Wales* (1969) in Longman's *World Landscapes* series and *Oxfordshire* (1974) in *The Making of the English Landscape* series for Hodder and Stoughton. The latter reflected his teaching and field classes around the University of Oxford. His other books related to the military history of South Africa, and his articles covered agricultural history and rural settlement in parts of England and Wales. He died in 1987, aged 57. See: J. Langton, 'Frank Vivien Emery, 1930–1987', *Transactions of the Institute of British Geographers*, NS 13 (1988), 240–4.

and writings of H. C. Darby and Carl Sauer, among other distinguished historical geographers and historians. As part of this special subject, Michael and Jack Langton led a very successful field week in Somerset each year, which embraced half of the time in the County Record Office to introduce students to archival evidence, and the remaining days in the field to interpret the county's varied landscapes. Not surprisingly, the Somerset Levels figured prominently in proceedings and Michael explained to the students how he had first encountered such a distinctive environment.

After a number of years, Michael turned his attention to rural geography, a new special subject in the Honour School, which complemented an option in urban geography taught by Colin Clarke, Ceri Peach and Ian Scargill. The rural course similarly spanned two years of study, with the first paper focusing on rural geography and countryside planning in the United Kingdom, and the second tracing comparable issues in the new world, with case studies from Australia and North America being analysed alongside examples from southern Africa, the latter being taught by Tony Lemon. However, the rural geography special subject disappeared in a revision of the honours syllabus some years before he took retirement in 2002. As the years passed, Michael's attention was drawn increasingly to his personal research projects and to his teaching of human geography at Oriel and St Anne's, with physical geography being covered by Nick Middleton. Countless tutees remember with genuine affection his scholarly support and wise advice, and recall his professionalism on fieldtrips in England and occasionally overseas. However, Michael was a library man rather than a fieldworker at heart.

He was devoted to his academic discipline and to his home college but he was wary of taking on major administrative roles that would sap his energies and deflect his attention from his research. He always took very seriously his tasks in the School of Geography, being a good lecturer and conscientious examiner, and an efficient chair of the Final Honours School as the exigencies of this rotating post required from time to time. He was never chair of the Sub-Faculty of Geography, Chair of the Anthropology and Geography Faculty Board, or Head of the School of Geography. He did, however, serve as Director of the M.Sc. course in Environmental Change and Management at the Environmental Change Unit, which began in October 1994 with fifteen students. Michael retained that position for the next four years.

Michael was proud of Oriel College and greatly enjoyed inviting colleagues old and new to dine with him there. He was particularly involved with projects to conserve its venerable buildings, whilst also finding ways to enable certain rooms to be modernised and be used more effectively. In the debate over admitting women students to Oriel, he—as father of two daughters—was in favour of change. Just as he never sought administrative roles in the School of Geography, he let it be known that others would serve Oriel College with greater distinction than he could muster. The Vice-Provostship came to him through seniority rather than choice, and in that role he was as approachable and considerate as ever as he oversaw the appointment of a new Provost. In all his collegiate and university dealings, Michael was a calm, courteous presence, whose company was enjoyable, relaxed and often entertaining. He was fully aware of the importance in 'a collegiate system [of] experience and tact ... to steer one through the sometimes labyrinthine complexities of committees and college–university relations'.[25] He was, indeed, reasonable in meetings and proceeded to do what had to be done, knowing that his personal research provided greater stimulation and satisfaction than administrative routine.

Over and above his teaching and research, Michael served the wider scholarly community in many ways. He was on the first editorial board of the *Journal of Historical Geography* from 1975 to 1977, and later assumed the arduous responsibility of editing the *Transactions of the Institute of British Geographers* (1983–8). His unquestionable talents and sense of judgement were sought by other journals and he agreed to serve as co-editor of *Progress in Human Geography* (1991–2001) and of *Global Environmental Change* (1993–7). He also belonged to the editorial boards of *Environmental History (USA)* and *Environmental History (UK)* and remained on the editorial advisory board of *Progress in Human Geography* after 2001. Countless authors around the world benefited from his advice and enthusiasm for their work. He was blessed with a genuine knack of finding ways to strengthen an argument and of finding words to make a point more conclusively. His letters were always enthusiastic, even when major revisions were required before resubmission, and his rejection notes were expressed with measured tact.

On behalf of the Institute of British Geographers, he edited an important collection of essays on wetlands, which was global in scale and interdisciplinary in perspective, containing chapters by physical scientists and economic geographers as well as practitioners of historical geography.[26] Perhaps not surprisingly, three of the eleven essays were his own work.

---

[25] M. Williams, 'Frank Vivien Emery', p. 454. These words, written about Emery, would be equally fitting in his own experience at Oriel and in the University of Oxford.
[26] M. Williams (ed.), *Wetlands: a Threatened Landscape* (Oxford, 1990); M. Williams, 'The human use of wetlands', *Progress in Human Geography*, 15 (1991), 1–22.

Reflecting on his own wetland research in the late 1950s, in which marshes were seen in 'negative' terms and ready for 'improvement' through drainage, he noted that if '*The Draining of the Somerset Levels* were to be written today it would include another chapter on wetland values and their conservation', and would also evaluate schemes for purposeful reflooding of fragile and cherished peat moors.[27] In 1993 another text appeared under his editorship, this time in the eleven-volume *Oxford Illustrated Encyclopaedia of World Geography* coordinated by Peter Haggett, FBA. This lavishly illustrated book presented major environmental issues, such as dwindling global resources, pollution, waste disposal, habitat and species destruction, and climate change to a wide audience, and raised the challenge of devising management strategies to attempt to halt, minimise and rectify the worst excesses of environmental degradation.[28]

Michael chaired the Historical Geography Research Group of the Institute of British Geographers from 1983 to 1986, and hosted an enjoyable international conference of historical geographers at Oriel College in 1983 that was both productive and convivial. A reception for participants at his family home is still recalled with appreciation and affection. He regularly attended similar specialist conferences held at universities across the Commonwealth, the USA and beyond.[29] With a growing international reputation and a stream of academic books and articles to his credit, Michael was elected to the fellowship of the British Academy in 1989, being only the sixth geographer to be so honoured, two decades after the election of H. C. Darby in 1968. He served as a member of Council (1993–6) and was a friendly and efficient chairman of the geography and social anthropology section (1994–7). Geographers in the Academy were delighted when he agreed to join Ron Johnston, FBA, to edit a volume to mark the Academy's centennial in 2003.[30] His own contribution was devoted to the creation of the cultural landscape in which he reviewed a wide swathe of research in historical geography, to conclude: 'It seems inescapable that landscapes are inseparable from human beings, who are their creators, workers, representers, and interpreters through time. When all is said and done, landscapes are an almost totally human construct.'[31]

[27] Williams, *Wetlands*, p. viii.

[28] M. Williams (ed.), *Planet Management* (Oxford, 1993).

[29] See, for example: M. Williams, 'On and beyond the fringe: CUKANZAS', Los Angeles, 1979, *Journal of Historical Geography*, 6 (1980), 65–8; 'The earth as transformed by human action: a symposium at Clark University, 1987', *Journal of Historical Geography*, 14 (1988), 410–12.

[30] R. Johnston and M. Williams (eds.), *A Century of British Geography* (Oxford, 2003).

[31] M. Williams, 'The creation of the humanized landscape', in Johnston and Williams (eds.), *A Century of British Geography*, pp. 167–212, p. 199.

He acknowledged that landscape study was less popular among Britain's human geographers in 2000 than earlier in the second half of the twentieth century, but it was his belief that 'landscapes will remain central to the British geographical enterprise if for no other reason than issues of environmental protection, heritage designation and preservation, regional planning and suburban "spill", the ownership of the countryside and public access to it, and national identity will loom larger in the future, not less'.[32]

From America to the World

In 1973–4, Michael had spent a sabbatical year as visiting professor at the University of Wisconsin at Madison. Work on *The Making of the South Australian Landscape* was progressing well and he was ready to embark on a new research topic. A conversation with Andrew Hill Clark, a distinguished professor of historical geography, encouraged him to develop his idea of tracing how forest clearance had operated not simply across a selected region but on the continental scale of North America. At that time, the theme was relatively novel and did not generate the degree of scholarly interest that would accumulate later. Clark advised him to study America's forests in an holistic way, with reference to regional and continental ecosystems and patterns of economic activity, rather than in the discrete, sectoral way that Darby had considered 'the clearing of the woods' without reference to other components in the landscapes of England, what else was changing in that complex array, and why those interwoven changes were taking place where they did and when they did.[33] Over the next decade and a half, Michael visited archives and libraries in Washington DC and elsewhere in the United States—occasionally benefiting from support from the British Academy—in order to complement the rich resources available in Oxford, London and elsewhere in the United Kingdom. He insisted that, other than the creation of cities, the greatest single factor in the evolution of the North American landscape was the clearing of forests that had once covered nearly half of the continental surface. In his exhaustive search of library holdings, he found that information before about 1840 was tantalisingly slight, and hence he had to rely on literary and topographic descriptions for whichever areas they

---

[32] Williams, 'The creation of the humanized landscape', p. 201.
[33] Further academic stimulation at Madison came from historian Susan Flader. See: S. Flader (ed.), *The Great Lakes Forest: an Environmental and Social History* (Minneapolis, 1983).

could be found. After that time, statistical and cartographic information increased rapidly so that the situation after 1880 had to be presented in a different way, by shifting from the individual and the local to the aggregate and the regional or even continental scale.

Americans and their Forests: an Historical Geography appeared in 1989 and was recognised as a masterpiece.[34] As the subtitle showed, Michael approached the topic as an historical geographer but he was well aware that he was fast approaching environmental history and perhaps even environmental science. He began by exploring the place of forests in American culture, tracing the significance of pioneer woodsmen, lumberjacks and settlers in the vast world of woodland and wilderness. Native tribes used fire to transform expanses of woodland for their subsistence economy, whilst early European settlers exploited forest products and began the protracted process of felling trees for harvesting timber and for creating farmlands that would span three hundred years.[35] Using woodcuts, photographs and over a hundred maps and diagrams, Michael revealed how North America's woodlands were at the heart of countless activities, ranging from naval stores and construction timber, to wood for charcoal and for making the sleepers on which iron rails would be nailed to make possible rapid communication across the continent. He showed that, toward the end of the nineteenth century, Americans came to realise that their forests were not a boundless resource and started to conserve the extensive portions that still remained. Michael's concluding message was one of cautious optimism, as he traced how regrowth of woodlands was advancing after 1950 in some regions. Whilst raising questions about the treatment of specific forest regions and the relative lack of attention given to Canada, reviewers hailed *Americans and their Forests* as a major synthesis that would inspire future generations of researchers, and praised its author for his courage in tackling so vast a topic. In 1990, Michael was awarded the Weyerhaeuser Prize of the American Forest and Conservation Society for his contribution to sylvicultural knowledge. The book generated such interest that a revised and slightly abridged version was issued in 2002.[36]

---

[34] M. Williams, *Americans and their Forests: an Historical Geography* (Cambridge, 1989); 'The clearing of the forests', in M. Conzen (ed.), *The Making of the American Landscape* (Boston, 1990), pp. 146–68.

[35] See also: M. Williams, 'Clearing the United States forests: pivotal years, 1810–1860', *Journal of Historical Geography*, 8 (1982), 12–28.

[36] M. Williams, *Americans and their Forests* (abridged edn.) (Cambridge, 2002).

Fortified by this reaction, Michael broadened his gaze and his reading to the challenge of charting deforestation on the global scale. The idea arose from a conversation with a publisher at the University of Chicago Press, during which Michael protested that such a project was 'simply too big for one person, encompassing as it would the whole earth through all time. Later she returned to the idea and suggested that I might know more about it than many. I agreed to try, having become convinced in the meantime that while it was probably a topic too big to be mastered, it was one that was too compelling to be ignored.'[37] In 2003, *Deforesting the Earth: from Prehistory to Global Crisis* appeared, running to 725 pages, embracing 200 illustrations, maps and tables, and drawing on a bibliography of 1,600 almost entirely English-language items. It is interesting to note that Michael gave the first word to H. C. Darby as he quoted a letter dated July 1954 that preceded the famous Wenner-Gren symposium at Princeton in 1955 devoted to 'Man's Role in Changing the Face of the Earth', where Darby met Carl Sauer, 'who impressed him greatly'.[38] The letter proclaimed: 'Probably the most important single factor that has changed the European landscape (and many other landscapes also) is the clearing of the woodland.'[39] In fifteen chapters, arranged in three parts, Michael surveyed ten thousand years to trace the effects of human-induced thinning, changing and clearing of forests on economies, societies and landscapes across the globe.

Beginning with 'Clearing in the deep past', he demonstrated that deforestation is not a recent phenomenon, as is popularly believed, but is as old as human occupation of the earth.[40] Five chapters examined the varying state of forests from the retreat of the glaciers through to medieval times, when woodlands were thinned or felled at times of population growth, and allowed to expand when population numbers declined in the wake of fire, plague, famine or the sword. In 'Reaching out: Europe and the wider world', Michael charted the internal and external expansion of European civilisation between 1500 and 1900, when deforestation accelerated in all regions undergoing demographic and economic growth, which was reflected through industrialisation, mechanisation, urbanisation,

---

[37] M. Williams, *Deforesting the Earth: from Prehistory to Global Crisis* (Chicago, IL, 2003), p. 479.
[38] W. L. Thomas (ed.), *Man's Role in Changing the Face of the Earth* (Chicago, IL, 1956); M. Williams, 'Henry Clifford Darby', p. 297.
[39] Cited in Williams, *Deforesting the Earth*, p. xv.
[40] See also: M. Williams, 'Deforestation: past and present', *Progress in Human Geography*, 13 (1989), 176–208; 'Dark ages and dark areas: global deforestation in the deep past', *Journal of Historical Geography*, 26 (2000), 28–46.

colonisation, navigation and trade.[41] Finally, in 'The global forest', he examined a veritable flood of documentation about contemporary environmental and forestry issues, ranging from scares about timber famine, through attempts at replanting and wise management of woodland resources, to recent onslaughts on tropical forests in Amazonia and Indonesia.[42] He concluded by reiterating his basic aims of helping readers to make sense of the momentous changes that have taken place, and of inviting reflection rather than offering prescriptions for action to resolve the grand ecological challenges posed by deforestation in our own time.

Once again, reviewers praised Michael's breadth of scholarship, his effective marshalling of evidence, and literary craftsmanship. They appreciated his forays into literature relating to developing parts of the world and the very recent past, whilst noting that he was most comfortable with the abundance of information relating to Europe and North America in the more distant past rather than in the last half century. Assimilating the flood of documentation on recent changes was acknowledged to be a superhuman and hence impossible task. Some critics remarked that *Deforesting the Earth* was old-fashioned historical geography, whose author was entranced by his sources and failed to develop—or even to declare—his theoretical position. Others said that sub-Saharan Africa and Latin America merited more attention, that attempts at statistical definition for various periods were inconsistent, and that the book's richly nuanced narrative made for exhausting reading. However, none disagreed with those who declared that Michael had produced a 'magnum opus', a '*tour de force*', and a 'monumental achievement'. One reviewer simply stated: 'Williams has given us a book for the ages, and it is something to stand back [from] and admire.'[43] *Deforesting the Earth* earned Michael the Weyerhaeuser Prize (2004) once again, and the Meridian Prize of the Association of American Geographers (2004) for 'the most scholarly work in geography' to appear during the preceding year. It was also runner-up in the 2004 British Academy Book Prize Competition. When the University of Chicago Press offered the opportunity of publishing an abbreviated edition in 2006, Michael slightly condensed his text, sacrificed many tables and figures, replaced the long bibliography with a bibliographical essay, and modified the discussion of prehistoric clearing and several other

[41] M. Williams, 'Ecology, imperialism and deforestation', in T. Griffiths and L. Robin (eds.), *Ecology and Empire: Environmental History of Settler Societies* (Seattle, 1998), pp. 169–84.
[42] See also: M. Williams, 'The end of modern history?', *Geographical Review*, 88 (1998), 275–300.
[43] G. Wynn, 'Review: *Deforesting the Earth*', *Canadian Geographer*, 47 (2003), 515.

themes to encapsulate results from new research.[44] A lengthy review article of these most recent findings was his last pronouncement on the topic.[45]

An endless interest in people

Despite his lifelong concern with landscapes and countless years devoted to silent reading in archives and libraries, in 2004 Michael confided to Les Heathcote, a fellow historical geographer, that he found 'people endlessly interesting'.[46] Two of his later projects demonstrate that very human concern. The first came in his commitment to putting into print the previously unpublished methodological essays of Sir Clifford Darby. Following Darby's death in 1992, Lady (Eva) Darby approached Professor Terry Coppock, FBA, to determine whether the sixteen essays dealing with Great Britain, France and the United States, and drafted in the late 1950s and 1960s, might be made ready for publication alongside a handful of contextual essays. Terry enlisted the help of Michael, Hugh Prince at UCL, and myself to check and if necessary correct Darby's text and to prepare the accompanying essays. When Terry died in 2000, Michael assumed the role of lead editor and, with financial support from the British Academy to employ a graduate student at the word processor, brought the volume to fruition. His contextual essay revealed the depth and breadth of his own knowledge of the historical geography of the USA, that had been reinforced by sabbatical years spent at Madison (1973, 1994), Chicago (1989) and Berkeley, California (1994).[47] Having already written the memorial essay on Darby for the British Academy, Michael now used a carefully crafted epilogue to trace the significance of Darby's work in giving shape and substance to the subdiscipline of historical geography, and explored his role in training a succession of young scholars.[48] Michael

---

[44] M. Williams, *Deforesting the Earth* (abridged edn.) (Chicago, IL, 2006).

[45] M. Williams, 'A new look at global forest histories of land clearing', *Annual Review of Environment and Resources*, 33 (2008), 345–67.

[46] Heathcote, 'Obituary: Michael Williams'.

[47] M. Williams, 'H. C. Darby and the historical geography of the United States', in M. Williams, with T. Coppock, H. Clout and H. C. Prince (eds.), *The Relations of History and Geography: Studies in England, France and the United States. Twelve Previously Unpublished Essays on Historical Geography by Henry Clifford Darby* (Exeter, 2002), pp. 186–202. The visit to Chicago enabled him to interact with historical geographer Michael Conzen, and during the second visit to Madison with William Cronon, the recently appointed Frderick Jackson Turner Professor of History, Geography and Environmental Studies.

[48] M. Williams, 'Henry Clifford Darby'; 'Epilogue: critique and evaluation', in Williams *et al.* (eds.), *The Relations of History and Geography*, pp. 203–11.

insisted that Darby should be appraised on his own terms and in his own time, and insisted that it was pointless to interrogate his writing through a turn-of-the-century lens since it had been drafted decades previously and conceptualised earlier still. Without doubt, Michael held Darby and his scholarship in high regard but, like others, he regretted that 'the changing landscape' was often devoid of the people, influenced by new ideas and ideologies, which brought about its transformation.[49] Michael's much appreciated editorial contribution to *The Relations of History and Geography: Studies in England, France and the United States* was arguably a labour of duty, rather than one of filial affection.[50]

By contrast, Michael's real passion in his final years centred on the work and life of Carl Ortwin Sauer (1889–1975) who had been a towering figure among cultural geographers and environmental thinkers, famed for his research on Central and Latin America, on the domestication of plants and animals, on the entry of man into the Americas, and the transformation of cultural landscapes across the globe. His work earned the deep respect of Darby who visited Sauer's base in the Department of Geography at the University of California, Berkeley in 1952 and again in 1959 and 1963, and quoted his work extensively in his own teaching and writing. Michael shared that same fascination and his undergraduate seminars on Sauer were among his most memorable at Oxford. However, he was far from satisfied with a critical reading of the great man's published work and delved deep into his life through interviews with members of Sauer's family, and with his former colleagues and students, as well as interrogating his voluminous archive in the Bancroft Library at Berkeley. Among this material are to be found hundreds of letters received by Sauer and numerous carbon copies of items dispatched by him, including early letters written in German to his parents. Since Michael's grasp of German was minimal, over a hundred of these personal letters were translated with love and dedication by Loré. Occasionally he had to reconstruct Sauer's views from the replies he received, since copies of the original letters could not be traced. The man who emerged from all this research was both an academic master who headed the distinctive 'Berkeley School' of cultural geographers, and an ageing individual who was frustrated by the demands of university administrators and disillusioned by new trends not only in geography but also in anthropology and in the social sciences at

---

[49] M. Williams, 'Historical geography and the concept of landscape', *Journal of Historical Geography*, 15: 92–104.
[50] On Darby's ideas and writings, see P. J. Perry, 'H. C. Darby and historical geography'.

large.[51] His life path was, indeed, 'endlessly interesting' and was captured in the monograph that had absorbed Michael in his latter years and was all but completed at the time of his death. Each of the fourteen chapters had been written and only the final checking of the text and the bibliography had to be done. Many geographers on both sides of the Atlantic and beyond hope that this volume will be delivered for publication soon,[52] since it will be an important contribution to the history of the discipline. In recognition of his sustained research, Michael had been invited to deliver his main findings at the twentieth 'Carl O. Sauer Memorial Lecture' at Berkeley on 26 October 2009, but his rapidly failing health meant that this had to be cancelled. By a cruel twist of fate, he died in Oxford on that very day, aged 74.

In memoriam

A few years ago, Michael told me that he was perplexed by many of the emerging strands of contemporary human geography and preferred to describe himself as an 'environmental historian', just as his preference was for reading historical rather than geographical journals.[53] Whatever his chosen title, he was a fine scholar whose research ranged in scale from the local in the Somerset Levels, through the regional in South Australia, to the continental in North America, and the global in *Deforesting the Earth*. His intellectual focus shifted over the years from research to elucidate 'the making of the landscape', to document-based syntheses of environmental change whose messages brought him closer to the fringes of environmental science. In 1991 he was awarded a D.Litt. from the University of Wales for his remarkable corpus of published work. He was a superb editor, a tactful chairman, an excellent teacher, and a caring supervisor of graduate students. In a non-imposing way, he shared his knowledge with doctoral candidates who drew inspiration from his enthusiasm for their work—as well as his own—and his attentiveness to their written style,

[51] M. Williams, 'The apple of my eye: Carl Sauer and historical geography', *Journal of Historical Geography*, 9 (1983), 1–28; 'Sauer and *Man's Role in Changing the Face of the Earth*', *Geographical Review*, 77 (1987), 218–31; 'Carl Sauer and the legacy of 'Man's Role', in K. Mathewson and M. S. Kenzer (eds.), *Culture, Land and Legacy: Perspectives of Carl Sauer and the Berkeley School of Geography* (Baton Rouge, 2003), pp. 217–32.
[52] By the University of Virginia Press.
[53] M. Williams, 'The relations of environmental history and historical geography', *Journal of Historical Geography*, 20 (1994), 3–21.

ensuring that they conveyed their message in the clearest way and with the maximum effect. He was not one to be swept along by new academic fashions but rather developed his own unique way of interrogating the subject through meticulous library work and careful sifting and reorganisation of information to tell the story. He was never hasty to judge, seeing the best in people around him, and always sure and clear in his decisions. During his Oxford years, he liked working on 'the big picture' and all his books witness how he managed to link past and present processes in his historical explorations, often making those enquiries relevant to the present day, although he never wrote explicitly about his methodological approaches. 'Landscape' was his lifelong interest, which he explored in several ways, by tracing its formation, assessing its multiple meanings, and reviewing the place of landscape study in historical geography, environmental history, cultural geography and landscape archaeology.[54]

To members of the School of Geography, Michael Williams was a courteous and hospitable colleague, and a single-minded and focused scholar of great international distinction. To Fellows of the British Academy, he was an effective member of Council, a business-like and expeditious chair of section, and an unfailingly friendly face. He is greatly missed by members of the 'wider family' of academics who had the privilege of knowing him, working with him, and laughing with him. Yet, Loré has confirmed:

> Although he loved his subject and his work, his close family was always more important to him. He took great pride in his daughters' careers, Cathy as a doctor and Tess as a lawyer. He was more proud of their achievement than his own. Not only did their achievements give cause for pride but they also brought a great deal of fun and love into both our lives. Because of them he acquired two sons-in-law who won his respect and love, and four lovely grandchildren. When he was in hospital, not able to sleep, he would visualize one grandchild at a time and imagine them playing.[55]

Viewed from whatever perspective, the life and work of Professor Michael Williams, historical geographer and environmental historian of great international renown, will not be forgotten by those who knew him or by the many more that have drawn inspiration from his publications.

HUGH CLOUT
Fellow of the Academy

---

[54] J. M. Powell, 'Professor Michael Williams, 1935–2009', *Australian Geographer*, 41 (2010), 425–7.
[55] Words written by Mrs Williams to be spoken at Michael's funeral.

Note. In preparing this essay, I have received invaluable help from Mrs Loré Williams; from Colin Clarke, Andrew Goudie, Jack Langton, Nick Middleton, Judith Pallot, Ceri Peach and Ian Scargill in Oxford; from Joe Powell, Peter Smailes, Gerard Ward and the late Les Heathcote in Australia; from Ron Johnston in Bristol, David Herbert in Swansea, Bill Mead and Hugh Prince in London, and Judith Tsouvalis in Lancaster; and from Diana Liverman in Arizona, and Philippe Le Billon in Vancouver. I extend my thanks to each of them.

DONALD WISEMAN

Donald John Wiseman
1918–2010

THE IMPACT OF HOME SURROUNDINGS on a child is apparent in the life of Donald Wiseman who ended his career as Professor of Assyriology in the University of London in 1982 and died on 4 February 2010. His father was Percy John Wiseman (1888–1948), his mother was Gertrude, née Savage. P. J. Wiseman was working as a senior accountant with the Royal Navy when he was transferred to help found the Accounts Branch of the Royal Air Force in 1918. From 1922–6 he served in Iraq and other areas of the Near East, rising to the rank of Air Commodore, honoured with the CBE (Military) in 1943. In Iraq he collected Babylonian antiquities, visiting, among other sites, (Sir) Leonard Woolley's excavations at Ur, so the young Donald grew up in a home where Babylonian bricks, cuneiform tablets, cylinder seals and Hebrew scrolls lay on the shelves. 'They whetted my appetite', he wrote later, 'for such things.' Donald was born on 25 October 1918, following Muriel (1914) and Phyllis (1916) and eventually became the middle child, when Ruth and David were born in 1921 and 1927 respectively.

The family moved to Upper Norwood, southeast London, in 1919, so Donald was educated locally at Dulwich College Preparatory School and then at Dulwich College (1931–6). By the time he entered the college, the family had taken up residence in Kent and then transferred to Lincolnshire, making it necessary that Donald board during term-time. He lodged with a widow living near the school who made him speak French and German at alternate meals, an exercise which benefited him throughout his life. Languages and history seem to have been his major subjects at school and he matriculated to gain a place at King's College London in 1936. Initially reading English History, Ancient History and Latin, his course changed after discussion with a friend of his father's.

Here the second aspect of the family demands attention. The Wiseman parents were regular members of 'Open Brethren' congregations, taking their children with them to Sunday services. 'The initial experience of family worship and regular churchgoing was a moulding factor in my life,' he stated, yet no pressure was put on the children to conform as they grew up, but Donald made his own commitment to Jesus as Lord and was baptised by immersion in 1932. Thereafter, his deep evangelical Christian faith underlay the whole of his life and work and brought him into contact with a wide range of people across the world. From his knowledge about Babylonia, Wiseman senior believed he could illumine understanding of the book of Genesis. In *New Discoveries about Babylonian in Genesis* (London, 1936) he argued that the recurrent phrase 'these are the generations of' marked the ends of sections in Genesis like colophons on cuneiform tablets. His second book, *Creation Revealed in Six Days* (London, 1946), propounded his thesis that the 'days' of Genesis 1 were days on which God's work of creation was revealed to early man. These works broke new ground in reading biblical texts beside Babylonian, that is, in the context of other ancient writings, but have not carried conviction. However, Donald supported his father's ideas and republished the two works in a single volume as *Clues to Creation in Genesis* (London, 1977).

One of the people Donald met was his father's friend W. J. Martin, Rankin Lecturer (later Senior Lecturer) in Hebrew and Ancient Semitic Languages at the University of Liverpool, 1937–70. He had taken a doctorate in Assyriology under Benno Landsberger at Leipzig, worked briefly on cuneiform tablets from Ur, and then was living at Hoylake on the Wirral. There low tides exposed long stretches of sand where he walked with Wiseman, talking about his future, persuading him that he should turn his attention to the world of the Bible and learn Semitic languages. King's College permitted him to change courses to read Hebrew with Assyrian, the first student to do so. He learnt Hebrew in the Faculty of Theology, winning the McCaul Hebrew prize, but Sidney Smith, Honorary Lecturer in Accadian Assyriology and Keeper of Egyptian and Assyrian Antiquities at the British Museum, was reluctant to make time to teach him, so put him in a class conducted by S. H. Hooke. When Hooke's elementary lessons failed to reach Wiseman's expectations, he persuaded Smith to teach him privately at the Museum for a while until Smith told him there was no point in continuing, as he would be killed in the imminent war, so stopped the classes. (Smith, who had himself served in the trenches and been wounded in the First World War, was now heavily occupied in rescuing Jewish scholars from Germany and ensuring safe storage for the Museum's collections.) Consequently, he passed the last eighteen months of his degree course studying cuneiform alone. He also attended courses given by V. Gordon Childe and Kathleen Kenyon at the Institute of Archaeology. The Professor of Hebrew at King's, S. L. Brown, successfully nominated Wiseman for the Hody Exhibition in Oriental languages at Wadham College, Oxford, but the prospect of war prevented him from taking it up.

He followed his father into the Royal Air Force and in September 1939 was commissioned as an Acting Pilot Officer, to be involved in various tests. March 1940 brought him, aged 21, to the position of Personal Assistant to Air Vice-Marshal Keith Park in which post he dealt with many visitors and inquiries from the King and Queen and Winston Churchill, as Park was in command of all fighter aircraft in southeast England. In Wiseman's opinion, Park's leadership 'saved not only our country, but the world', something only recently recognised with a statue in Waterloo Place, London, not far from the British Academy. Wiseman was posted to Gravesend, then to Malling, where he flew several sorties in a night fighter wing and reported his observations to such effect that he was transferred to HQ Fighter Command at Bentley Priory, Stanmore, to handle information derived from the Ultra Intelligence operation which decoded the German Enigma signals. Thence he was eventually appointed to work under Field-Marshal (later Lord) Alexander as Chief Intelligence Officer, Mediterranean Allied Tactical Air Force, with the rank of Group Captain (1942), to plan landings in North Africa. He sailed to Gibraltar carrying maps and plans and on to Algiers. In North Africa he continued to relay information from Ultra that enabled the forces to advance along the coast to Tunis, taking part in reconnaissance and other activities. As the Allied forces moved into Sicily he was based near Syracuse. Flying back there from an inspection, the plane he was in made a crash landing, injuring his legs. He insisted on staying to recover locally, rather than being evacuated to Algiers, and was back at work two months later, moving with Alexander up Italy, during which time he learnt Italian. On the basis of Ultra information he opposed the bombing of Monte Cassino. He was twice mentioned in despatches; in March 1943 he was awarded the OBE (Military) in recognition of his services and in 1944, to his great surprise, the USA Bronze Star for 'rare analytical and organizational genius ... selfless and earnest work' which enabled the planning of 'the air operations which brought victory to the Allied Forces in Italy'. As the forces progressed through Italy, he participated in the surrender of German troops at Bolsano, his knowledge of German giving him an advantage in negotiations with Generals von Pohl and Wolff. Rejecting offers of a career in the RAF, on 28 October 1945 he was demobilised with the rank of Group Captain and moved quickly to take up his place at Oxford. Throughout his war service he seized any opportunity to meet other Christian officers and men, to attend local church services, to call on missionaries and to share his faith with others.

Already knowing Hebrew and Babylonian, he was able to appreciate the erudite lectures of Godfrey Driver on the Book of Job and to progress quickly in reading cuneiform texts with Oliver Gurney, although Gurney went to do research in Ankara, leaving Donald to study on his own, as he had at King's, and to teach a new student, James Kinnier Wilson, who was to become Eric Yarrow Lecturer in Assyriology at Cambridge (1955–89).

As he completed his finals in 1948, a letter arrived from Sidney Smith offering him an Assistant Keepership in the British Museum's Department of Egyptian and Assyrian Antiquities, a post he took up at the end of May. Meanwhile, he had become engaged to be married to Mary Catherine Ruoff, a nurse trained at St Bartholomew's Hospital, whom he had met while she was taking a Health Visitor's course in Oxford. Their wedding took place in Enfield on 18 September 1948 and they made their home in Finchley, North London.

When he entered the Museum, Smith entrusted to him the 460 cuneiform tablets Sir Leonard Woolley had unearthed at Tell Atchana, ancient Alalakh on the Orontes, between 1937 and 1949. There are two groups, one written about 1600 and the other about 1450 BC. He was told a large proportion of them was due to be returned to Antakya Museum after about eighteen months, so he had to do his work in that time. In the end, he would work on them, between other duties, for about four years to make a pioneering edition of texts from eras and a region that had produced no others at that time. (The tablets from Mari offered some points of comparison for the earlier group, those from Ugarit some for the later, but they had been published only in a limited quantity at the time.) To comply with the time limit, Wiseman followed the example of his senior colleague Cyril Gadd who had used a catalogue style to publish tablets from sites in eastern Syria a few years earlier, giving full texts of major or typical items, summarising the types and contents, listing the proper names and making hand copies of many.[1] His volume *The Alalakh Tablets*

---

[1] C. J. Gadd, 'Texts from Chagar Bazar and Tall Brak', *Iraq*, 7 (1940), 22–61.

was published in 1953 (London), he having corrected the proofs while excavating in Iraq. Although not a complete publication, it aroused much interest and has continued to stimulate doctoral theses and other studies ever since.

As tens of thousands of the Museum's cuneiform tablets had never been identified by more than a simple registration, Wiseman made a habit of cataloguing twenty-five after the Museum had closed to the public each day. This process gave him knowledge of a miscellany of texts which he edited over the years. A very significant product was the location of over 1,500 astronomical diaries and related observations which recorded historical and economic details as well as movements of heavenly bodies during the last half of the first millennium BC. T. G. Pinches had made copies of the majority between 1895 and 1900 which had never reached publication. These he handed to Abraham J. Sachs of Brown University to publish.[2] The cuneiform collections also held manuscripts of the Babylonian Chronicle series which had remained unedited. Gadd, who had translated one,[3] urged him to publish four more. They relate events in the reigns of Nebuchadnezzar and his father, Nabopolassar, and of Neriglissar. Important as all are for Babylonian history, the monograph *Chronicles of Chaldaean Kings (626–556 B.C.) in the British Museum* (London, 1956) gained wide publicity because one entry told of the capture of 'the city of Judah' (i.e. Jerusalem) on 15–16 March 597 BC, this precise date clarifying the chronology of the last decades of that kingdom's history and so of several biblical passages. That brief entry made this the most widely known and cited of all Wiseman's works.

When M. E. L. Mallowan opened his excavations at Nimrud, Iraq, he needed an epigraphist, so the Museum lent Wiseman for the second season in 1950, then the third and the fifth seasons (1951, 1953), He joined in the work of the expedition wholeheartedly, putting his practical skills at its disposal and making a lasting friendship with Mallowan and his wife, Agatha Christie. Nimrud yielded large quantities of inscriptions, on clay tablets, stone slabs and other surfaces. With his accustomed industry, he used the catalogue pattern he had adopted in *The Alalakh Tablets* to ensure the new discoveries were quickly available to scholars at large. Major documents warranted more extensive treatment, among them being the Banquet Stele of Ashurnasirpal, commemorating a festival and its menu for 69,574 people, and the *de luxe* ivory writing boards made for

[2] *Late Babylonian Astronomical and Related Texts Copied by T. G. Pinches and J. N. Strassmeier, Prepared for publication by A. J. Sachs with the co-operation of J. Schaumberger* (Providence, RI, 1955).
[3] C. J. Gadd, *The Fall of Nineveh* (London, 1923).

Sargon II to contain hundreds of lines of astronomical omens in minute script on a wax coating, now largely destroyed.[4] The greatest prize was the Library of the Temple of Nabu, unearthed in 1955–7. About 250 damaged tablets were recovered. They include copies of standard Babylonian books which enabled lines missing from other copies to be restored (e.g. Epic of Gilgamesh, The Poem of the Righteous Sufferer). Political upheavals in Iraq and other tasks hindered access to the tablets kept in the Iraq Museum, so the definitive edition was not completed until 1996, in collaboration with J. A. Black.[5] Eight tablets lay smashed in a throne room next to the Nabu Temple and formed a discrete group, initially identified by Barbara Parker as treaty texts. After long hours of patient treatment by the Department's conservator, C. A. Bateman, and of reconstruction and comparison, Wiseman reconstructed the eight tablets from 350 pieces and issued *The Vassal Treaties of Esarhaddon* in 1958 (as volume 20.1 of *Iraq*). These are treaties imposed by Sennacherib's son on Median princes to ensure their support for the peaceful succession of his son Ashurbanipal to the throne of Assyria. The stipulations are reinforced by a long series of vivid and frightful curses on any traitor, using a number of unusual phases. Given that no up-to-date dictionary of the language existed at the time of his work, the achievement is the more remarkable. A German colleague commented on the 'astonishing speed' of the publication, whilst making numerous small corrections,[6] while Mallowan, the Director of the Nimrud excavations, wrote of Donald being 'faced with problems which might have occupied many for a lifetime'.[7] Wiseman saw similarities between the treaties with their curses and Old Testament covenants, notably in the book of Deuteronomy, suggesting that the Assyrian texts continued a tradition seen in Hittite treaties of Late Bronze Age and Old Testament covenants 'some of which may well have originated in the second millennium BC'.[8] He explored some of the parallels in a paper read to the Society for Old Testament Study in January 1958, which he did not publish.

An Assistant Keeper's tasks included answering inquiries from the public and Wiseman noted from his official diaries that he had dealt with over 10,000 in his fourteen years at the Museum. In addition, there were

---

[4] D. J. Wiseman, 'A New Stela of Aššur-naṣir-pal from Nimrud', *Iraq*, 14 (1952), 24–44; 'Assyrian writing boards', *Iraq*, 17 (1955), 3–13.

[5] D. J. Wiseman and J. A. Black, *Literary Texts from the Temple of Nabu.* Cuneiform Texts from Nimrud, 4 (London, 1996).

[6] R. Borger, 'Zu den Asarhaddon-Verträge aus Nimrud', *Zeitschrift für Assyriologie,* 54 (1961), 173–96.

[7] D. J. Wiseman, *Vassal Treaties of Esarhaddon* (London, 1958), p. ii.

[8] Ibid., pp. 26–30.

numerous written requests for information of all sorts relating to the collections or from colleagues for collation of passages on tablets. There was also a constant flow of scholars coming to study in the department to whom he gave courteous attention and whatever help he could, advising W. G. Lambert, for example, in the techniques of copying tablets. This interaction helped to rebuild contacts with Continental Assyriologists prevented during the war years. The Museum sent him as a representative to the annual Rencontres Assyriologiques Internationales, occasions which he also used to strengthen such relationships.

Another duty was arranging exhibits. The Room of Writing was Wiseman's notable achievement. Largely devoted to displaying the history and scope of cuneiform texts, it presented a wall of bricks bearing royal inscriptions, a selection of cylinder seals, and a case devoted to the early history of the alphabet with the famous sphinx from the Sinai bearing the oldest intelligible inscription in letters ancestral to ours, 'LB 'LT' 'for the lady (goddess)'. The room was dismantled; the cuneiform writings are incorporated elsewhere, but the early history of the alphabet is, regrettably, not so well presented.

As well as identifying cuneiform texts, he paid attention to the Museum's large collection of cylinder seals and inaugurated the *Catalogue of Western Asiatic Seals in the British Museum*, with volume I: *Cylinder Seals, Uruk-Early Dynastic Periods* in 1962. Five more volumes have been published by other experts. Earlier, he had issued a more 'popular' picture book, *Cylinder Seals of Western Asia* (London, 1959), with photographs by W. and B. Forman made from old, worn plaster impressions. His desire to spread knowledge of ancient Mesopotamia is evident in that and in the booklet *Fifty Masterpieces of Ancient Near Eastern Art*, written with his colleague R. D. Barnett (London, 1960).

That desire was met in a different way when he accepted the Chair of Assyriology in the University of London (School of Oriental and African Studies: SOAS) in 1961. He had done a limited amount of teaching while in the Museum's employ, notably when there was an hiatus in the lectureship in Assyriology at Cambridge, one of the students being T. C. Mitchell, later to be Keeper of Western Asiatic Antiquities at the British Museum. Now free from the restrictions of the Museum service, his life took on a new dimension, and he could roam over all the wide areas of teaching and research that interested him. His Inaugural Lecture was published as *The Expansion of Assyrian Studies*.[9] Postgraduate students were quickly

---

[9] In 1962 by Oxford University Press for the School of Oriental and African Studies.

attracted to the weekly seminars he organised in which he could integrate Mesopotamian history, literature and customs with biblical. His academic standing and warm personality drew younger and more established scholars to spend sabbatical leave to study with him, notably Israelis who took leading positions in those studies in their own universities: Hayim Tadmor, Hanoch Reviv, Bustenay Oded, Zafrira Ben Barak, Victor Hurowitz. One of them admired him as 'hospitable and scholarly'. Among others who came for graduate studies were from Iraq (Amir Sulaiman, Ali Yasin Ahmed), from France (Maurice Couve de Murville) and the USA (David Baker). He cooperated happily with H. W. F. Saggs, Lecturer in Assyriology 1953–66, and, after Saggs was appointed to a chair at Cardiff, fostered the careers of younger Assyriologists—Alan Millard, Nicholas Postgate, Martin Selman and Johanna Firbank—with one-year appointments. In 1964, he was able to secure a permanent post for David Hawkins, who eventually succeeded to the Chair as Professor of Ancient Anatolian Languages in 1996.

The study of Assyriology in post-war Europe was the subject of an investigation for the Council of Europe's Council for Cultural Co-operation to 'indicate the facilities, research orientation and needs of member countries'. Wiseman produced the report *European Research Resources: Assyriology* in 1967 on the basis of a questionnaire answered by forty universities and through personal correspondence. Its conclusions were predictable and sanguine: the subject should be taught in all faculties of Ancient History, Linguistics, Law, and Science and History of Science; additional posts should be established in museums and libraries as well as universities, with research fellowships; interchange of students for special themes of study should be fostered. What impact the report had is impossible to measure. It would be timely for the successor body in the EU to commission a new report.

SOAS gave leave to attend the Assyriological Rencontres, to lecture abroad and to join excavations. Thus he was able to serve as epigraphist for the British School of Archaeology in Iraq's work at Tall al-Rimah in 1966,[10] and to further the work of the School in Baghdad (see below). Beside worldwide lecture tours, one taking him to New Zealand where he was delighted to meet Sir Keith Park again, he led tours to the Holy Land and made a memorable three-week visit to Japan with his wife as the guests of HIH Prince Mikasa in 1983. That invitation posed a problem, what could a British university professor take as a gift to a Japanese

---

[10] 'The Tell al Rimah tablets, 1966', *Iraq*, 20 (1968), 175–205.

prince? A cuneiform tablet his father had acquired, part of an ancient Babylonian dictionary, was the answer Wiseman found. The tablet entered the collection of the Middle East Culture Centre which Prince Mikasa had founded. At SOAS he willingly assumed administrative duties as Senior Tutor, serving on the governing body and the editorial board of the School's *Bulletin,* becoming Head of the Department of the Languages and Cultures of the Near and Middle East in 1981. That was the time when the government of Margaret Thatcher cut university funds and redundancies became inevitable. Rather than see the careers of younger teachers cut short, Wiseman took early retirement, aged 64, in 1982, with Edward Ullendorff and other senior members. Pressed by colleagues, he submitted his published work and received a D.Lit. from the university in 1969, the same year in which 'to my surprise' he was elected to the British Academy.

His Fellowship opened new possibilities for him to advance archaeological work in the Near East. From 1984 to 1987 he served on the Academy's Standing Committee for the Schools and Institutes, which initiated inspections of each in the context of a wider examination of their roles in undertaking and facilitating British work overseas. He was a key member of the inspection team that visited the Schools in Jerusalem (of which he was a Trustee from 1974–94), Baghdad (during the Iran–Iraq War), Amman and Nairobi, and was active in the drafting of the 1985 Report which guided the Academy's policy over the next decade. He served on the Academy's Council during the Presidency of Sir Isaiah Berlin, who invited him to hold office as Vice-President in 1976–7. He particularly remembered from this time the negotiation of a formal Agreement between the British Academy and the Academy of Sciences of the USSR for the exchange of scholars from the two countries. He served, too, on the Academy's Schweich Lecture Committee.

Mallowan excavated at Nimrud under the aegis of the British School of Archaeology in Iraq. That organisation, founded in memory of Gertrude Bell in 1932, was to become one of Wiseman's central preoccupations. For twenty-five years, from 1953 to 1978, he was the main editor of the journal *Iraq* (volumes 15–40), jointly with Mallowan until 1971, then with J. D. Hawkins, maintaining its position as one of the leading journals in the field. He joined the School's Council in 1955, was elected Vice-Chairman in 1966, Chairman in 1970 until he became Vice-President in 1988, and President from 1993 to 2000. As in every committee on which he served, he was as regular in attendance as other engagements allowed, expressing his sensible and practical views considerately. As A. R. George has written, 'In presiding over meetings, he displayed characteristic good nature and detachment,' with the ability to draw discussions to clear conclusions. (Although he remarked to the writer more than once that he sometimes talked too much!) From 1961 to 1964 he was Joint Director with David Oates, then and later travelling to Baghdad on the School's behalf, making excursions to its fieldwork, copying tablets and maintaining connections with Iraqi colleagues. Despite the closure of the School by Iraqi authorities in 1973, a base and activities continued under the name The British Archaeological Expedition to Iraq until 1997. Wiseman was convinced that the School's policy of avoiding any activity or research into the country's recent history, politics or social affairs was a reason its presence was tolerated. The School dedicated volume 50 (1988) of *Iraq* to him and to Barbara Lady Mallowan, and affixed a letter of greeting on his eightieth birthday to volume 60 (1998).

Soon after arriving in Oxford in 1945, Wiseman joined the Oxford Inter-Collegiate Christian Union, enthusiastically engaging in its evangelistic meetings. He was soon approached to travel to America to be a delegate of the Inter-Varsity Fellowship (now the Universities and Colleges Christian Fellowship) to the founding of the International Fellowship of Evangelical Students at Harvard in 1948. That gave him the opportunity to go to major centres of Assyriological studies in the United States as well, so he met several of the leading scholars of the time (A. Goetze, F. J. Stephens, F. R. Steele, S. N. Kramer, and W. F. Albright). In Britain the Inter-Varsity Fellowship had founded Tyndale House in Cambridge as a residential library for Biblical Research. J. N. D. Anderson was its first Warden and he and Wiseman were to become colleagues later in London University where Anderson lectured in Law at SOAS before taking the directorship of the Institute for Advanced Legal Studies in 1959.[11] Wiseman saw Tyndale House with the Tyndale Fellowship for Biblical Research as a prime resource for building positive biblical scholarship and training young scholars (among them, at different times, K. A. Kitchen and H. G. M. Williamson), so he gave much time and thought to it, especially as Chairman from 1957 to 1986, guiding it through a period of reorganisation, strengthening the emphasis on biblical studies in conjunction with the New Testament scholar F. F. Bruce.[12] As in every society he joined, Wiseman readily attended to practical aspects as well as matters of policy, suggesting, for example, how an extension to the library might be neatly fitted into the

---

[11] See *Proceedings of the British Academy*, 90 (1996), 251–63.
[12] See *Proceedings of the British Academy*, 80 (1991), 245–60.

grounds. Members of the Tyndale Fellowship Old Testament Study Group dedicated a small volume of essays to him in 1994 as a mark of appreciation.[13]

In his autobiography, Wiseman states that, while at Oxford, 'I felt a call to apply my interest in Biblical languages and an understanding of the culture of the ancient Near East to the better understanding of the Bible and to further this among educated Christians.' This became a major complement to his academic Assyriology. In 1927, his father had read a paper on 'Babylon in the days of Hammurapi and Nebuchadrezzar' to the Victoria Institute (founded in 1865, now known as Faith and Thought) which convened to 'investigate ... important questions of Philosophy and Science, especially those bearing upon Holy Scripture', and another on 'Archaeology and literary criticism of the Old Testament' in 1945,[14] so it was a natural forum for Donald to present 'Some recent trends in Biblical archaeology' in 1950 and further papers in 1954, 1955 and 1956, the last, 'The place and progress of Biblical archaeology', being The Gunning Prize Essay.[15] He lectured frequently on the topic in many places and was often invited to contribute to Bible dictionaries and handbooks by editors in Britain and America. In 1958, at the urging of the publisher, he wrote *Illustrations from Biblical Archaeology* (London), describing and illustrating numerous discoveries in a clear, straightforward style. At the outset he made his attitude to the subject plain, 'confirmation of the biblical narrative' may be 'expected and found in contemporary documents' (p. 6), but concluding, yet 'great care is needed, both in the selection of facts from archaeology as a whole, and in the integration of the evidence with the proved results of Old Testament scholarship' and quoting Sir Frederic Kenyon (President of the Victoria Institute 1946–52) on the positive role of archaeological research for biblical interpretation (p. 102). Thus he distanced himself from those who too enthusiastically take archaeological discoveries as a means to 'prove the Bible is true', expecting, rather, to find corroboration of biblical statements in the ancient sources, using the term 'confirmation' repeatedly. At the same time, he avoided forcing either the biblical text to fit with some discovery, or adducing a discovery to illuminate the Scriptures without good reason. Changes in the interpretation of some findings were to be expected and he was ready to take them into

---

[13] R. S. Hess, G. J. Wenham, P. E. Satterthwaite (eds.), *He Swore an Oath: Biblical Themes from Genesis 12–50* (Exeter, 1994).
[14] *Journal of the Transactions of the Victoria Institute*, 59 (1927), 121–36; 77 (1945), 101–11.
[15] *Journal of the Transactions of the Victoria Institute*, 82 (1951), 1–17; 87 (1955), 14–25; 88 (1956), 26–36.

account if he found them justified. Eager to give reliable information to Bible students, he undertook 152 entries (amounting to about 70,000 words) for *The New Bible Dictionary* (edited by J. D. Douglas; London, 1962), a reference volume which proved its worth so that he revised and added some for the second edition (1982) and was Consulting Editor for the three-volume *Illustrated Bible Dictionary* (Leicester, 1980), drawing on his extensive knowledge of the British Museum's collections. His academic competence in this area was acknowledged when the Society for Old Testament Study invited him to edit a collection of essays by its members under the title *Peoples of Old Testament Times* (Oxford, 1973, repr. 1975). The Society elected him its President for 1980.

However, when two American authors, John van Seters and T. L. Thompson, published doctoral theses launching wholesale attacks against the use of texts and material remains to 'confirm' a background for the Patriarchal Narratives of Genesis in the early second millennium BC, championed notably by the Johns Hopkins' scholar William Foxwell Albright, he wrote forcefully to correct some of the erroneous assertions they made. In particular, in an essay entitled 'They lived in tents',[16] he demonstrated adequate evidence for tent-life in the early second millennium BC, denied by J. van Seters, and contributed 'Abraham reassessed' to a volume conceived as a response to the attacks, *Essays on the Patriarchal Narratives*, which he edited with the present writer.[17]

First-hand knowledge of the cuneiform tablets in the British Museum, his edition of the Babylonian Chronicle texts and a visit to a conference on Babylon in 1979 at the invitation of the Iraqi authorities provided resources for the British Academy Schweich Lectures he delivered in 1983 on 'Nebuchadrezzar and Babylon' in which he drew together textual and material evidence for the king's works, arguing that the famous 'Hanging Gardens' should be located nearer to the Euphrates than usually supposed, and explaining the relevance of discoveries at Babylon for biblical exegesis.[18]

His regular, attentive reading of the Hebrew Bible led him to make several fresh proposals for understanding the text. Most notable is his perception that the sentence in Daniel 6: 28, 'So Daniel prospered during the reign of Darius and the reign of Cyrus the Persian', has a syntactic parallel in 1 Chronicles 5: 26, 'So the God of Israel stirred up the spirit of

[16] G. A. Tuttle (ed.), *The Bible and Near Eastern Studies: Essays in Honor of William Sanford LaSor* (Grand Rapids, MI, 1978), pp. 195–200.
[17] (Leicester, 1980; repr. Winona Lake, IN, 1983).
[18] *Nebchadrezzar and Babylon* (London, 1985; pb. edn., 1991).

Pul, king of Assyria, and the spirit of Tiglath-pileser, king of Assyria' (AV, RV). Since, in the latter, Pul and Tiglath-pileser are names for the same man, so Darius and Cyrus might be names for one man in Daniel 6. The particle linking them, rendered 'and' in the old translations, serves both as the simple conjunction and as an explanatory one in Hebrew and in Aramaic, allowing the rendering, 'during the reign of Darius, that is the reign of Cyrus ...' just as 1 Chronicles 5: 26 is now rendered, '... the spirit of Pul ... that is the spirit of Tiglath-pileser'. In this way, the long-standing problem of the identity of Darius the Mede, held by many biblical scholars to be a sign of the historical ignorance of the book's author, might be resolved. However, no other documents refer to Cyrus by the name Darius, so this has to remain hypothetical, yet one that should not be lightly discounted.[19]

Concern for a clear understanding of Scripture naturally led Wiseman to involvement in Bible translation, an activity which he had seen in his teacher (Sir) Godfrey Driver's involvement with the New English Bible. The British and Foreign Bible Society welcomed him to its Translation Committee when it was engaged in 'anglicizing' the Good News Bible and, as the United Bible Society, to its Translation Advisory Group, which took him to various countries to discuss methods and policies of translating. His most significant activity in this area grew from a meeting in 1966 with some American evangelical scholars in New York who were contemplating a new translation of the Bible to replace the archaic language of the King James Version, incorporating the best current knowledge of biblical languages. A Committee on Bible Translation was formed which allocated the books of Kings and Chronicles to him to translate—a large section of the Old Testament. His drafts were revised by another translator, then by the whole committee. The year 1978 saw the *New International Version Bible* (NIV) released in the USA and February 1979 the issue of a British edition. At short notice, Wiseman had been asked to replace American expressions with British, a task which he completed within a few weeks, helped by a few specialists in English and friends with suitable experience. As a result of his representations to the Gideons, the NIV is the version of the Bible now placed in hotel rooms across the country.

---

[19] 'Darius the Mede', *Christianity Today*, 2.4 (25 Nov. 1957), 7–10; 'Some historical problems in the Book of Daniel', in Donald J. Wiseman, Terence C. Mitchell, Ray Joyce, William J. Martin, Kenneth A. Kitchen, *Notes on Some Problems in the Book of Daniel* (London, 1956), pp. 9–16, expanded by James M. Bulman, 'The identification of Darius the Mede', *Westminster Theological Journal*, 35 (1973), 247–67; Brian E. Colless, 'Cyrus the Persian as Darius the Mede in the Book of Daniel', *Journal for the Study of the Old Testament*, 56 (1992), 113–26.

Another body to which he gave time was the Scripture Gift Mission which circulates Bibles and selections of biblical texts in many languages. A former colleague wrote:

> He became a Member of Association in 1952, a Council Member in 1961, and Chairman of Council in 1978—a position which he occupied with distinction for 14 years. He was, during that time, also a member of the Translations Committee until his retirement in 1994. His scholarly and wise contribution to the work of SGM generally, and his remarkable insights into the problems of Scripture translation were outstanding and, though they may not be aware of it, many peoples of the world owe him a tremendous debt for Scriptures in their own languages which are linguistically correct and culturally acceptable.[20]

His final publication was a volume on the biblical books of 1 and 2 Kings in the Tyndale Old Testament Commentary series of which he had been General Editor since its inception in 1967.[21] In it he shows his awareness of the main currents of Old Testament research and supports his conviction that the books report accurate historical information with numerous references to ancient Near Eastern sources. The comments he makes demonstrate that he saw no reason to move from the position he held at the start of his career. As he closed his autobiography, he stated, 'It has been my experience that the Bible, rightly understood, does not clash with any finds when they are rightly understood in their context.'

His copies of cuneiform inscriptions are, in most cases, still basic for primary studies, although some of his editions have been superseded by re-examination and the advance of knowledge, while others have been incorporated in new standard texts (e.g. the Banquet Stele of Ashur-nasir-pal, the Vassal Treaties of Esarhaddon, the Nimrud piece of the Epic of Gilgamesh[22]). For a large quantity of other texts, his publications still serve. The role he played in speedily making important written documents available to the scholarly world was admirable and deserves to be imitated! His sober and positive use of ancient texts in biblical interpretation, conservative as many may perceive it, also deserves imitation in a field where the accumulation of hypotheses can only mislead students and the wider public.

---

[20] Norman Brown, personal communication.

[21] *1 and 2 Kings* (Leicester, 1993).

[22] See A. K. Grayson, *Assyrian Rulers of the Early First Millennium BC, 1 (1114–859 BC)*, Royal Inscriptions of Mesopotamia, Assyrian Periods, 2 (Toronto, 1991), pp. 288–93; Kazuko Watanabe, *Die adê-Vereidigung anlässlich der Thronfolgerung Asarhaddons*, Baghdader Mitteilungen, Beiheft, 3 (Berlin, 1987); Andrew R. George, *The Babylonian Gilgamesh Epic* (Oxford, 2003), p. 536, MS g, Pl. 46.

Wiseman was energetic, unstinting in his efforts to further a project—Mallowan wrote of him, 'none has worked harder in the cause of our excavations'—diligent in every activity, a great enthusiast and generous encourager of others.[23] He is remembered for his kindness to all his students, his stimulus to the clever and his patience with the slow, totally sincere, unselfishly concerned for the good of others, a gentleman who was good company, enjoying laughter and life. He was never reluctant to state his Christian beliefs, without any suggestion that he expected his students to conform to them, rather, he respected their convictions and they respected him for that—Roman Catholics, Muslims, Japanese and Jews. He did not stand on ceremony or give himself airs. One Israeli scholar was surprised when he arrived to visit the Wisemans to see the professor emerge in oily overalls from beneath his car. Another former Israeli student observed, 'He really was a wise man!' In his later years he was immobilised partly as a consequence of his wartime injury, cared for lovingly by his wife Mary until her death in February 2006, and their three daughters.

ALAN MILLARD
University of Liverpool

Note. Wiseman's Memoirs, *Life Above and Below*, privately published in 2003, are the major source for this obituary and all unattributed quotations are taken from it. Additional information is drawn from obituaries by A. R. George in *Iraq*, 72 (2010), v–viii, by T. C. Mitchell in *Faith and Thought*, 48 (April 2010), 3–6. See also M. J. Selman, 'Donald J. Wiseman', in W. Elwell and J. Weaver (eds.), *Bible Interpreters of the Twentieth Century* (Grand Rapids, MI, 1999), pp. 299–311.

[23] M. E. L. Mallowan, *Nimrud and its Remains* (London, 1966), p. 15.